THE NEW COMPREHENSIVE
AMERICAN RHYMING
DICTIONARY

THE NEW COMPREHENSIVE AMERICAN RHYMING DICTIONARY

SUE YOUNG

AVON BOOKS ◆ NEW YORK

AVON BOOKS, INC.
1350 Avenue of the Americas
New York, New York 10019

Copyright © 1991 by Sue Daugherty Young
Published by arrangement with William Morrow and Company, Inc.
ISBN: 0-380-71392-6
www.avonbooks.com

Published in hardcover by William Morrow and Company, Inc.; for information address Permissions Department, William Morrow and Company, Inc., 1350 Avenue of the Americas, New York, New York 10019.

The William Morrow and Company edition contains the following Library of Congress Cataloging in Publication Data:

Young, Sue (Sue Daugherty)
  The New Comprehensive American rhyming dictionary / by Sue Young.
    p.   cm.
  Includes index.
1. English language—Rhyme—Dictionaries. 2. English language—United States—Rhyme—Dictionaries. 3. Americanisms—Dictionaries.
I. Title.
PE1519.Y68   1991   90-19165
423'.1   dc20   CIP

First Avon Books Trade Paperback Printing: November 1991

AVON TRADEMARK REG. U.S. PAT. OFF. AND IN OTHER COUNTRIES, MARCA REGISTRADA, HECHO EN U.S.A.

Printed in the U.S.A.

20 19 18 17 16 15 14

Acknowledgments

———— • ————

The author wishes to acknowledge the invaluable help of the following people:

Charles E. Young for his conviction that this work should be published.

The late Norman Cousins for his belief in this project, and his willingness to go out of his way for a friend.

Jackie Reynolds for her advice and guidance on the mysteries of the computer.

INTRODUCTION

Rhyming is not the exclusive territory of established poets, professional songwriters, and advertising people. Rhyming is for everyone—an appreciative friend, a frustrated lover, an exasperated student, a smitten construction worker, an inspired coach, a traveling salesman, a happy truck driver, a devoted mate.

This book is written for all of these people. Rappers will appreciate the variety of slang terms. Songwriters will find that because of its simple organization and offering of phrases, it makes rhyming faster so that they will not lose their train of thought. The casual rhymer, the amateur lyricist, the advertising genius, the limerick lover, will also find it expedites the creative process.

Rhyming is fun and should be easy. Years ago, however, when I attempted to use rhyming dictionaries, I found them difficult to work with, unimaginative, and terribly outdated. My graduate studies in linguistics at UCLA convinced me that a totally different kind of dictionary was possible—one that would be easy to use, with rhyming words and phrases in modern American/English.

Americans have their own way of pronouncing the English language. I wanted to accommodate American pronunciation by rhyming words as we actually say them, not as they are spelled. For example, for most of us, *pretty* rhymes with *giddy*; for some, *pretty* rhymes with *witty*. In this book you would look up whichever sound works for you. Close sounds are cross-referenced for your convenience.

A unique aspect of this dictionary is that it includes *phrases* as well as *words*. These phrases are quite common to all Americans. For instance, *Fourth of July* rhymes with *chicken pot pie, in a pig's eye, little white lie, Mr. Nice Guy, never say die,* etc. We use many phrases as single-word ideas, such as *hole-in-one,* which rhymes with *hot dog bun, 9–1–1, Air Force One, hit-and-run,* etc. One could say that this book is an offering of ideas that rhyme.

This collection of words and phrases represents twenty years of research, of listening to how we Americans talk, of always having a pencil ready to jot down a clever rhyme heard or seen anywhere—on the street, on airplanes, in theaters, on bathroom walls.

You will find a lot of slang in this book because Americans feel comfortable with slang. You will find much humor in this book because humor is an important part of American life, and because some of the most unexpected words and phrases turn up together, such as *genitalia* and *never fail ya.*

Some words will not be found in this dictionary. No, I have not omitted a word just because some people might find it naughty. Where would limericks be if it were not for spicy language? However, I have tried to omit words that are clearly reflective of racial or ethnic prejudice.

As you use this book, you will probably think of some rhyming words and phrases that are missing, but I suspect I have included some that may have eluded you.

Have fun!

—SUE YOUNG

HOW TO USE THIS BOOK

———•———

Rhyming is really very simple and lots of fun. Rhymes sound best when they are based on an accented vowel sound of a word. For example, *hysteria* ends with the sound *Ē-u*. So does *idea*. However, the two words don't rhyme very well. *Hysteria* (AR-ē-u) sounds much better with *malaria*, and *idea* (Ē-u) sounds better with *tortilla*. That is because you are starting your rhyming sound with an accented vowel.

Here are some examples of rhyming an accented vowel sound:

hysterical	**(AR-i-kul)**	numerical
perpendicular	**(IK-ū-lur)**	vehicular
trick or treated	**(ĒD-ud)**	overheated
global	**(ŌB-ul)**	noble
introduction	**(UK-shun)**	liposuction

Rhyming sounds start with a word's accented vowel and contain the rest of the word. To select the accented vowel sound of the word with which you wish to rhyme, first listen to the word. What syllable sounds strongest? In single-syllable words there is no question of which is the accented vowel sound since there is only one choice. In multisyllable words, however, sometimes more than one syllable is stressed. For example, the word *dis-a-ppoint* has three syllables, two of them accented:

dis and *point*. Rhyming sounds start with a vowel, not a consonant. For the word *disappoint*, the rhyming sounds would be either *isappoint* or *oint*. The sound *isappoint* rhymes with *miss a point*, but not much else. *Oint* would be the easier rhyming sound to find. This sound is shown as *ŌĒNT*, and it would indicate that *disappoint* could rhyme with *anoint*, *West Point*, *out of joint*, *turning point*, *get to the point*, etc.

Some multisyllable words have only one accented vowel sound. For example, if you listen to the word *per-sim-mon*, you will hear that the accented vowel sound is *im*. Your rhyming sound will start with *im* and contain the rest of the word: *immon*. This is shown as *IM-un*, and it would indicate that *persimmon* could rhyme with *lemon*, *swimmin'*, *women*, etc..

Another example is the phrase, *maid-en aunt*. The accented syllables of this phrase are *maid* and *aunt*. If you choose *maid* then the rest of the word must follow and your rhyming sound would be *aid-en-aunt*. This limits your choices considerably to things like *fadin' aunt*. However, if you choose *aunt* to rhyme with, and look up the sound *ANT*, you can rhyme *maiden aunt* with *disenchant*, *gallivant*, and *sycophant*. Or, depending on your pronunciation of *aunt*, you can look up the sound *ONT* and rhyme *maiden aunt* with *confidante*, *debutante*, and *nonchalant*.

In selecting your rhyming sound, you often have choices. You can try them all. If the more complicated sound is either not listed or too limited, then try the simpler one.

To use this dictionary you don't have to know anything except what sound you want to rhyme with and what letters represent that sound. I have used a simplified system for all sounds. Letters representing vowel and consonant sounds are shown in the Sound Chart on page 11.

Word rhymes in this book are based on the pronunciation used by the majority of Americans.

The advantage of favoring sound over spelling is that it affords a wider selection of words to rhyme. For example, in many rhyming dictionaries, *incredible* and *forgettable* would not be listed together because they are not spelled the same. However, most Americans say them alike. In this book they are represented by the sound *ED-u-bul*. If you happened to look under *ET-u-bul*, you would be directed to *ED-u-bul*.

Many of us can say words that we cannot spell. Here are some examples of hard-to-spell words and where you would find them:

Word	Sound Heading
asthma	AZ-mu
medallion	AL-yun
acquiesce	ES
syphon	ĪF-un
vociferous	IF-ur-us
hors d'oeuvre	URV

Because rhyming sounds begin with vowels, they can be divided into the five vowel categories. Examples are:

Section A   long Ā sounds   as in *shame* (**ĀM**), *aching* (**ĀK-ēng**), *glacier* (**ĀSH-ur**)

short A sounds   as in *fashion* (**ASH-un**), *camera* (**AM-ur-u**), *brat* (**AT**)

short AR sounds   as in *their* (**AR**), *declare* (**AR**), *hair* (**AR**)

ÄR sounds   as in *sorry* (**ÄR-ē**), *tomorrow* (**ÄR-ō**), *partner* (**ÄRT-nur**)

Section E   long Ē sounds   as in *tingle* (**ĒNG-ul**), *league* (**ĒG**), *torpedo* (**ĒD-ō**)

short E sounds   as in *pet* (**ET**), *edible* (**ED-ub-ul**), *beggar* (**EG-ur**)

Section I   long Ī sounds   as in *idle* (**ĪD-ul**), *aye* (**Ī**), *tightly* (**ĪT-lē**)

short I sounds   as in *symbol* (**IM-bul**), *fitted* (**ID-ud**), *quibble* (**IB-ul**)

Section O   long Ō sounds   as in *alone* (**ŌN**), *linoleum* (**ŌL-ē-um**), *coaster* (**ŌS-tur**)

short O sounds   as in *odd* (**OD**), *often* (**OF-un**), *father* (**OTHE-ur**)

ŌĒ sounds   as in *joint* (**ŌĒNT**), *destroyer* (**ŌĒ-ur**), *oil* (**ŌĒL**)

OR sounds   as in *horse* (**ŌRS**), *snore* (**ŌR**), *war* (**ŌR**)

OW sounds   as in *ouch* (**OWCH**), *hour* (**OWR**), *proud* (**OWD**)

Section U long Ū sound   as in *juice* (**ŪS**), *few* (**Ū**), *blooper*
(**ŪP-ur**)

short U sound   as in *lumber* (**UMB-ur**), *jump*
(**UMP**), *truck* (**UK**)

flat Û sound   as in *put* (**ÛT**), *good* (**ÛD**), *pushy*
(**ÛSH-ē**)

short UR sound   as in *her* (**UR**), *urge* (**URJ**), *refer*
(**UR**)

All sounds are listed alphabetically, with short vowel sounds immediately following long vowel sounds. For instance, the *A* listing would read: A, ĀB, AB, ĀB-ē, AB-ē, etc. The beginning of a rhyming sound indicates where it is listed. For example, to rhyme a word with *about*, the sound to look up would be *OWT*. More examples are given on page 12.

Many plurals and past tenses of words are also offered so you can be more precise in available rhymes. Some examples are:

cat	(AT)	cats	(ATS)
chew	(Ū)	chewed	(ŪD)
check	(EK)	checks	(EX)
stir	(UR)	stirred	(URD)

All words ending with a particular sound are grouped together regardless of the number of syllables in the words. In the column of words, there will be a space between syllables. Here are two examples:

OK-ru-tēz	**ED-i-kut**
Socrates	etiquette
	predicate
Hippocrates	
	Connecticut
mediocrities	

For rapid scanning of all sounds offered, please refer to the Sound Index beginning on page 579.

Sound Chart

Consonant Sounds

B	as in *b*aker
C	will only be seen as an S or K sound
CH	as in *ch*ur*ch*
D	as in *d*ad*d*y
F	as in *f*inally
G	hard G only, as in *g*ate
H	as in *h*arbor, *j*alapeño, and *wh*o
J	*as in* **G**eorge and *j*ump
JH	as in gara*g*e
K	as in *c*at, *k*itchen, and *qu*iche
KW	as in *qu*ick
L	as in *l*imp
M	as in *m*ixture
N	as in *n*ut
P	as in *p*eewee
Q	will only be seen as KW
R	as in *r*affle
S	as in *s*imple and *c*inch
SH	as in *sh*ort
T	as in *t*ravel
TH	as in *th*ought, *th*ing
THE	as in loa*the*, ra*the*r

V	as in *v*alley
W	as in *wh*ich and *w*ait
X	as in flu*x* and ja*cks*
Y	as in *y*ellow
Z	as in *z*eal
ZH	as in camou*fl*age

Vowel Sounds

Ā	as in b*a*by, l*a*dle
A	as in *a*pple, g*a*llon
AR	as in h*air*, th*ere*
ÄR	as in h*ar*p, s*o*rry
Ē	as in *e*vil, th*i*ng
E	as in *e*ver, *e*dge
Ī	as in *i*cy, *eye*, compl*y*
I	as in *i*mp, dr*i*bble
Ō	as in *o*ver, b*oa*t
O	as in *o*ff, f*a*ther
ÕĒ	as in *oi*ly, j*oi*nt
ŌR	as in sh*or*t, w*ar*m
OW	as in h*ou*r, pl*ow*
OO	will be seen in Ū and Û
Ū	as in *u*tility, g*oo*se, h*u*man
U	as in j*u*mp, m*o*ther, c*u*t
Û	as in b*oo*k, p*u*t, w*oo*den
UR	as in h*er*, *er*mine, f*ur*

The following are some sample words and how they are listed:

Sample Words	**Where to look**
daddy	A D - ē
fracture	A K - c h u r
sorry	Ä R - ē
carriage	A R - i j
beagle	Ē G - u l

careen	Ē N
ring	Ē N G
niño	Ē N - y ō
metric	E T - r i k
idol	Ī D - u l
antiquity	I K - w i - d ē
continue	I N - y ū
additional	I S H - u n - u l
pliant	Ī - u n t
noisy	Ō Ē Z - ē
college	O L - i j
electronics	O N - i x
portion	Ō R S H - u n
cuddle	U D - u l
proverbial	U R B - ē - u l
turkey	U R K - ē
solution	Ū S H - u n
foot	Û T
mutiny	Ū T - i n - ē
Caruso	Ū S - ō
school	Ū L
choosy	Ū Z - ē

A SOUNDS

Ā

a
bay
bray
clay
day
fay
Faye
flay
fray
gay
grey
gray
hay
hey
jay
j
k
Kay
lei
lay
may
Mae
nay
neigh
pay
play

pray
prey
ray
re
say
slay
sleigh
spay
spray
stay
stray
sway
Shea
tray
trey
they
way
weigh
whey
yea

AA

au lait
at bay
all-day
array
amscray
astray

allay
après
away
aweigh
affray
Amway
assay
ashtray
archway
breath spray
buffet
Bombay
backpay
ballet
beret
birthday
Broadway
bidet
bobsleigh
betray
bouquet
bluejay
breezeway
blasé
cachet
café
causeway
cherchez

cliché
croquet
chalet
Camay
crochet
child's play
convey
display
D-day
deejay
driveway
defray
decay
daresay
downplay
delay
dismay
doomsday
doorway
entrée
épée
endplay
essay
foul play
field day
fair play
fairway
frappé
filet
freeway
foreplay
foyer
flambé
gourmet
gainsay
gateway
give way
gangway
glacé
headway
hair spray
halfway
hallway
hurray
hearsay

horseplay
highway
heyday
inlay
inveigh
ice tray
lamé
leeway
long-play
make hay
Manet
mislay
my way
midday
melee
mainstay
misplay
Mayday
make way
no way
nosegay
naysay
Norway
okay
olé
outlay
outré
outweigh
one-way
obey
prepay
power play
plissé
payday
portray
pâté
pathway
per se
parquet
purvey
parlay
puree
parfait
passé
pince-nez

plié
Pompeii
raceway
roadway
railway
runway
repay
risqué
roué
replay
replay
role-play
someway
stingray
squeeze play
sick pay
sick bay
subway
segue
soufflé
sauté
stairway
soiree
sachet
survey
sashay
screenplay
très gai
tramway
touché
Taipei
toupee
today
two-way
wordplay
washday
weekday
waylay
workday
x-ray

A-OK
all the way
AMA
attaché

arete
appliqué
ABA
beast of prey
break of day
blow away
breakaway
by the way
bird of prey
Bastille Day
croupier
Cartier
come what may
cosmic ray
crème brûlée
cabaret
castaway
cloisonné
CIA
Christmas Day
consommé
canapé
CPA
Chevrolet
cutaway
décolleté
déclassé
dapple-gray
day by day
die away
DOA
double play
disobey
déjeuner
disarray
devotee
divorcée
day-to-day
dossier
distingué
everyday
expressway
ETA
easy way
esposé

émigré
every way
fiancée
Father's Day
FHA
faraway
fadeaway
foldaway
fire away
feet of clay
getaway
gamma ray
grandstand play
Grand Marnier
giveaway
holiday
Hemingway
hit the hay
here to stay
hideaway
interplay
in the way
Judgment Day
Labor Day
lackaday
lead astray
layaway
lump of clay
latter-day
lead the way
macramé
matinée
Mother's Day
Monterey
MIA
Milky Way
Mandalay
métier
make one's way
negligee
New Year's Day
nasal spray
NBA
night and day
overstay

out of play
overplay
only way
overpay
overlay
on display
off Broadway
pass away
popinjay
present-day
passion play
photoplay
passageway
pave the way
play-by-play
PTA
protégé
Perrier
repartee
runaway
résumé
ricochet
right-of-way
right away
recherché
stowaway
swing and sway
silver gray
Santa Fe
San Jose
straightaway
silver tray
Triple A
time of day
towaway
throwaway
touchdown play
tooth decay
tape delay
triple play
takeaway
take-home pay
thataway
USA
underplay

underway
V-J Day
V-E Day
waste away
waterway
wile away
wedding day
workaday
yesterday
yea or nay

April Fools' Day
any which way
atelier
anchors away
alackaday
battleship gray
born yesterday
bridal bouquet
café au lait
call it a day
carry the day
cabriolet
carried away
children at play
Champs Élysées
communiqué
couturier
catch of the day
cocktail buffet
day after day
dead giveaway
devil to pay
Et tu, Brute?
every which way
far and away
go all the way
games people play
habitué
happy birthday
in a bad way
instant replay
in the worst way
late in the day
naiveté

out of the way
overtime pay
papier-mâché
Pouilly-Fuissé
rub the wrong way
red letter day
roll in the hay
SPCA
sommelier
St. Patrick's Day
tattletale gray
UCLA
vitamin A
water ballet
YMCA

American way
be that as it may
deodorant spray
go out of one's way
in a family way
look the other way
morality play
petit déjeuner
pass the time of day
Sadie Hawkins Day
TWA
up up and away

YWCA

ĀB

Abe
babe
Gabe

Honest Abe
newborn babe

AB

blab
cab
crab
dab

drab
fab
flab
gab
grab
jab
lab
nab
scab
slab
stab
tab

Ahab
backstab
confab
keep tab(s)
prefab
rehab
sand dab
sand crab
smack-dab

fiddler crab
gift of gab
horseshoe crab
olive drab
photo lab
taxicab
up for grab(s)

pick up the tab

ĀB-ē

baby
maybe
rabie(s)
scabie(s)

AB-ē

abbey
Abby
blabby
cabby
crabby

drabby
flabby
gabby
grabby
jabby
scabby
shabby
tabby

Dear Abby

AB-ēng

blabbing
crabbing
dabbing
gabbing
grabbing
jabbing
nabbing
scabbing
stabbing

backstabbing
gut-grabbing

AB-ē-nus

blabbiness
crabbiness
flabbiness
gabbiness
grabbiness
shabbiness

AB-eth
(See AB-uth)

ĀB-ē-un

babyin'
Fabian

Arabian

Saudi Arabian

AB-ē-ur

blabbier
crabbier
drabbier
flabbier
gabbier
grabbier
scabbier
shabbier

AB-in
(See AB-un)

AB-in-et
(See AB-un-ut)

AB-it
(See Ab-ut)

ĀB-lē

ably
stably

ĀB-lēng

abling
cabling
labeling
stabling
tabling

disabling
enabling
mislabeling

AB-lēng

babbling
dabbling

AB-lish

babblish
establish

disestablish
reestablish

AB-u-bul

blabbable
dabbable
grabbable
jabbable
nabbable
stabbable

ĀB-ul

able
Abel
cable
fable
gable
label
Mabel
sable
stable
table

card table
crap table
disable
enable
end table
horse stable
mislabel
pool table
round table
timetable
turntable
times table
unstable
unable
wait table(s)

Aesop's fable
billiard table
coffee table
Cain and Abel
dressing table

jumper cable
on the table
Ping-Pong table
TV cable
turn the table(s)
training table
union label
warning label

conference table
designer label
head of the table
telephone cable
under the table
willing and able

AB-ul

babble
drabble
dabble
gabble
rabble
Scrabble
shabble
scabble

gibble-gabble
Tower of Babel

ĀB-uld

cabled
fabled
gabled
labeled
tabled

disabled
enabled
mislabeled

AB-uld

babbled
dabbled

AB-ū-lus

fabulous
sabulous

AB-un

blabbin'
cabin
crabbin'
dabbin'
grabbin'
jabbin'
nabbin'
scabbin'
stabbin'

AB-un-ut

blabbin' it
cabinet
dabbin' it
gabbin' it
jabbin' it
nabbin' it
stabbin' it

ĀB-ur

labor
neighbor
saber

belabor
day labor
false labor
good neighbor
hard labor
slave labor

next-door neighbor

AB-ur

blabber
clabber
crabber
dabber

drabber
gabber
grabber
jabber
nabber
stabber

bejabber(s)
backstabber

jibber-jabber
money grabber

AB-ur-āt

collaborate
elaborate

AB-urd

blabbered
clabbered
jabbered

ĀB-ur-ēng

laboring
neighboring

belaboring

AB-ur-ēng

blabbering
clabbering
jabbering

AB-ut

abbot
Abbott
blab it
dab it
grab it
habit
jab it
nab it
rabbit

sabot
stab it

bad habit
cohabit
drug habit
inhabit
jackrabbit
Welsh rabbit

Easter rabbit
force of habit
kick the habit
out of habit
riding habit

creature of habit

AB-uth

blabbeth
Sabbath

AB-yū-lus
(See AB-u-lus)

ACH

batch
catch
hatch
klatsch
latch
match
natch
patch
Satch
scratch
snatch
thatch

armpatch
attach
crosspatch
door latch
detach
Dogpatch

dispatch
from scratch
knee patch
love match
mismatch
no match
nuthatch
potlatch
rematch
rescratch
repatch
unlatch

boxing match
booby hatch
coffee klatsch
cradle-snatch
cabbage patch
down the hatch
elbow patch
escape hatch
Got a match?
mix and match
overmatch
perfect match
polo match
reattach
safety catch
shouting match
shooting match
tennis match
unattach
up to scratch

no strings attach(ed)
not up to scratch
semidetach(ed)
strawberry patch
three on a match

ACH-bak

hatchback
snatch back

attach back

ACH-ē

catchy
patchy
scratchy

Apache

Tallahatchee

ACH-ēng

batching
catching
hatching
latching
matching
patching
scratching
snatching
thatching

attaching
back scratching
detaching
dispatching
eye-catching
mismatching
rematching
repatching
rescratching
unlatching

cradle-snatching
mix-and-matching
overmatching
reattaching

ACH-et
(See ACH-ut)

ACH-ē-ust

catchiest
scratchiest

ACH-lus

catchless
latchless
matchless
patchless
scratchless

ACH-ment

attachment
detachment

reattachment

ACH-u-bul

catchable
hatchable
latchable
matchable
patchable
scratchable
snatchable
thatchable

attachable
detachable
dispatchable
rematchable
rescratchable
repatchable
unlatchable
unmatchable

mix-and-matchable
reattachable
unattachable

ACH-up

catsup
catch up
hatch up
latch up
match up
patch up

scratch up

play catch-up

ĀCH-ur

nature

denature
good nature

back to nature
call of nature
human nature
legislature
Mother Nature
nomenclature
second nature

ACH-ur

catcher
hatcher
latcher
matcher
patcher
scratcher
stature
snatcher
thatcher

attacher
back scratcher
cowcatcher
detacher
dispatcher
dogcatcher
egg hatcher
eye-catcher
flycatcher
mismatcher
purse snatcher
plot hatcher
rematcher
unlatcher

body snatcher
cradle-snatcher

mix-and-matcher
reattacher
unattacher

ACH-ur-āt

maturate
saturate

ACH-ur-ē

hatchery
thatchery

ACH-ut

catch it
hatch it
hatchet
latch it
match it
patch it
ratchet
scratch it
snatch it
thatch it

attach it
detach it
dispatch it
mismatch it
rematch it
repatch it
unlatch it

mix and match it
reattach it
unattach it

bury the hatchet

ACH-uz

batches
catches
hatches
klatches
latches

Natchez
patches
scratches
snatches
thatches

attaches
detaches
dispatches
knee patches
love matches
mismatches
nuthatches
potlatches
rematches
rescratches
repatches
unlatches

boxing matches
booby hatches
coffee klatches
perfect matches
reattaches
shouting matches
tennis matches
unattaches

batten down the
  hatches

ĀD

AID(S)
aid
aide
ade
blade
braid
bayed
brayed
daid
fade
flayed
frayed
grade
glade

grayed
haid
jade
laid
lade
maid
made
neighed
paid
played
preyed
prayed
raid
staid
sleighed
shade
suede
swayed
spade
sprayed
stayed
they'd
trade
wade
weighed

afraid
assayed
air raid
arrayed
abrade
arcade
allayed
blockade
barmaid
Band-Aid
brocade
brigade
betrayed
bridesmaid
Belgrade
conveyed
cascade
crusade
charade

crocheted
degrade
downgrade
dissuade
defrayed
displayed
decayed
delayed
dismayed
evade
essayed
fair trade
first aid
grenade
gay blade
hurrayed
high grade
homemade
housemaid
handmade
inlaid
invade
inveighed
Kool-Aid
Kincaid
limeade
lampshade
milkmaid
manmade
misplayed
mermaid
nightshade
nursemaid
outweighed
old maid
okayed
obeyed
parlayed
postpaid
parade
pomade
prepaid
persuade
pervade
portrayed

pureed
repaid
remade
relaid
replayed
relayed
stockade
self-made
segued
surveyed
sashayed
sunshade
sautéed
switchblade
steep grade
tirade
top grade
upgrade
unswayed
unmade
unpaid
upbraid
waylaid
well-made
x-rayed

apartheid
ace of spade(s)
Adelaide
accolade
appliquéd
balustrade
barricade
chambermaid
custom-made
carriage trade
centigrade
colonnade
cavalcade
disobeyed
disarrayed
dairymaid
escapade
escalade
even trade

everglade
fire brigade
foreign aid
foreign trade
final grade
Gatorade
hand grenade
hearing aid
hit parade
lemonade
legal aid
marmalade
make the grade
masquerade
motorcade
Medicaid
metermaid
Minute Maid
marinade
overpaid
overlaid
overstayed
promenade
panty raid
palisade
ready-made
retrograde
renegade
Rubbermaid
ricocheted
razor blade
Rose Parade
stock-in-trade
shoulder blade
serenade
tape delayed
teacher's aid
tailormade
ultrasuede
undismayed
unafraid
underlaid
underplayed
underpaid
welfare aid

bucket brigade
balance of trade
Easter parade
fanfaronade
government aid
jack-of-all-trade(s)
penny arcade
restraint of trade
visual aid

call a spade a spade
ticker-tape parade

AD

add
ad
bad
brad
cad
Chad
clad
dad
fad
gad
grad
had
lad
mad
pad
plaid
sad
scad(s)
shad
tad

bedpad
Baghdad
cornpad
crash pad
check pad
comrade
Carlsbad
crawdad
doodad
desk pad

egad
forbade
footpad
gone mad
granddad
hexad
ink pad
launch pad
like mad
nomad
not bad
note pad
post-grad
Sinbad
scratch pad
too bad
triad
unclad
want ad

boiling mad
Galahad
heating pad
have it bad
hopping mad
ivy-clad
ironclad
launching pad
landing pad
Leningrad
mom and dad
not so bad
shoulder pad
steno pad
Trinidad
undergrad

classified ad
Olympiad
stark raving mad
scantily clad

helicopter pad
sanitary pad

ĀD-ā

gray day
heyday
May Day
payday
playday

ĀD-ē

braidy
Beatty
eighty
Grady
Haiti
Katie
lady
matey
Sadie
shady
weighty

bag lady
church lady
First Lady
landlady
old lady
unshady

AD-ē

batty
bratty
baddy
caddie
catty
chatty
daddy
fatty
faddy
gaddy
Hattie
laddie
matty
natty
patty

paddy
ratty
tatty

big daddy
golf caddie
granddaddy
rice paddy
tea caddy

Cincinnati
finnan haddie
sugar daddy

ĀD-en
(See ĀD-un)

AD-en
(See AD-un)

ĀD-ēng

aiding
braiding
baiting
fading
freighting
grading
grating
hating
lading
mating
plaiting
plating
raiding
rating
shading
spading
sating
skating
slating
stating
trading
waiting
wading

abrading
abating
blockading
berating
cascading
crusading
charading
castrating
checkmating
collating
creating
cremating
debating
donating
deflating
dilating
degrading
downgrading
dissuading
elating
equating
evading
fixating
frustrating
floodgating
gradating
gyrating
invading
ice-skating
inflating
locating
mandating
migrating
misstating
negating
orating
outdating
placating
prostrating
probating
prorating
prostrating
pulsating
parading
persuading

pervading
relating
rebating
rotating
sedating
serrating
stagnating
stalemating
translating
tailgating
tirading
upgrading
upbraiding
updating
vacating
vibrating

abrogating
acerbating
abnegating
abdicating
animating
arbitrating
actuating
annotating
activating
acclimating
adulating
advocating
amputating
agitating
aggravating
aspirating
allocating
barricading
bifurcating
castigating
calibrating
calculating
captivating
cogitating
carbonating
circulating
complicating
celebrating

constipating
compensating
contemplating
confiscating
correlating
conjugating
congregating
credit rating
concentrating
copulating
cultivating
culminating
cumulating
decimating
delegating
decorating
devastating
deviating
deprecating
dehydrating
demonstrating
designating
defecating
dedicating
dislocating
dissipating
demarcating
detonating
dominating
duplicating
educating
elongating
emanating
emulating
enervating
emigrating
extricating
elevating
escalating
escapading
fluoridating
fabricating
fascinating
federating
formulating

fornicating
fluctuating
fumigating
generating
germinating
graduating
gravitating
hesitating
hibernating
hyphenating
integrating
intimating
illustrating
immigrating
impregnating
insulating
implicating
imitating
instigating
indicating
incubating
inundating
iterating
infiltrating
isolating
irrigating
irritating
jubilating
lacerating
liquidating
laminating
legislating
litigating
liberating
lubricating
masticating
masturbating
meditating
medicating
mediating
moderating
menstruating
mitigating
modulating
motivating

mutilating
masquerading
navigating
nauseating
operating
overrating
obfuscating
obligating
oscillating
overstating
pantyraiding
palpitating
permeating
perforating
penetrating
percolating
predicating
perorating
postulating
pollinating
procreating
promulgating
profligating
propagating
retrograding
radiating
relegating
recreating
remonstrating
roller-skating
relocating
regulating
reinstating
renovating
ruminating
satiating
scintillating
salivating
saturating
segregating
separating
simulating
silver-plating
speculating
syndicating

stimulating
stipulating
subjugating
sublimating
strangulating
suffocating
serenading
tabulating
terminating
titillating
tête-à-têteing
tolerating
twitterpating
underrating
understating
undulating
validating
venerating
vacillating
ventilating
vindicating
violating

abominating
abbreviating
accelerating
accumulating
accentuating
accommodating
affiliating
adulterating
adjudicating
alleviating
alienating
articulating
agglutinating
anticipating
annihilating
appreciating
appropriating
associating
asphyxiating
assassinating
authenticating
capitulating

consolidating
coagulating
cross-ventilating
conciliating
communicating
commemorating
cooperating
commiserating
congratulating
coordinating
contaminating
deliberating
depopulating
debilitating
delineating
depreciating
decaffeinating
discriminating
domesticating
elaborating
ejaculating
elucidating
emancipating
eliminating
emaciating
encapsulating
equivocating
eradicating
extrapolating
excruciating
exacerbating
exhilarating
exterminating
exaggerating
expectorating
exasperating
evaporating
evacuating
facilitating
felicitating
gesticulating
hallucinating
infatuating
incarcerating
indoctrinating

impersonating
ingratiating
insider trading
initiating
illuminating
inoculating
irradiating
investigating
interrogating
intoxicating
invalidating
invigorating
intimidating
insinuating
luxuriating
lady-in-waiting
manipulating
matriculating
miscegenating
miscalculating
necessitating
negotiating
officiating
orientating
perambulating
participating
perpetuating
precipitating
pontificating
prevaricating
procrastinating
proliferating
prognosticating
recaptivating
recriminating
redecorating
reciprocating
recuperating
refrigerating
repudiating
reiterating
rejuvenating
remunerating
resuscitating
retaliating

regurgitating
reverberating
subordinating
substantiating

ameliorating
discombobulating
differentiating
hyperventilating
misappropriating
rehabilitating
reinvigorating

AD-ēng

adding
batting
chatting
gadding
madding
matting
padding
patting
ratting
slatting
splatting
tatting

chitchatting
combatting
floor matting
footpadding
hellcatting
tomcatting

pitterpatting
photostatting

AD-ē-nus

battiness
brattiness
cattiness
chattiness
fattiness
nattiness
rattiness

ĀD-ē-u

stadia

Arcadia

ĀD-ē-ul

gradial
radial

ĀD-ē-um

radium
stadium

palladium

ĀD-ē-un

Arcadian
Canadian

ĀD-ē-unt

gradient
radiant

ĀD-ēz

eighties
Hades
Katie's
ladies
maties

bag ladies
Euphrates
landladies
Mercedes

AD-ēz

baddies
caddies
daddies
fatties
laddies

paddies
patties

AD-i-fī
(See AD-u-fī)

AD-ik
(See AD-uk)

AD-ik-lē

radically

erratically
fanatically
grammatically
mathematically
sporadically

AD-ik-u

Attica

sciatica

AD-ik-ul

radical

erratical
fanatical
grammatical
mathematical
sporadical
sabbatical

problematical
ungrammatical

ĀD-in
(See ĀD-un)

AD-in
(See AD-un)

AD-ish

baddish
brattish
caddish
cattish
fattish
faddish
flattish
gaddish
maddish
plaidish
radish

chitchattish
high-hattish
horseradish

aristocratish

ĀD-ist
(See ĀD-ust)

AD-ist
(See AD-ust)

AD-it
(See AD-ut)

AD-i-tūd

attitude
gratitude
latitude
platitude

beatitude
ingratitude

ĀD-iv

dative
native

creative
debative

dilative
elative
frustrative
go native
rotative
translative

animative
cogitative
complicative
circulative
compensative
copulative
cumulative
contemplative
calculative
deprecative
designative
dominative
duplicative
emanative
explicative
educative
emulative
federative
gravitative
hesitative
imitative
implicative
incubative
innovative
irritative
iterative
irrigative
judicative
lacerative
legislative
meditative
modulative
mitigative
medicative
procreative
qualitative
quantitative
radiative

recreative
regulative
stimulative
speculative
segregative
simulative
suffocative
terminative
uncreative
vegetative
violative
ventilative
anticipative
administrative
adjudicative
appreciative
accelerative
associative
communicative
discriminative
elucidative
enumerative
enunciative
exonerative
incriminative
illuminative
investigative
manipulative
opinionative
recuperative
recriminative
remunerative
retaliative

AD-ix
(See AD-ux)

ADJ
(See AJ)

AD-lē

badly
Bradley

gladly
madly
sadly

ĀD-lēng

cradling
ladling

encradling

AD-lēng

battling
Gatling
paddling
rattling
saddling
straddling
tattling

skedaddling
unsaddling

AD-lur

addler
Adler
battler
paddler
rattler
saddler
straddler
tattler

cage rattler
skedaddler
unsaddler

baby rattler

ĀD-nus

frayedness
staidness

afraidness

AD-nus

badness
gladness
madness
sadness

ĀD-ō

Cato
credo
dado
NATO
Plato
Play-Doh

Laredo
potato
tomato
tornado

couch potato
hot potato
small potato(es)

AD-ō

shadow

eye shadow
foreshadow

Colorado
overshadow

ĀD-u

Ada
beta
data
eta
feta
theta

Alpha Beta

AD-u

data
strata

Nevada
pro rata
sub strata

Sierra Nevada

ĀD-u-bul

aidable
baitable
braidable
cratable
datable
gradable
gratable
raidable
shadable
skateable
slatable
statable
tradable
wadable

abatable
awaitable
blockadable
collatable
creatable
crematable
degradable
debatable
deflatable
dilatable
donatable
dissuadable
elatable
evadable
equatable
frustratable
invadable
inflatable
ligatable
locatable
mandatable
narratable
negatable

paradable
placatable
persuadable
probatable
rebatable
relatable
rotatable
sedatable
translatable
upgradable
updatable
upbraidable
vacatable
vibratable

arbitratable
activatable
annotatable
advocatable
amputatable
agitatable
aggravatable
allocatable
barricadable
marinadable
promenadable
serenadable

biodegradable

AD-u-bul

addable
battable
mattable
paddable
pattable
rattable

compatible
combatable

ĀD-ud

aided
braided
baited

faded
graded
grated
hated
jaded
laded
mated
plaited
plated
raided
rated
shaded
spaded
sated
skated
slated
stated
traded
waited
waded

abraded
abated
blockaded
berated
cascaded
crusaded
castrated
collated
created
cremated
debated
donated
deflated
dilated
degraded
downgraded
dissuaded
elated
equated
evaded
frustrated
gradated
gyrated
invaded

ice-skated
inflated
located
mandated
migrated
misstated
negated
orated
outdated
placated
prostrated
probated
prorated
pulsated
paraded
persuaded
pervaded
related
rebated
rotated
sedated
serrated
stagnated
translated
tailgated
upgraded
updated
vacated
vibrated

abrogated
abnegated
abdicated
animated
arbitrated
annotated
activated
acclimated
advocated
amputated
agitated
aggravated
aspirated
allocated
barricaded

castigated
calibrated
calculated
captivated
cogitated
carbonated
circulated
complicated
celebrated
constipated
compensated
contemplated
confiscated
conjugated
concentrated
copulated
cultivated
culminated
decimated
delegated
decorated
devastated
deviated
deprecated
dehydrated
demonstrated
designated
defecated
dedicated
dislocated
dissipated
detonated
dominated
duplicated
educated
elongated
emanated
emulated
emigrated
extricated
elevated
escalated
fluoridated
fabricated
fascinated

federated
formulated
fornicated
fluctuated
fumigated
generated
germinated
graduated
gravitated
hesitated
hibernated
hyphenated
integrated
intimated
illustrated
immigrated
impregnated
insulated
implicated
imitated
instigated
indicated
incubated
inundated
iterated
infiltrated
isolated
irrigated
irritated
lacerated
liquidated
laminated
litigated
liberated
lubricated
masticated
masturbated
meditated
medicated
mediated
moderated
menstruated
mitigated
modulated
motivated

mutilated
masqueraded
navigated
nauseated
operated
overrated
obfuscated
obligated
oscillated
overstated
palpitated
permeated
perforated
penetrated
percolated
predicated
postulated
pollinated
procreated
promulgated
profligated
propagated
radiated
relegated
recreated
roller-skated
relocated
regulated
reinstated
renovated
ruminated
satiated
salivated
saturated
segregated
separated
simulated
silver-plated
speculated
syndicated
stimulated
stipulated
subjugated
sublimated
strangulated

suffocated
serenaded
tabulated
terminated
titillated
tolerated
underrated
understated
undulated
validated
venerated
vacillated
ventilated
vindicated
violated

abbreviated
accelerated
accumulated
accentuated
accommodated
affiliated
adulterated
adjudicated
alleviated
alienated
articulated
agglutinated
anticipated
annihilated
appreciated
appropriated
associated
asphyxiated
assassinated
authenticated
capitulated
consolidated
communicated
commemorated
cooperated
commiserated
congratulated
coordinated
contaminated

deliberated
depopulated
debilitated
delineated
depreciated
decaffeinated
dilapidated
discriminated
domesticated
elaborated
ejaculated
elucidated
emancipated
eliminated
emaciated
encapsulated
equivocated
eradicated
extrapolated
exacerbated
exhilarated
exterminated
exaggerated
expectorated
exasperated
evaporated
evacuated
facilitated
felicitated
gesticulated
hallucinated
infatuated
incarcerated
indoctrinated
impersonated
ingratiated
initiated
iluminated
inoculated
irradiated
investigated
interrogated
intoxicated
invalidated
invigorated

intimidated
insinuated
manipulated
matriculated
miscegenated
miscalculated
necessitated
negotiated
officiated
orientated
participated
perpetuated
precipitated
pontificated
prevaricated
procrastinated
proliferated
prognosticated
recaptivated
redecorated
reciprocated
recuperated
refrigerated
repudiated
reiterated
rejuvenated
remunerated
resuscitated
retaliated
regurgitated
reverberated
substantiated

ameliorated
discombobulated
differentiated
hyperventilated
misappropriated
rehabilitated
reinvigorated

AD-ud

added
batted
chatted

gadded
matted
padded
patted
ratted
slatted
tatted

chitchatted
combatted

photostatted

AD-u-fi

gratify
ratify

beatify

AD-uk

attic
haddock
static

asthmatic
chromatic
climatic
dogmatic
dramatic
erratic
emphatic
ecstatic
fanatic
lymphatic
mathematic
pneumatic
pragmatic
rheumatic
sporadic
Sabbatic
stigmatic
sciatic
schematic
Socratic
somatic

thematic
traumatic

automatic
Asiatic
autocratic
animatic
acrobatic
aromatic
astigmatic
Adriatic
bureaucratic
charismatic
democratic
diplomatic
enigmatic
emblematic
Instamatic
mathematic
numismatic
operatic
photostatic
pancreatic
problematic
plutocratic
symptomatic
systematic
thermostatic
undramatic
ungrammatic

aristocratic
axiomatic
anathematic
idiocratic
idiomatic
melodramatic
psychosomatic
undiplomatic

idiosyncratic
semiautomatic

AD-uk-lē

statically
dramatically

dogmatically
erratically
emphatically
ecstatically
fanatically
mathematically
pragmatically
sporadically

automatically
autocratically
charismatically
democratically
diplomatically
enigmatically
systematically
undramatically
ungrammatically

aristocratically
melodramatically
undiplomatically

idiosyncratically

ĀD-ul

cradle
fatal
ladle
natal

cat's cradle
encradle
prenatal
postnatal

gravy ladle
rock the cradle
rob the cradle

AD-ul

addle
battle
cattle
chattel
paddle

prattle
rattle
straddle
saddle
tattle

astraddle
dog-paddle
death rattle
embattle(d)
pitched battle
skedaddle
Seattle
sidesaddle
unsaddle

baby rattle
fiddle-faddle
ice cream paddle
losing battle
tittle-tattle

AD-uld

addled
battled
paddled
prattled
rattled
straddled
saddled
tattled

dog-paddled
embattled
skedaddled
unsaddled

ĀD-ul-ēng
(See ĀD-lēng)

AD-ul-ēng
(See AD-lēng)

ĀD-um

aid 'em
ate 'em
braid 'em
datum
date 'em
fade 'em
flayed 'em
grade 'em
grayed 'em
hate 'em
laid 'em
lade 'em
made 'em
paid 'em
played 'em
raid 'em
rate 'em
slayed 'em
shade 'em
swayed 'em
spade 'em
sprayed 'em
stratum
trade 'em
weighed 'em

assayed 'em
arrayed 'em
allayed 'em
blockade 'em
betrayed 'em
conveyed 'em
crocheted 'em
degrade 'em
downgrade 'em
dissuade 'em
displayed 'em
delayed 'em
dismayed 'em
evade 'em
hurrayed 'em
handmade 'em
invade 'em
misplayed 'em

outweighed 'em
okayed 'em
obeyed 'em
parlayed 'em
postpaid 'em
parade 'em
persuade 'em
pervade 'em
portrayed 'em
pureed 'em
repaid 'em
remade 'em
relaid 'em
replayed 'em
relayed 'em
relate 'em
segued 'em
surveyed 'em
sautéed 'em
substratum
upgrade 'em
unswayed 'em
upbraid 'em
verbatim
waylaid 'em
x-rayed 'em

appliquéd 'em
barricade 'em
custom-made 'em
disobeyed 'em
disarrayed 'em
seriatim
ultimatum

AD-um

at 'em
add 'em
Adam
atom
bat 'em
datum
drat 'em
had 'em
madam

pat 'em
pad 'em

begat 'em
combat 'em
forbade 'em
macadam

baby-sat 'em

AD-um-ē

bad o' me

academy
anatomy

ĀD-un

aidin'
braidin'
fadin'
gradin'
laden
maiden
raidin'
shadin'
tradin'
wadin'

blockadin'
cascadin'
crusadin'
degradin'
downgradin'
dissuadin'
evadin'
fair maiden
iron maiden
invadin'
paradin'
persuadin'
pervadin'
upgradin'
unladen

heavy-laden
overladen

AD-un

addin'
gaddin'
gladden
madden
paddin'
sadden

Aladdin
Macfadden
readdin'

AD-un-ēng

gladdening
maddening
saddening

ĀD-ur

aider
ate 'er
baiter
braider
cater
crater
dater
date 'er
fader
freighter
gator
gaiter
grader
grater
greater
hater
hate 'er
later
made 'er
nadir
Nader
rater
rate 'er
raider
satyr

shader
Seder
skater
staider
stater
straighter
trader
trade 'er
traitor
tater
waiter
wader

abater
awaiter
await 'er
blockader
berater
curator
crusader
castrator
checkmate 'er
collator
creator
cremator
charader
dictator
degrader
debater
Decatur
downgrader
dissuader
deflator
dilator
donator
dumb waiter
elater
evader
equator
fixator
fur trader
filtrator
frustrater
gyrator
head waiter

horse trader
invader
inflator
ice skater
locator
legator
mandator
migrator
man-hater
negator
narrator
outdater
ornater
parader
placater
persuader
prostrater
probater
prorater
pulsator
rebater
relater
rotator
spectator
sedator
slave trader
stock trader
tailgater
tirader
theater
testator
translator
upgrader
updater
unbraider
vacater
vibrator

aspirator
arbitrator
aviator
alligator
abnegator
abdicator
animator

annotator
actuator
activator
adulator
acclimater
advocator
agitator
aggravator
allocator
barricader
cavalcader
castigator
calibrator
calculator
carburetor
captivator
circulator
celebrator
compensator
cogitator
contemplator
confiscator
commentator
correlator
conjugator
concentrator
copulator
cultivator
culminator
cumulator
delegator
deviator
deprecator
dehydrator
demonstrator
designator
defecator
dedicator
dislocater
dissipater
duplicator
decimator
decorator
devastator
dominator

detonator
emanator
emigrator
extricator
educator
emulator
enervator
elevator
escalator
estimator
excavator
escapader
fabricator
formulator
fornicator
fumigator
fluoridater
fascinator
fluctuator
gladiator
generator
gravitator
hesitater
hibernator
hyphenator
illustrator
implicator
imitator
instigator
integrator
indicator
incubator
inundater
irrigator
irritator
isolator
immigrator
impregnator
insulator
iterater
infiltrator
innovator
lacerator
laminator
legislator

liberator
lubricator
liquidator
litigator
masquerader
masticator
masturbator
meditator
medicator
mediator
mitigator
motivator
mutilator
moderator
modulator
navigator
nominator
nauseator
operator
obligator
oscillator
overstater
palpitater
permeater
perforator
penetrator
perpetrator
perorator
postulator
pollinator
procreator
propagator
percolator
predicator
promulgator
roller skater
radiator
relegator
relocater
regulator
recreator
reinstater
renovator
ruminator
salivater

see you later
saturater
scintillator
segregator
separator
simulator
serenader
speculator
stimulater
stipulator
syndicator
suffocater
subjugator
sublimater
tabulator
terminator
titillater
tolerator
underrater
understater
undulator
validator
vacillator
ventilator
vindicator
violator
woman hater

associator
abominator
abbreviator
accelerator
accumulator
adulterator
accentuator
accommodator
affiliator
appropriator
adjudicator
alleviator
alienator
annihilator
appreciator
asphyxiator
authenticator

articulator
anticipator
assassinator
conciliator
capitulator
crane operator
consolidator
communicator
cooperator
commiserator
contaminator
cross ventilator
congratulator
coordinator
devaluator
depreciator
debilitator
delineator
discriminator
domesticator
deliberator
elaborator
elucidator
ego inflater
emancipator
encapsulator
ego deflator
eradicator
extrapolator
exacerbator
evaluator
exhilarator
exterminator
exaggerator
evaporator
evacuator
ejaculator
eliminator
emaciator
equivocator
expectorator
facilitator
gesticulator
hallucinator
humiliator

infatuator
incarcerator
indoctrinator
ingratiator
initiator
inoculator
investigator
interrogator
intoxicator
invigorator
intimidator
insinuator
impersonator
illuminator
irradiator
invalidator
luxuriator
manipulator
matriculator
miscegenator
miscalculator
negotiator
necessitator
officiator
orientator
perambulator
perpetuator
pontificator
proliferator
participator
precipitator
prevaricator
procrastinator
prognosticator
recaptivator
recriminator
reciprocator
refrigerator
repudiator
rejuvenator
remunerator
resuscitator
reiterator
retaliator
regurgitator

recuperator
reverberator
smooth operator
sooner or later

ameliorator
big-time operator
beauty operator
differentiator
discombobulator
hyperventilator
misappropriator
rehabilitator
reinvigorator

common denominator
telephone operator

elevator operator
interior decorator

AD-ur

adder
batter
badder
bladder
chatter
clatter
dratter
fatter
flatter
gadder
gladder
hatter
had 'er
ladder
latter
madder
matter
patter
padder
platter
ratter
spatter
splatter
sadder

smatter
shatter
tatter
yatter

gallbladder
gray matter
have at 'er
mad hatter
meat platter
no matter
rope ladder
stepladder
wildcatter

antimatter
hook and ladder
ironcladder
laughing matter
pitter-patter
printed matter
subject matter
spin the platter
up the ladder

corporate ladder
family matter
gist of the matter
mad as a hatter

AD-urd

battered
chattered
clattered
flattered
mattered
pattered
spattered
splattered
shattered
tattered

AD-ur-ē

battery
chattery

cattery
clattery
flattery
mattery
spattery
tattery

assault and battery

ĀD-ur-ēng

catering
waitering

AD-ur-ēng

chattering
clattering
flattering
mattering
pattering
spattering
splattering
smattering
shattering

unflattering

pitterpattering

AD-ur-īz

bat 'er eyes
badder eyes
drat 'er eyes
madder eyes
satirize
sadder eyes

AD-urn

pattern
slattern
Saturn

AD-ur-ul

lateral

bilateral
collateral

unilateral

AD-ur-ur

batterer
chatterer
flatterer
patterer
splatterer
shatterer

ĀD-us

aid us
ate us
bait us
date us
grade us
hate us
jade us
made us
mate us
paid us
played us
rate us
shade us
swayed us
sprayed us
trade us
weighed us
status

await us
berate us
blockade us
betrayed us
castrate us
create us
deflate us
degrade us

downgrade us
dissuade us
displayed us
delayed us
dismayed us
evade us
elate us
frustrate us
hiatus
invade us
inflate us
locate us
mandate us
negate us
outdate us
okayed us
obeyed us
parade us
persuade us
pervade us
portrayed us
placate us
prostrate us
repaid us
relate us
rotate us
surveyed us
stagnate us
upgrade us
update us

disobeyed us
overpaid us
overrate us
serenade us
underpaid us
underrate us

AD-us

at us
add us
had us
lattice
pad us
pat us

stratus
status

combat us
free gratis
forbade us

apparatus
baby-sat us

ĀD-ust

greatest
latest
sadist
staidest
straightest

crusadist
charadist

AD-ust

baddest
fattest
faddist
flattest
maddest
saddest

combatist

AD-ut

adit
add it
at it
bat it
drat it
had it
mat it
pad it
pat it
rat it

combat it
forbade it

baby-sat it
photostat it

AD-ux

attics
addicts

asthmatics
dramatics
fanatics

Appomattox
acrobatics
mathematics

Ā-est
(See Ā-ust)

ĀF

chafe
safe
strafe
waif

failsafe
play safe
unsafe
vouchsafe

AF

calf
chaff
gaffe
graph
half
laugh
staff
staph
WAF

behalf
carafe
distaff
decaf

Falstaff
Flagstaff
giraffe
half-staff
horselaugh
last laugh
one-half
riffraff

autograph
belly laugh
better half
chief of staff
epitaph
fatted calf
homograph
holograph
half-and-half
lithograph
monograph
overstaff
paragraph
photograph
phonograph
polygraph
seismograph
telegraph
understaff

addressograph
cardiograph
mimeograph
time and a half

AF-ē

daffy
Jaffe
taffy

ĀF-ēng

chafing
strafing

vouchsafing

AF-ēng

gaffing
laughing
staffing

autographing
overstaffing
paragraphing
photographing
telegraphing

AF-ik
(See AF-uk)

AF-i-kul
(See AF-u-kul)

AF-lēng

baffling
raffling

AFS

chaffs
crafts
drafts
gaffes
grafts
graphs
laughs
rafts
shafts
staffs
wafts

carafes
giraffes

autographs
arts and crafts
belly laughs
epitaphs
homographs
handicrafts

holographs
overstaffs
overdrafts
paragraphs
photographs
phonographs
polygraphs
seismographs
telegraphs
understaffs

mimeographs

AFT

aft
craft
daft
draft
draught
gaffed
graft
laughed
raft
shaft
staffed
Taft
waft

abaft
aircraft
bank draft
crankshaft
downdraft
first draft
life raft
mine shaft
spacecraft
skin graft
unstaffed
updraft
witchcraft
woodcraft

arts and craft(s)
autographed
bellylaughed

fore and aft
get the shaft
handicraft
hovercraft
overstaffed
overdraft
photographed
telegraphed
understaffed
watercraft

antiaircraft
mimeographed

AFT-ē

crafty
drafty

AFT-ed
(See AFT-ud)

AFT-ēng

crafting
drafting
grafting
rafting
wafting

skin grafting

overdrafting

whitewater rafting

AFT-u-bul

craftable
draftable
graftable
shaftable
waftable

AFT-ud

crafted
drafted

grafted
rafted
shafted
wafted

AFT-un

caftan
craftin'
draftin'
graftin'
shaftin'

overdraftin'

AFT-ur

after
crafter
dafter
drafter
grafter
laughter
rafter
shafter

come after
hereafter
run after
thereafter
take after

ever after
handicrafter
hereinafter
morning after
overdrafter
pick up after
thereinafter

forever after

AF-ub-lē

affably
laughably

AF-u-bul

affable
laughable
staffable

unlaughable
unstaffable

autographable
paragraphable
photographable
telegraphable

unparagraphable
unphotographable

AF-uk

graphic
Sapphic
traffic

air traffic
seraphic
ungraphic

biographic
calligraphic
demographic
geographic
holographic
lithographic
one-way traffic
photographic
pornographic
phonographic
seismographic
stenographic
telegraphic

choreographic

autobiographic

AF-u-kul

biographical
demographical

geographical
pornographical
typographical

bibliographical

autobiographical

ĀF-ul

playful
sleighful
strayful
trayful

bouquetful

AF-ul

baffle
raffle

AF-uld

baffled
raffled
scaffold

ĀF-ur

chafer
safer
strafer
Schaefer
wafer

unsafer
vouchsafer

AF-ur

chaffer
gaffer
grapher
laugher
staffer

horselaugher

autographer
belly laugher
overstaffer
paragrapher
understaffer

mimeographer

ĀG

Craig
Greg
Hague
keg
leg
plague
vague

bootleg
bum leg
beer keg
pegleg

break a leg
pull one's leg
shake a leg

bubonic plague
daddy longleg(s)

AG

bag
brag
crag
drag
fag
flag
gag
hag
jag
lag
nag
rag
sag
slag
shag

skag
scrag
stag
swag
snag
tag
wag
zag

airbag
barf bag
beanbag
dishrag
douche bag
dogtag
feedbag
fleabag
flight bag
grab bag
gasbag
glad rag(s)
handbag
ice bag
jig jag
jet lag
mailbag
mixed bag
Maytag
main drag
nametag
old bag
price tag
ragtag
ragbag
red tag
scuzzbag
sandbag
scumbag
sleazebag
tote bag
teabag
trashbag
time-lag
unsnag
washrag

wigwag
white flag
windbag
zigzag

airsick bag
bowling bag
carpetbag
chew the rag
crying jag
checkered flag
ditty bag
doggie bag
duffel bag
garment bag
in the bag
luggage tag
lollygag
litterbag
laundry bag
moneybag(s)
punching bag
running gag
saddlebag
shopping bag
sleeping bag
•scalawag

American flag

AG-ē

Aggie
baggy
craggy
draggy
faggy
gaggy
haggy
laggy
Maggie
naggy
saggy
snaggy
swaggy
shaggy

waggy

jig-jaggy
wigwaggy
zigzaggy

ĀG-en
(See ĀG-un)

AG-en
(See AG-un)

ĀG-ēng

legging
plaguing

bootlegging

AG-ēng

bagging
bragging
dragging
flagging
gagging
jagging
lagging
nagging
sagging
swagging
snagging
tagging
wagging
zagging

sandbagging
unsnagging
wigwagging
zigzagging

carpetbagging
lollygagging

AG-ē-nus

bagginess
cragginess
sagginess
swagginess
shagginess

AG-lēng

haggling
straggling
snaggling
waggling

AG-nun

Cro-Magnon
I. Magnin

ĀG-ō

sago

lumbago
plumbago

San Diego
Winnebago

ĀG-runt

flagrant
fragrant
vagrant

ĀG-u

Omega

rutabaga

Alpha Tau Omega

AG-u-bul

baggable
draggable
flaggable

gaggable
saggable
swaggable
snaggable
taggable
waggable

AG-ud

jagged
ragged

ĀG-ul

bagel

finagle
inveigle

AG-ul

gaggle
haggle
straggle
snaggle
waggle .

bedraggle
rehaggle

wiggle waggle

AG-ul-ēng
(See AG-lēng)

ĀG-un

plaguin'
pagan
Reagan

bootleggin'

Copenhagen

AG-un

braggin'
baggin'

dragon
draggin'
flagon
gaggin'
laggin'
naggin'
saggin'
snaggin'
swaggin'
waggin'
wagon

bandwagon
chuck wagon
jigjaggin'
snapdragon
sandbaggin'
tail waggin'
Volkswagen
zigzaggin'

battlewagon
carpetbaggin'
covered wagon
lollygaggin'
paddy wagon
station wagon

fix someone's wagon

AG-un-ē

agony
dragony
wagony

AG-un-ist

braggin'est
draggin'est
gaggin'est
naggin'est
saggin'est
waggin'est

antagonist
protagonist
zigzaggin'est

AG-un-ul

diagonal
hexagonal
octagonal
pentagonal

ĀG-ur

plaguer
vaguer

bootlegger

AG-ur

bagger
bragger
dagger
dragger
flagger
gagger
jagger
lagger
nagger
swagger
snagger
stagger
sagger
tagger
wagger

brown bagger
four bagger
foot dragger
sandbagger
tail wagger
wigwagger
zigzagger

cloak-and-dagger
carpetbagger
lollygagger

AG-urd

haggard
laggard

swaggered
staggered

ĀG-ur-ē

Gregory
vagary

AG-ur-ēng

staggering
swaggering

AG-urt

braggart
swaggart

AG-ur-us

stagger us

Pythagoras

ĀG-us

plague us

Las Vegas

AG-ut

agate
bag it
drag it
faggot
flag it
gag it
maggot
nag it
snag it
swag it
shag it
tag it
wag it

sandbag it
unsnag it

Ā-ik
(See Ā-uk)

Ā-is
(See Ā-us)

Ā-i-tē
(See Ā-u-dē)

ĀJ

age
cage
gauge
page
rage
sage
stage
wage

assuage
birdcage
backstage
Bronze Age
downstage
Dark Age(s)
enrage
engage
front page
gas gauge
Ice Age
outrage
offstage
of age
old age
onstage
ribcage
rampage
Stone Age
school age
space age
sound stage
teenage
ten-gauge

upstage

awkward age
act one's age
all the rage
Broadway stage
center stage
come of age
disengage
golden age
gilded cage
Iron Age
just a stage
lion cage
legal age
middle age
over age
reengage
title page
under age
weather gauge

minimum wage
temperature gauge

AJ

badge
cadge
Madge

ĀJ-ēng

aging
caging
gauging
paging
raging
staging
waging

assuaging
enraging
engaging
outraging
rampaging

upstaging

disengaging

ĀJ-es
(See ĀJ-us)

AJ-et
(See AJ-ut)

AJ-ik

magic
tragic

black magic
untragic

AJ-ik-lē

magically
tragically

AJ-il
(See AJ-ul)

AJ-in-ul
(See AJ-un-ul)

ĀJ-lus

ageless
cageless
gaugeless
pageless
stageless
wageless

ĀJ-ment

assuagement
enragement
engagement

disengagement
preengagement

AJ-ud-ē

gadgety
tragedy

AJ-ul

agile
fragile
Madge 'll

ĀJ-un

agin'
Cajun
cagin'
gaugin'
pagin'
ragin'
stagin'
wagin'

assuagin'
contagion
engagin'
enragin'
rampagin'
upstagin'

disengagin'

AJ-un

cadgin'

imagine

AJ-un-ul

paginal
vaginal

ĀJ-ur

ager
cager
gauger
major

pager
rager
sager
stager
wager

assuager
backstager
drum major
engager
enrager
outrager
rampager
teenager
upstager

disengager
Ursa Major

AJ-ur

badger
cadger

ĀJ-ur-ēng

majoring
wagering

ĀJ-us

age us
cage us
gauge us
page us

assuage us
contagious
courageous
engage us
enrage us
outrage us
outrageous
Pantages
rampageous
upstage us

advantageous

disengage us
reengage us

disadvantageous

ĀJ-us-lē

contagiously
courageously
outrageously
rampageously

advantageously

AJ-ut

cadge it
gadget

AJ-u-tē
(See AJ-u-dē)

ĀJ-uz

ages
cages
gauges
pages
rages
sages
stages
wages

assuages
birdcages
Dark Ages
enrages
engages
outrages
rampages
upstages

disengages
lion cages
Middle Ages
reengages

Rock of Ages
yellow pages

ĀK

ache
bake
Blake
brake
break
cake
drake
fake
flake
jake
lake
make
quake
rake
sake
slake
snake
stake
steak
spake
shake
sheik
take
wake

air brake
awake
at stake
beefsteak
big break
beefcake
backache
cornflake(s)
cheesecake
cupcake
clambake
daybreak
earthquake
earache
forsake
fair shake

fast break
firebreak
fruitcake
Great Lake(s)
grubstake
headache
hot cake
housebreak
handshake
heartache
heartbreak
intake
jailbreak
keepsake
lunch break
milkshake
mandrake
muckrake
mistake
namesake
newsbreak
opaque
outbreak
partake
pancake
remake
retake
shortcake
snowflake
sweepstake(s)
toothache
tax break
tough break
uptake
yeastcake

bellyache
birthday cake
coffee cake
coffee break
doubletake
give and take
get a break
merrymake
make or break

no great shake(s)
overtake
on the take
on the make
pat-a-cake
piece of cake
pull up stake(s)
pepper steak
rattlesnake
stomachache
station break
sugarbake
shake and bake
service break
take the cake
take a break
undertake
wide-awake
wedding cake

apply the brake
commercial break
devil's food cake
for goodness sake
for pity sake
gimme a break
jump in the lake

icing on the cake
potato pancake
slow on the uptake
upside-down cake

nutty as a fruitcake

AK

back
black
clack
claque
crack
flack
hack
jack
knack
lack

lac
pack
plaque
quack
rack
sac
sack
shack
smack
stack
slack
snack
tack
thwack
track
wrack
whack
wack
yak

Amtrak
alack
attack
aback
bushwhack
backpack
bounce back
backtrack
buyback
bivouac
bootblack
bareback
brushback
blackjack
cognac
cold pack
Cossack
cutback
comeback
call back
clothes rack
drawback
Dry Sack
fall back
flapjack

feedback
fast track
fastback
fight back
flashback
fullback
greenback
give back
hatrack
hijack
horseback
humpback
hunchback
hatchback
haystack
halfback
hardtack
hold back
Iraq
icepack
jet black
knapsack
Kodak
kayak
kickback
keep track
look back
laugh track
lose track
lunch sack
laid-back
lampblack
mudpack
outback
on track
offtrack
one-track
playback
pitch-black
pay back
quack quack
ransack
right track
rat pack
retrack

rickrack
repack
racetrack
rollback
smokestack
setback
soundtrack
short stack
six-pack
slow track
soft pack
skyjack
switchback
swayback
shellac
sidetrack
shoerack
sad sack
scatback
slapjack
thumbtack
throwback
talk back
Tic Tac
take back
tie rack
tie tack
unpack
wisecrack
way back
wingback
wolf pack
wrong track
zwieback

almanac
applejack
bric-a-brac
ball the jack
back to back
blow one's stack
ball and jack
Cadillac
cardiac
cul-de-sac

caddie shack
chili mac
camelback
crackerjack
diamondback
gunnysack
heart attack
Hackensack
hit the sack
inside track
jumping jack
lumberjack
maniac
money back
Navy Jack
out of whack
off the track
off-the-rack
paperback
paddywhack
piggyback
paper sack
Pontiac
quarterback
razorback
railroad track
single-track
turtleback
union jack
warning track
zodiac

Adirondack
amnesiac
behind one's back
biofeedback
cigarette pack
counterattack
clickety-clack
flat on one's back
hard nut to crack
insomniac
knife in the back
little grass shack
on the attack

pat on the back
panic attack
shirt off one's back
sharp as a tack
scratch someone's back
stab in the back
taken aback
tough nut to crack
take up the slack
yakkity-yak

aphrodisiac
alas and alack
dipsomaniac
Farmer's Almanac
hemophiliac
hypochondriac
kleptomaniac
sacroiliac

megalomaniac
needle in a haystack
sign of the zodiac

Cyrano de Bergerac
Monday morning
    quarterback

ĀK-āt

placate
vacate

AK-chur

fracture

manufacture

AK-chū-ul

actual
factual

contractual
transactual

counterfactual
satisfactual

ĀK-ē

achy
caky
flaky
quaky
shaky
snaky

headachy

AK-ē

blackie
clacky
Jackie
khaki
lackey
quacky
sacky
tacky
wacky

by cracky
knickknacky

ticky tacky

ĀK-en
(See ĀK-un)

AK-en
(See AK-un)

ĀK-ēng

aching
baking
braking
breaking
caking
faking
flaking
making
quaking
raking

snaking
staking
shaking
taking
waking

awaking
breathtaking
backbreaking
backaching
cake baking
earthshaking
forsaking
groundbreaking
handshaking
housebreaking
heartaching
heartbreaking
jailbreaking
lovemaking
leavetaking
mistaking
muckraking
painstaking
partaking
remaking
retaking

bellyaching
crazymaking
epoch-making
merrymaking
movie making
overtaking
patty-caking
undertaking

AK-ēng

backing
blacking
clacking
cracking
hacking
jacking
lacking

packing
quacking
racking
sacking
shacking
smacking
stacking
slacking
snacking
thwacking
tacking
tracking
whacking
wracking
yakking

attacking
backpacking
bushwacking
backtracking
hijacking
lipsmacking
ransacking
repacking
retracking
sidetracking
skyjacking
thumbtacking
unpacking
wisecracking

lumberjacking
piggybacking
pistolpacking
quarterbacking
reattacking

counterattacking
yakkity-yakking

ĀK-ē-nus

achiness
flakiness
quakiness
snakiness
shakiness

AK-ē-nus

khakiness
sackiness
tackiness
wackiness

**AK-et
(See AK-ut)**

**AK-et-ē
(See AK-ud-ē)**

ĀK-ful

acheful
wakeful

AK-ij

brackage
package
slackage

**ĀK-il-ē
(See ĀK-ul-ē)**

**ĀK-in
(See ĀK-un)**

**AK-in
(See AK-un)**

AK-ish

blackish
brackish

**AK-it
(See AK-ut)**

AK-lē

blackly

abstractly
compactly
exactly

not exactly

matter-of-factly

AK-lēng

cackling
crackling
spackling
shackling
tackling

AK-mē

acme
back me
crack me
lack me
pack me
sack me
smack me
track me
whack me

AK-nē

acne
hackney

AK-nus

blackness
slackness

abstractness
compactness
exactness

ĀK-ō

Waco

Arroyo Seco

AK-ō

whacko

tobacco

ĀK-owt

breakout
fake out
flake out
make out
shake out
stakeout
takeout

AK-owt

blackout
back out
sack out

AK-pot

black pot
crackpot
jackpot

AK-run

Akron
saccharin

AKS
(See AX)

AK-shun

action
faction
fraction
traction

abstraction
attraction
compaction
class action

court action
contraction
distraction
detraction
extraction
infraction
impaction
in traction
inaction
live action
protraction
refraction
reaction
retraction
Swiss action
subtraction
see action
transaction
take action

chain reaction
calefaction
covert action
counteraction
direct action
gut reaction
interaction
malefaction
out of action
police action
prolonged-action
retroaction
reflex action
satisfaction
stupefaction
star attraction

dissatisfaction
drug interaction
piece of the action

affirmative action

AK-shun-ul

factional
fractional

reactional
transactional

AK-shus

factious
fractious

AK-sun
(See AX-un)

ĀKT

ached
baked
faked
flaked
quaked
raked
snaked
staked
waked

honeybaked
sugarbaked

AKT

act
backed
clacked
cracked
fact
hacked
lacked
packed
pact
quacked
racked
sacked
stacked
slacked
smacked
snacked
tact
tract

tacked
tracked
whacked
wracked
yakked

attract
abstract
attacked
backpacked
backtracked
bivouacked
barebacked
contract
class act
contact
compact
distract
detract
enact
exact
extract
first act
hijacked
half-cracked
humpbacked
handpacked
hunchbacked
impact
in tact
infract
in fact
jam-packed
known fact
last act
Mann Act
protract
playact
react
refract
retract
ransacked
repacked
redact
subtract

sex act
swaybacked
sidetracked
shellacked
transact
thumbtacked
unpacked
unbacked
untracked
wisecracked

artifact
cataract
counteract
final act
interact
inexact
overact
point of fact
reenact
retroact
riot act
vacuum-packed

after the fact
before the fact
clickety-clacked
clean up one's act
counterattacked
Miranda Act
matter of fact
overreact

AKT-ēng

acting

attracting
contracting
contacting
compacting
distracting
detracting
extracting
exacting
enacting
impacting

protracting
playacting
reacting
refracting
retracting
subtracting
transacting

counteracting
interacting
overacting
reenacting

overreacting

AKT-ful

factful
packed full
tactful

distractful
detractful
untactful

AKT-ī

black tie
blacked eye
cacti

**AKT-i-bul
(See AKT-u-bul)**

AKT-ik

lactic
tactic

climactic
didactic
galactic
syntactic

chiropractic
prophylactic

intergalactic

AKT-i-kul

practical
tactical

impractical
syntactical

AKT-is
(See AKT-us)

AKT-iv

active
tractive

abstractive
attractive
contractive
distractive
enactive
inactive
protractive
reactive
refractive
subtractive

counteractive
hyperactive
overactive
retroactive

radioactive

AKT-iv-nus

activeness
tractiveness

attractiveness
inactiveness
reactiveness

hyperactiveness

radioactiveness

AKT-lē
(See AK-lē)

AKTS
(See AX)

AKT-u-bul

actable

attractable
contactable
contractable
compactible
distractable
detractable
enactable
exactable
extractable
impactable
reactable
subtractable
transactable

AKT-u-kul
(See AKT-i-kul)

AKT-ul

dactyl
tactile

AKT-ur

actor
backed 'er
cracked 'er
factor
hacked 'er
packed 'er
sacked 'er
smacked 'er
tractor
tracked 'er
whacked 'er

abstractor
attractor

attacked 'er
contractor
contactor
compactor
distracter
detractor
enactor
exacter
extractor
ham actor
impactor
Max Factor
protractor
refractor
retractor
reactor
subtractor
sidetracked 'er
transactor
unpacked 'er

benefactor
counteractor
chiropractor
interactor
overactor
RH factor
trash compactor
windchill factor

character actor
finagle factor
overreactor

AKT-ur-ē

factory

olfactory
refractory

calefactory
satisfactory

AKT-us

backed us
cactus

lacked us
practice
smacked us
sacked us
tracked us
whacked us

attract us
attacked us
contact us
distract us
impact us
malpractice
subtract us
unpacked us

counteract us
out of practice

AK-u-dē

clackety
rackety

AK-uj
(See AK-ij)

AK-ul

cackle
crackle
jackal
mackle
spackle
shackle
tackle

debacle
hamshackle
ramshackle
unshackle

block and tackle
flying tackle
fishing tackle
tabernacle

ĀK-u-lē

achily
snakily
shakily

AK-ū-lur

spectacular
vernacular

ĀK-un

achin'
bacon
bakin'
breakin'
cakin'
fakin'
flakin'
Macon
makin'
quakin'
rakin'
shaken
shakin'
snakin'
stakin'
takin'
taken
waken
wakin'

awaken
backachin'
forsakin'
forsaken
handshakin'
heartbreakin'
housebreakin'
jailbreakin'
Jamaican
muckrakin'
mistaken
mistakin'
partakin'

partaken
remakin'
retaken
retakin'
unshaken
untaken
well-taken

bellyachin'
eggs and bacon
godforsaken
merrymakin'
overtaken
patty-cakin'
reawaken
undertaken
unforsaken
unpartaken

bring home the bacon

AK-un

blacken
backin'
clackin'
crackin'
hackin'
lackin'
packin'
quackin'
rackin'
slacken
smackin'
snackin'
stackin'
tackin'
trackin'
whackin'
wrackin'
yakkin'

attackin'
bushwhackin'
backtrackin'
backpackin'
hijackin'

ransackin'
repackin'
skyjackin'
sidetrackin'
unpackin'
wisecrackin'

paddywhackin'
piggybackin'
quarterbackin'
counterattackin'
clickety-clackin'
yakkity-yakkin'

AK-un-ēng

blackening
slackening

ĀK-up

breakup
bake up
cake up
flake up
makeup
rake up
shakeup
take up
wake up

kiss and make up
pancake makeup

AK-up

backup
crackup
hack up
jack up
pack up
rack up
shack up
stack up
tack up

ĀK-ur

acher
acre
baker
breaker
faker
fakir
Laker(s)
maker
nacre
quaker
raker
shaker
staker
taker
waker

awaker
backbreaker
bone-breaker
bookmaker
cakebaker
caretaker
dressmaker
dreammaker
deal maker
earthshaker
film maker
forsaker
grubstaker
haymaker
handshaker
heartacher
homebreaker
heartbreaker
homemaker
housebreaker
ice breaker
icemaker
jawbreaker
kingmaker
lawbreaker
lovemaker
lawmaker
leavetaker

muckraker
mistaker
matchmaker
moonraker
mythmaker
noisemaker
newsmaker
partaker
peacemaker
pacemaker
playmaker
remaker
risk taker
rule breaker
strikebreaker
shoemaker
salt shaker
tiebreaker
windbreaker
wiseacre
winemaker
watchmaker

boilermaker
bellyacher
cabinetmaker
census taker
crazymaker
coffeemaker
circuit breaker
image maker
moviemaker
mischiefmaker
moneymaker
merrymaker
noisemaker
overtaker
patty-caker
pepper shaker
Studebaker
troublemaker
undertaker

movers and shaker(s)
policymaker

AK-ur

backer
blacker
cracker
clacker
hacker
lacquer
packer
quacker
racker
sacker
stacker
slacker
snacker
smacker
tacker
tracker
thwacker
whacker
yakker

attacker
backpacker
backtracker
bootblacker
bivouacker
bushwhacker
firecracker
hijacker
lipsmacker
linebacker
nutcracker
repacker
ransacker
sidetracker
safecracker
skyjacker
thumbtacker
unpacker
wisecracker

animal cracker
counterattacker
yakkity-yakker

AK-urd

lacquered
placard
Packard

ĀK-ur-ē

bakery
fakery

AK-ur-ē

crackery
daiquiri
quackery
Thackeray
Zachary

gimcrackery

AK-ur-un

lacquerin'
saccharin

ĀK-us

break us
fracas
make us
shake us
stake us
take us
wake us

forsake us
grubstake us
mistake us
remake us

overtake us

AK-us

Bacchus
back us
crack us

lack us
pack us
sack us
smack us
stack us
thwack us
track us
wrack us
whack us

attack us
unpack us

AK-ust

blackest
slackest

AK-ut

bracket
back it
crack it
hack it
jacket
lack it
packet
pack it
placket
racket
racquet
sack it
smack it
stack it
track it
whack it

attack it
bushwhack it
fur jacket
flight jacket
hijack it
lifejacket
ransack it
repack it
straitjacket

sidetrack it
unpack it
wall bracket

dinner jacket
smoking jacket
tennis racket
yellowjacket

counterattack it

AK-ut-ē
(See AK-ud-ē)

AK-yūl-ur
(See AK-ūl-ur)

ĀL
(See alsoĀ-ul)

ale
ail
bail
bale
Braille
dale
fail
frail
gale
grail
hail
hale
jail
kale
mail
male
nail
pale
pail
quail
rail
sail
scale
sale
snail

stale
shale
tale
they'll
tail
trail
vale
veil
wail
whale
Wale(s)
Yale

Airedale
airmail
avail
assail
arrayal
bewail
bulk mail
bangtail
blackmail
bobtail
betrayal
Clydesdale
coattail
curtail
cattail
cocktail
doornail
ducktail
derail
detail
dovetail
defrayal
exhale
E-mail
entail
female
fire sale
fish scale
for sale
fan mail
fishtail
fantail

guardrail
grand scale
handrail
hobnail
hate mail
hightail
hangnail
inhale
impale
jump bail
junk mail
large-scale
make sail
outsail
on sale
pigtail
payscale
prevail
percale
pass-fail
portrayal
regale
rattail
resale
retail
shirttail
smallscale
sperm whale
set sail
shavetail
travail
thumbnail
turn tail
toenail
telltale
to scale
unveil
upscale
unfail(ing)
V-mail
wholesale
white sale

Abigail
bill of sale

Bloomingdale('s)
cottontail
Chippendale
clearance sale
countervail
cotton bale
drag one's tail
express mail
estate sale
fairy tale
fingernail
garage sale
ginger ale
heads or tail(s)
hill and dale
Holy Grail
in detail
killer whale
lonesome trail
monorail
nature trail
never fail
nightingale
overscale
Prince of Wale(s)
press-on nail
out on bail
ride the rail(s)
rummage sale
sliding scale
tattletale
tip the scale
trim the sail(s)
tooth and nail
take the veil
under sail
vapor trail
without fail
water pail
yellowtail
year-end sale

beyond the pale
cat o' nine tail(s)
Grimm's fairy tale(s)

registered mail
thin as a rail
to no avail
white tie and tail(s)

dead as a doornail

bright-eyed and bushy
    tail(ed)
two shakes of a lamb's
    tail

have a tiger by the tail

AL

Al
Cal
gal
Hal
pal
Sal
shall
Val

banal
canal
corral
chorale
decal
locale
low-cal
morale
pen pal

chaparral
ear canal
femme fatale
musicale
root canal
rationale

Erie Canal
Guadalcanal

ĀL-ā

melee
Pele
waylay

AL-ā

allay
ballet
chalet

ĀL-burd

frail bird
jailbird
pale bird
railbird

ĀLD

ailed
bailed
baled
failed
hailed
jailed
mailed
nailed
paled
railed
sailed
scaled
tailed
trailed
veiled

airmailed
assailed
bewailed
blackmailed
curtailed
derailed
detailed
dovetailed
exhaled
entailed

inhaled
impaled
outsailed
prevailed
regaled
retailed
unveiled

overscaled

bright-eyed and
    bushy-tailed

Ā-lē

Bailey
daily
gaily
scaly
snaily

Disraeli
Israeli
shillelagh
unscaly

ukulele

Barnum and Bailey

AL-ē

alley
Bali
challis
dally
galley
rally
sally
tally
valley

blind alley
back alley
Death Valley
pep rally
Rudy Vallee
Svengali

ship's galley

bowling alley
dilly dally
football rally
Mexicali
shilly shally
Tin Pan Alley
up one's alley

Silicon Valley

ĀL-ē-en
(See ĀL-ē-un)

AL-ē-ēng

dallying
rallying
sallying
tallying

AL-ek
(See AL-uk)

ĀL-em
(See ĀL-um)

Ā-lēn

praline
saline

ĀL-ēng

ailing
bailing
baling
failing
galing
hailing
jailing
mailing
nailing

paling
railing
sailing
scaling
tailing
trailing
wailing

airmailing
assailing
bewailing
blackmailing
curtailing
derailing
detailing
dovetailing
exhaling
entailing
hightailing
handrailing
inhaling
impaling
outsailing
prevailing
regaling
retailing
unveiling
unfailing

countervailing
never failing

AL-ēng

palling

corralling

AL-en-jur

challenger
Salinger

AL-ens
(See AL-uns)

AL-ent
(See AL-unt)

AL-et
(See AL-ut)

ĀL-ē-u
(See ĀL-yu)

AL-ē-um

dally 'em
rally 'em
tally 'em
Valium

ĀL-ē-un

alien
thalian

Australian
Pygmalion

Episcopalian

AL-ē-un

dallyin'
galleon
rallyin'
tallyin'

AL-ex
(See AL-ux)

AL-i-bul
(See AL-u-bul)

AL-id
(See AL-ud)

AL-ik
(See AL-uk)

AL-i-mōn-ē

alimony
palimony

ĀL-is
(See ĀL-us)

AL-is
(See AL-us)

AL-is-is
(See AL-us-uz)

AL-it-ē
(See AL-ud-ē)

AL-ix
(See AL-ux)

AL-jik

neuralgic
nostalgic

AL-ku-mē

alchemy
talcumy

ĀL-ment

ailment

curtailment
derailment
impalement

ĀL-nus

frailness
maleness
paleness
staleness

Ā-lō

halo
lay low
pay low
stay low
way low

AL-ō

aloe
callow
fallow
gallow(s)
Gallo
hallow
sallow
shallow
shall owe
tallow

marshmallow

ALP

Alp
help
scalp

AL-tō

alto

contralto
Rialto

Palo Alto

ĀL-u

gala

Consuela

Venezuela

AL-u

Allah
calla

Fala
gala

impala
Valhalla

AL-ū .

shall you
value

corral you
devalue
face value

ĀL-ub-ul

failable
jailable
mailable
nailable
sailable
scalable
tailable
trailable

available
assailable
curtailable
derailable
inhalable
impalable
regalable
retailable

unavailable
unassailable

AL-ub-ul

fallible

corralable
infallible

AL-ud

ballad
pallid

salad
valid

fruit salad
invalid
love ballad
tossed salad

AL-ud-ē

malady

banality
brutality
centrality
causality
egality
fatality
finality
frugality
formality
legality
locality
morality
mentality
mortality
normality
neutrality
plurality
rascality
reality
tonality
totality
vocality
vitality

abnormality
actuality
bestiality
criminality
cordiality
commonality
geniality
generality
hospitality
immorality
informality

immortality
illegality
joviality
liberality
mutuality
nationality
personality
punctuality
principality
partiality
practicality
rationality
sexuality
speciality
sensuality
triviality
technicality
visuality
whimsicality

asexuality
bisexuality
congeniality
conviviality
eventuality
impartiality
irrationality
instrumentality
municipality
originality
spirituality
sentimentality
universality

artificiality
confidentiality
constitutionality
individuality
superficiality
territoriality

AL-uk

Alec
Gallic
phallic

cephalic
italic
metallic
smart alec

ĀL-um

fail 'em
hail 'em
jail 'em
mail 'em
nail 'em
sail 'em
Salem
scale 'em
tail 'em

AL-un

Alan
gallon
pallin'
talon

corralin'

ĀL-uns

assailants
exhalants
inhalants
surveillance

AL-uns

balance
talents
valance

off balance

counterbalance
hidden talents

ĀL-unt

assailant
exhalant

inhalant
surveillant

AL-unt

gallant
talent

AL-up

gallop
scallop

keep morale up

ĀL-ur

ailer
Baylor
bailer
failer
fail 'er
frailer
flailer
hailer
haler
jailer
jail 'er
mailer
nailer
nail 'er
paler
railer
sail 'er
sailor
scaler
staler
tailor
Taylor
tailer
tail 'er
trailer
wailer
whaler

airmailer
availer

avail 'er
assailer
bewailer
blackmailer
curtailer
derailer
detailer
dovetailer
exhaler
entailer
femaler
hightailer
inhaler
impaler
prevailer
regaler
regale 'er
retailer
unveiler
wholesaler

never fail 'er
overscaler
tattletaler

AL-ur

pallor
valor

corral 'er

AL-ur-ē

calorie
gallery
salary
Valerie

art gallery
rogue's gallery

ĀL-us

ail us
fail us
hail us

jail us
mail us
nail us
sail us
tail us
veil us

airmail us
avail us
assail us
blackmail us
curtail us
derail us
impale us
outsail us
regale us
unveil us

never fail us

semper fidelis

AL-us

Alice
callous
callus
chalice
Dallas
malice
phallus
palace

corral us
with malice

digitalis

aurora borealis

AL-u-sē

callousy
fallacy

ĀL-ust

frailest
malest

palest
stalest

AL-ust

ballast
calloused

AL-us-uz

Alice's
calluses
chalices
malices
palaces

analysis
dialysis
paralysis

AL-ut

ballot
mallet
palate
palette
pallet
shallot
valet

corral it
so shall it

croquet mallet
cast a ballot
secret ballot

AL-ux

Alex

italics
metallics
smart alecs

ĀL-yu

ail ya
fail ya

hail ya
jail ya
mail ya
nail ya
tail ya
trail ya

azalea
Australia
assail ya
blackmail ya
curtail ya
derail ya
impale ya
outsail ya
regalia
regale ya
unveil ya

Bacchanalia
genitalia
never fail ya
Saturnalia

paraphernalia

AL-yū
(See AL-ū)

AL-yun

galleon
scallion
stallion

black stallion
battalion
Italian
medallion
rapscallion

ĀLZ

ales
ails
bails
bales

dales
fails
gales
grails
hails
hales
jails
mails
males
nails
pales
pails
quails
rails
sails
scales
sales
snails
tales
tails
trails
vales
veils
wails
whales
Wales

Airedales
airmails
assails
arrayals
bewails
bangtails
blackmails
bobtails
betrayals
Clydesdales
coattails
curtails
cattails
cocktails
doornails
ducktails
derails
details

dovetails
defrayals
exhales
entails
females
fish scales
fishtails
fantails
guardrails
hangnails
inhales
impales
outsails
pigtails
prevails
portrayals
regales
rattails
resales
retails
shirttails
thumbnails
toenails
unveils

Bloomingdale's
cottontails
Chippendale's
countervails
fairy tales
fingernails
heads or tails
hills and dales
monorails
never fails
nightingales
Prince of Wales
press-on nails
ride the rails
rummage sales
tattletales
trim the sails

cat o' nine tails
Grimm's fairy tales
white tie and tails

ĀM

aim
blame
came
claim
dame
fame
frame
flame
game
Jame(s)
lame
maim
Mame
name
same
shame
tame

A-frame
acclaim
aflame
became
big game
brand name
ball game
chess game
con game
card game
defame
door frame
disclaim
dad-blame
exclaim
for shame
first name
fair game
inflame
misname
mainframe
nickname
old flame
pen name
pet name
quitclaim

reclaim
rename
surname
skin game
selfsame
shell game
tradename
take aim
time frame
untame
war game

all the same
change of name
claim to fame
counterclaim
guessing game
given name
Hall of Fame
just the same
maiden name
married name
middle name
Notre Dame
overcame
parlor game
play the game
proper name
picture frame
put to shame
ready, aim
stake a claim
windowframe
waiting game

all in the game
Court of St. Jame(s)
confidence game
eternal flame
name of the game
Olympic flame
Olympic game(s)
video game
wordly acclaim

ahead of the game
low-down dirty shame

AM

am
bam
cam
cram
clam
damn
dam
dram
gram
gam
ham
jam
jamb
lamb
lam
ma'am
Pam
pram
ram
Sam
scam
sham
slam
scram
swam
tam
tram
wham
yam

door jamb
exam
flimflam
grandslam
gawddamn
hot damn
logjam
madame
outswam
program
Potsdam
Siam
toe jam
wham bam

whim-wham

Abraham
anagram
Amsterdam
Birmingham
body slam
Buckingham
cablegram
candied yam
diaphragm
diagram
epigram
give a damn
hologram
in a jam
kilogram
leg of lamb
little slam
monogram
myelogram
mammogram
milligram
nanogram
on the lam
rack of lamb
Rotterdam
telegram
traffic jam
tinker's dam
Uncle Sam

battering ram
cherchez la femme
ideogram
oral exam
Omar Khayyam

happy as a clam
parallelogram

water over the dam

AMB-ē

Bambi

namby-pamby

AMB-lēng

ambling
gambling
Grambling
rambling
scrambling

unscrambling

AMB-lur

ambler
gambler
rambler
scrambler

tinhorn gambler

AMB-ul

amble
bramble
Campbell
gamble
gambol
ramble
scramble
shamble

ashamble
preamble
unscramble

in a shamble(s)
skimble-scamble

AMB-uld

ambled
gambled
gamboled
rambled
scrambled

AMB-ur

amber
clamber

ĀMD

aimed
blamed
claimed
famed
framed
lamed
maimed
named
shamed
tamed

acclaimed
dad-blamed
defamed
disclaimed
exclaimed
far-famed
inflamed
misnamed
nicknamed
reclaimed
renamed
unnamed

AMD

crammed
damned
dammed
jammed
rammed
scammed
slammed
scrammed

gawddamned
programmed

diagrammed
monogrammed

ĀM-ē

Amy
gamey
Jamie
Mamie

cockamamie

AM-ē

chamois
clammy
Grammy
hammy
jammie(s)
mammy
Tammy
whammy

flimflammy
Miami
unclammy

double whammy

ĀM-ēng

aiming
blaming
claiming
framing
flaming
gaming
laming
maiming
naming
shaming
taming

acclaiming
defaming
disclaiming
exclaiming
inflaming
misnaming
nicknaming
reclaiming
renaming

AM-ēng

cramming
clamming
damning
damming
hamming
jamming
lambing
ramming
scamming
slamming
scramming
whamming

programming

diagramming
telegramming

**AM-el
(See AM-ul)**

Ā-ment

payment
raiment

backpayment
betrayment
defrayment
prepayment
portrayment
repayment

ĀM-ful

blameful
shameful

**AM-ik
(See AM-uk)**

**AM-in
(See AM-un)**

AM-in-āt

laminate

contaminate

AM-in-u

lamina
stamina

AM-ish

clammish
famish
hammish

**AM-it
(See AM-ut)**

**AM-it-ē
(See AM-ud-ē)**

ĀM-lus

aimless
blameless
claimless
dameless
fameless
frameless
flameless
gameless
nameless
shameless

ĀM-nus

lameness
sameness

AM-ō

ammo
whammo

AMP

amp
camp
clamp
champ
cramp
damp
gramp
lamp
ramp
scamp
stamp
tramp
tamp
vamp

bootcamp
decamp
encamp
food stamp
heatlamp
on-ramp
off-ramp
revamp
sunlamp
unclamp

aide-de-camp
postage stamp
prison camp
rubber-stamp
summer camp
saddle tramp
trailer camp
Van de Kamp
writer's cramp

heavyweight champ
surgical clamp

AMP-ē

campy
crampy
scampi
vampy

AMP-en
(See AMP-un)

AMP-ēng

camping
clamping
champing
cramping
stamping
tamping
tramping
vamping

decamping
encamping
revamping
unclamping

rubber-stamping

AMP-lē

amply
damply

AMP-lēng

sampling
trampling

AMP-on

camp on
clamp on
cramp on
stamp on
tampon
tramp on

AMP-ul

ample
sample
trample

example

floor sample
free sample

for example

AMP-un

campin'
clampin'
crampin'
champin'
dampen
stampin'
vampin'

decampin'
encampin'
revampin'
unclampin'

AMP-ur

camper
clamper
cramper
damper
hamper
pamper
stamper
scamper
tamper
tramper
vamper

clothes hamper
day camper
decamper
encamper
foot stamper
revamper

AMP-urd

hampered
pampered
scampered
tampered

AMP-ur-ēng

hampering
pampering
scampering
tampering

AMP-us

campus
cramp us
grampus
stamp us
tramp us
vamp us

off-campus
revamp us

AM-stur

hamster
lamster

AM-u

gamma

pajama

Alabama
cinerama
diorama
futurama
melodrama
panorama

ĀM-u-bul

blameable
claimable
frameable
nameable
shameable
tameable

acclaimable
defameable

disclaimable
exclaimable
nicknameable
reclaimable
renameable
unnameable
untameable

AM-u-bul

crammable
dammable
jammable
rammable
slammable

programmable

diagrammable
monogrammable
telegrammable

AM-u-dē

amity

calamity

AM-uk

hammock

ceramic
dynamic
Islamic

panoramic

aerodynamic
thermodynamic

AM-ul

camel
mammal
trammel

enamel

ĀM-un

aimin'
blamin'
claimin'
Damon
framin'
flamin'
gamin'
lamin'
maimin'
namin'
shamin'

acclaimin'
defamin'
disclaimin'
exclaimin'
highwayman
inflamin'
misnamin'
nicknamin'
reclaimin'
renamin'

AM-un

dammin'
damnin'
famine
gamin
hammin'
jammin'
rammin'
salmon
slammin'
scrammin'

backgammon
examine
flimflammin'
smoked salmon

cross-examine
diagrammin'
feast or famine
reexamine

ĀM-unt

claimant
payment
raiment

disclaimant
down payment

ĀM-ur

aimer
blamer
claimer
framer
flamer
gamer
Kramer
lamer
maimer
namer
shamer
tamer

acclaimer
defamer
disclaimer
exclaimer
inflamer
misnamer
reclaimer

AM-ur

crammer
clamor
damner
dammer
grammar
glamour
hammer
jammer
rammer
slammer
stammer
scrammer
whammer

yammer

door slammer
enamor
flimflammer
grandslammer
jackhammer
programmer
sledgehammer
windjammer

Arm and Hammer
diagrammer
katzenjammer
monogrammer

AM-ur-ē

clamory
mammary
stammery

AM-ur-ēng

clamoring
hammering
jammering
stammering
yammering

enamoring

AM-ur-u

camera
Tamara

AM-ur-un

Cameron
clamorin'
hammerin'
jammerin'
stammerin'
yammerin'

enamorin'

AM-ur-us

amorous
clamorous
glamorous
hammer us

enamor us
unglamorous

ĀM-us

Amos
blame us
claim us
frame us
famous
lame us
maim us
name us
shame us
shamus
tame us

acclaim us
became us
defame us
inflame us
misname us
mandamus
nickname us
reclaim us
unfamous
world-famous

ignoramus
overcame us

AM-ut

cram it
dammit
gamut
ham it
jam it
ram it
slam it

wham it

outswam it
program it

diagram it
monogram it
run the gamut

AM-u-tē
(See AM-u-dē)

AM-u-tōr-ē

amatory
flammatory

inflammatory

ĀN

bane
brain
Cain
chain
crane
cane
deign
Dane
drain
feign
grain
gain
Jane
lane
lain
Maine
main
mane
plane
plain
pane
pain
rain
rein
reign

strain
skein
stain
swain
sane
slain
Spain
Seine
sprain
train
twain
vain
vane
vein
wane

arcane
abstain
again
attain
airbrain
airplane
arraign
bi-plane
brain drain
birdbrain
bloodstain
butane
champagne
campaign
constrain
contain
cocaine
chow mein
complain
choke chain
detain
domain
disdain
dog chain
detrain
deplane
explain
engrain
Elaine

eye strain
food chain
free rein
freight train
fast lane
germane
grosgrain
Great Dane
gold chain
humane
hairbrain
inane
in vain
insane
left brain
Lorraine
lamebrain
mundane
membrane
migraine
maintain
Mark Twain
mule train
obtain
ordain
octane
pertain
peabrain
ptomaine
Plain Jane
profane
propane
right brain
refrain
restrain
regain
remain
retain
retrain
romaine
raise Cain
slow lane
seaplane
Spillane
sustain

tearstain
tire chain
terrain
urbane
Ukraine
unchain

acid rain
aquaplane
appertain
ascertain
aeroplane
ball and chain
candy cane
Charlemagne
country lane
Coeur d'Alene
cellophane
down the drain
daisy chain
entertain
featherbrain
feel no pain
freezing rain
fast-food chain
foreordain
gravy train
growing pain(s)
give free rein
hurricane
hydroplane
inhumane
lovers' lane
monoplane
Novocain
overstrain
once·again
preordain
potty-train
passing lane
pink champagne
quiche Lorraine
rattlebrain
rock cocaine
right as rain

scatterbrain
sugar cane
Solarcaine
smear campaign
toilet-train
windowpane
weathervane
whooping crane
wagon train

auf Wiedersehen
Alsace-Lorraine
against the grain
bicycle lane
capital gain
memory lane
legerdemain
no pain, no gain
public domain
sympathy pain
varicose vein

Calamity Jane
eminent domain
money down the drain
polyurethane

political campaign

AN

an
Anne
ban
bran
can
Cannes
clan
fan
flan
Fran
Jan
man
Nan
pan
plan
ran

scan
span
Stan
tan
than
van

ashcan
adman
ape-man
afghan
best man
Batman
bagman
bedpan
began
CAT scan
cave man
con man
Chopin
cancan
divan
dauphin
dishpan
deadpan
dustpan
fan-tan
floor plan
flight plan
front man
G-man
Gauguin
game plan
he-man
headman
handspan
hangman
house plan
health plan
hit man
iceman
Iran
Japan
Koran
lifespan

lead man
lawman
main man
milkman
Moran
madman
Milan
merman
odd man
oil can
oat bran
oilman
outran
Pac-man
point man
rattan
sedan
Saipan
sauce pan
stunt man
Spokane
suntan
sandman
sampan
soup can
sports fan
Sudan
spray can
trashcan
time plan
tin can
test ban
trashman
timespan
taipan
wise man
wild man
young man
yes man

anchorman
also-ran
candy man
caravan
coq au vin

Dapper Dan
exhaust fan
fellowman
family man
frying pan
garbageman
garbage can
grand old man
hatchet man
handyman
hit the fan
in the can
Ketchikan
kick the can
Ku Klux Klan
leading man
ladies' man
middleman
man-to-man
master plan
moving van
marzipan
overran
Pakistan
payment plan
Peter Pan
pension plan
repairman
roasting pan
right-hand man
superman
spick-and-span
triggerman
trimaran
workingman

as best one can
attention span
aerosol can
Afghanistan
confidence man
company man
catamaran
catch-as-catch-can
dirty old man

forgotten man
four-letter man
flash-in-the-pan
Good Humor man
gingerbread man
installment plan
medicine man
moo goo gai pan
newspaperman
orangutan
watering can

deliveryman
second story man
undercover man

ĀN-bō

main beau
plain beau
rainbow
sane beau
vain beau

ANCH

branch
blanch
Blanche
ranch

dude ranch

avalanche
cattle ranch
chicken ranch
olive branch

ANCH-ē
(See ANSHē)

ANCH-ēng

branching
blanching
ranching

ANCH-ul

financial
substantial

circumstantial

ANCH-un

branchin'
blanchin'
mansion
ranchin'
stanchion

expansion

ANCH-ur

blancher
rancher

ĀND

brained
chained
craned
caned
deigned
drained
feigned
gained
laned
maned
planed
paned
pained
rained
reined
reigned
strained
stained
sprained
trained
veined
waned

abstained

attained
arraigned
campaigned
constrained
contained
complained
detained
deplaned
explained
engrained
hairbrained
maintained
obtained
ordained
pertained
refrained
restrained
regained
remained
retained
retrained
sustained
tearstained
unchained

addlebrained
appertained
ascertained
entertained
foreordained
preordained
rattlebrained
scatterbrained
toilet-trained

AND

and
band
banned
brand
bland
canned
fanned
grand
gland

hand
land
manned
planned
panned
sand
stand
strand
spanned
tanned

armband
badland(s)
by hand
backhand
brass band
bandstand
cabstand
cowhand
command
crash-land
dance band
deck hand
demand
dreamland
deadpanned
disband
expand
firebrand
farmhand
firsthand
free hand
forehand
flat land
gladhand
grandstand
headband
hour hand
hired hand
hatband
homeland
handstand
kickstand
Lapland
last stand

longhand
left hand
newsstand
name-brand
on hand
outmanned
offhand
old hand
off-brand
quicksand
right hand
remand
shorthand
stagehand
suntanned
thirdhand
Thailand
unhand
unmanned
withstand
wasteland
waistband
wristband
watchband

at firsthand
ampersand
bellyland
beforehand
baby grand
Beulah Land
bottomland
borderland
close-at-hand
cap in hand
caravanned
contraband
countermand
Dixieland
Disneyland
fairyland
fatherland
force one's hand
four-in-hand
gerrymand

goal line stand
hat in hand
hotdog stand
helping hand
hand-in-hand
high command
hinterland
heavy hand
Holy Land
Krugerrand
lend a hand
motherland
marching band
minute hand
no man's land
near at hand
overland
on demand
out of hand
openhand
overhand
one-night stand
Promised Land
Rio Grande
rubberband
reprimand
show of hand(s)
sleight of hand
show one's hand
shortwave band
secondhand
take in hand
tip one's hand
taxi stand
take a stand
TV stand
take the stand
underhand
upper hand
understand
undermanned
wonderland
witness stand

analysand

bird in the hand
chain of command
Dixieland band
fat of the land
fantasyland
generic brand
hamburger stand
installment plan
law of the land
lay of the land
misunderstand
newspaper stand
pay on demand
umbrella stand

eat out of one's hand
never-never land
on the other hand
supply and demand
second in command

AND-ē

Andy
bandy
brandy
candy
dandy
Gandhi
handy
Mandy
randy
sandy

expandy
jim-dandy
rock candy
unhandy

cotton candy
fine and dandy
handy-andy

Yankee Doodle Dandy

AND-ed
(See AND-ud)

AND-em
(See AND-um)

AND-ēng

banding
branding
handing
landing
sanding
standing
stranding

backhanding
bandstanding
commanding
crash-landing
demanding
disbanding
expanding
freestanding
forced landing
grandstanding
gladhanding
longstanding
outstanding
remanding
soft landing
upstanding
unhanding
withstanding

belly-landing
countermanding
gerrymanding
notwithstanding
reprimanding
three-point landing
understanding

instrument landing
misunderstanding

AND-ēz

Andes
bandies

brandies
candies
dandies

Fernandez

AND-id
(See AND-ud)

AND-ish

blandish
brandish
grandish

Miles Standish
outlandish

AND-it
(See AND-ut)

AND-lē
(See AN-lē)

AND-lēng

dandling
handling

mishandling
manhandling
panhandling

AND-lur

Chandler
dandler
handler

mishandler
manhandler
panhandler

AND-ment

commandment
disbandment

countermandent
Ten Command-
   ment(s)

AND-ō

Brando
bandeau

commando
Fernando
Orlando

accelerando

AND-ru

Sandra

Cassandra

Alexandra

AND-stand

bandstand
grandstand
handstand
planned stand

AND-sum
(See AN-sum)

AND-u

panda

Amanda
Miranda
Uganda
veranda

jacaranda
memoranda
propaganda

AND-u-bul

bandable
brandable

landable
sandable
standable

commandable
demandable
expandable
remandable
withstandable

countermandable
reprimandable
understandable

AND-ud

banded
branded
candid
handed
landed
sanded
stranded

backhanded
commanded
crash-landed
demanded
disbanded
expanded
forehanded
high-handed
left-handed
one-handed
offhanded
remanded
righthanded
two-handed
unsanded
unbranded

belly-landed
countermanded
caught red-handed
empty-handed
evenhanded
gerrymanded

heavy-handed
openhanded
overhanded
reprimanded
single-handed
underhanded

AND-ul

candle
Crandall
dandle
Handel
handle
Randall
sandal
scandal
vandal

door handle
love handle(s)
mishandle
manhandle
panhandle

Roman candle

fly off the handle

AND-ul-īz

scandalize
vandalize

AND-ul-us

handle us
scandalous

mishandle us
manhandle us

AND-um

banned 'em
brand 'em
canned 'em
hand 'em

manned 'em
panned 'em
random
tandem
tanned 'em

command 'em
demand 'em
expand 'em
outmanned 'em

countermand 'em
memorandum
reprimand 'em
understand 'em

misunderstand 'em

AND-un

bandin'
brandin'
handin'
landin'
standin'
strandin'

abandon
backhandin'
commandin'
demandin'
disbandin'
expandin'
remandin'
withstandin'

countermandin'
gay abandon
gerrymandin'
reprimandin'
understandin'

ĀND-ur

brained 'er
chained 'er
drained 'er
pained 'er

strained 'er
stained 'er
trained 'er

arraigned 'er
contained 'er
detained 'er
maintained 'er
obtained 'er
ordained 'er
restrained 'er
regained 'er
remainder
retained 'er
sustained 'er
unchained 'er

entertained 'er

AND-ur

bander
brander
blander
candor
canned 'er
dander
gander
grander
hander
pander
sander
stander
strander
slander

Auslander
Ann Lander(s)
bystander
backhander
commander
demander
disbander
expander
grandstander
handstander
Icelander

lefthander
Laplander
meander
outlander
philander
righthander
unhander
unhand 'er

Alexander
countermander
coriander
gerrymander
high commander
oleander
reprimander
salamander
understander

misunderstander
misunderstand 'er

AND-urd

pandered
standard
slandered

gold standard
meandered
substandard

double standard

AND-ur-ēng

pandering
slandering

meandering

gerrymandering

AND-ur-un

Mandarin
panderin'
slanderin'

meanderin'

gerrymanderin'

AND-ur-ur

panderer
slanderer

meanderer
philanderer

gerrymanderer

AND-urz

branders
Flanders
ganders
panders
slanders

Ann Landers
Auslanders
bystanders
commanders
demanders
disbanders
expanders
Laplanders

AND-ust

blandest
grandest

propagandist

AND-ut

bandit
brand it
banned it
canned it
fanned it
hand it
land it
manned it

panned it
sand it
stand it
spanned it
tanned it

backhand it
crashland it
command it
demand it
deadpanned it
disband it
expand it
remand it
suntanned it
unhand it
withstand it

countermand it
gerrymand it
one-armed bandit
overhand it
underhand it
understand it

misunderstand it

make out like a bandit

ANDZ
(See ANZ)

ĀN-ē

brainy
grainy
Janie
rainy
veiny
zany

Delaney

Allegheny
miscellany

AN-ē

any
Annie
canny
clanny
cranny
Danny
fanny
granny
nanny

uncanny

frangipani
hootenanny
Orphan Annie

AN-el
(See AN-ul)

ĀN-ēng

braining
chaining
craning
caning
deigning
draining
feigning
gaining
planing
paining
raining
reining
reigning
straining
staining
spraining
training

abstaining
attaining
arraigning
campaigning
containing

complaining
detaining
detraining
deplaning
explaining
maintaining
obtaining
ordaining
pertaining
refraining
restraining
regaining
remaining
retaining
retraining
spring training
sustaining
unchaining

appertaining
ascertaining
entertaining
foreordaining
overstraining
preordaining

on-the-job training

sensitivity training

AN-ēng

banning
canning
Channing
fanning
manning
panning
planning
scanning
spanning

cancanning
deadpanning

ĀN-ē-nus

braininess
graininess
raininess
zaniness

AN-et
(See AN-ut)

ĀN-ē-u

mania

Albania
Romania
Sylvania
Tasmania

dipsomania
egomania
kleptomania
Lusitania
Lithuania
pyromania
Pennsylvania
Transylvania

bibliomania
megalomania
oniomania

ĀN-ē-um

cranium

geranium
titanium
uranium

ĀN-ē-un

Albanian
Romanian
Tasmanian
Ukranian

Agajanian

Lithuanian
Pomeranian
Pennsylvanian
subterranean

Mediterranean

ĀN-ē-us

brainy us

extraneous
spontaneous

instantaneous
miscellaneous
simultaneous
subterraneous
subcutaneous

contemporaneous
extemporaneous

ĀN-ful

gainful
painful
vainful

attainful
complainful
detainful
disdainful
obtainful
refrainful
restrainful
sustainful
ungainful
unpainful

entertainful

ANG

bang
brang
clang
dang
fang

gang
hang
rang
sang
slang
sprang
stang
swang
tang
twang
whang
Wang
yang

big bang
chain gang
defang
gang bang
harangue
meringue
mustang
outrang
poontang
road gang
shebang
slam bang
whiz-bang

boomerang
hunger pang
overhang
paperhang
yin and yang

lemon meringue
orangutang

go out with a bang

ANG-ē

clangy
fangy
slangy
tangy
twangy

Ubangi

ANG-ēng

banging
clanging
ganging
hanging
tanging
twanging
whanging

defanging
haranguing

boomeranging
overhanging
paperhanging

ANG-lē

dangly
gangly
jangly
spangly
tangly

ANG-lēng

angling
dangling
gangling
jangling
mangling
strangling
tangling
wrangling
wangling

entangling
untangling

ANG-lur

angler
dangler
jangler
mangler
strangler
tangler

wrangler
wangler

entangler
untangler

disentangler

ANG-ō

mango
tango

Durango
fandango

Pago Pago

ANG-ul

angle
bangle
dangle
jangle
mangle
spangle
strangle
tangle
wrangle
wangle

atangle
Bojangle(s)
entangle
quadrangle
rectangle
right angle
triangle
untangle
wide-angle

disentangle
intertangle
jingle jangle
play the angle(s)

ANG-ū-lāt

strangulate
triangluate

ANG-uld

angled
dangled
jangled
spangled
tangled
wrangled
wangled

entangled
newfangled
starspangled
untangled

disentangled
intertangled

ANG-ū-lur

angular

quadrangular
rectangular
triangular

ANG-ur

anger
Bangor
banger
clanger
dang 'er
hanger
hangar
hang 'er
languor
rang 'er
sang 'er

clothes hanger
cliffhanger
chain-ganger

defanger
haranguer
whiz-banger

airplane hangar
boomeranger
Bible-banger
paperhanger

Harvey Wallbanger

ANG-wij

language
slanguage

ANG-wish

anguish
languish

ANG-yū-lur (See ANG-ū-lur)

AN-i-bul (See AN-u-bul)

AN-i-gun

brannigan
Flannigan

shenanigun

AN-ik

manic
panic
tannic

Britannic
botanic
Germanic
galvanic
Hispanic
mechanic
morganic

organic
satanic
Titanic
tyrannic
volcanic

inorganic
Messianic
oceanic
puritanic

transoceanic

AN-i-kul
(See AN-u-kul)

ĀN-il
(See ĀN-ul)

AN-il
(See AN-ul)

AN-i-mus

magnanimous
unanimous

pusillanimous

ĀN-is
(See ĀN-us)

AN-is
(See AN-us)

ĀN-ish

brainish
Danish
sanish

AN-ish

banish
clannish

mannish
Spanish
vanish

AN-ish-ēng

banishing
vanishing

AN-ist-ur

bannister
canister

AN-it
(See AN-ut)

AN-i-tē
(See AN-u-dē)

AN-ix

panics

Hispanics
mechanics

ĀNJ

change
grange
mange
range
strange

arrange
close range
downrange
derange
exchange
estrange
free-range
long-range
loose change
oil change
shortchange

small change
sex change

diaper change
driving range
disarrange
exact change
firing range
for a change
interchange
never change
out of range
prearrange
post exchange
rearrange
rifle range
stock exchange

foreign exchange

ĀNJD

changed
ranged

arranged
deranged
exchanged
estranged

disarranged
interchanged
prearranged
rearranged

ĀNJ-ē

mangy
rangy

ĀNJ-ēng

changing
ranging

arranging
exchanging
free-ranging

disarranging
diaper-changing
everchanging
interchanging
prearranging
rearranging

ANJ-ent
(See ANJ-unt)

ANJ-i-bul
(See ANJ-u-bul)

ĀNJ-ment

arrangement
derangement
estrangement

disarrangement
flower arrangement
prearrangement
rearrangement

ĀNJ-u-bul

changeable

arrangeable
exchangeable
estrangeable
unchangeable

interchangeable
prearrangeable
rearrangeable

ANJ-u-bul

frangible
tangible

intangible
infrangible
refrangible

ANJ-unt

plangent
tangent

ĀNJ-ur

changer
danger
granger
manger
ranger
stranger

arranger
deranger
estranger
endanger
exchanger
shortchanger

diaper changer
disarranger
forest ranger
interchanger
money changer
out of danger
perfect stranger
rearranger

dog in the manger

ĀNJ-ur-us

dangerous

endanger us

ANK

bank
blank
crank
clank
dank
drank
frank
franc

flank
hank
lank
prank
plank
rank
swank
sank
shank
stank
spank
shrank
tank
thank
yank

air tank
blood bank
drunk tank
embank
Fairbank(s)
fog bank
fish tank
gangplank
gas tank
handcrank
high rank
kerplank
outrank
outflank
outdrank
point-blank
pull rank
preshrank
sandbank
sperm bank
snowbank
think tank

break the bank
draw a blank
data bank
holding tank
overdrank
play a prank
riverbank

savings bank
Sherman tank
septic tank
walk the plank
water tank

blankety-blank
Halloween prank
memory bank

have oneself to thank
military rank

ANK-ē

blanky
clanky
cranky
Frankie
hankie
lanky
swanky
Yankee

damyankee

hanky-panky

ANK-ēng

banking
blanking
cranking
clanking
franking
ranking
spanking
tanking
thanking
yanking

handcranking
high-ranking
outranking
outflanking

investment banking

ANK-et
(See ANK-ut)

ANK-ful

prankful
tank full
thankful

ANK-lus

bankless
rankless
tankless
thankless

ANKT

banked
blanked
cranked
clanked
flanked
ranked
spanked
tanked
thanked
yanked

handcranked
outranked
outflanked
unranked

sacrosanct

ANKT-um

banked 'em
flanked 'em
ranked 'em
sanctum
spanked 'em
thanked 'em
yanked 'em

outranked 'em

outflanked 'em

innersanctum

ANK-u

Sanka

Casablanca
lingua franca

ANK-ul

ankle
Frankel
rankle

ANK-ur

anchor
banker
blanker
cranker
canker
clanker
danker
drank 'er
franker
flanker
hanker
lanker
pranker
rancor
ranker
sank 'er
swanker
shrank 'er
spanker
tanker
thanker
yanker

drop anchor
embanker
oil tanker
outranker
outflanker

up anchor
weigh anchor

ANK-urd

anchored
hankered
rancored
tankard

ANK-ur-ēng

anchoring
hankering
rancoring

ANK-ur-us

anchor us
hankerous
rancor us

cantankerous

ANK-ut

blanket
bank it
crank it
drank it
flank it
rank it
spank it
shrank it
sank it
thank it
yank it

horseblanket
handcrank it
outrank it
outflank it
wet blanket

security blanket

ĀN-lē

gainly
mainly
plainly
sanely
vainly

arcanely
germanely
humanely
inanely
insanely
mundanely
profanely
urbanely
ungainly

inhumanely
scatterbrainly

AN-lē

blandly
grandly
manly
Stanley

ĀN-lus

brainless
chainless
caneless
gainless
maneless
planeless
rainless
strainless
stainless
trainless
veinless

attainless

ĀN-ment

abstainment
attainment

arraignment
constrainment
containment
detainment
ordainment
retainment
sustainment

ascertainment
entertainment

ĀN-ō

bueno
Drano

volcano

AN-ō

piano
soprano

ĀNS

faints
feints
paints
plaints
saints
taints

acquaints
constraints
complaints
restraints
repaints

fingerpaints
patron saints
reacquaints

Latter Day Saints

ANS

ants
aunts

cants
can'ts
chance
chants
dance
France
grants
glance
lance
manse
pants
plants
prance
rants
shan'ts
stance
slants
trance

askance
Air France
advance
breakdance
barn dance
by chance
decants
entrance
eggplants
enchants
expanse
enhance
folk dance
flash dance
finance
fat chance
fan dance
freelance
hat dance
houseplants
implants
knee pants
last chance
land grants
mischance
main chance

no chance
off chance
perchance
power plants
romance
replants
rain dance
recants
supplants
slim chance
square dance
stretch pants
sweat pants
side-glance
tap dance
toe dance
transplants
tap pants
war dance

at a glance
ballroom dance
belly dance
circumstance
disenchants
disco dance
even chance
fancy pants
fighting chance
game of chance
high finance
hula dance
happenstance
in a trance
in advance
Ile de France
only chance
outside chance
old-maid aunts
sycophants
sidelong glance
stand a chance
sporting chance
smarty-pants
song and dance

take a chance
training pants
underpants
wear the pants

ants in one's pants
ghost of a chance
hypnotic trance
kick in the pants
medicine dance
on the off chance
St. Vitus' dance

pomp and
    circumstance

by the seat of the
    pants

ANS-ē

antsy
chancy
fancy
Nancy
prancy

unfancy

fancy-schmancy
flight of fancy
necromancy
passing fancy

ANS-el
(See ANS-ul)

ANS-el-ur
(See ANS-ul-ur)

ANS-ēng

chancing
dancing
glancing
prancing

advancing
breakdancing
entrancing
enhancing
financing
freelancing
romancing
rain dancing
square dancing
tap dancing
toe dancing

belly dancing
high financing

AN-shē

banshee
can she?

Comanche

**AN-shul
(See AN-chul)**

**AN-shun
(See AN-chun)**

ANS-ment

advancement
entrancement
enhancement

ANST

chanced
danced
glanced
lanced
pranced

advanced
against
breakdanced
entranced

enhanced
financed
romanced
square danced
tap danced

belly danced
up against

AN-sul

cancel
chancel

ANS-u-lot

dance a lot
Lancelot
prance a lot
pants a lot

AN-sul-ur

chancellor
canceller
cancel 'er

AN-sum

and some
ban some
brand some
handsome
hansom
land some
man some
plan some
ransom
ran some
span some
stand some
strand some
transom
tan some

began some
command some

demand some
expand some
king's ransom
outran some
unhandsome

hold for ransom
overran some

high, wide, and
　handsome
misunderstand some

AN-sum-ur

handsomer
ransom 'er

AN-sur

answer
cancer
chancer
dancer
glancer
lancer
prancer

advancer
enhancer
enchants 'er
entrancer
financer
freelancer
fan dancer
romancer
supplants 'er
square dancer
tap dancer
toe dancer

belly dancer
disenchants 'er
disco dancer
gandy dancer
go-go dancer
taxi dancer

exotic dancer
know all the answer(s)
tropic of Cancer

AN-sur-us

answer us
cancerous

ĀNT

ain't
cain't
faint
feint
mayn't
paint
plaint
quaint
saint
tain't
taint

acquaint
constraint
complaint
grease paint
restraint
repaint
war paint

fingerpaint
get acquaint(ed)
patron saint
reacquaint
self-restraint

Latter Day Saint

ANT

ant
aunt
Brandt
can't
cant
chant

grant
pant
plant
rant
slant
scant
shan't

aslant
decant
enchant
eggplant
houseplant
implant
land grant
power plant
pissant
replant
Rembrandt
recant
supplant
transplant

Charlie's aunt
disenchant
gallivant
hair transplant
heart transplant
maiden aunt
overplant
rubberplant
sycophant
take for grant(ed)

century plant

Gregorian chant

ĀNT-ē

dainty
fainty
sainty
veinte

undainty

ANT-ē

aunty
anti
ante
Dante
panty
shanty
scanty
slanty

Ashanti

penny ante
vigilante

ĀNT-ēng

fainting
feinting
painting
tainting

acquainting
repainting

fingerpainting
reacquainting

ANT-ēng

canting
chanting
granting
panting
planting
ranting
slanting

decanting
enchanting
implanting
replanting
recanting
supplanting
transplanting

disenchanting

gallivanting
overplanting

ANTH-u

Samantha

agapantha
pyrocantha

ANT-ik

antic
frantic

Atlantic
gigantic
pedantic
romantic
semantic

sycophantic
transatlantic
unromantic

ANT-ik-lē

frantically

gigantically
pedantically
romantically

ANT-is
(See ANT-us)

ANT-lur

antler

dismantler

ĀNTS
(See ĀNS)

ANTS
(See ANS)

ANTS-ē
(See ANS-ē)

ANT-u

Santa

Atlanta

ĀNT-ud

fainted
feinted
painted
sainted
tainted

acquainted
repainted

fingerpainted
get acquainted
reacquainted

ANT-ud

canted
chanted
granted
panted
planted
ranted
slanted

decanted
enchanted
implanted
recanted
supplanted
transplanted

disenchanted
gallivanted
overplanted

take for granted

ANT-uk
(See ANT-ik)

ANT-ul

mantel
mantle

dismantle

ANT-u-lōp

antelope
cantaloupe

ANT-um

bantam
chant 'em
grant 'em
plant 'em
phantom
slant 'em

enchant 'em
implant 'em
replant 'em
supplant 'em
transplant 'em

disenchant 'em

ĀNT-ur

fainter
feinter
painter
quainter
tainter

acquaint 'er

fingerpainter
reacquaint 'er

ANT-ur

banter
canter
cantor
chanter
granter

panter
planter
ranter
slanter
scanter

decanter
enchanter
implanter
recanter
replanter
supplanter
transplanter

disenchanter
gallivanter
tam-o'-shanter

ANT-ur-ēng

bantering
cantering
cantoring

ANT-us

grant us
plant us
slant us

Atlantis
enchant us
supplant us
transplant us

disenchant us
praying mantis

ĀNT-ust

faintest
quaintest

AN-u

Anna
manna
Vanna

Amana
bandanna
banana
cabana
Diana
hosanna
Havana
lantana
Montana
Nirvana
savannah
Susanna

go banana(s)
Indiana
Pollyanna
Susquehanna
Santa Ana
poinciana
top banana
Tex-Arkana

Americana
Louisiana

AN-u-bul

bannable
cannibal
cannable
Hannibal
plannable
scannable
spannable
tannable

AN-u-dē

sanity
vanity

humanity
inanity
insanity
profanity
urbanity

Christianity
inhumanity

AN-u-gun
(See AN-i-gun)

AN-uk
(See AN-ik)

AN-u-kul

manacle

botanical
Britannical
mechanical
organical
satanical
tyranical

puritanical

ĀN-ul

anile
anal

attainal
migrainal
maintainal
obtainal

AN-ul

annal
anil
anile
channel
flannel
panel

empanel

jury panel
TV channel

AN-ul-ēng

channeling
paneling

AN-ul-ist

analyst
panelist

AN-um

annum
ban 'em
can 'em
fan 'em
man 'em
pan 'em
ran 'em
span 'em
tan 'em

outran 'em
per annum

AN-u-mus
(See AN-i-mus)

AN-un

bannin'
cannon
canon
cannin'
Dannon
fannin'
mannin'
pannin'
plannin'
Shannon
spannin'
tannin'

ĀN-ur

brain 'er
chain 'er

drainer
feigner
gainer
planer
pain 'er
reiner
reigner
strainer
stainer
saner
slain 'er
sprainer
trainer
vainer
waner

abstainer
attainer
arraigner
campaigner
constrainer
container
complainer
detainer
deplaner
explainer
humaner
half gainer
inaner
insaner
mundaner
maintainer
obtainer
ordainer
profaner
refrainer
restrainer
regainer
remainer
retainer
sustainer
urbaner
unchainer

ascertainer
entertainer

inhumaner
overstrainer

AN-ur

banner
canner
fanner
manner
manor
planner
panner
ran 'er
scanner
spanner
tanner

cancanner
deadpanner
outran 'er
suntanner

bedside manner
city planner
overran 'er
table manner(s)

lord of the manor

"The Star-Spangled
    Banner"

AN-urd

bannered
mannered

ill-mannered
well-mannered

ĀN-ur-ē

granary

chicanery

AN-ur-ē

cannery
Flannery
tannery

ĀN-us

anus
brain us
chain us
drain us
gayness
grayness
heinous
pain us
stain us
slain us
strain us
train us

contain us
detain us
maintain us
ordain us
restrain us
retain us
retrain us
sustain us
Uranus

entertain us
overstrain us

AN-us

anise
ban us
can us
fan us
Janice
tan us

AN-ut

ban it
can it

fan it
granite
Janet
man it
planet
pan it
plan it
ran it
scan it
span it
tan it

began it

overran it
pomegranate
solid granite

AN-u-tē
(See AN-u-dē)

AN-ū-ul

annual
manual

ANX

banks
blanks
cranks
clanks
francs
flanks
Manx
pranks
ranks
shanks
spanks
tanks
thanks
yanks

air tanks
break ranks
bloodbanks

close ranks
drunk tanks
embanks
Fairbanks
fog banks
gangplanks
handcranks
outranks
outflanks
sandbanks
sperm banks
shoot blanks
snowbanks
think tanks

data banks
septic tanks

AN-yul

Daniel
granule
spaniel

Jack Daniel('s)
Nathaniel

cocker spaniel

AN-yun

banyan
canyon

companion
Grand Canyon

AN-yū-ul
(See AN-ū-ul)

ANZ

Anne's
bans
bands
brands
brans

cans
clans
fans
flans
Fran's
glands
hands
mans
lands
pans
plans
sands
scans
stands
spans
strands
Stan's
tans
vans

brass bands
badlands
cowhands
commands
crash-lands
change hands
divans
dance bands
deckhands
demands
disbands
expands
flight plans
gladhands
grandstands
headlands
hired hands
hold hands
newsstands
name-brands
old hands
rattans
sedans
sampans
shake hands

stagehands
trash cans
taipans
unhands
wastelands
waistbands
watchbands

ampersands
bellylands
baby grands
countermands
caravans
dishpan hands
fairylands
frying pans
gerrymands
goal-line stands
moving vans
one-night stands
rubberbands
reprimands
show of hands
shortwave bands
trimarans
tie one's hands
understands
wonderlands

analysands
generic brands
misunderstands
throw up one's hands

laying on of hands

ANZ-ē

pansy

chimpanzee

ANZ-u

stanza

bonanza

organza

extravaganza

ANZ-us

bans us
cans us
fans us
hands us
Kansas
pans us
stands us
tans us

Ā-of

day off
layoff
payoff
playoff
stray off

Ā-on

crayon
lay on
play on
prey on
pray on
pay on
rayon
stay on
spray on

ĀP

ape
cape
crepe
drape
gape
grape
nape
rape
shape
scrape

scape
tape

agape
escape
egg-shape
go ape
heart-shape
landscape
misshape
pear-shape
reshape
red tape
seascape
shipshape
sour grape(s)
Scotch tape
undrape

bow and scrape
demo tape
fire escape
in good shape
in a scrape
out of shape
seedless grape
tickertape

bent out of shape
magnetic tape
videotape
whip into shape

AP

cap
clap
crap
chap
flap
gap
hap
Knapp
lap
map
nap
rap

slap
scrap
sap
strap
snap
tap
trap
wrap
yap
zap

aflap
ASCAP
agap
bad rap
bootstrap
burlap
backslap
bra strap
blackstrap
catnap
cold snap
chinstrap
claptrap
deathtrap
dognap
dunce cap
entrap
enwrap
foolscap
firetrap
gas cap
giftwrap
heel tap
hubcap
icecap
jockstrap
kidnap
kneecap
mishap
madcap
mayhap
mousetrap
mudflap
mantrap

nightcap
on tap
old chap
perhap(s)
recap
rat trap
redcap
roadmap
resnap
stop gap
skullcap
sandtrap
speed trap
satrap
snowcap
steel trap
T-strap
unwrap
uncap
unstrap
unsnap
wiretap
Winesap
whitecap

bottlecap
baseball cap
beat the rap
booby trap
cradle cap
Dimetapp
gingersnap
gender gap
handicap
interlap
missile gap
nurse's cap
overlap
rattletrap
shut one's trap
Saran Wrap
shoulder strap
thinking cap
thunderclap
tender trap

take the rap
take a nap
tourist trap
weather map
whippersnap

not give a snap
spaghetti strap

feather in one's cap
generation gap
mind like a steel trap

credibility gap
physical handicap

AP-chur

capture
rapture

enrapture
recapture

AP-ē

crappy
flappy
gappy
happy
nappy
pappy
sappy
scrappy
snappy
trappy
yappie

grandpappy
slaphappy
unhappy

make it snappy
trigger-happy

**ĀP-en
(See ĀP-un)**

**AP-en
(See AP-un)**

ĀP-ēng

aping
draping
gaping
raping
shaping
scraping
taping

escaping
landscaping
misshaping
reshaping
Scotch taping
undraping

videotaping

AP-ēng

capping
chapping
clapping
crapping
flapping
gapping
lapping
mapping
napping
rapping
slapping
scrapping
sapping
strapping
snapping
tapping
trapping
wrapping
yapping
zapping

backslapping

catnapping
dognapping
entrapping
enwrapping
giftwrapping
kidnapping
recapping
tooth-capping
toe-tapping
unwrapping
uncapping
unstrapping
unsnapping
wiretapping

boobytrapping
handicapping
interlapping
overlapping

AP-ē-nus

crappiness
happiness
sappiness

unhappiness

ĀP-ē-ur

crepier
drapier
rapier

AP-ē-ur

crappier
flappier
happier
nappier
sappier
snappier
yappier

slaphappier
unhappier

AP-id
(See AP-ud)

AP-il-ē
(See AP-u-lē)

ĀP-in
(See ĀP-un)

AP-in
(See AP-un)

ĀP-ist

Papist
rapist

escapist
landscapist

AP-lē

aptly
raptly

AP-lēng

grappling
sapling

AP-lin
(See AP-lun)

AP-lun

chaplain
Chaplin
grapplin'
Kaplan

ĀP-lus

capeless
drapeless
grapeless

shapeless
tapeless

AP-lus

capless
hapless
mapless
napless
strapless
snapless
wrapless

ĀPS

apes
capes
crepes
drapes
gapes
grapes
napes
rapes
shapes
scrapes
traipse
tapes

escapes
landscapes
misshapes
reshapes
sour grapes
Scotch tapes
undrapes

fire escapes
tickertapes

videotapes

APS

apse
caps
claps
craps

chaps
flaps
gaps
laps
lapse
maps
naps
raps
saps
straps
slaps
scraps
snaps
schnapps
taps
traps
wraps
yaps
zaps

adapts
backslaps
bootstraps
burlaps
chinstraps
claptraps
collapse
catnaps
death traps
dunce caps
entraps
elapse
enwraps
fire traps
giftwraps
gas caps
heel taps
hub caps
ice caps
Jap flaps
jockstraps
kidnaps
kneecaps
mishaps
mousetraps

mudflaps
madcaps
nightcaps
perhaps
rat traps
recaps
relapse
road maps
red caps
resnaps
skullcaps
sandtraps
speed traps
stop gaps
time lapse
T-straps
unwraps
unstraps
unsnaps
uncaps
wiretaps
whitecaps

bottlecaps
baseball caps
booby traps
gingersnaps
handicaps
interlaps
overlaps
rattletraps
shoulder straps
thunderclaps
under wraps

memory lapse
spaghetti straps

APS-ēng

lapsing

collapsing
elapsing
relapsing

AP-shun

caption

adaption
contraption
closed caption

ĀPT

aped
caped
draped
gaped
raped
shaped
scraped
taped

escaped
egg-shaped
landscaped
pear-shaped
reshaped
undraped

videotaped

APT

apt
capped
clapped
crapped
chapped
flapped
gapped
lapped
mapped
napped
rapt
rapped
slapped
scrapped
sapped
strapped
snapped

tapped
trapped
wrapped
yapped
zapped

adapt
catnapped
entrapped
kidnapped
recapped
unwrapped
unstrapped

handicapped
interlapped
overlapped

APT-lē
(See AP-lē)

APT-un

captain

adaptin'

APT-ur

apter
captor
chapter
capped 'er
rapter
rapped 'er
snapped 'er
slapped 'er
scrapped 'er
strapped 'er
tapped 'er
wrapped 'er
zapped 'er

adapter
entrapped 'er
kidnapped 'er
unwrapped 'er

final chapter
handicapped 'er
overlapped 'er

ĀP-u-bul

capable
drapable
rapable
shapable
scrapable
tapable

escapable
incapable
reshapeable
undrapable
unshapeable

inescapable

AP-ud

rapid
sapid
vapid

ĀP-ul

maple
Naple(s)
papal
staple

AP-ul

apple
chapel
dapple
grapple

bad apple
Big Apple
pineapple

Adam's apple
wedding chapel

AP-uld

dappled
grappled

AP-u-lē

crappily
happily
Napoli
scrappily
sappily
snappily

slaphappily
unhappily

AP-ul-us

grapple us

Annapolis

Minneapolis

Indianapolis

ĀP-un

apin'
drapin'
gapin'
rapin'
shapen
shapin'
scrapin'
tapin'

escapin'
misshapen
reshapin'
unshapen
undrapin'

AP-un

clappin'
crappin'
flappin'

gappin'
happen
lappin'
lapin
mappin'
nappin'
rappin'
slappin'
scrappin'
strappin'
snappin'
tappin'
trappin'
wrappin'
yappin'
zappin'

catnappin'
entrappin'
kidnappin'
recappin'
unwrappin'
wiretappin'

handicappin'
overlappin'

ĀP-ur

aper
caper
draper
gaper
paper
raper
shaper
scraper
sapor
taper
tapir
vapor

crepe paper
escape 'er
flypaper
landscaper
misshaper

notepaper
newspaper
reshaper
rice paper
scratch paper
sandpaper
skyscraper
tar paper
undraper
wallpaper
white paper

funny paper(s)
toilet paper
walking paper(s)

videotaper

AP-ur

capper
clapper
crapper
chapper
dapper
flapper
gapper
mapper
napper
rapper
slapper
scrapper
strapper
tapper
trapper
wrapper
yapper
zapper

backslapper
catnapper
dognapper
entrapper
enwrapper
gum wrapper
giftwrapper
kidnapper

knee-slapper
madcapper
recapper
red snapper
toe tapper
unwrapper
uncapper
unstrapper
wiretapper

handicapper
overlapper
plain brown wrapper
whippersnapper

ĀP-ur-ē

drapery
napery
papery
tapery
vapory

sandpapery

ĀP-ur-ēng

capering
papering
tapering

wallpapering

ĀP-ur-us

saporous
vaporous

ĀP-ust
(See ĀP-ist)

AR
(Also see Ā-ur)

air
bare
bear

blare
care
cher
chair
dare
e'er
err
ere
fair
fare
flair
flare
glare
hare
hair
heir
lair
mare
ne'er
pair
pear
pare
prayer
rare
scare
swear
square
stare
snare
spare
stair
share
tear
there
they're
their
ware
wear
where

au pair
armchair
Adair
aware
airfare

affair
Bel-Air
bus fare
brood mare
beware
carfare
compare
child care
declare
day care
despair
desk chair
ensnare
elsewhere
eclair
flatware
fore'er
forbear
fanfare
fresh air
foursquare
forswear
footwear
gray hair
glassware
hardware
howe'er
highchair
health care
hot air
horsehair
impair
lounge chair
longhair
mohair
midair
March hare
mon cher
nightmare
no fair
nowhere
outwear
outstare
prepare
Pierre

plane fare
plowshare
repair
run scare(d)
software
sportswear
spare pair
somewhere
threadbare
time share
town square
train fare
take care
Times Square
unbare
unfair
whate'er
whene'er
welfare
warfare
wheelchair

angel hair
au contraire
anywhere
billionaire
bill of fare
bring to bear
barber chair
bruin bear
Camembert
car repair
camel hair
curl one's hair
c'est la guerre
country fair
Delaware
debonair
derriere
dance on air
doctrinaire
disrepair
dentist chair
easy chair
étagère

everywhere
endowed chair
earthenware
formalwear
Fred Astaire
float on air
Frigidaire
fair and square
grizzly bear
ground-to-air
here and there
ill-prepare(d)
laissez-faire
love affair
lion's share
legionnaire
Medicare
millionaire
mal de mer
maidenhair
not all there
nail repair
nom de guerre
overbear
over there
open-air
on the air
put on air(s)
potty-chair
questionnaire
room to spare
rocking chair
savoir faire
say a prayer
silverware
solitaire
son and heir
swivel chair
teddy bear
take a chair
thoroughfare
The Lord's Prayer
then and there
tear one's hair
unaware

underwear
wash and wear
walk on air
when or where
women's wear
wear and tear
zillionaire

auto repair
beyond compare
breath of fresh air
chargé d'affaires
concessionaire
devil-may-care
electric chair
full of hot air
hearing impair(ed)
intensive care
loaded for bear
long underwear
lighter-than-air
musical chair(s)
pied-à-terre
private affair
ready-to-wear
Smokey the Bear
surface-to-air
up in the air

castles in the air
extraordinaire
Ghirardelli Square
Londonderry Air
multimillionaire
neither here nor there

ÄR

are
bar
car
char
czar
far
jar
mar

Mar(s)
par
r
star
scar
spar
tsar
tar
yare

all-star
afar
armoire
attar
ajar
bête noire
bizarre
bonsoir
boxcar
boudoir
bazaar
cigar
costar
club car
crossbar
coaltar
crowbar
dinar
disbar
five-star
film star
flatcar
feldspar
four-star
guitar
gold star
jaguar
lumbar
lone star
lodestar
memoir
North Star
PR
polestar
pace car

quasar
Renoir
so far
sports car
sandbar
sitar
sidecar
streetcar
snack bar
stock car
tin star
track star
three R('s)
tartare
used car

au revoir
armored car
below par
battlestar
behind bar(s)
commissar
candy bar
cattle car
caviar
cinnabar
CPR
chocolate bar
cookie jar
cable car
Christmas star
compact car
DAR
dinosaur
evening star
fading star
falling star
football star
handlebar
Hershey bar
isobar
insofar
ice cream bar
lucky star
morning star

minibar
minotaur
Mason jar
movie star
no fumar
near and far
no host bar
oyster bar
on a par
objet d'art
pass the bar
police car
pinot noir
registrar
repertoire
railroad car
R and R
rising star
rent-a-car
reservoir
rouge et noir
superstar
seminar
salad bar
shooting star
steak tartare
scimitar
singles bar
sissy bar
trolley car
VCR
wishing star
Zanzibar

bulletproof car
carry too far
hardy har har
mayonnaise jar
parallel bar(s)
radio car
USSR

close but no cigar
wish upon a star

AR-āt

aerate
narrate
serrate

ÄRB

barb
garb

rhubarb

ÄRB-ul

garble
marble
warble

ÄRB-ur

arbor
barber
harbor

Ann Arbor
Pearl Harbor
safe harbor

ÄRB-urd

arbored
barbered
harbored
starboard

ÄRB-ur-ēng

barbering
harboring

ÄRCH

arch
March
march
parch
starch

cornstarch
death march
grand march
outmarch

Golden Arch(es)
Ides of March
wedding march

metatarsal arch

ÄRCH-ē

Archie
starchy

ÄRCH-ēng

arching
marching
parching
starching

outmarching

ÄRCH-ur

archer
marcher
parcher
starcher

departure
outmarch 'er

point of departure

ARD

aired
bared
blared
cared
chaired
dared
erred
fared
flaired

glared
paired
pared
scared
squared
stared
snared
spared
shared

compared
declared
despaired
ensnared
impaired
outstared
prepared
repaired
run scared
unbared

ill-prepared

hearing-impaired

ÄRD

bard
barred
card
chard
charred
guard
hard
jarred
lard
marred
nard
pard
parred
shard
scarred
sparred
starred
tarred
yard

armed guard
armguard
barnyard
blackguard
boneyard
Bernard
bank guard
backyard
bombard
blowhard
canard
churchyard
cue card
Coast Guard
courtyard
charge card
co-starred
dockyard
diehard
discard
disbarred
face card
flash card
green card
graveyard
jail guard
jacquard
junkyard
lifeguard
mag card
nose guard
on guard
off guard
old guard
petard
playyard
placecard
postcard
regard
rail guard
retard
Scotchgard
scorecard
stand guard
safeguard

stockyard
shipyard
shin guard
trump card
vanguard
wild card

avant-garde
birthday card
bodyguard
battle-scarred
boulevard
business card
bumper guard
baseball card
color guard
colombard
Christmas card
credit card
calling card
crossing guard
disregard
drawing card
greeting card
house of card(s)
in the card(s)
leotard
landing card
Master Card
no holds barred
prison guard
palace guard
report card
St. Bernard
Scotland Yard
tub of lard
take it hard
union card
Visa card

idiot card
library card
National Guard
the whole nine yard(s)

security guard

ÄRD-ē

arty
hardy
hearty
Marty
party
Sardi
smarty
tardy

Bacardi
foolhardy
hen party
Lombardi
stag party
search party
third party
tea party

birthday party
cocktail party
Grand Old Party
guilty party
hale and hearty
injured party
office party
party smarty
slumber party
throw a party

ÄRD-ed
(See ÄRD-ud)

ÄRD-en
(See ÄRD-un)

ÄRD-ēng

carding
charting
darting
farting
guarding
Harding

parting
smarting
starting

bombarding
departing
discarding
imparting
lifeguarding
outsmarting
regarding
restarting
retarding
safeguarding

disregarding

ÄRD-ent
(See ÄRD-unt)

ÄRD-ē-nus

artiness
hardiness
heartiness
smartiness

ÄRD-ē-un

guardian
partyin'

Edwardian

ÄRD-ik

arctic

antarctic
cathartic
Sephardic

ÄRD-ik-ul

article
particle

ÄRD-i-zun

artisan
partisan

bipartisan

ÄRD-lē

hardly
Yardley

ÄRD-lus

cardless
guardless
yardless

regardless

ÄRD-ō

ritardo
Lombardo
Ricardo

ARD-ū

dare do
hairdo
ne'er do
rare do

ÄRD-u

Sparta

Jakarta

Magna Carta

ÄRD-ud

carted
charted
carded
darted
farted
guarded

parted
smarted
started

blackhearted
bombarded
downhearted
departed
discarded
fainthearted
good-hearted
hardhearted
halfhearted
imparted
jumpstarted
kindhearted
lifeguarded
lighthearted
outsmarted
restarted
regarded
retarded
softhearted
stouthearted
Scotchgarded
safeguarded
uncharted
unguarded
wholehearted
warmhearted

brokenhearted
chickenhearted
disregarded
lionhearted
openhearted

ÄRD-uk
(See ÄRD-ik)

ÄRD-uk-ul
(See ÄRD-i-kul)

ÄRD-um

cart 'em
chart 'em
guard 'em
jarred 'em
marred 'em
part 'em
stardom
scarred 'em
start 'em

bombard 'em
discard 'em
jumpstart 'em
lifeguard 'em
outsmart 'em
postpartum
restart 'em
regard 'em

bodyguard 'em
disregard 'em

ÄRD-un

garden
guardin'
harden
pardon

bombardin'
discardin'
rose garden
regardin'
retardin'
safeguardin'

bodyguardin'
beg your pardon
disregardin'

Elizabeth Arden

ÄRD-un-ēng

gardening
hardening
pardoning

ÄRD-unt

ardent

retardant

ÄRD-ur

ardor
barter
barred 'er
carder
carter
charter
darter
farter
guarder
garter
harder
jarred 'er
larder
martyr
marred 'er
parter
starter
smarter
starred 'er
tarred'er
Tartar
tarter

bombarder
co-starred 'er
discarder
disbarred 'er
departer
imparter
regarder
retarder
restarter
safeguard 'er
self-starter
slow starter
try harder

cream of tartar
disregarder

ÄRD-ur-dum

bartered 'em
chartered 'em
martyrdom

ÄRD-ur-ē

artery
martyry

ÄRD-ur-ēng

bartering
chartering
martyring

ÄRD-ust

artist
chartist
hardest
smartest
stardust
tartest

con artist

AR-ē

airy
aerie
berry
blary
Barry
bury
cherry
Carrie
carry
dairy
fairy
ferry
Gerry
Gary
glary
hairy
Harry

Kerry
Larry
Mary
marry
merry
nary
parry
prairie
Perry
scary
sherry
tarry
Terry
vary
very
wary

bayberry
binary
contrary
canary
cranberry
Du Barry
good fairy
gooseberry
hand-carry
library
miscarry
mulberry
make merry
primary
raspberry
rosemary
remarry
strawberry
tooth fairy
unvary
unwary

aviary
adversary
airy-fairy
apiary
arbitrary
actuary
antiquary

boysenberry
bloody Mary
beriberi
commentary
cash and carry
cautionary
commissary
cackleberry
culinary
Canterbury
cemetery
customary
capillary
corollary
coronary
dromedary
dietary
dignitary
dysentery
dictionary
emissary
estuary
fragmentary
fetch and carry
functionary
February
hari kari
honorary
Holy Mary
huckleberry
intermarry
January
legendary
literary
luminary
Londonderry
loganberry
lapidary
missionary
Mata Hari
mortuary
military
monetary
monastery
mercenary

momentary
necessary
ordinary
planetary
pulmonary
salutary
secretary
secondary
statuary
salivary
sanitary
stationary
sanctuary
seminary
stationery
sedentary
solitary
sumptuary
tertiary
tributary
Tipperary
temporary
topiary
Typhoid Mary
visionary
voluntary
Virgin Mary

apothecary
contemporary
constabulary
discretionary
disciplinary
extemporary
extraordinary
fiduciary
hereditary
involuntary
incendiary
itinerary
imaginary
obituary
pecuniary
precautionary
proprietary

preliminary
probationary
reactionary
sugarplum fairy
subsidiary
Tom, Dick, and
  Harry
unsanitary
unnecessary
unordinary
vocabulary
veterinary

beneficiary
cat and the canary
evolutionary
eat, drink, and be
  merry
intermediary
private secretary
revolutionary
supernumerary
undersecretary

eleemosynary
plenipotentiary

ÄR-ē

jarry
quarry
starry
sorry
sari

curare
Campari
Ferrari
safari
so sorry
volare

calamari
Mata Hari

writ of certiorari

AR-ēd

buried
carried
ferried
harried
married
parried
tarried
varied

miscarried
remarried
unvaried
unmarried

intermarried

AR-ē-ēng

burying
carrying
ferrying
marrying
parrying
tarrying
varying

card-carrying
miscarrying
remarrying
unvarying

intermarrying

AR-ē-et
(See AR-ē-ut)

AR-e-fi
(See AR-u-fi)

AR-el
(See AR-ul)

ÄR-el
(See ÄR-ul)

AR-em
(See AR-um)

AR-en
(See AR-un)

AR-ēng

airing
baring
blaring
bearing
caring
chairing
daring
erring
faring
flaring
glaring
herring
pairing
paring
scaring
swearing
squaring
staring
snaring
sparing
sharing
tearing
wearing

ballbearing
comparing
declaring
despairing
ensnaring
forswearing
forbearing
impairing
long-wearing
outwearing
outstaring
preparing

repairing
red herring
seafaring
talebearing
uncaring
unerring

overbearing

revenue sharing

ÄR-ēng

barring
charring
jarring
marring
starring
scarring
sparring
tarring

co-starring
disbarring

AR-ēng-lē

blaringly
daringly
glaringly
sparingly

AR-ent
(See AR-unt)

AR-en-ur
(See AR-un-ur)

ÄR-ē-ō

barrio
Mario

Lothario
scenario

impresario

worst-case scenario

AR-e-sē
(See AR-u-sē)

AR-est
(See AR-ust)

AR-et
(See AR-ut)

AR-ē-u

area

Bavaria
Bay Area
Bulgaria
fringe area
hysteria
malaria
wisteria

honoraria
mass hysteria

disaster area

AR-ē-ul

aerial
Ariel
burial

malarial

actuarial
secretarial

AR-ē-um

bury 'em
barium
ferry 'em
marry 'em

vary 'em

aquarium
solarium
terrarium
vivarium

honorarium
planetarium
sanitarium

AR-ē-un

Aryan
buryin'
carryin'
carrion
clarion
ferryin'
marryin'
Marian
parryin'
tarryin'
varyin'

agrarian
barbarian
Bulgarian
Bavarian
card-carryin'
Caesarean
contrarian
grammarian
Hungarian
librarian
miscarryin'
ovarian
remarryin'
sectarian
unvaryin'

antiquarian
centenarian
intermarryin'
libertarian
nonsectarian
proletarian

Unitarian
vegetarian

authoritarian
abecedarian
disciplinarian
humanitarian
nonagenarian
octogenarian
parliamentarian
quadragenarian
sexagenarian
totalitarian
veterinarian

attitudinarian
latitudinarian
septuagenarian
valetudinarian

AR-ē-ur

airier
barrier
burier
bury 'er
blarier
carrier
carry 'er
ferrier
glarier
hairier
harrier
marrier
merrier
marry 'er
scarier
terrier
tarrier
varier
warier

card carrier
contrarier
fox terrier
germ carrier
hod carrier

mail carrier
miscarrier
remarry 'er
sound barrier
troop carrier
unvarier

aircraft carrier
letter carrier
legendarier
ordinarier
sanitarier
sonic barrier
sedentarier

the more the merrier

ÄR-ē-ur

jarrier
starrier
sorrier

AR-ē-us

bury us
carry us
ferry us
marry us
vary us
various

Aquarius
barbarious
gregarious
hilarious
nefarious
precarious
remarry us
vicarious

multifarious
Stradivarius
Sagittarius

AR-ē-ut

bury it
carry it

chariot
Harriet
lariat
marry it
vary it

Iscariot

proletariat
secretariat

AR-ēz

Aries
aeries
berries
buries
cherries
carries
dairies
fairies
ferries
marries
parries
prairies
tarries
varies

bayberries
canaries
good fairies
libraries
miscarries
mulberries
primaries
raspberries
remarries
strawberries
tooth fairies

aviaries
adversaries
apiaries
boysenberries
bloody Marys
cackleberries
commentaries

commissaries
cemeteries
corollaries
coronaries
dromedaries
dignitaries
dictionaries
estuaries
emissaries
Februarys
functionaries
honoraries
intermarries
Januarys
luminaries
loganberries
mortuaries
missionaries
monasteries
mercenaries
secretaries
sanctuaries
seminaries
temporaries
topiaries
tributaries
visionaries
Virgin Marys

apothecaries
contemporaries
itineraries
obituaries
preliminaries
subsidiaries
vocabularies

beneficiaries
intermediaries
revolutionaries
supernumeraries
undersecretaries

plenipotentiaries

ÄRF

arf
barf
scarf

AR-fōr

care for
therefore
wherefore

prepare for

say a prayer for

AR-ful

careful
chairful
prayerful

despairful
uncareful

ÄR-gō

Argo
argot
cargo
Fargo
largo
Margo

embargo
Key Largo
Wells Fargo

supercargo

ÄR-gun

argon
bargain
jargon

plea-bargain

AR-i-bul
(See AR-u-bul)

AR-if
(See AR-uf)

AR-if-ī
(See AR-uf-ī)

AR-ij

carriage
marriage

disparage
miscarriage
mixed marriage

baby carriage
horseless carriage

divorceless marriage

AR-ik
(See AR-uk)

AR-i-ku

Erica

America

AR-ik-ul

clerical

generical
hysterical
Homerical
numerical

esoterical

AR-il
(See AR-ul)

AR-il-ē
(See AR-ul-ē)

AR-il-us
(See AR-ul-us)

AR-in
(See AR-un)

AR-i-nur
(See AR-u-nur)

AR-is
(See AR-us)

AR-ish

barish
bearish
cherish
fairish
garish
glarish
perish
rarish
squarish

foursquarish
nightmarish

publish or perish

AR-ish-ēng

cherishing
perishing

ÄR-ist

farest

bizarrest
guitarist

AR-is-un

garrison
harassin'

Harrison

comparison
embarrassin'

by comparison

Ā-rīt

gay right(s)
may write
playwright
play right
say right
stay right
weigh right

AR-it
(See AR-ut)

AR-it-ē
(See AR-ud-ē)

AR-i-tōr-ē
(See AR-u-tōr-ē)

AR-it-u-bul
(See AR-ud-u-bul)

AR-i-tun
(See AR-u-tun)

AR-it-us
(See AR-ud-us)

ÄRJ

barge
charge
large
Marge
sarge

at large
discharge
depth charge
enlarge
in charge
recharge
surcharge
take charge
top sarge

by and large
cover charge
overcharge
trumped-up charge
undercharge

carrying charge

ambassador-at-large

ÄRJ-ēng

barging
charging

discharging
enlarging
recharging
surcharging

overcharging
undercharging

ÄRJ-u-bul

chargeable

dischargeable
enlargeable
rechargeable

ÄRJ-un

bargin'
chargin'
margin

dischargin'
enlargin'

rechargin'
surchargin'

overchargin'
superchargin'
underchargin'

ÄRJ-ur

barger
charger
larger

discharger
enlarger
recharger

supercharger

ÄRK

arc
ark
bark
Clark
dark
hark
lark
mark
marc
narc
park
shark
spark
stark

aardvark
bulwark
black mark
bookmark
birthmark
ballpark
Bismarck
benchmark
card shark
chop mark
check mark

debark
Deutsche mark
Denmark
embark
earmark
footmark
hallmark
hashmark
landmark
loan shark
monarch
Ozark
poolshark
postmark
pockmark
pitch-dark
quote mark
remark
smudge mark
skylark
skid mark
stretch mark
trademark
theme park

accent mark
beauty mark
baseball park
Central Park
Cutty Sark
doublepark
disembark
easy mark
fingermark
great white shark
hierarch
in the dark
Joan of Arc
killer shark
leave one's mark
matriarch
meadowlark
make one's mark
Noah's ark
oligarch

on the mark
patriarch
question mark
trailer park
valet park
watermark

amusement park
high-water mark
Lewis and Clark
man-eating shark
national park
shot in the dark
strawberry mark
unkind remark

exclamation mark
happy as a lark
punctuation mark
whistle in the dark

AR-kās

fair case
rare case
staircase

unfair case

ÄRK-ē

Arkie
car key
sparky

autarchy
anarchy
malarkey
monarchy

hierarchy
matriarchy
oligarchy
patriarchy

ÄRK-en
(See ÄRK-un)

ÄRK-ēng

arcing
barking
harking
marking
parking
sparking

debarking
embarking
earmarking
no parking
postmarking
remarking

doubleparking
disembarking

ÄRK-et
(See ÄRK-ut)

ÄRK-ik

anarchic

hierarchic
matriarchic
oligarchic
patriarchic

ÄRK-lē

Barkley
darkly
starkly

ÄRK-nus

darkness
starkness

ÄRKT

arced
barked
harked

marked
parked
sparked

debarked
embarked
earmarked
postmarked
pockmarked
remarked

disembarked
doubleparked
watermarked

ÄRK-ul

sparkle

hierarchal
matriarchal
oligarchal
patriarical

ÄRK-un

barkin'
darken
harken
markin'
parkin'
sparkin'

debarkin'
embarkin'
remarkin'

doubleparkin'
disembarkin'
valet parkin'

ÄRK-un-ēng

darkening
harkening

ÄRK-ur

barker
darker

marker
parker
spark 'er
starker

ÄRK-us

carcass
mark us
Marcus
park us
spark us

doublepark us
disembark us
Neiman-Marcus
valet-park us

ÄRK-ust

darkest
starkest

anarchist

matriarchist
patriarchist

ÄRK-ut

market
mark it
park it
spark it

blackmarket
bear market
bull market
earmark it
flea market
postmark it
stockmarket

ÄRL

Carl
gnarl
snarl

ensnarl
unsnarl

ARL-ē

barely
fairly
rarely
squarely

unfairly

ÄRL-ē

barley
Charlie
Farley
gnarly
parley
snarly

bizarrely

good-time Charlie

ÄRL-ēng

darling
gnarling
snarling
starling

ensnarling
my darling
unsnarling

AR-les
(See AR-lus)

ÄR-let
(See ÄR-lut)

AR-līn

airline
hairline

rare line
snare line

ÄRL-ō

Arlo
Barlow
Carlo
Harlow
Marlow

Monte Carlo

ÄRL-um

Harlem
snarl 'em

ensnarl 'em

ÄRL-ur

gnarler
parlor
snarler

ensnarler
unsnarler

beauty parlor
massage parlor

AR-lus

airless
careless
chairless
glareless
hairless
heirless
prayerless

affairless

ÄRL-ut

Charlotte
harlot
snarl it

scarlet
starlet

ensnarl it
unsnarl it

ÄRLZ

Charles
Carl's
gnarls
snarls

ensnarls
Prince Charles
unsnarls

ÄRM

arm
charm
farm
harm
marm

alarm
disarm
forearm
fat farm
firearm
gendarme
truck farm
schoolmarm
sidearm
stud farm
strongarm
unharm
unarm
yardarm

arm in arm
buy the farm
bet the farm
chicken farm
coat of arm(s)
dairy farm
false alarm

funny farm
fire alarm
lucky charm
open arm(s)
smoke alarm
snooze alarm
three-alarm
take up arm(s)
twist one's arm
up in arm(s)
underarm

burglar alarm
comrade-in-arm(s)
cause for alarm
long as one's arm
right to bear arm(s)
shot in the arm
silent alarm
twist someone's arm
travel alarm

ÄRMD

armed
charmed
farmed
harmed

alarmed
disarmed
unharmed

ÄRM-ē

army
arm me
charm me
farmy
harm me

alarm me
disarm me
schoolmarmy

Salvation Army

ÄRM-ēng

arming
charming
farming
harming

alarming
disarming
truck farming
uncharming

ÄRM-ent
(See ÄRM-unt)

ÄRM-ful

armful
charmful
harmful

unharmful

ÄRM-int
(See ÄRM-unt)

ÄRM-lus

armless
charmless
farmless
harmless

AR-mun

airman
chairman

repairman

ÄRM-un

armin'
barman
Carmen
charmin'
farmin'

harmin'

alarmin'

disarmin'

ÄRM-unt

garment

varmint

disbarment

undergarment

ÄRM-ur

armer

armor

charmer

farmer

harmer

alarmer

disarmer

snake charmer

strongarm 'er

chicken farmer

plate of armor

three-alarmer

ÄRN

barn

darn

yarn

consarn(ed)

goldarn

give a darn

spin a yarn

ÄRN-ē

barny

blarney

carny

garni

Killarney

chili con carne

ÄRN-ish

barnish

garnish

tarnish

varnish

revarnish

untarnish

ÄRN-ur

darner

garner

yarner

consarn 'er

goldarn 'er

AR-nus

bareness

fairness

rareness

squareness

awareness

threadbareness

unfairness

debonairness

unawareness

ÄR-nus

darn us

farness

harness

bizarreness

AR-ō

arrow

barrow

farrow

faro

harrow

Karo

marrow

narrow

pharaoh

sparrow

tarot

bolero

bone marrow

Camaro

dinero

Pierce-Arrow

ranchero

Romero

straight arrow

sombrero

torero

vaquero

wheelbarrow

bow and arrow

caballero

Clarence Darrow

straight and narrow

Atascadero

Embarcadero

Rio de Janeiro

ÄR-ō

borrow

charro

morrow

Poirot

sorrow

Ferraro

reborrow

tomorrow

beg, steal, or borrow

Kilimanjaro

AR-ō-ēng

harrowing
narrowing

AR-ō-in
(See AR-ō-un)

Ā-rōl

hay roll
payroll
may roll

AR-ō-un

heroin
heroine
harrowin'
narrowin'

ÄRP

carp
harp
sharp
tarp

cardsharp
look sharp
mouthharp

razor sharp

ÄRP-ē

harpie
sharpie

ÄRP-ist

harpist
sharpest

ÄRP-ur

Harper
sharper

ÄRS

farce
parse
sparse

ÄRS-el
(See ÄRS-ul)

ÄRSH

harsh
marsh

démarche

ÄRSH-ul

martial
marshal
Marshall
partial

court-martial
fire marshal
grand marshal
impartial

federal marshal
fair and impartial

ÄRS-i-tē
(See ÄRS-u-dē)

ÄRS-lē

parsley
sparsely

ÄRS-u-dē

farcity
sparsity
varsity

ÄRS-ul

parcel
tarsal

metatarsal
part and parcel

ÄRS-un

arson
Carson
Larsen
parson
parsin'

ÄRT

art
cart
chart
dart
fart
heart
hart
mart
part
smart
start
tart

apart
Bernhardt
Bogart
bit part
by heart
best part
depart
Descartes
dogcart
eye chart
faint heart
flow chart
folk art
flower cart
fresh start
fine art

false start
golf cart
go-cart
get smart
hard heart
health chart
headstart
impart
jump-start
kind heart
K Mart
light heart
late start
Mozart
outsmart
op art
pop art
Pop Tart
pushcart
rampart
restart
soft heart
Stuttgart
sweetheart
street smart
tea cart
take heart
upstart

applecart
abstract art
à la carte
bleeding heart
Bonaparte
broken heart
cross one's heart
Cuisinart
counterpart
change of heart
Eberhardt
flying start
fall apart
from the heart
graphic art
heart to heart

have a heart
lose one's heart
lonely heart
martial art
minimart
natal chart
open heart
Purple Heart
pastry cart
pick apart
running start
supermart
shopping cart
take apart
take to heart
vital part
weatherchart
work of art

break someone's heart
for the most part
manual art
performing art
replacement part
state of the art
with all one's heart

artificial heart
till death do you part

Associate of Art(s)
organization chart
upset the applecart

from the bottom of
   one's heart

ÄRT-ē
(See ÄRD-ē)

ÄRT-ed
(See ÄRD-ud)

ÄRT-en
(See ÄRT-un)

ÄRT-ēng
(See ÄRD-ēng)

ÄRT-ē-nus
(See ÄRD-ē-nus)

ÄRT-ik
(See ÄRD-ik)

ÄRT-ik-ul
(See ÄRD-i-kul)

ÄRT-ist
(See ÄRD-ust)

ÄRT-iz-un
(See ÄRD-iz-un)

ÄRT-lē

partly
smartly

ÄRT-lus

artless
cartless
chartless
dartless
heartless
startless

sweetheartless

ÄRT-ment

apartment
compartment
department
my heart meant

fire department
glove compartment

War Department

co-op apartment
luggage compartment

ÄRT-nur

heartener
partner

kindergartner
silent partner
sparring partner

ÄRT-nus

smartness
tartness

upstartness

ART-ō

Alberto
concerto
Umberto

ÄRT-rij

cartridge
partridge

ÄRTS

arts
carts
charts
darts
farts
hearts
harts
marts
parts
smarts
starts
tarts

departs

flow charts
flowercharts
fine arts
false starts
golf carts
go-carts
headstarts
imparts
jumpstarts
K Marts
late starts
outsmarts
Pop Tarts
pushcarts
restarts
ramparts
sweethearts
tea carts
upstarts

applecarts
bleeding hearts
broken hearts
counterparts
fits and starts
graphic arts
heart of hearts
knave of hearts
lonely hearts
martial arts
off the charts
private parts
queen of hearts
running starts
supermarts
shopping carts
weathercharts

bachelor of arts
liberal arts
performing arts
replacement parts

artificial hearts
patron of the arts

associate of arts

ÄRT-u
(See ÄRD-u)

ÄRT-ud
(See ÄRD-ud)

ÄRT-um
(See ÄRD-um)

ÄRT-un

Barton
carton
cartin'
chartin'
dartin'
fartin'
hearten
marten
Martin
partin'
Spartan
smarten
startin'
tartan

dishearten
departin'
false startin'
impartin'
milk carton
outsmartin'
restartin'

kindergarten

ÄRT-ur
(See ÄRD-ur)

ÄRT-ur-dum
(See ÄRD-ur-dum)

ÄRT-ur-ē
(See ÄRD-ur-ē)

ÄRT-ur-ēng
(See ÄRD-ur-ēng)

AR-u

Cara
Clara
era
Sarah

Herrera
mascara
Sahara

Riviera
Santa Clara
Theda Bara

Scarlett O'Hara

ÄR-u

aura
Laura

tiara

Masai Mara
sayonara

Guadalajara

AR-ub

Arab
carob
cherub
scarab

AR-u-bul

airable
arable
bearable
barable

darable
flairable
parable
pairable
sharable
squarable
scarable
sparable
swearable
snarable
terrible
tearable
wearable

declarable
ensnarable
forebearable
impairable
outwearable
outstarable
repairable
unbearable
unsharable
untearable
unwearable

AR-ud

arid
Herod
Jared

AR-u-dē

charity
clarity
parody
parity
rarity
verity

austerity
asperity
barbarity
celerity
disparity

dexterity
hilarity
prosperity
posterity
polarity
sincerity
severity
temerity
vulgarity

angularity
circularity
insincerity
jocularity
popularity
regularity
similarity
singularity
solidarity
secularity

ambidexterity
dissimilarity
familiarity
faith, hope, and
    charity
irregularity
particularity
peculiarity
unpopularity

AR-ud-ēng

ferreting
meriting
parroting

inheriting

AR-u-div

narrative

comparative
declarative
imperative
preparative

AR-u-du-bul

charitable
ferretable
meritable
veritable

inheritable

AR-u-dus

ferret us
meritous

emeritus
inherit us

disinherit us

AR-uf

sheriff
seraf
tariff

AR-u-fī

clarify
rarefy
scarify
terrify
verify

AR-u-gon

Aragon
paragon
tarragon

AR-uk

barrack
cleric
Derek
derrick
Eric

barbaric
generic

hysteric
Homeric
numeric
oil derrick

esoteric

AR-ul

aril
barrel
carol
Carole
carrel
Cheryl
Darryl
feral
Merrill
peril
sterile

apparel
imperil
pork barrel

Christmas carol

lock, stock, and barrel

bottom of the barrel

ÄR-ul

gnarl
quarrel
laurel
snarl

ensnarl
unsnarl

rest on one's laurel(s)

AR-uld

barrelled
carolled
Gerald
herald

Harold
Fitzgerald
imperilled

AR-u-lē

airily
merrily
scarily
verily
warily

AR-ul-ēng

barreling
caroling

imperiling

AR-u-lus

garrulous
perilous
querulous

imperil us

AR-um

air 'em
bare 'em
bear 'em
carom
dare 'em
harem
pair 'em
scare 'em
snare 'em
spare 'em
share 'em
tear 'em
wear 'em

compare 'em
declare 'em
ensnare 'em
impair 'em

outwear 'em
prepare 'em
repair 'em
unbare 'em

harum scarum

AR-um-ē

fair o' me
Jeremy
Laramie
square o' me

aware o' me
beware o' me
unfair o' me

AR-un

Aaron
airin'
baron
barin'
barren
bearin'
carin'
chairin'
darin'
Erin
farin'
flarin'
glarin'
heron
Karen
parin'
pairin'
rarin'
Sharon
sparin'
starin'
swearin'
sharin'
tearin'
wearin'

comparin'

declarin'
despairin'
ensnarin'
impairin'
outwearin'
outstarin'
preparin'
repairin'
unbarin'

overbearin'
robber baron

AR-und

errand
gerund

AR-un-et

baronet
clarinet
wear a net

AR-uns

Clarence
parents

forbearance
forswearance
grandparents
godparents
knight-errants
transparence

foster parents
heir apparents

AR-unt

arrant
errant
parent

apparent
grandparent
godparent

inherent
knight-errant
transparent

foster parent
great-grandparent
heir apparent

single parent
unapparent
working parent

AR-unts
(See AR-uns)

AR-un-ur

barrener
chairin' 'er
darin' 'er
mariner
sparin' 'er
sharin' 'er
wearin' 'er

AR-unz

Aaron's
barons
errands
Erin's
gerunds
herons
Sharon's

AR-ur

bearer
barer
blarer
carer
darer
error
fairer
farer
flarer

glarer
parer
pairer
rarer
scarer
sharer
squarer
sparer
starer
swearer
tearer
terror
wearer

comparer
cropsharer
declarer
despairer
ensnarer
forbearer
impairer
night terror
outstarer
preparer
pallbearer
repairer
seafarer
threadbarer
tale bearer
torchbearer
unfairer
wayfarer

car repairer
holy terror
overbearer
Reign of Terror
standard bearer
trial and error
wash and wearer

comedy of error(s)

AR-us

bear us
dare us

ferrous
Harris
harass
heiress
pair us
Paris
share us
spare us
scare us
terrace

compare us
ensnare us
embarrass
impair us
outwear us
outstare us
prepare us
repair us

plaster of Paris

ÄR-us

are us
bar us
jar us
mar us
scar us
star us
Taurus

co-star us
Centaurus
disbar us
thesaurus

brontosaurus

tyrannosaurus

AR-u-sē

clerisy
heresy
Pharisee

AR-u-sēng

harassing
terracing

embarrassing

AR-us-ment

harassment

embarrassment

AR-ust

barest
fairest
rarest
squarest

foursquarest
threadbarest

ÄR-ust
(See ÄR-ist)

AR-us-un
(See AR-is-un)

AR-u-tē
(See AR-u-dē)

AR-ut

air it
bear it
bare it
blare it
carrot
caret
carat
claret
dare it
flair it
ferret
garret

karat
merit
pare it
parrot
pair it
scare it
spare it
swear it
square it
share it
snare it
tear it
wear it

compare it
demerit
declare it
ensnare it
forbear it
inherit
impair it
prepare it
repair it
unbare it

badge of merit
disinherit
on one's merit

twenty-four carat

**AR-ut-ēng
(See AR-ud-ēng)**

**AR-u-tiv
(See AR-u-div)**

AR-u-tōr-ē

territory

declaratory
preparatory

**AR-u-tu-bul
(See AR-u-du-bul)**

AR-u-tun

ferretin'
garrotin'
meritin'
parrotin'
Sheraton

inheritin'
Samaritan

disinheritin'
Good Samaritan

ÄRV

carve
Marv
scarve(s)
starve

ÄRV-ēng

carving
starving

woodcarving

ÄRV-on

carve on
Darvon
starve on

ÄRV-un

carvin'
Marvin
starvin'

AR-wā

airway
fairway
stairway

ÄRX

arcs
arks

barks
larks
Marx
marks
narcs
parks
sharks

bookmarks
birthmarks
cardsharks
checkmarks
debarks
Deutsche marks
earmarks
footmarks
hallmarks
hashmarks
Karl Marx
landmarks
loan sharks
monarchs
poolsharks
postmarks
pockmarks
quote marks
remarks
skid marks
stretch marks
trademarks
theme parks

beauty marks
doubleparks
easy marks
Groucho Marx
matriarchs
patriarchs
question marks

ĀS

ace
base
bass
brace

case	footrace	bouillabaisse
chase	freebase	basket case
face	glass case	change of pace
grace	give chase	commonplace
lace	horserace	data base
mace	home base	doublespace
pace	in case	every place
place	keep pace	freckleface
plaice	lose face	flying ace
race	last place	funny face
space	misplace	face-to-face
trace	no place	fall from grace
vase	neckbrace	hiding place
	outpace	human race
air base	off-base	hatchet face
apace	paleface	interface
arms race	Park Place	interlace
abase	power base	interspace
birthplace	retrace	innerspace
backspace	replace	jewelry case
briefcase	rat race	just in case
boldface	staircase	know one's place
bookcase	sackrace	marketplace
crawlspace	showcase	meeting place
car race	save face	makeup case
crankcase	straight face	not a trace
cardcase	suitcase	outerspace
disgrace	shoelace	out of place
doughface	showplace	pokerface
dog race	snail's pace	paper chase
dollface	typeface	polling place
drag race	touch base	pillow case
dogface	two-face	pennant race
displace	third base	Queen Anne's lace
debase	test case	relay race
deface	unlace	resting place
efface	workplace	steeplechase
encase		show one's face
enlace	aerospace	self-efface
erase	anyplace	storage space
embrace	angel face	saving grace
fireplace	about-face	stock-car race
first base	breathing space	set the pace
fast pace	babyface	upper case

way off base
wild-goose chase

blue in the face
cigarette case
chariot race
egg on one's face
everyplace
federal case
get to first base
in any case
jumping-off place
put through one's
    pace(s)
satin and lace
slap in the face
vanity case
watering place

kick over the trace(s)
open-and-shut-case
political race
wide-open space

arsenic and old lace
America's Cup Race

between a rock and a
    hard place

AS

ass
brass
bass
class
crass
gas
glass
grass
lass
mass
pass
sass

amass
alas

big brass
bluegrass
bypass
crevasse
cut glass
crabgrass
eyeglass
en masse
fat ass
first class
harass
high class
hourglass
impasse
jive-ass
jackass
low class
lardass
morass
molass(es)
nerve gas
outclass
press pass
plateglass
smart ass
surpass
seabass
stained glass
spyglass
spun glass
trespass
top brass
tear gas
third class
wise-ass
world class

bring to pass
boarding pass
bonny lass
cabin class
cocktail glass
clump of grass
cook with gas
come to pass

demitasse
drag one's ass
fiberglass
horse's ass
heart bypass
isinglass
looking glass
laughing gas
lower-class
middle-class
make a pass
mountain pass
out of gas
overpass
parking pass
poison gas
sassafras
second class
smooth as glass
sleeping gas
underpass
upper-class
working-class

head of the class
natural gas
pain in the ass
run out of gas
step on the gas
snake in the grass
head off at the pass
magnifying glass
pheasant under glass

coronary bypass

AS-ā

assay
class A
glacé
passe

AS-chun

bastion
Sebastian

ĀS-ē

Casey
Gracie
lacy
Macy('s)
precis
racy
spacy
Tracy

Dick Tracy

AS-ē

brassy
classy
chassis
gassy
grassy
glassy
lassie
sassy

unclassy
ungrassy
unsassy

classy chassis
fat and sassy
Tallahassee

ĀS-ē-āt
(See ĀSH-ē-āt)

AS-el
(See AS-ul)

ĀS-en
(See ĀS-un)

AS-en
(See AS-un)

ĀS-ēng

acing
basing
bracing
casing
chasing
facing
gracing
lacing
pacing
placing
racing
spacing
tracing

disgracing
displacing
debasing
defacing
enlacing
erasing
embracing
freebasing
horseracing
misplacing
outpacing
retracing
replacing
unlacing

doublespacing
interfacing
interlacing
pillowcasing
self-effacing
single-spacing
stock-car racing
steeplechasing

chariot racing

AS-ēng

gassing
massing
passing

sassing

amassing
bypassing
harassing
outclassing
surpassing
trespassing

ĀS-ens
(See ĀS-uns)

ĀS-ent
(See ĀS-unt)

AS-ē-nus

brassiness
classiness
gassiness
glassiness
sassiness

AS-et
(See AS-ut)

AS-ez
(See As-uz)

ĀS-ful

faceful
graceful
spaceful

disgraceful
ungraceful

ASH

ash
bash
brash
cache

cash
crash
clash
dash
flash
gnash
gash
hash
lash
mash
plash
rash
sash
stash
splash
slash
smash
trash
thrash

abash
backsplash
backlash
cold cash
eyelash
gate crash
hard cash
hot flash
mishmash
moustache
news flash
panache
rehash
splish splash
sour mash
sling hash
slapdash
tonguelash
unlash
Wabash
whiplash

balderdash
corned beef hash
Calabash
diaper rash

false eyelash
make a splash
petty cash
ready cash
succotash

handlebar moustache

ASH-ē

ashy
clashy
flashy
mashie
plashy
splashy
trashy

ĀSH-ē-āt

satiate

emaciate
expatiate
ingratiate
the way she ate

ĀSH-en
(See ĀSH-un)

ASH-en
(See ASH-un)

ASH-ēng

bashing
cashing
crashing
clashing
dashing
flashing
gnashing
hashing
lashing
mashing
stashing

splashing
slashing
smashing
trashing
thrashing

gay-bashing
rehashing
tonguelashing
unlashing

ĀSH-ē-ō

ratio

fellatio
Horatio

ASH-ful

bashful
brashful
rashful
splashful

ASH-ist

brashest
fascist
rashest

ASH-lē

Ashley
brashly
rashly

ASH-nus

brashness
rashness

ĀSH-u

geisha

acacia
Croatia

ĀSH-ul

facial
glacial
racial
spatial

palatial

interracial

ĀSH-un

Haitian
nation
ration
station

Alsatian
carnation
cognation
citation
crustacean
castration
creation
collation
cremation
cessation
causation
deflation
Dalmatian
dilation
damnation
donation
duration
dictation
elation
eustachian
foundation
frustration
formation
fire station
filtration
flotation
flirtation
fixation
gyration

gas station
gradation
gestation
hydration
inflation
location
libation
ligation
migration
mutation
notation
oration
ovation
prostration
pulsation
probation
plantation
quotation
relation
rotation
space station
summation
starvation
substation
taxation
tarnation
vacation
vocation
vibration
vexation
way station

abdication
application
allocation
avocation
altercation
appellation
allegation
aviation
adulation
acclamation
animation
affirmation
assignation

alteration
admiration
aspiration
adoration
aberration
arbitration
affectation
agitation
augmentation
annotation
adaptation
amputation
aggravation
annexation
complication
convocation
commendation
congregation
castigation
conjugation
correlation
compilation
cancellation
consolation
contemplation
calculation
conflagration
circulation
consummation
confirmation
conformation
combination
culmination
condemnation
carbonation
coronation
consternation
celebration
calibration
consecration
corporation
concentration
condensation
compensation
conversation

cogitation
capitation
consultation
confrontation
connotation
cultivation
captivation
crop rotation
conservation
dedication
duplication
dislocation
demarcation
degradation
delegation
deviation
distillation
desolation
defamation
designation
domination
destination
detonation
dissipation
declaration
desecration
dehydration
desperation
decoration
demonstration
dispensation
denotation
dissertation
devastation
derivation
deprivation
elevation
exportation
emulation
estimation
explanation
emanation
emigration
expiration
exploration

expectation
exploitation
exaltation
excitation
exultation
excavation
fabrication
fumigation
fascination
formulation
filling station
federation
figuration
fomentation
fermentation
fluctuation
generation
gravitation
graduation
hyphenation
hibernation
habitation
hesitation
incubation
indication
implication
inundation
irrigation
instigation
inhalation
installation
immolation
isolation
insulation
intimation
inflammation
information
indignation
inclination
integration
imitation
irritation
immigration
inspiration
infiltration

illustration
importation
indentation
infestation
innovation
jubilation
lubrication
liquidation
litigation
legislation
lamination
lumination
liberation
laceration
limitation
levitation
lamentation
League of Nation(s)
masturbation
medication
mitigation
mediation
menstruation
ministration
mutilation
malformation
machination
moderation
maturation
meditation
molestation
motivation
nomination
obligation
ovulation
occupation
operation
orchestration
observation
provocation
procreation
propagation
population
pagination
preparation

perspiration
perforation
peroration
penetration
perpetration
palpitation
presentation
punctuation
preservation
pollination
retardation
recreation
radiation
revelation
regulation
reformation
resignation
ruination
reparation
respiration
restoration
registration
recitation
reputation
renovation
reservation
relaxation
syndication
segregation
speculation
simulation
stimulation
stipulation
syncopation
service station
separation
saturation
sanitation
segmentation
salutation
situation
salivation
trepidation
Third World nation
tracking station

tabulation
transformation
termination
toleration
transplantation
transportation
undulation
usurpation
vindication
validation
variation
ventilation
violation
vaccination
veneration
vegetation
visitation
valuation

adjudication
amplification
authentication
accreditation
accommodation
appreciation
affiliation
alleviation
abbreviation
asphyxiation
annihilation
assimilation
articulation
accumulation
amalgamation
approximation
appropriation
alienation
abomination
assassination
anticipation
acceleration
alliteration
adulteration
administration
argumentation

accentuation
authorization
analyzation
beautification
Beat Generation
by acclamation
clarification
classification
configuration
certification
communication
consolidation
co-education
conciliation
congratulation(s)
capitulation
coordination
contamination
confederation
consideration
conglomeration
cooperation
commiseration
collaboration
corroboration
commemoration
commensuration
continuation
centralization
civilization
crystallization
Christianization
columnization
colonization
canonization
dignification
domestication
delineation
depreciation
denunciation
defoliation
disembarkation
disconsolation
dissemination
discrimination

denomination
determination
deliberation
deceleration
degeneration
discoloration
debilitation
decapitation
documentation
dramatization
exacerbation
eradication
equivocation
emaciation
enunciation
expropriation
ejaculation
emasculation
elimination
extermination
emancipation
exasperation
exhilaration
exaggeration
enumeration
exoneration
evaluation
extenuation
edification
fortification
falsification
felicitation
facilitation
formalization
fraternization
glorification
gay liberation
gratification
gesticulation
humiliation
hallucination
habituation
humanization
harmonization
intoxication

invalidation
intimidation
investigation
interrogation
irradiation
infuriation
ingratiation
initiation
interrelation
incrimination
illumination
indoctrination
impersonation
incarceration
insemination
incineration
imagination
inebriation
invigoration
incorporation
inauguration
improvisation
interpretation
inhabitation
instrumentation
insinuation
idealization
idolization
justification
luxuriation
Lost Generation
legalization
modification
mortification
multiplication
misapplication
magnification
matriculation
miscalculation
manipulation
misinformation
manifestation
minimization
modernization
magnetization

nullification
notification
necessitation
normalization
neutralization
officiation
origination
obliteration
ornamentation
organization
proliferation
pressurization
purification
prognostication
preoccupation
prevarication
pronunciation
perambulation
predomination
procrastination
predestination
participation
premeditation
precipitation
penalization
patronization
polarization
pasteurization
paralyzation
qualification
ratification
reciprocation
recommendation
radio station
renunciation
rejuvenation
repudiation
retaliation
repatriation
recrimination
renomination
reverberation
refrigeration
regeneration
remuneration

recuperation
reiteration
resuscitation
regurgitation
regimentation
representation
realization
simplification
signification
solicitation
sanctification
sophistication
substantiation
Serbo-Croatian
stabilization
summer vacation
supplementation
sedimentation
standardization
socialization
sterilization
symbolization
scrutinization
solemnization
synchronization
summarization
sensitization
standing ovation
transfiguration
tranquilization
United Nation(s)
unification
utilization
urbanization
vilification
verification
versification
vituperation
vocalization
vandalization
verbalization
victimization

antagonization
amelioration

adult education
alphabetization
anesthetization
circumstantiation
college education
commercialization
covert operation
capitalization
characterization
categorization
disqualification
diversification
differentiation
discontinuation
decentralization
demoralization
demobilization
disorganization
deodorization
desensitization
deterioration
exemplification
electrification
excommunication
experimentation
familiarization
generalization
high school education
indemnification
intensification
identification
intermediation
insubordination
inside information
intimate relation(s)
indetermination
inconsideration
incapacitation
immortalization
liberalization
militarization
misrepresentation
mispronunciation
monopolization
nationalization

naturalization
no-win situation
personification
prestidigitation
parks and recreation
popularization
reconciliation
recapitulation
reconsideration
rehabilitation
reorganization
revitalization
solidification
self-determination
systematization
unsophistication
under obligation
visualization
workman's
    compensation
women's liberation

Americanization
double-digit inflation
intercommunication
liberal education
materialization
physical education
spiritualization
statute of limitation(s)

artifical respiration
individualization
intellectualization

Articles of
    Confederation
artificial insemination

ASH-un

ashen
bashin'
cashin'
crashin'
clashin'
dashin'

fashion
flashin'
gashin'
gnashin'
hashin'
lashin'
mashin'
passion
ration
stashin'
splashin'
slashin'
smashin'
trashin'
thrashin'

compassion
dispassion
grand passion
high fashion
rehashin'
splish splashin'
unlashin'

out of fashion

ASH-und

fashioned
rationed

impassioned
old-fashioned

ĀSH-un-ēng

rationing
stationing

ASH-un-ēng

fashioning
rationing

ĀSH-unt

patient

impatient

somnifacient

ĀSH-un-ul

notational
probational
sensational
vocational
vibrational

congregational
convocational
conversational
confrontational
educational
generational
informational
inspirational
motivational
observational
occupational
recreational
transformational

co-educational
denominational
improvisational
organizational
representational

ASH-un-ul

national
rational

irrational

international
supranational

ASH-un-ul-īz

nationalize
rationalize

ASH-un-ut

cashin' it
crashin' it
fashion it
mashin' it
passionate
ration it
slashin' it
smashin' it
trashin' it

compassionate
dispassionate

ĀSH-ur

glacier

erasure

ASH-ur

basher
brasher
crasher
clasher
dasher
flasher
gnasher
gasher
hasher
lasher
masher
rasher
stasher
slasher
splasher
smasher
thrasher

gate-crasher
price slasher
unlasher

atom smasher
haberdasher

party crasher

potato masher

ĀSH-us

gracious
spacious

audacious
bodacious
capacious
curvaceous
fallacious
flirtatious
good gracious
Horatius
Ignatius
loquacious
mendacious
nugacious
predacious
pugnacious
rapacious
salacious
sagacious
sequacious
tenacious
ungracious
veracious
voracious
vivacious
vexatious

efficacious
goodness gracious
ostentatious
perspicacious
pertinacious
saponaceous

ĀSH-us-nus

graciousness
spaciousness

audaciousness

curvaceousness
fallaciousness
mendaciousness
sagaciousness
tenaciousness
ungraciousness
vivaciousness

ASH-ust
(See ASH-ist)

ASH-uz

ashes
bashes
caches
cashes
crashes
clashes
dashes
flashes
gnashes
gashes
hashes
lashes
mashes
plashes
rashes
sashes
stashes
splashes
slashes
smashes
trashes
thrashes

eyelashes
hot flashes
mishmashes
moustaches
news flashes
rehashes
unlashes
whiplashes

AS-ibul
(See AS-u-bul)

AS-id
(See AS-ud)

AS-if-ī
(See AS-uf-ī)

ĀS-ik

basic
play sick

AS-ik

classic
hassock

neoclassic

AS-il
(See AS-ul)

ĀS-in
(See ĀS-un)

AS-in
(See AS-un)

AS-in-āt

fascinate

assassinate

ĀS-is
(See ĀS-us)

ĀS-ist

basest
racist

AS-it
(See AS-ut)

AS-it-ē
(See AS-ud-ē)

ĀS-iv

abrasive
assuasive
dissuasive
evasive
invasive
persuasive
pervasive

AS-iv

massive
passive

impassive

ASK

ask
Basque
bask
cask
flask
mask
task

facemask
gas mask
hip flask
ski mask
unmask
wine cask

take to task
water flask

Halloween mask

ASK-ēng

asking
basking
masking

ASK-et
(See ASK-ut)

ASK-ō

fiasco
Tabasco

ASK-ot

ascot
mascot

ASK-u

Alaska
Nebraska

baked Alaska

ASK-u-bul

askable
maskable

ASK-ur

asker
basker
masker

just ask 'er
unmasker

Madagascar

ASK-us

ask us
mask us

Damascus
unmask us

ASK-ut

ask it
basket
casket
gasket
mask it

breadbasket
unmask it
workbasket
wastebasket

blow a gasket
Easter basket

a tisket, a tasket
hell in a handbasket

AS-lē

crassly
ghastly
lastly
vastly

downcastly
steadfastly

ĀS-lus

baseless
faceless
graceless
spaceless
tasteless
traceless
waistless

ĀS-ment

basement
casement
placement

abasement
debasement
defacement
displacement

effacement
encasement
embracement
misplacement
replacement

bargain basement

ĀS-ō

beso
peso
queso
say so

AS-ō

basso
lasso

El Paso

ASP

asp
clasp
gasp
grasp
hasp
rasp

agasp
hand clasp
last gasp
unclasp

ASP-ē

graspy
raspy

ASP-ēng

clasping
gasping
grasping
rasping

unclasping

ASP-u-bul

claspable
graspable

ASP-un

Aspen
claspin'
gaspin'
graspin'
raspin'

unclaspin'

ASP-ur

clasper
Casper
gasper
grasp 'er
Jasper
rasper

ĀST

aced
baste
braced
cased
chaste
chased
faced
graced
haste
laced
paced
paste
placed
raced
spaced
taste
traced
waste
waist

abased

barefaced
boldfaced
bad taste
displaced
disgraced
distaste
debased
defaced
effaced
enlaced
erased
encased
embraced
fastpaced
full-faced
good taste
lambaste
lay waste
misplaced
moonfaced
make haste
outpaced
palefaced
posthaste
retraced
redfaced
replaced
showcased
shamefaced
straitlaced
two-faced
toothpaste
unlaced
unchaste
wasp waist

acquired taste
aftertaste
babyfaced
cut-and-paste
double-faced
dirty-faced
frecklefaced
go to waste
haste makes waste

interspaced
interfaced
interlaced
pure and chaste
pantywaist

hazardous waste
nuclear waste

AST

blast
cast
caste
classed
fast
gassed
grassed
glassed
last
mast
massed
past
passed
sassed
vast

aghast
avast
amassed
at last
bombast
broadcast
contrast
dad-blast(ed)
downcast
fat-assed
full blast
forecast
gymnast
hold fast
half past
halfmast
half-assed
harassed
half caste

lambaste
miscast
newscast
outlast
outclassed
outcast
play cast
repast
surpassed
smart-assed
steadfast
sandblast
stand fast
tight-assed
typecast

all-star cast
at long last
colorcast
colorfast
die is cast
flabbergast
hard and fast
middle-classed
overcast
simulcast
telecast
unsurpassed
upper-classed

before the mast
enthusiast
get nowhere fast
iconoclast

ĀST-ē

hasty
pasty
tasty

AST-ē

Asti
blasty
fasty

nasty

angioplasty

ĀST-ed
(See ĀST-ud)

AST-ed
(See AST-ud)

ĀST-ēng

basting
Hasting(s)
pasting
tasting
wasting

lambasting
winetasting

AST-ēng

blasting
casting
fasting
lasting

bombasting
broadcasting
contrasting
flycasting
forecasting
lambasting
longlasting
miscasting
outlasting
sandblasting
typecasting

everlasting
flabbergasting
simulcasting
telecasting

ĀST-ful

tasteful
wasteful

distasteful

AST-ik

drastic
gas stick
plastic
spastic

bombastic
elastic
fantastic
gymnastic
monastic
sarcastic
scholastic

orgiastic

enthusiastic
ecclesiastic
interscholastic
iconoclastic

trip the light fantastic

AST-ik-ul

bombastical
elastical
fantastical
monastical
scholastical

enthusiastical
ecclesiastical

AST-īz

chastise
cast eyes
fast eyes
glassed eyes

AST-lē
(See AS-lē)

ĀST-lus
(See ĀS-lus)

AST-of

blastoff
castoff
last off
passed off

AST-u

hasta
Shasta

canasta

ĀST-ud

basted
pasted
tasted
wasted

highwaisted
longwaisted
shortwaisted
untasted

AST-ud

blasted
fasted
lasted
masted

bombasted
broadcasted
contrasted
dad-blasted
forecasted
lambasted
outlasted

sandblasted

flabbergasted

AST-uk
(See AST-ik)

ĀST-ur

aced 'er
baster
chaster
chased 'er
faced 'er
paced 'er
paster
placed 'er
raced 'er
taster
traced 'er
waster

disgraced 'er
embraced 'er
lambaster
unchaster
winetaster

AST-ur

aster
Astor
blaster
castor
caster
gassed 'er
faster
laster
master
pastor
past 'er
plaster
passed 'er
sassed 'er
vaster

broadcaster

bandmaster
bypassed 'er
corn plaster
contraster
choirmaster
disaster
dance master
forecaster
headmaster
harassed 'er
Mixmaster
mud plaster
newscaster
old master
outlast 'er
outclassed 'er
postmaster
pastmaster
paymaster
ringmaster
steadfaster
sandblaster
scoutmaster
schoolmaster
surpassed 'er
taskmaster
toastmaster
typecaster

alabaster
flabbergaster
ghetto blaster
lath and plaster
lord and master
mustard plaster
quartermaster
simulcaster

weather forecaster

AST-urd

bastard
dastard
mastered

pastored
plastered

AST-ur-ēng

mastering
pastoring
plastering

ĀS-u

Asa
mesa

cabeza

ĀS-u-bul

chasable
faceable
paceable
placeable
traceable

displaceable
defaceable
erasable
embraceable
misplaceable
outpaceable
retraceable
replaceable
unplaceable
unlaceable

interlaceable
irreplaceable

AS-u-bul

passable
sassable

amassable
bypassable
harassable
impassable
irascible

outclassable
surpassable
trespassable

AS-ud

acid
flaccid
placid

antacid
Lake Placid

AS-ud-ē

acidy
Cassidy

audacity
capacity
edacity
mendacity
pugnacity
sagacity
tenacity
voracity
vivacity
veracity

incapacity
perspicacity

Hop-a-long Cassidy

AS-u-fī

classify
pacify

declassify
reclassify

**AS-uk
(See AS-ik)**

AS-ul

castle
facile

hassle
passel
tassel
vassal

Newcastle
sandcastle

ĀS-un

basin
bracin'
chasin'
caisson
chasten
facin'
gracin'
hasten
Jason
lacin'
mason
pacin'
placin'
racin'
spacin'
tracin'

disgracin'
displacin'
debasin'
defacin'
enlacin'
erasin'
embracin'
horseracin'
misplacin'
outpacin'
retracin'
replacin'
showcasin'
stonemason
unlacin'
washbasin

about-facin'
interfacin'
interlacin'

self-effacin'
wild-goose chasin'

AS-un

fasten
massin'
passin'
sassin'

assassin
amassin'
bypassin'
harassin'
in passin'
outclassin'
refasten
surpassin'
trespassin'
unfasten

AS-un-āt
(See AS-in-āt)

ĀS-un-ēng

chastening
hastening

ĀS-uns

nascence
naissance

adjacence
complaisance

ĀS-unt

nascent

adjacent
complacent
complaisant
renascent

ĀS-ur

ace 'er
bracer
chaser
facer
lacer
macer
pacer
placer
racer
spacer
tracer

abaser
beer chaser
backspacer
boy chaser
car racer
disgracer
displacer
drag racer
debaser
defacer
effacer
encaser
enlacer
eraser
embracer
freebaser
girl chaser
horseracer
misplacer
man chaser
outpacer
retracer
replacer
showcase 'er
skin bracer
skirt chaser
unlacer

doublespacer
interfacer
interlacer
interspacer

relay racer
self-effacer
wild-goose chaser
woman chaser

ambulance chaser

AS-ur

crasser
gasser
Nasser
passer
sasser
Vassar

amasser
bypasser
harasser
outclass 'er
surpasser
trespasser

antimacassar

AS-ur-āt

lacerate
macerate

ĀS-us

ace us
basis
brace us
chase us
face us
grace us
mace us
pace us
place us
race us
space us
trace us

abase us
disgrace us
deface us

displace us
debase us
erase us
embrace us
misplace us
oasis
outpace us
retrace us
replace us
showcase us
unlace us

AS-us

gas us
pass us

harass us
outclass us
Parnassus
surpass us

ĀS-ust
(See ĀS-ist)

AS-ut

Bassett
facet
gas it
pass it
tacit

harass it
surpass it

AS-uz

asses
brasses
classes
gasses
glasses
grasses
lasses
masses

passes
sasses

amasses
bypasses
dark glasses
eyeglasses
field glasses
fat asses
harasses
hourglasses
impasses
jackasses
jive-asses
lardasses
morasses
molasses
outclasses
Onassis
press passes
surpasses
smart asses
spyglasses
trespasses
top brasses

boarding passes
bonny lasses
cocktail glasses
demitasses
granny glasses
huddled masses
horn-rimmed glasses
horses' asses
looking glasses
lower classes
mountain passes
middle classes
opera glasses
overpasses
parking passes
underpasses
upper classes
working classes

rose-colored glasses

magnifying glasses

AS-wurd

class word
password
sass word

backassward

ĀT

ate
bait
bate
crate
date
eight
fate
freight
gait
gate
grate
great
hate
Kate
late
mate
pate
plait
plate
rate
sate
skate
slate
state
strait
straight
trait
wait
weight

abate
aerate
Allstate

await
belate(d)
bedmate
birth date
back date
birthrate
blind date
birthweight
berate
bookplate
castrate
court date
cheapskate
clean slate
cellmate
cakeplate
checkmate
classmate
collate
create
cremate
Colgate
cut-rate
dead weight
debate
date bait
due date
death rate
donate
deflate
dilate
elate
equate
estate
first date
first mate
flat rate
flyweight
filtrate
first-rate
fixate
frustrate
floodgate
gold plate
gradate

gyrate
home state
hot plate
helpmate
home plate
ice skate
ingrate
inflate
innate
inmate
ill-fate(d)
jailbait
Kuwait
lightweight
lactate
ligate
locate
live bait
mandate
migrate
misstate
narrate
negate
orate
ornate
out late
outdate
outwait
playmate
placate
prostrate
probate
prorate
prostate
pulsate
prime rate
primate
postdate
predate
prom date
Phi Bete
rebate
relate
rotate
R-rate(d)

sedate
sleep state
soulmate
serrate
shipmate
stagnate
stalemate
translate
tailgate
third rate
testate
update
upstate
vacate
V-eight
vibrate
X-rate(d)

abrogate
acerbate
abnegate
abdicate
animate
arbitrate
acetate
aviate
actuate
annotate
activate
apartheid
acclimate
antedate
adulate
act of fate
advocate
amputate
antiquate
agitate
aggravate
aspirate
allocate
bifurcate
bantamweight
boiler plate
castigate

calibrate
candidate
calculate
captivate
cogitate
carbonate
circulate
complicate
celebrate
constipate
contemplate
chief of state
confiscate
correlate
conjugate
congregate
concentrate
copulate
cultivate
culminate
cumulate
consummate
decimate
delegate
double-date
decorate
devastate
deviate
deprecate
dehydrate
demonstrate
designate
defecate
dedicate
dislocate
dissipate
demarcate
detonate
dominate
duplicate
dinner date
educate
exchange rate
elongate
emanate

emulate
enervate
emigrate
extricate
elevate
escalate
estimate
excavate
featherweight
fashion plate
figure skate
fluoridate
fourth estate
fabricate
fascinate
federate
formulate
fornicate
fluctuate
fumigate
generate
guesstimate
Golden Gate
granulate
germinate
graduate
gravitate
heavyweight
hesitate
heavy date
hibernate
hyphenate
interstate
integrate
in a state
Irangate
intimate
illustrate
immigrate
impregnate
insulate
implicate
imitate
instigate
indicate

incubate

inundate

iterate

infiltrate

innovate

irrigate

irritate

isolate

interstate

jubilate

lacerate

liquidate

laminate

legislate

litigate

liberate

lubricate

lower plate

license plate

Lone Star State

lie in state

middleweight

masticate

masturbate

magistrate

meditate

medicate

mediate

moderate

menstruate

mitigate

modulate

motivate

mutilate

navigate

nauseate

nominate

operate

out-of-date

obfuscate

obligate

osculate

oscillate

overstate

overrate

orchestrate

overweight

out-of-state

pass the plate

partial plate

paper plate

police state

palpitate

permeate

perforate

penetrate

percolate

predicate

Pearly Gate(s)

paperweight

populate

perpetrate

perorate

potentate

postulate

pollinate

procreate

promulgate

profligate

propagate

punctuate

pull one's weight

real estate

running mate

rollerskate

radiate

relegate

re-create

remonstrate

relocate

reprobate

regulate

reinstate

renovate

ruminate

satiate

scintillate

salivate

saturate

segregate

separate

simulate

speculate

syndicate

stimulate

stipulate

subjugate

sublimate

strangulate

suffocate

second-rate

ship of state

situate

silverplate

syncopate

self-portrait

section eight

solid-state

starting gate

tabulate

terminate

titillate

target date

tête-à-tête

tolerate

twitterpate

underrate

underweight

understate

undulate

up to date

upper plate

ululate

validate

venerate

vacillate

ventilate

vindicate

violate

vaccinate

welfare state

Watergate

at any rate

abominate

abbreviate
accelerate
accumulate
accentuate
accommodate
affiliate
adulterate
adjudicate
alleviate
alienate
articulate
aggulinate
anticipate
annihilate
appreciate
appropriate
associate
asphyxiate
assassinate
authenticate
collection plate
capitulate
consolidate
coagulate
cross-ventilate
carbohydrate
conciliate
communicate
commemorate
cooperate
commiserate
congratulate
cohabitate
coordinate
contaminate
defibrillate
deliberate
depopulate
debilitate
delineate
depreciate
decaffeinate
dilapidate
discriminate
domesticate

easy to take
elaborate
ejaculate
elucidate
emancipate
eliminate
emaciate
encapsulate
equivocate
eradicate
extrapolate
exacerbate
exhilarate
exterminate
exaggerate
expectorate
exasperate
evaporate
evacuate
fish or cut bait
facilitate
felicitate
gesticulate
hallucinate
humiliate
infatuate
incarcerate
indoctrinate
impersonate
ingratiate
initiate
illuminate
inoculate
irradiate
investigate
interrogate
intoxicate
invalidate
invigorate
intimidate
insinuate
Kaopectate
luxuriate
manipulate
matriculate

miscegenate
miscalculate
necessitate
officiate
obliterate
orientate
perambulate
public debate
participate
perpetuate
peregrinate
precipitate
pontificate
prevaricate
procrastinate
proliferate
prognosticate
pull one's own weight
recaptivate
recriminate
redecorate
reciprocate
recuperate
refrigerate
repudiate
reiterate
rejuvenate
remunerate
resuscitate
retaliate
regurgitate
reverberate
subordinate
substantiate
somnambulate
United State(s)
unsaturate

ameliorate
catatonic state
discombobulate
Department of State
differentiate
give someone the gate
hyperventilate

misappropriate
overcompensate
rehabilitate
reinvigorate

fickle finger of fate
political debate
polyunsaturate(d)
Secretary of State

AT

at
bat
brat
cat
chat
drat
fat
frat
flat
gat
gnat
hat
mat
pat
prat
rat
sat
spat
slat
splat
stat
tat
that
vat

at bat
bobcat
begat
brass hat
bark at
brickbat
chitchat
cocked hat
combat

cravat
congrat(s)
deep fat
dingbat
drowned rat
doormat
fire hat
format
fall flat
fat cat
floormat
hellcat
hepcat
high hat
hardhat
Jack Sprat
kersplat
low-fat
love pat
laugh at
muskrat
nonfat
old hat
old bat
placemat
packrat
polecat
peek at
straw hat
stand pat
stray cat
sneeze at
slap at
sun hat
top hat
that's that
tomcat
wombat
wildcat
wink at
white rat
yell at

alley cat
army brat

Arafat
autocrat
automat
acrobat
bureaucrat
bacon fat
baccarat
baby-sat
baby fat
chew the fat
copy cat
chicken fat
cowboy hat
desert rat
democrat
drowning rat
dirty rat
diplomat
fireside chat
fraidy cat
habitat
hobie cat
kitty cat
laundromat
pussycat
pass the hat
Photostat
plutocrat
pitapat
pitterpat
rheostat
smell a rat
scaredy cat
sailor hat
stovepipe hat
tit for tat
this and that
thermostat
technocrat
vampire bat
where it's at
wear two hat(s)
welcome mat

aristocrat

blind as a bat
cold-water flat
calico cat
go to the mat
in nothing flat
Jehoshaphat
right off the bat
talk through one's hat
ten-gallon hat
under one's hat

career diplomat

at the drop of one's
  hat
jumpin' Jehoshaphat

ATCH
(See ACH)

ĀT-ē
(See ĀD-ē)

AT-ē
(See AD-ē)

ĀT-ed
(See ĀD-ud)

AT-ed
(See AD-ud)

ĀT-en
(See ĀT-un)

AT-en
(See AT-un)

ĀT-ēng
(See ĀD-ēng)

AT-ēng
(See AD-ēng)

ĀT-ent
(See ĀT-unt)

AT-ent
(See AT-unt)

AT-ē-nus
(See AD-ē-nus)

ĀT-est
(See ĀD-ust)

AT-est
(See AD-ust)

ĀT-ēz
(See ĀD-ēz)

AT-ēz
(See AD-ēz)

ĀT-ful

fateful
grateful
hateful
plateful
waitful

ungrateful

ĀTH

faith
saith

ATH

bath
hath
lath
math
path
wrath

birdbath
bypath
bike path
bloodbath
footbath
flight path
footpath
glide path
new math
sponge bath
steam bath
sitz bath
warpath

aftermath
bubble bath
bridle path
cross one's path
garden path
Grapes of Wrath
psychopath
primrose path
take a bath
Turkish bath

osteopath
sociopath

down the garden path
off the beaten path

ATH-ē

Cathy

Abernathy

ĀTHE

bathe
lathe
scathe

sunbathe
unscathe(d)

ĀTHE-ēng

bathing
lathing
scathing

sunbathing

ATHE-ur

blather
gather
lather
rather
slather

regather
woolgather

shaving lather

ATHE-ur-ēng

blathering
gathering
lathering
slathering

regathering
woolgathering

ATH-ik

telepathic
psychopathic

AT-i-bul
(See AD-u-bul)

AT-i-fi
(See AD-u-fi)

AT-ik
(See AD-uk)

AT-ik-lē
(See AD-ik-lē)

AT-ik-u
(See AD-ik-u)

AT-ik-ul
(See AD-ik-ul)

Ā-tīm

daytime
gay time
Maytime
playtime
pay time
stay time
sway time

delay time

AT-in
(See AT-un)

AT-i-num

battin 'em
fatten 'em
flatten 'em
platinum
sat in 'em

AT-is
(See AD-us)

AT-ish
(See AD-ish)

AT-it
(See AD-ut)

AT-it-ūd
(See AD-it-ūd)

ĀT-iv
(See ĀD-iv)

AT-ix
(See Ad-ux)

ĀT-lē

greatly
lately
stately

innately
irately
ornately
sedately

Johnny-come-lately

AT-lēng
(See AD-lēng)

AT-les
(See AT-lus)

ĀT-līn

dateline
freightline
great line
stateline
straight line

AT-lur
(See AD-lur)

ĀT-lus

baitless
dateless
freightless
fateless
gateless
mateless
plateless
rateless
skateless
stateless
traitless
weightless

helpmateless
playmateless
rebateless

AT-lus

atlas
batless
hatless

ĀT-ment

batement
statement

abatement
bank statement
beratement
deflatement
elatement
inflatement
misstatement
rotatement

noise abatement
opening statement

ĀT-nus

greatness
lateness
straightness

irateness
innateness
ornateness
sedateness

AT-nus

fatness
flatness

ĀT-ō
(See ĀD-ō)

AT-rik

hat trick
Patrick

Fitzpatrick
theatric

geriatric
psychiatric
pediatric

ĀT-rix

matrix

aviatrix

AT-rix

hat tricks
Patrick's

theatrics

geriatrics
pediatrics

ĀT-run

matron
patron

AT-sō

fatso

is that so?

ĀT-u
(See ĀD-u)

AT-u
(See AD-u)

ĀT-ub-ul
(See ĀD-ub-ul)

AT-ub-ul
(See AD-ub-ul)

ĀT-ud
(See ĀD-ud)

AT-ud
(See Ad-ud)

AT-u-fī
(See AD-u-fī)

ĀT-ul
(See ĀD-ul)

AT-ul
(See AD-ul)

ĀT-um
(See ĀD-um)

AT-um
(See AD-um)

Manhattan
pig Latin

ĀT-unt

blatant
latent
natant

AT-unt

patent

combatant

ĀT-ur
(See ĀD-ur)

AT-ur
(See AD-ur)

AT-urd
(See AD-urd)

AT-ur-ē
(See AD-ur-ē)

ĀT-ur-ēng
(See ĀD-ur-ēng)

AT-ur-ēng
(See AD-ur-ēng)

AT-ur-īz
(See AD-ur-īz)

AT-urn
(See AD-urn)

AT-ur-ul
(See AD-ur-ul)

AT-um-ē
(See AD-um-ē)

ĀT-un

baitin'
Clayton
cratin'
Creighton
datin'
Dayton
gratin'
hatin'
matin'
platin'
ratin'
satin'
skatin'
slatin'
statin'
Satan
straighten
straiten
waitin'

AT-un

batten
battin'
chattin'
fatten
flatten
Latin
platen
Patton
rattin'
splattin'
satin
tattin'

chitchattin'
combattin'

AT-ur-ur
(See AD-ur-ur)

ĀT-us
(See ĀD-us)

AT-us
(See AD-us)

Ā-u

Isaiah
La Brea
Malaya

Kilauea
Himalaya
Mauna Kea

Ā-ub-ul

flayable
layable
payable
playable
sayable
sprayable
swayable
weighable

betrayable
conveyable
defrayable
downplayable
delayable
misplayable
okayable
obeyable
prepayable
portrayable
repayable
replayable
relayable
surveyable
waylayable

Ā-u-dē

gaiety
laity

spontaneity

homogeneity

Ā-uk

laic

archaic
Judaic
mosaic
prosaic

algebraic

Ā-ul (See ĀL)

Ā-um

graham
lay 'em
mayhem
pay 'em
play 'em
say 'em
spray 'em
sway 'em
weigh 'em

Ā-uns

abeyance
conveyance

in abeyance

Ā-ur
(See also AR)

Bayer
flayer
gayer
grayer

layer
mayor
Mayer
payer
prayer
player
strayer
stayer
sprayer
slayer
weigher

bricklayer
betrayer
conveyor
defrayer
doomsayer
delayer
displayer
essayer
hoorayer
naysayer
obeyer
purveyor
portrayer
surveyor
soothsayer
taxpayer
team player
top layer
waylayer
cassette player
ozone layer
record player

inversion layer

Ā-urz

Bayers
flayers
layers
mayors
payers
prayers
players

sprayers
slayers
weighers

bricklayers
betrayors
conveyors
doomsayers
delayers
naysayers
purveyors
portrayers
surveyors
soothsayers
taxpayers
waylayers

Ā-us

dais
gray us
lay us
pay us
play us
slay us
spray us
sway us
stay us
weigh us

allay us
betray us
convey us
display us
decay us
downplay us
dismay us
delay us
mislay us
okay us
outweigh us
obey us
portray us
replay us
repay us
waylay us

disobey us
Menelaus
overplay us
overpay us
San Andreas
underpay us

Ā-ust

gayest
grayest

essayist
risquéest

Ā-u-tē
(See Ā-u-dē)

ĀV

brave
cave
crave
gave
grave
knave
lave
nave
pave
rave
save
slave
shave
stave
they've
wave
waive

airwave
behave
brainwave
concave
close shave
conclave
cold wave
deprave

enclave
engrave
enslave
forgave
heat wave
make wave(s)
new wave
repave
shortwave
soundwave
shockwave

aftershave
body wave
fingerwave
galley slave
misbehave
microwave
Pic 'N' Save
rant and rave
scrimp and save
tidal wave

cradle-to-grave
Indian brave
permanent wave

one foot in the grave

turn over in one's
grave

AV

calve
have
halve
salve

ĀVD

braved
craved
laved
paved
raved
saved

slaved
shaved
staved
waved
waived

behaved
depraved
engraved
enslaved
repaved

misbehaved
microwaved
scrimped and saved

ĀV-ē

gravy
navy
wavy

unwavy

AV-ē

savvy

unsavvy

rikky tikky tavvy

ĀV-el
(See ĀV-ul)

AV-el
(See AV-ul)

ĀV-en
(See ĀV-un)

ĀV-ēng

braving
craving
paving

raving
saving
slaving
shaving
waving
waiving

behaving
depraving
engraving
enslaving
flag waving
face-saving
repaving

daylight saving(s)
finger waving
laborsaving
microwaving
misbehaving

ranting and raving

ĀV-ē-u

Moldavia

Scandinavia

ĀV-ē-un

avian

Moldavian

Scandinavian

AV-ij

ravage
savage

AV-il
(See AV-ul)

ĀV-in
(See ĀV-un)

AV-is
(See ĀV-us)

AV-is
(See AV-us)

AV-ish

lavish
ravish

AV-ish-ēng

lavishing
ravishing

ĀV-it

brave it
crave it
gave it
pave it
save it
shave it
wave it
waive it

engrave it
enslave it
forgave it
repave it

affidavit

AV-it-ē
(See AV-ud-ē)

ĀV-ment

pavement

depravement
enslavement
repavement

pound the pavement

AV-u

Java
lava

AV-ud-ē

cavity
gravity

depravity

law of gravity

center of gravity

ĀV-ul

navel
naval

AV-ul

cavil
gavel
gravel
ravel
travel

unravel

AV-ul-ēng

gaveling
traveling

unraveling

ĀV-un

bravin'
cravin'
craven
cavin'
graven
haven
pavin'
raven
ravin'

savin'
shaven
slavin'
shavin'
wavin'
waivin'

behavin'
depravin'
engravin'
enslavin'
face-savin'
flag-wavin'
smooth-shaven
unshaven

misbehavin'
microwavin'
riboflavin

ĀV-ur

braver
craver
favor
flavor
gave 'er
graver
paver
quaver
raver
savor
saver
shaver
slaver
waiver
waver

behaver
concaver
disfavor
depraver
engraver
enslaver
find favor
face-saver
flag-waver

forgave 'er
lifesaver
place saver
repaver
timesaver

curry favor
demiquaver
little shaver
misbehaver
out of favor
rant and raver

hemidemisemiquaver

AV-ur

halver
have 'er
slaver

cadaver
palaver

ĀV-urd

favored
flavored
savored
wavered

ĀV-ur-ē

Avery
bravery
flavory
knavery
quavery
savory
slavery
wavery

depravery
pro-slavery
unsavory
unbravery

anti-slavery

ĀV-ur-ēng

favoring
flavoring
quavering
savoring
wavering

disfavoring
unwavering

AV-ur-is
(See AV-ur-us)

ĀV-ur-it

favorite
flavor it
favor it
gave 'er it
savor it

forgave 'er it

AV-urn

cavern
tavern

ĀV-ur-u-bul

favorable
flavorable
savorable

unfavorable

AV-ur-us

avarice

cadaverous

ĀV-us

Avis
Davis
gave us

save us
shave us

enslave us
forgave us

AV-us

have us
Travis

ĀV-ust

bravest
gravest

ĀV-yur

savior
save your(s)

behavior

good behavior
misbehavior

AX

acts
ax
backs
blacks
clacks
claques
cracks
fax
flax
facts
hacks
jacks
knacks
lacks
lax
Max
pacts
packs
plaques
quacks

racks
Saks
sacks
sax
sacs
shacks
snacks
stacks
smacks
slacks
tacks
tax
tracts
tracks
whacks
wracks
wax
yaks

abstracts
Ajax
attracts
attacks
barebacks
bushwhacks
backpacks
bivouacs
beeswax
bootblacks
brass tacks
borax
backtracks
climax
compacts
cutbacks
clothes racks
class acts
contracts
cognacs
comebacks
contacts
drawbacks
distracts
detracts
enacts

Ex-Lax
extracts
earwax
exacts
flapjacks
flashbacks
fast tracks
floorwax
fullbacks
greenbacks
hijacks
humpbacks
hatchbacks
haystacks
halfbacks
hunchbacks
hatracks
impacts
ice packs
knapsacks
kickbacks
kayaks
known facts
knickknacks
lilacs
laugh tracks
make tracks
mudpacks
playbacks
protracts
playacts
poll tax
pickax
ransacks
relax
reacts
retracts
racetracks
repacks
rat packs
rollbacks
syntax
sound tracts
sex acts
swaybacks

sidetracks
subtracts
shellacs
surtax
sales tax
six packs
sin tax
sad sacks
smokestacks
setbacks
skyjacks
switchbacks
shoe racks
thorax
transacts
thumbtacks
throwbacks
train tracks
tie racks
unpacks
wisecracks
wet backs
wolf packs

artifacts
almanacs
Cracker Jacks
battle-ax
city tax
candle wax
counteracts
caddie shacks
Cadillacs
cardiacs
cataracts
cul-de-sacs
diamondbacks
gunnysacks
heart attacks
income tax
interacts
jumping jacks
lumberjacks
maniacs
moustache wax

needle tracks
overtax
overacts
paper sacks
Pontiacs
parallax
paperbacks
piggybacks
quarterbacks
razorbacks
railroad tracks
reattacks
reenacts
sealing wax
to the max
turtlebacks
thermofax
union jacks

clickety-clacks
counterattacks
cigarette packs
down to brass tacks
dead in one's tracks
insomniacs
overreacts
property tax
panic attacks
whole ball of wax
withholding tax
yakkity-yaks

aphrodisiacs
dipsomaniacs
hypochondriacs
hemophiliacs
inheritance tax
kleptomaniacs
right side of the tracks
sacroiliacs
slip between the
   cracks
wrong side of the
   tracks

megalomaniacs

AXD

axed
faxed
laxed
taxed
waxed

relaxed

overtaxed

AX-ē

flaxy
maxi
Maxie
taxi
waxy

**AX-en
(See AX-un)**

AX-ēng

axing
faxing
taxing
waxing

leg waxing
relaxing

overtaxing
thermofaxing

AX-ē-um

axiom
taxi 'em

**AX-im
(See AX-um)**

**AX-is
(See AX-us)**

AX-u-bul

faxable
taxable
waxable

climaxable
relaxable

AX-um

ax 'em
backs 'em
cracks 'em
fax 'em
hacks 'em
lacks 'em
maxim
packs 'em
racks 'em
sacks 'em
stacks 'em
smacks 'em
tax 'em
tracks 'em
tacks 'em
whacks 'em
wracks 'em
wax 'em

AX-un

flaxen
faxin'
Jackson
Saxon
taxin'
waxen
waxin'

climaxin'
relaxin'

Anglo-Saxon
overtaxin'

AX-ur

axer
backs 'er
faxer
hacks 'er
laxer
packs 'er
sacks 'er
smacks 'er
taxer
tracks 'er
waxer

attracts 'er
attacks 'er
distracts 'er
relaxer

AX-us

axis
ax us
backs us
cracks us
fax us
hacks us
lacks us
packs us
sacks us
smacks us
tracks us
tax us

attracts us
attacks us
bushwhacks us
contacts us
distracts us
hijacks us
impacts us
relax us
skyjacks us
sidetracks us

unpacks us
prophylaxis

ĀZ

a's
bays
brays
braise
blaze
clays
chaise
craze
days
daze
faze
frays
flays
gaze
graze
glaze
gays
grays
haze
Hayes
jays
j's
k's
lays
leis
laze
maize
maze
neighs
nays
pays
plays
prays
phrase
phase
praise
raze
raise
rays

slays
sleighs
spays
stays
sprays
strays
sways
smaze
trays
treys
ways
weighs
yeas

aways
arrays
always
archways
allays
affrays
assays
ashtrays
ablaze
amscrays
amaze
appraise
by-ways
bouquets
buzzphrase
berets
birthdays
bidets
bobsleighs
betrays
blue blaze(s)
breath sprays
ballets
bluejays
cafés
catch phrase
crochets
clichés
conveys
chalets
causeways

defrays
dog days
displays
decays
delays
dismays
doorways
deejays
driveways
downplays
endplays
entrées
essays
Fridays
filets
forays
foyers
frappés
freeways
foreplays
flambés
fairways
gourmets
glacés
gangways
gateways
hair sprays
hurrays
horseplays
highways
heydays
hallways
inlays
inveighs
ice trays
lamés
melees
malaise
misplays
Mondays
mainstays
mores
mislays
nosegays
okays

obeys
outlays
outweighs
one-ways
olés
paydays
portrays
pâtés
parquets
parfaits
prepays
purveys
parlays
raceways
railways
runways
roués
repays
replays
relays
rephrase
role plays
Sundays
subways
self-praise
stargaze
school days
segues
soufflés
stairways
sachets
soirees
skygaze
stingrays
surveys
sashays
sideways
Tuesdays
touchés
Thursdays
toupees
todays
two ways
trailblaze
upraise

unfaze
Wednesdays
waylays
wash days
weekdays
workdays
x-rays

attachés
appliqués
bag some rays
bouillabaise
breakaways
castaways
cosmic rays
canapés
Chevrolets
cutaways
croupiers
cabarets
consommes
CPAs
disobeys
disarrays
divorcées
dossiers
devotees
everydays
exposés
financées
getaways
gamma rays
giveaways
grab some rays
hollandaise
holidays
hideaways
interplays
lyonnaise
matinées
mayonnaise
macramés
nasal sprays
negligees
nowadays

overstays
overpraise
overpays
overlays
overplays
photoplays
paraphrase
protégées
passageways
popinjays
power plays
repartees
runaways
résumés
ricochets
reappraise
Saturdays
swing both ways
stowaways
silver trays
swings and sways
tape delays
throwaways
triple plays
underplays
underpraise
workadays
waterways
yesterdays

bridal bouquets
coin a phrase
communiqués
couturiers
café-au-laits
cocktail buffets
have it both ways
heavenly days
habitués
happy birthdays
instant replays
red-letter days
UCLA's

deodorant sprays
legal holidays

prepositional phrase
ultraviolet rays

AZ

as
has
jazz
razz

topaz
pizazz
whereas

all that jazz
Alcatraz

razzmatazz

ĀZD

braised
blazed
crazed
dazed
fazed
gazed
grazed
glazed
lazed
phrased
phased
praised
razed
raised

amazed
appraised
rephrased
stargazed
trailblazed
unfazed

AZD

jazzed
razzed

ĀZ-ē

crazy
daisy
hazy
lazy

stir-crazy

Bel Paese
push up daisie(s)
upsy-daisy

fresh as a daisy

AZ-ē

has he
jazzy
snazzy

pizazzy

ĀZ-el
(See ĀZ-ul)

ĀZ-en
(See ĀZ-un)

ĀZ-ēng

braising
blazing
dazing
fazing
gazing
grazing
glazing
hazing
lazing
phrasing
phasing
praising
razing
raising

amazing

appraising
rephrasing
stargazing
trailblazing
upraising

freshman hazing
overpraising
paraphrasing
reappraising

ĀZH-u

Asia

aphasia
aphagia
astasia
abasia
dysplasia
fantasia
gymnasia
Malaysia

Anastasia
athanasia
euthanasia
Southeast Asia

ĀZH-un

Asian
suasion

abrasion
Caucasion
dissuasion
evasion
Eurasian
equation
invasion
occasion
persuasion
pervasion

on occasion

ĀZH-ur

leisure
measure
pleasure
treasure

displeasure
my pleasure
tape measure
with pleasure

beyond measure
countermeasure
for good measure
hidden treasure

measure for measure

ĀZH-ur-ēng

leisuring
measuring
pleasuring
treasuring

ĀZH-ur-u-bul

measurable
pleasurable
treasurable

displeasurable
immeasurable

ĀZH-ur-ur

measurer
pleasurer
treasurer

ĀZ-il
(See ĀZ-ul)

AZ-lĕng

dazzling
frazzling

bedazzling

razzledazzling

ĀZ-ment

amazement
appraisement

reappraisement

AZ-mu

asthma
plasma

ĀZ-ul

basil
basal
hazel
nasal

appraisal
postnasal
St. Basil
witch hazel

reappraisal

AZ-ul

dazzle
frazzle
razzle

bedazzle

razzle-dazzle

AZ-um

chasm
has 'em
jazz 'em
plasm
razz 'em
spasm

orgasm

phantasm
sarcasm

pleonasm
protoplasm

enthusiasm
iconoclasm
razzamatazz 'em

ĀZ-un

blazon
brazen
blazin'
braisin'
dazin'
fazin'
gazin'
grazin'
glazin'
lazin'
phrasin'
praisin'
phasin'
raisin
raisin'
razin'

amazin'
appraisin'
emblazon
fund-raisin'
hair-raisin'
rephrasin'
stargazin'
skygazin'
trailblazin'
upraisin'

overpraisin'
paraphrasin'
reappraisin'
underpraisin'

ĀZ-ur

braiser
blazer
dazer
fazer
frays 'er
flays 'er
Frazer
gazer
grazer
glazer
laser
praiser
phaser
phraser
pays 'er
plays 'er
razor
raze 'er
raiser
slays 'er
sprays 'er
sways 'er
weighs 'er

amazer
appraiser
betrays 'er
blue blazer
displays 'er
delays 'er
dismays 'er
fund-raiser
hair-raiser
hell-raiser
okays 'er
obeys 'er
outweighs 'er
portrays 'er
repays 'er
rephraser
stargazer
skygazer
self-praiser
straight razor

surveys 'er
tape measure
trailblazer
upraiser
waylays 'er
x-rays 'er

crystal gazer
disobeys 'er
overpraiser
overpays 'er
overplays 'er
paraphraser
reappraiser
safety razor
underplays 'er

AZ-ur

has 'er
jazzer
razzer

AZ-urd

hazard
mazzard

haphazard

E SOUNDS

Ē

b
be
bee
brie
c
Cree
d
e
fee
flee
free
flea
g
gee
glee
he
key
knee
Lee
lea
me
mi
nee
oui
p
plea

pea
pee
quay
sea
see
spree
she
si
ski
t
ti
tea
tee
tree
thee
three
v
vee
wee
we
whee
ye
z

A.D.
at sea
A.P.
agree

Big C
B.C.
chickpea
confit
Capri
carefree
Chablis
card-key
chi chi
Dead Sea
D.C.
Dufy
deep-sea
Dundee
degree
decree
debris
esprit
ennui
emcee
finis
foresee
feel free
Grand Prix
goatee
greens fee
home free
he/she

high tea
ID
lessee
low-key
look-see
marquee
Marie
M.D.
marquis
MP
must-see
on dit
off-key
oui, oui
P.E.
précis
PC
passkey
peewee
queen bee
QT
RV
Red Sea
rent-free
settee
salt-free
scot-free
sweet pea
show-me
sightsee
stud fee
tehee
trick knee
tab key
tepee
TB
TV
TD
TP
turnkey
toll-free
tax-free
three-D
VP
wee wee

would-be

ABC
addressee
assignee
apogee
absentee
attendee
awardee
abductee
après-ski
amputee
bumblebee
bon ami
bourgeoisie
blackeyed pea
BBC
busy bee
bonhomie
BLT
conferee
COD
c'est la vie
chimpanzee
chickadee
Cherokee
coterie
cop a plea
cup of tea
Christmas tree
do re mi
disagree
DDT
departee
duty-free
dungaree
devotee
DMV
excuse me
escapee
FOB
fricassee
fleur de lis
fancy free
finder's fee

FCC
first-degree
family tree
Galilee
GOP
guarantee
herbal tea
housemaid's knee
Holy See
honeybee
honoree
if need be
jamboree
jubilee
LSD
let it be
LL.D.
licensee
MIT
maître d'
MVP
money tree
minor key
MSG
nominee
NBC
nth degree
oversee
oversea(s)
Ph.D.
pedigree
potpourri
pardon me
PCP
peony
refugee
Rosemarie
referee
RIP
repartee
sans souci
so help me
shopping spree
sugar-free
SST

shivaree
spelling bee
Twiddledee
third-degree
Tennessee
USC
used to be
up a tree
undersea
user's fee
vis-à-vis
VIP
worry-free
worker bee
water ski
Waikiki
XYZ
Zuider Zee

admission fee
A T & T
AC-DC
asap
Aegean Sea
BYOB
BMOC
consent decree
Chef Boy Ar Dee
college degree
evacuee
employee
fait accompli
fiddle-de-dee
family tree
land of the free
long time no see
master's degree
maintenance-free
one's cup of tea
RSVP
ROTC
the powers that be
the royal *we*
to a degree
vitamin B

VSOP

between you and me
chicken fricassee
cherries jubilee
golden jubilee
under lock and key
Washington, D.C.
water on the knee

agree to disagree
easy as ABC
footloose and fancy
    free
moneyback guarantee
NAACP

political refugee
the editorial *we*

EB

deb
ebb
neb
reb
web

celeb
cobweb

ĒB-ē

CB
freebie
he be
Phoebe

heebie-jeebie(s)

ĒB-ēng

ebbing
webbing

ĒB-ō

gazebo
placebo

ĒB-ru

Libra
zebra

ĒB-u

Reba
Sheba

amoeba
Bathsheba

EB-ul

pebble
rebel
treble

ĒCH

beach
beech
breach
bleach
each
leech
peach
preach
reach
screech
speech
teach

beseech
free speech
impeach
Jones Beach
outreach
reteach

Georgia peach
keynote speech
Muscle Beach
overreach
part of speach

freedom of speech

figure of speech
Miami Beach

ECH

catch
etch
fetch
ketch
kvetch
lech
retch
stretch
sketch
tetch(ed)
vetch
wretch

homestretch
outstretch
unstretch

bitter vetch
thumbnail sketch

ĒCH-ē

chi chi
ichi
litchi
peachy
preachy
screechy
speechy

seviche

ECH-ē

catchy
stretchy
sketchy

Hetch Hetchy

ĒCH-ēng

beaching
breaching

bleaching
preaching
reaching
screeching
teaching

beseeching
impeaching

overreaching

ECH-ēng

catching
etching
fetching
retching
stretching

ĒCHT

beached
breached
bleached
preached
reached
screeched

beseeched
impeached

ECHT

etched
fetched
retched
stretched
sketched
tetched

outstretched

ĒCH-ub-ul

beachable
breachable
bleachable
preachable

reachable
screechable
teachable

beseechable
impeachable
unreachable
unteachable

unimpeachable

ECH-ub-ul

catchable
etchable
fetchable
stretchable
sketchable

ECH-un

etchin'
fetchin'
Gretchen
lechin'
retchin'
stretchin'
sketchin'

ĒCH-ur

beacher
bleacher
breacher
creature
feature
leecher
preacher
reacher
screecher
teacher

beseecher
impeacher
outreacher

double feature
facial feature

ECH-ur

catcher
etcher
fetcher
Fletcher
lecher
retcher
stretcher
sketcher

ECH-ur-ē

lechery
treachery

ECH-ur-us

lecherous
treacherous

ĒD

bleed
bead
breed
cede
creed
deed
feed
freed
greed
heed
keyed
knead
kneed
lead
mead
need
plead
peed
reed
read
screed
seed
steed

Swede
speed
skied
treed
tweed
weed

accede
agreed
birdseed
concede
Candide
crossbreed
decreed
exceed
full speed
force-feed
good deed
Godspeed
hayseed
hand-feed
high speed
halfbreed
knock-kneed
inbreed
impede
indeed
lipread
Lockheed
mislead
milkweed
misread
misdeed
nosebleed
proofread
precede
proceed
recede
reseed
ragweed
succeed
stampede
secede
speedread
seaweed

spoonfeed
teheed
trust deed
top seed
top speed
three-speed
ten-speed
whoopeed
weak-kneed

antecede
apple seed
centipede
chickenfeed
cottonseed
disagreed
filigreed
guaranteed
go to seed
intercede
locoweed
overfeed
off one's feed
pedigreed
refereed
supersede
tumbleweed
title deed
third-degreed
underfeed
up to speed
widow's weed(s)
worry bead(s)

fiddle-de-deed
unpedigreed
velocipede

ED

bread
bred
bled
bed
dead
dread

Ed
fed
fled
head
led
lead
med
Ned
pled
read
red
said
stead
shed
sped
spread
sled
shred
Ted
thread
tread
wed
zed

airhead
abed
ahead
break bread
bunkbed
bald head
beachhead
bulkhead
blackhead
bobsled
bedspread
biped
bonehead
big head
bloodshed
bullhead(ed)
behead
blockhead
co-ed
car bed
Club Med

crossbred
cokehead
corn bread
cornfed
cowshed
deadhead
deathbed
dog sled
drop dead
daybed
dopehead
egghead
embed
forehead
French bread
flatbed
fathead
hardhead
homestead
hotbed
highbred
hot head
hophead
inbred
instead
ill-bred
jughead
lunkhead
misread
meth head
moped
moosehead
outspread
Op-Ed
pinhead
premed
pothead
proofread
purebred
point spread
redhead
rewed
retread
sorehead
stone dead

shortbread
spearhead
sweetbread
spoonfed
swellhead
skinhead
see red
sickbed
unsaid
unread
unwed
well-read
well-bred
warhead
widespread
woodshed
wingspread
well-fed

acid-head
Actifed
arrowhead
blunderhead
bottlefed
baby bed
city-bred
country-bred
copperhead
dunderhead
Diamond Head
daily bread
double bed
empty head
featherbed
fountainhead
figurehead
flower bed
go ahead
Grateful Dead
garlic bread
gingerbread
hammerhead
hang one's head
infrared
in the red

keep one's head
knucklehead
king-sized bed
knock 'em dead
lose one's head
letterhead
maidenhead
monkey bread
newlywed
overfed
overhead
riverbed
sourdough bread
Sudafed
sleepyhead
straight-ahead
trundle bed
thoroughbred
underfed
use one's head
watershed
waterbed

at loggerhead(s)
come to a head
early to bed
full speed ahead
go to one's head
hospital bed
hole in the head
middle-age spread
over one's head
out of one's head
paint the town red
rocks in the head
soft in the head
stand in good stead
turn someone's head

in over one's head
wrong side of the bed

hit the nail on the
    head
off the top of one's
    head

ĒD-ē

beady
fleety
greedy
meaty
needy
reedy
seedy
speedy
sweetie
treaty
tweety
weedy

entreaty
graffiti
hayseedy
peace treaty
Tahiti
unneedy
unheedy

yes indeedy

ĒD-ē

bready
Betty
Eddie
Ettie
eddy
fretty
Getty
heady
jetty
petty
petit
pretty
ready
sweaty
steady
teddy

already
Andretti
Brown Betty

confetti
get ready
go steady
machete
spaghetti
unready
unsteady

cappelletti
rough and ready

all right already

ĒD-ē-ēng

readying
steadying

ĒD-ē-ent
(See ĒD-ē-unt)

ĒD-en
(See ĒD-un)

ĒD-en
(See ĒD-un)

ĒD-ēng

bleeding
beading
breeding
beating
bleating
cheating
ceding
eating
feeding
fleeting
feting
greeting
heeding
heating
Keating
leading

meeting
needing
pleading
pleating
reading
speeding
seating
seeding
sheeting
sleeting
tweeting
treating
weeding

acceding
breast-feeding
child-beating
competing
completing
conceding
crossbreeding
chance meeting
depleting
defeating
deleting
exceeding
entreating
excreting
good breeding
impeding
inbreeding
lipreading
misreading
misleading
mind reading
mistreating
preceding
prayer meeting
proceeding
proofreading
receding
reseeding
repeating
retreating
reheating

succeeding
stampeding
seceding
secreting
spoon-feeding
town meeting
unheeding

business meeting
interceding
overeating
overfeeding
overheating
superseding
take a beating
trick or treating
undereating
underfeeding

ED-ēng

breading
bedding
betting
dreading
fretting
getting
heading
jetting
netting
petting
shedding
setting
spreading
sledding
sweating
shredding
threading
treading
wedding
wetting
whetting

abetting
begetting
bedwetting

bloodletting
bobsledding
besetting
beheading
forgetting
homesteading
jet setting
June wedding
offsetting
place setting
resetting
regretting
retreading
subletting
snow-sledding
spearheading
upsetting

heavy petting
off-track betting
pirouetting
paper shredding
shotgun wedding
silhouetting

idyllic setting
mosquito netting

ĒD-ē-nus

beadiness
greediness
meatiness
neediness
seediness
speediness

ED-ē-nus

breadiness
headiness
pettiness
prettiness
readiness
steadiness
sweatiness

ĒD-ē-u

media

mass media
perfidia
multimedia

encyclopedia

ĒD-ē-um

medium
tedium

happy medium

ĒD-ē-un

median

comedian
tragedian

ĒD-ē-uns

expedience
ingredients
obedience

disobedience

ĒD-ē-unt

mediant

expedient
ingredient
obedient

disobedient

ĒD-ē-ur

beadier
fleetier
greedier
meteor
meatier
needier

seedier
speedier
weedier

ED-ē-ur

breadier
headier
pettier
prettier
readier
sweatier
steadier

ĒD-ē-us

greedy us
speedy us
tedious

ĒD-ē-ut

immediate

intermediate

ĒD-ēz

sweeties
speedies
treaties
Wheaties

entreaties
peace treaties

diabetes

ED-ēz

Betty's
Eddie's
eddies
jetties
readies
steadies
teddies

machetes

ĒD-ful

deedful
greedful
heedful
needful
pleadful

ED-ib-ul
(See ED-ub-ul)

ĒD-ik

comedic

orthopedic

ED-ik

medic

ascetic
athletic
aesthetic
cosmetic
emetic
frenetic
genetic
hermetic
kinetic
magnetic
phonetic
prophetic
phrenetic
pathetic
poetic
splenetic
synthetic

alphabetic
apathetic
anesthetic
arithmetic
copacetic
diabetic
dietetic
diuretic

energetic
empathetic
hypothetic
parenthetic
paramedic
sympathetic
theoretic
unpoetic

apologetic
antipathetic
peripatetic

ED-i-kāt

dedicate
medicate
predicate

ED-i-ket
(See ED-i-kut)

ED-ik-lē

medically

aesthetically
prophetically
pathetically
poetically
synthetically

alphabetically
hypothetically
parenthetically
theoretically

apologetically

ED-i-kul

medical

aesthetical
heretical
prophetical
pathetical

poetical
synthetical

alphabetical
apathetical
arithmetical
diabetical
hypothetical
parenthetical
theoretical

apologetical

ED-i-kut

etiquette
predicate

Connecticut

ĒD-i-lē
(See ĒD-u-lē)

ED-i-lē
(See ED-u-lē)

ED-i-ment

sediment

impediment

ĒD-ish

Swedish
sweetish
tweedish

elitish
petitish
upbeatish

ED-ish

deadish
fetish
reddish

wettish

coquettish

ED-is-un

Edison
jettison
medicine

ED-it
(See ED-ut)

ED-it-ur
(See Ed-ut-ur)

ĒD-ix

edicts

orthopedics

ED-ix

medics

ascetics
athletics
cosmetics
emetics
genetics
synthetics

cybernetics
diabetics
diuretics

paramedics

EDJ
(See EJ)

ED-lē

deadly
medley
Smedley

ĒD-lēng

needling
seedling
wheedling

ĒD-lĕng

meddling
nettling
peddling
settling

unsettling

ĒD-līn

breadline
deadline
headline
redline

ĒD-lok

deadlock
headlock
shed lock
wedlock

out of wedlock

ĒD-lur

needler
wheedler

ĒD-lur

meddler
peddler
settler

fruit peddler
flesh peddler
unsettler

influence peddler

ĒD-lus

beadless
heedless
creedless
leadless
needless
seedless
steedless
weedless

ĒD-nus

deadness
redness

ĒD-ō

Frito
Lido
neat-o
Quito
Tito
veto

bandito
Benito
burrito
finito
libido
torpedo
Toledo
tuxedo

Hirohito
incognito
pocket veto

ĒD-ō

ghetto
meadow

falsetto
Gepetto
larghetto
libretto
palmetto

stiletto

amaretto
Rigoletto

ĒD-ō-ēng

vetoing

torpedoing

ĒD-u

cheetah
Leda
pita
Rita
Theda

Aida
Addida(s)
corrida
Juanita
Lolita
Reseda

incognita
margarita
manzanita
señorita

fajita pita
la dolce vita
Santa Anita

ĒD-u

Etta
feta
Greta

vendetta

Marietta

ĒD-ub-ul

breedable
beatable

cheatable
eatable
feedable
heedable
heatable
leadable
meetable
readable
seatable
treatable
weedable

completable
defeatable
deletable
exceedable
impedible
recedable
repeatable
stampedable
unbeatable

ED-ub-ul

beddable
breadable
bettable
credible
edible
gettable
pettable
spreadable
sheddable
shreddable
threadable
weddable
wettable

beheadable
forgettable
homesteadable
incredible
offsettable
resettable
regrettable
ungettable

upsettable
unsheddable

unforgettable

ĒD-ud

beaded
bleated
ceded
cheated
deeded
feted
fetid
greeted
heated
heeded
kneaded
meted
needed
pleaded
pleated
seeded
seated
sleeted
treated
tweeted
weeded

acceded
conceded
competed
completed
conceited
depleted
defeated
deepseated
deleted
exceeded
excreted
entreated
impeded
maltreated
mistreated
preceded
proceeded

repeated
retreated
reheated
reseated
receded
reseeded
succeeded
steam-heated
stampeded
seceded
secreted
unseated

anteceded
incompleted
interceded
overheated
superseded
trick-or-treated

ED-ud

breaded
bedded
dreaded
fetid
fretted
headed
jetted
netted
petted
sweated
shedded
sledded
shredded
threaded
wedded
wetted
whetted

abetted
airheaded
bigheaded
bullheaded
beheaded
embedded

hard-headed
homesteaded
hot-headed
indebted
lightheaded
retreaded
regretted
spearheaded
subletted
unleaded

bayonetted
levelheaded
pirouetted
silhouetted

ĒD-ul

betel
beetle
fetal
needle
tweedle
wheedle

pins and needle(s)

ED-ul

fettle
Gretel
kettle
mettle
metal
medal
meddle
nettle
petal
pedal
peddle
settle
treadle

backpedal
base metal
fine fettle
gun metal

gold medal
pot metal
rose petal
soup kettle
sheet metal
soft pedal
teakettle
unsettle

heavy metal
on one's mettle

ĒD-ul-ē

fleetily
greedily
speedily

ED-ul-ē

pettily
prettily
readily
sweatily
steadily

ĒD-ul-dum

needled 'em
Tweedledum
wheedled 'em

ED-ul-sum

meddlesome
nettlesome
peddle some
settle some

ED-ūl-us

credulous
schedule us

incredulous

ĒD-um

bleed 'em
beat 'em
cede 'em
cheat 'em
eat 'em
feed 'em
freedom
fete 'em
greet 'em
heat 'em
lead 'em
meet 'em
need 'em
read 'em
seat 'em
treat 'em

concede 'em
deplete 'em
decreed 'em
defeat 'em
delete 'em
exceed 'em
impede 'em
mistreat 'em
mislead 'em
precede 'em
repeat 'em
reheat 'em
succeed 'em
secrete 'em
spoon-feed 'em
stampede 'em

arboretum
overfeed 'em
overheat 'em
refereed 'em
supersede 'em
trick-or-treat 'em
third-degreed 'em
warrantied 'em

academic freedom

ĒD-un

bleedin'
Eden
feedin'
leadin'
needin'
pleadin'
readin'
speedin'
Sweden
weedin'

misleadin'

Garden of Eden

ED-un

beddin'
deaden
dreadin'
headin'
leaden
redden
sleddin'
shreddin'
threadin'
treadin'
weddin'

bobsleddin'
beheadin'
embeddin'
homesteadin'

Armageddon

ĒD-uns

credence

antecedents
intercedents

ĒD-unt

needn't

antecedent
intercedent

ĒD-ur

beader
bleater
beater
bleeder
cedar
cheater
deeder
eater
feeder
fleeter
greeter
heater
heeder
liter
leader
lieder
meter
meet 'er
neater
needer
pleader
pleater
Peter
reader
speeder
sweeter
seater
teeter
treater
weeder

acceder
anteater
browbeater
born leader
Beefeater
bandleader
car heater

cheerleader
competer
completer
child beater
crossbreeder
conceder
defeater
discreter
deleter
depleter
eliter
entreater
excreter
egg beater
exceeder
fire eater
group leader
gang leader
inbreeder
impeder
misreader
misleader
mind reader
man-eater
mistreater
petiter
preceder
proofreader
proceeder
palm reader
ringleader
retreater
receder
reheater
repeater
stampeder
secretor
speed reader
St. Peter
succeeder
seceder
scout leader
song leader
spoon-feed 'er
saltpeter

two-seater
team leader
unseater
wife-beater

bittersweeter
centimeter
indiscreter
interceder
incompleter
kilometer
lotus eater
milliliter
overfeeder
overeater
overheater
parking meter
superseder
trick-or-treater

follow the leader

ED-ur

bettor
better
cheddar
deader
debtor
dreader
fretter
fetter
getter
header
letter
netter
petter
redder
setter
shedder
shredder
sweater
treader
threader
wetter
wed 'er

whetter

abettor
bedwetter
begetter
beheader
call letter(s)
chain letter
crank letter
dead letter
forgetter
form letter
fan letter
goal setter
go-getter
jet setter
love letter
newsletter
pacesetter
typesetter
trendsetter
vote-getter

doubleheader
go one better
Irish Setter
man of letter(s)
paper shredder
to the letter

appetite whetter
cardigan sweater

ED-urd

bettered
fettered
lettered

unlettered
unfettered

ĒD-ur-ē

cedary
eatery
teetery

ĒD-ur-ēng

metering
petering
teetering

ED-ur-ēng

bettering
fettering
lettering

ĒD-ur-ship

leadership
readership

ED-ur-un

betterin'
letterin'
veteran

ED-ur-ut

better it
preterit

confederate
inveterate

ĒD-us

beat us
bleed us
breed us
cheat us
feed us
fete us
freed us
fetus
greet us
heed us
heat us
lead us
meet us
need us
read us

seat us
treat us
treed us
treatise

crossbreed us
complete us
deplete us
defeat us
entreat us
exceed us
impede us
mistreat us
misread us
mislead us
precede us
stampede us
spoon-feed us
succeed us
unseat us

diabetes
overheat us
overfeed us
refereed us
supersede us
trick-or-treat us
underfeed us

ED-us

bet us
bred us
bled us
dread us
fed us
get us
lettuce
let us
met us
net us
pet us
read us
set us
shred us
shed us

wet us
wed us

abet us
behead us
beget us
beset us
forget us
misread us
offset us
upset us

bayonet us
overfed us
underfed us

aid and abet us

ĒD-ust

fetist
fleetest
neatest
sweetest

completest
discretest
defeatist
elitist
petitest
upbeatest

ED-ust

deadest
reddest

ĒD-us-uz

fetuses
treatises

ED-ut

bet it
bled it
bred it
credit

dread it
edit
fed it
fret it
fled it
get it
head it
led it
let it
met it
net it
pet it
read it
said it
spread it
shred it
set it
thread it
wed it
wet it
whet it

accredit
crossbred it
co-edit
don't sweat it
discredit
forget it
offset it
retread it
reset it
regret it
upset it

ED-ut-ēng

editing
crediting

ED-ut-iv

sedative

competitive
repetitive

ED-ut-ud

credited
edited

accredited

ED-ut-ur

creditor
editor
predator

co-editor
competitor
discreditor

ĒD-uz

cheetahs
Rita's

Adidas
Lolitas

margaritas
manzanitas
señoritas

fajita pitas

ED-wûd

deadwood
Ed would
redwood

ED-yū-lus
(See Ed-ū-lus)

Ē-ēng

being
fleeing
freeing
keying
kneeing
peeing

seeing
skiing
teeing
treeing

agreeing
decreeing
foreseeing
well-being

human being
overseeing
reparteeing
refereeing
water skiing

ĒF

beef
brief
chief
grief
leaf
reef
sheaf
thief

belief
caliph
car thief
chipped beef
corned beef
debrief
fig leaf
flyleaf
fire chief
good grief
gold leaf
loose-leaf
motif
O'Keefe
roast beef
relief
sneak thief
Van Cleef

bas relief

coral reef
cloverleaf
disbelief
handkerchief
leitmotif
misbelief
neckerchief
petty thief
side of beef

apéritif
baron of beef
barrier reef
comic relief
Hail to the Chief
Indian chief

Commander-in-Chief
Great Barrier Reef

turn over a new leaf

EF

chef
clef
deaf
f
Jeff
ref

French chef
stone deaf
tone deaf

master chef
Mutt and Jeff
RAF
UNICEF

ĒF-ē

beefy
Fifi
leafy

EF-en
(See EF-un)

ĒF-ēng

beefing
briefing
leafing

debriefing

EF-ēng

cheffing
reffing

ĒF-lē

briefly
chiefly

EFT

cheffed
cleft
deft
left
reffed
theft

bereft
grand theft

hang a left
nothing left
petty theft
right and left

EFT-ē

hefty
lefty

EF-un

cheffin'
deafen
reffin'

ĒF-ur

beefer
briefer

reefer
debriefer

EF-ur

deafer
heifer
zephyr

EF-ur-uns

deference
preference
reference

cross-reference

frame of reference

ĒG

klieg
league

bush league
big league
blitzkrieg
colleague
fatigue
intrigue
sitzkrieg

Captain Queeg
Ivy League
Little League

battle fatigue

EG

beg
dreg(s)
egg
Greg
keg
leg
Meg
peg

yegg

bad egg
boiled egg
beer keg
frogs' leg(s)
goose egg
good egg
nest egg
pegleg
renege
sea leg(s)

break a leg
Easter egg
lay an egg
mumblepeg
powder keg
pull one's leg
soft-boiled egg
shake a leg
scrambled egg
Winnipeg
wooden leg

daddy longleg(s)
take down a peg

cost an arm and a leg

EG-ē

eggy
leggy
Peggy

ĒG-ēng

blitzkrieging
fatiguing
intriguing

EG-ēng

begging
egging
legging

pegging

reneging

ĒG-ō

ego
me go
sego
we go

amigo

alter ego

ĒG-ul

beagle
eagle
legal
regal
Segal
sea gull

bald eagle
illegal
spread-eagle
unregal

extralegal
paralegal

ĒG-u-lē

legally
regally

illegally

ĒG-ur

eager
meager

big leaguer
bush leaguer
beleaguer
fatiguer
intriguer

little leaguer
major leaguer
overeager

EG-ur

beggar
egger
pegger

McGregor
reneger

ĒG-ur-lē

eagerly
meagerly

Ē-ist

deist
freest
theist

Ē-i-tē
(See Ē-u-dē)

ĒJ

liege
siege

besiege
prestige

noblesse oblige

EJ

dredge
edge
fledge
hedge
ledge
pledge
sledge
veg

wedge

allege
on edge

leading edge
on the edge
razor's edge
window ledge

EJD

dredged
edged
hedged
pledged
wedged

alleged
full-fledged
gilt-edged

double-edged

ĒJ-ē

Fiji
Gigi
ouija
PG
squeegee

EJ-ē

edgy
hedgy
Reggie
veggie
wedgie

EJ-ēng

dredging
edging
pledging
wedging

alleging

ĒJ-i-bul
(See EJ-u-bul)

ĒJ-ik

strategic

parapalegic

ĒJ-is
(See ĒJ-us)

EJ-u-bul

dredgeable
hedgeable
legible

allegible
illegible

ĒJ-un

legion
region

besiegin'
collegian
Norwegian

foreign legion

American Legion

EJ-ur

dredger
edger
hedger
ledger
pledger
wedger

alleger

ĒJ-us

aegis

besiege us
egregious

ĒK

beak
bleak
chic
cheek
clique
creak
creek
deke
eek
eke
freak
geek
Greek
leak
leek
meek
peek
peak
pique
reek
seek
speak
sleek
sneak
squeak
streak
shriek
sheik
teak
tweak
week
weak
wreak

antique
bespeak
batik
boutique

blue streak
critique
hell week
mystique
midweek
misspeak
oblique
pipsqueak
physique
reseek
Twin Peak(s)
technique
unchic
unique
workweek

acid freak
Battle Creek
Chesapeake
cheek-to-cheek
hide-and-seek
Holy Week
magnifique
Mozambique
Martinique
rosy cheek
spring a leak
so to speak
take a peek
tongue in cheek
take a leak
up the creek
widow's peak
yellow streak

peck on the cheek
quarterback sneak

EK

beck
Czech
check
deck
fleck
heck

neck
peck
sec
speck
trek
tech
wreck

Aztec
blank check
breakneck
bedeck
bad check
claim check
Cal. Tech.
coat check
cross check
crew neck
flight deck
fly speck
gooseneck
henpeck
hat check
hi-tech
kopeck
marked deck
OPEC
on deck
poop deck
parsec
paycheck
Quebec
redneck
raincheck
roughneck
Star Trek
shipwreck
spotcheck
sales check
trainwreck
tape deck

break one's neck
body check
bottleneck
cashier's check

countercheck
Chiang Kai-Shek
discotheque
doublecheck
hit the deck
hunt and peck
keep in check
Kohoutek
leatherneck
neck and neck
quarterdeck
rubberneck
rubber check
save one's neck
stack the deck
total wreck
traveler's check
triple sec
turtleneck
what the heck

certified check
pain in the neck
promenade deck
take a rain check
Toulouse-Lautrec
up to one's neck
win by a neck

play with a full deck
security check

EK-chur

lecture

conjecture

architecture

EK-chur-ur

lecturer

conjecturer

EK-chū-ul
(See EX-ū-ul)

ĒK-ē

cheeky
creaky
freaky
geeky
leaky
sneaky
squeaky
streaky
tiki

Kon Tiki
pipsqueaky
uncreaky
unleaky
unsneaky

wikiwiki

ĒK-en
(See ĒK-un)

ĒK-ēng

creaking
eking
freaking
leaking
peeking
peaking
piquing
reeking
seeking
speaking
sneaking
squeaking
streaking
shrieking
tweaking
wreaking

bespeaking
critiquing
misspeaking
self-seeking

public speaking
strictly speaking

manner of speaking

EK-ēng

checking
decking
necking
pecking
trekking
wrecking

bedecking
henpecking
spotchecking

bodychecking
bottlenecking
doublechecking
rubbernecking

ĒK-ē-nus

cheekiness
creakiness
freakiness
geekiness
leakiness
sneakiness
squeakiness

ĒK-lē

bleakly
meekly
sleekly
weekly
weakly

bi-weekly
obliquely
uniquely

EK-lē

abjectly
correctly

directly
erectly

circumspectly
incorrectly
indirectly

EK-lus

checkless
feckless
neckless
necklace
speckless
reckless

ĒK-nus

bleakness
meekness
Preakness
sleekness
weakness

obliqueness
uniqueness

EK-nus

abjectness
correctness
directness
erectness

ĒK-ō

Chico
picot
pekoe
tricot

Tampico

Puerto Rico

EK-ō

deco
echo

Greco

art deco
El Greco

Marimekko

EK-owt

checkout
deck out
peck out

stick one's neck out

ĒKS
(See ĒX)

EKS
(See EX)

EK-shun

section

abjection
affection
bisection
complexion
cross-section
collection
connection
confection
conception
C-section
correction
defection
direction
dissection
deflection
dejection
detection
erection
ejection
election
infection

inspection
inflection
injection
mid-section
objection
perfection
projection
protection
reflection
refection
rejection
subjection
selection
trajection

art collection
circumspection
disinfection
disaffection
disconnection
fuel injection
genuflection
indirection
introspection
intersection
interjection
imperfection
insurrection
misdirection
predilection
recollection
reelection
redirection
retrospection
right direction
resurrection
rhythm section
smoking section
vivisection
wrong direction

house of correction
nonsmoking section
sense of direction

natural selection

environmental
   protection

alienation of affection

EK-shun-ist

perfectionist
projectionist
protectionist

insurrectionist

EK-shun-ul

sectional

correctional
directional

insurrectional

EK-shun-ut

section it

affectionate

EK-shur
(See EK-chur)

EK-shū-ul
(See EX-ū-ul)

ĒKT

creaked
eked
freaked
leaked
peeked
reeked
sneaked
squeaked
streaked
shrieked

tweaked

critiqued

EKT

checked
decked
flecked
Hecht
necked
pecked
sect
specked
trekked
wrecked

abject
affect
bedecked
bisect
collect
connect
correct
cross-checked
defect
direct
dissect
deflect
deject
detect
eject
erect
effect
elect
expect
goosenecked
henpecked
hi-teched
infect
insect
inflect
inspect
inject
neglect
object

perfect
project
prefect
protect
prospect
reflect
respect
reject
roughnecked
rednecked
select
suspect
subject
shipwrecked
spot-checked
stiff-necked
traject
unchecked

architect
birth defect
bottlenecked
circumspect
call collect
dialect
dial direct
dark-complect(ed)
disrespect
disconnect
disinfect
doublechecked
genuflect
hunt-and-peck(ed)
incorrect
in effect
indirect
insurrect
introspect
intersect
intellect
interject
light-complect(ed)
misdirect
retrospect
recollect

resurrect
reelect
redirect
rubbernecked
self-respect
sound effect
side effect
take effect

cause-and-effect
Doppler effect
in retrospect
religious sect
ripple effect
special effect

domino effect

EKT-ēng

affecting
bisecting
collecting
connecting
correcting
defecting
directing
dissecting
deflecting
detecting
ejecting
erecting
effecting
electing
expecting
infecting
inflecting
inspecting
injecting
neglecting
objecting
perfecting
projecting
protecting
prospecting
reflecting

respecting
rejecting
selecting
suspecting
subjecting

disconnecting
disinfecting
genuflecting
intersecting
interjecting
misdirecting
recollecting
resurrecting
reelecting
redirecting

EKT-ful

dejectful
expectful
neglectful
protectful
respectful
reflectful
selectful

disrespectful
introspectful
retrospectful

EKT-ī

necktie
wrecked eye

corpus delicti

EKT-i-fi
(See EKT-u-fi)

EKT-ik

hectic

eclectic
unhectic

apoplectic
dialectic

EKT-iv

abjective
affective
collective
corrective
connective
defective
directive
deflective
detective
elective
effective
infective
inflective
invective
objective
protective
perspective
prospective
reflective
respective
subjective
selective

circumspective
disinfective
ineffective
irrespective
insurrective
interjective
introspective
retrospective
unprotective

overprotective
private detective

EKT-lē
(See EK-lē)

EKT-nus
(See EK-nus)

EKT-rik

electric

Selectric

EKT-u-bul

affectable
bisectable
collectible
connectable
correctable
directable
delectable
dissectable
deflectable
detectable
ejectable
expectable
erectable
electable
infectable
objectable
perfectable
projectable
protectable
reflectable
rejectable
respectable
selectable
subjectable

disrespectable
disconnectable
disinfectable
intersectable
interjectable
resurrectable
reelectable

EKT-ud

affected
bisected
collected
connected

corrected
defected
directed
dissected
deflected
dejected
detected
ejected
erected
effected
elected
expected
infected
inflected
inspected
injected
neglected
objected
perfected
projected
protected
prospected
reflected
respected
rejected
selected
suspected
trajected

dark-complected
disinfected
disconnected
genuflected
intersected
interjected
light-complected
misdirected
recollected
resurrected
reelected
redirected
undirected
undetected
unaffected
unreflected

unexpected
unsuspected

EKT-u-fī

rectify

objectify
subjectify

EKT-u-kul

spectacle

dialectical

apoplectical

EKT-um

checked 'em
decked 'em
necked 'em
pecked 'em
rectum
wrecked 'em

affect 'em
bisect 'em
collect 'em
connect 'em
correct 'em
cross-checked 'em
deflect 'em
direct 'em
dissect 'em
detect 'em
eject 'em
erect 'em
elect 'em
expect 'em
henpecked 'em
infect 'em
inspect 'em
inject 'em
neglect 'em
perfect 'em
project 'em

protect 'em
respect 'em
reject 'em
subject 'em
shipwrecked 'em
select 'em
suspect 'em
spot-checked 'em

disconnect 'em
disinfect 'em
intersect 'em
misdirect 'em
recollect 'em
reelect 'em
redirect 'em

EKT-um-ē

check to me

mastectomy
object to me
vasectomy

appendectomy
hysterectomy
tonsillectomy

hemorrhoidectomy

EKT-ur

checked 'er
decked 'er
Hector
nectar
necked 'er
pecked 'er
rector
sector
specter
wrecked 'er

affect 'er
bisector
collector
connector

corrector
cross-checked 'er
defector
director
dissector
deflector
detector
erector
elector
expect 'er
eject 'er
inspector
infector
inflector
injector
neglect 'er
objector
perfecter
projector
protector
reflector
respect 'er
reject 'er
subject 'er
suspect 'er
selector

chief inspector
disinfector
disconnector
genuflector
intersector
interjector
lie detector
misdirect 'er
private sector
public sector
recollector
resurrector
reelect 'er
smoke detector
stage director

metal detector

conscientious objector

EKT-ur-ē

rectory

directory
projectory
trajectory

EKT-ur-ul

pectoral

electoral

EKT-ur-ut

sector it

electorate
expectorate
protectorate

EKT-us

checked us
decked us
necked us
pecked us
wrecked us

affect us
bedecked us
collect us
connect us
correct us
cross-checked us
direct us
detect us
eject us
elect us
expect us
henpecked us
infect us
inspect us
inject us
neglect us
perfect us
prospectus

protect us
respect us
reject us
select us
suspect us

disconnect us
disinfect us
misdirect us
resurrect us
reelect us
redirect us

ĒK-u

eureka
paprika
swastika
Topeka

Costa Rica
Tanganyika

EK-u

Decca
Mecca

Rebecca

ĒK-u-bul

leakable
seekable
speakable
streakable

critiqueable
unspeakable

EK-u-bul

checkable
neckable
peckable
peccable
trekkable
wreckable

bedeckable
henpeckable
impeccable

EK-ū-div

consecutive
executive

EK-ul

freckle
heckle
Jekyll
speckle
shekel

EK-ūl-ur

secular

molecular

ĒK-un

beacon
creakin'
deacon
ekin'
freakin'
leakin'
peekin'
peakin'
reekin'
speakin'
sneakin'
squeakin'
streakin'
shriekin'
tweakin'
weaken

critiquin'
Mohican
reseekin'

EK-un

beckon
checkin'
deckin'
peckin'
reckon
trekkin'
wreckin'

henpeckin'
spot-checkin'

rubberneckin'

EK-und

beckoned
fecund
reckoned
second

split second

nanosecond

ĒK-un-ēng

beaconing
weakening

EK-un-ēng

beckoning
reckoning

day of reckoning

EK-up

checkup
wreck up

from the neck up
yearly checkup

ĒK-ur

beaker
bleaker

creaker
eker
leaker
meeker
peeker
piquer
reeker
seeker
speaker
sleeker
sneaker
squeaker
streaker
shrieker
tweaker
weaker

critiquer
loudspeaker
obliquer
uniquer

fortune seeker
office seeker

after dinner speaker
graduation speaker

EK-ur

Becker
checker
check 'er
deck 'er
decker
necker
neck 'er
pecker
trekker
wreck 'er
wrecker

exchequer
henpecker
hat checker
homewrecker
woodpecker

Black and Decker
double-decker

EK-urd

checkered
deckered
record

track record

broken record
double-deckered
off-the-record

EK-urz

checkers
neckers
peckers
trekkers
wreckers

henpeckers
homewreckers
woodpeckers

Chinese checkers
double-deckers

ĒK-ust

bleakest
chicest
meekest
sleekest
weakest

obliquest

EK-ū-tiv
(See EK-ū-div)

ĒK-wul

equal
sequel

unequal

separate but equal

ĒK-wens
(See ĒK-wuns)

ĒK-wuns

frequence
sequence

ĒL

deal
eel
feel
heal
heel
he'll
keel
kneel
meal
peel
peal
reel
real
seal
steal
steel
spiel
squeal
she'll
teal
veal
wheel
we'll
wheal
zeal

appeal
bastille
big wheel
big deal
chenille
cornmeal

Camille
congeal
cartwheel
conceal
castile
freewheel
fifth wheel
four-wheel
fair deal
for real
genteel
good deal
high heel
ideal
misdeal
mobile
newsreel
New Deal
ordeal
oatmeal
O'Neill
pinwheel
piecemeal
reveal
repeal
reseal
raw deal
redeal
square deal
square meal
schlemiel
unreal
unpeel
unreel
unseal

at the wheel
bloodmobile
bookmobile
balance wheel
commonweal
camomile
cop a feel
Christmas seal
cut a deal

dirty deal
double-deal
dishabille
even keel
eye appeal
Ferris wheel
glockenspiel
lemon peel
mercantile
movie reel
no big deal
Oldsmobile
paddlewheel
package deal
pimpmobile
sex appeal
spinning wheel
stainless steel
snob appeal
steering wheel
snowmobile
wheel and deal
wagonwheel

automobile
Achilles' heel
official seal

on an even keel

slippery as an eel

EL

bell
belle
cell
dell
dwell
ell
fell
gel
hell
jell
knell
l
Nell

quell
sell
shell
smell
spell
swell
tell
well
yell

Adele
brain cell
bluebell
blood cell
bombshell
befell
Chanel
compel
clamshell
catch hell
cartel
Cornell
cowbell
doorbell
dispel
do tell
Di-gel
dumbbell
eggshell
expel
excel
foretell
farewell
gazelle
groundswell
hotel
halfshell
hardsell
hard-shell
ink well
impel
jail cell
lapel
misspell
Maxwell

motel
nutshell
noel
oh well
oil well
pell mell
propel
pastel
rappel
retell
Raquel
resell
rebel
repel
raise hell
sea shell
softsell
sleighbell
soft-shell
schoolbell
unshell
unwell

bagatelle
caramel
caravel
clientele
citadel
cancer cell
cockleshell
carousel
cast a spell
chanterelle
diving bell
dinner bell
demoiselle
Dardanelle(s)
fare-thee-well
infidel
Isabel
jingle bell
Jezebel
kiss and tell
muscatel
magic spell

NFL
oversell
parallel
personnel
Packard Bell
padded cell
prison cell
red blood cell
Raphael
show and tell
Southern belle
Tinker Bell
tortoise shell
undersell
very well
wedding bell(s)
wishing well
William Tell
Zinfandel

artesian well
cold day in hell
clear as a bell
Liberty Bell
mademoiselle
Pacific Bell
saved by the bell

farmer in the dell
isolation cell

AWOL
like a bat out of hell

ELCH

belch
squelch
welch

ĒLD

field
healed
heeled
peeled
pealed

reeled
sealed
steeled
shield
wheeled
wield
yield

airfield
afield
appealed
backfield
congealed
cornfield
concealed
four-wheeled
high-heeled
infield
minefield
midfield
outfield
revealed
resealed
repealed
repeeled
Springfield
unsealed
windshield
well-heeled

battlefield
Bakersfield
far afield
Marshall Field
play the field
unrevealed
vacuum sealed

ELD

belled
geld
held
jelled
meld
quelled

spelled
shelled
weld
welled
yelled

beheld
compelled
dispelled
expelled
excelled
hand-held
impelled
misspelled
propelled
rappelled
rebelled
repelled
upheld
withheld

paralleled
Rosenfeld

unparalleled

ĒLD-ēng

fielding
shielding
wielding
yielding

unyielding

ELD-ēng

gelding
melding
welding

ĒLD-u-bul

fieldable
shieldable
wieldable

unwieldable

ĒLD-ud

fielded
shielded
wielded
yielded

ELD-um

held 'em
jelled 'em
meld 'em
quelled 'em
seldom
yelled 'em

beheld 'em
compelled 'em
dispelled 'em
expelled 'em
excelled 'em
impelled 'em
misspelled 'em
propelled 'em
repelled 'em
upheld 'em
withheld 'em

paralleled 'em
very seldom

ĒLD-ur

fielder
healed 'er
shielder
wielder
yielder

concealed 'er
infielder
revealed 'er

ELD-ur

belled 'er
elder
held 'er

melder
spelled 'er
welder

beheld 'er
compelled 'er
expelled 'er
excelled 'er
impelled 'er
propelled 'er
repelled 'er
upheld 'er
withheld 'er

ĒLDZ (See ĒLZ)

**ELDZ
(See ELZ)**

ĒL-ē

deelie
dele
eely
feely
freely
mealy
really
steely
squealy
wheelie

genteelly
ideally
oh really?
Swahili

campanile
pop a wheelie

EL-ē

belly
deli
Delhi
jelly

Kelly
Nellie
Shelley
smelly
telly

beer belly
New Delhi
pork belly
potbelly

Amboseli
Botticelli
jelly-belly
nervous Nellie
yellow-belly

Machiavelli

peanut butter and jelly

**EL-e-gāt
(See EL-u-gāt)**

ĒL-ēng

ceiling
dealing
feeling
healing
heeling
keeling
kneeling
peeling
pealing
reeling
sealing
stealing
steeling
spieling
squealing
wheeling

appealing
congealing
cartwheeling
concealing

Darjeeling
freewheeling
gut feeling
misdealing
revealing
repealing
resealing
redealing
unpeeling
unfeeling
unsealing

dirty dealing
double-dealing
hit the ceiling
sinking feeling

cathedral ceiling
once more with
   feeling
wheeling and dealing

EL-ēng

dwelling
jelling
quelling
selling
shelling
smelling
spelling
swelling
telling
yelling

compelling
dispelling
expelling
excelling
foretelling
foul smelling
hardselling
impelling
misspelling
no telling
propelling
retelling

reselling
rebelling
repelling
rappelling
sweet smelling
softselling

overselling
paralleling
underselling

ĒL-ē-nus

mealiness
steeliness
squealiness

EL-et
(See El-ut)

EL-e-tun
(See EL-u-tun)

ĒL-ē-u
(See ĒL-yu)

ELF

elf
shelf
self

bookshelf
herself
himself
itself
myself
thyself
yourself

on the shelf

ELF-ish

elfish
selfish

shellfish

unselfish

EL-i-bul
(See EL-u-bul)

EL-ik

relic

angelic
smart aleck

psychedelic

Ē-līn

beeline
feline

EL-ish

hellish
relish
swellish
wellish

embellish

EL-ish-ment

relishment

embellishment

EL-ist

cellist
swellest

unwellest

EL-it
(See El-ut)

EL-it-ē
(See EL-ud-ē)

ĒL-ix

Felix
helix
he licks
she licks

EL-jun

Belgian
Elgin

ELM

elm
helm
realm
whelm

overwhelm
underwhelm

coin of the realm

ELM-ur

Delmer
Elmer

overwhelm 'er
underwhelm 'er

ĒL-ō

be low
filo
Hilo
kilo
ski low

EL-ō

bellow
cello
fellow
hello
Jell-O
mellow

sell low
yellow

bedfellow
bordello
good fellow
Longfellow
marshmallow
Othello
Odd Fellow(s)
unmellow

Donatello
Monticello
Pocatello

EL-ō-ēng

bellowing
mellowing
yellowing

ELP

help
kelp
Phelp(s)
whelp
yelp

hired help
self-help

ELP-ur

helper
whelper
yelper

plumber's helper

ELS

belts
else
melts
pelts
welts

fan belts
life belts
or else
seatbelts

garter belts
patty melts
someone else

everything else
somebody else

anybody else

ELS-ē

Chelsea
Elsie
Kelsey

ELS-ur

belts 'er
melts 'er
pelts 'er
seltzer

ELT

belt
Celt
dealt
dwelt
felt
knelt
melt
pelt
svelte
smelt
welt

black belt
Corn Belt
fan belt
farm belt
heartfelt
misspelt
misdealt

redealt
sunbelt
seatbelt
unsmelt
unfelt

Cotton Belt
garter belt
patty melt
Roosevelt

ELT-ēng

belting
melting
pelting
welting

ELTH

health
stealth
wealth

board of health
commonwealth
mental health

clean bill of health

ELTH-ē

healthy
stealthy
wealthy

unhealthy
unwealthy

ELTS
(See ELS)

ELTS-ur
(See ELS-ur)

ELT-ur

belter
helter
melter
pelter
shelter
smelter
swelter
welter

bomb shelter
tax shelter

helter skelter

animal shelter

ELT-ur-ēng

sheltering
sweltering
smeltering

ĒL-u

Gila
Sheila

tequila

Monongahela

EL-u

Della
Ella
fella
Stella

Daniella
rubella
umbrella

a cappella
citronella
Cinderella
Campanella
Isabella
mozzarella

salmonella
tarantella

ĒL-u-bul

dealable
feelable
healable
peelable
sealable
stealable
wheelable

appealable
concealable
revealable
repealable
resealable
unpeelable
unsealable

EL-u-bul

fellable
jellable
quellable
sellable
spellable
smellable
swellable
tellable
yellable

compellable
dispellable
expellable
excellable
foretellable
impellable
indelible
misspellable
propellable
retellable
repellable
unspellable
unquellable

EL-ud-ē

melody

fidelity

high fidelity
infidelity

EL-u-gāt

delegate
relegate

EL-uk
(See EL-ik)

EL-um

quell 'em
sell 'em
smell 'em
spell 'em
tell 'em
vellum

antebellum
cerebellum

EL-un

dwellin'
Ellen
felon
Helen
jellin'
melon
sellin'
smellin'
spellin'
swellin'
tellin'
yellin'

compellin'
dispellin'
expellin'

foretellin'
impellin'
propellin'
Magellan
misspellin'
no tellin'
retellin'
resellin'

watermelon

convicted felon

EL-un-ē

felony
Melanie

EL-unt

appellant
propellant
repellant

EL-up

develop
envelop

redevelop

ĒL-ur

dealer
eeler
feeler
healer
kneeler
peeler
pealer
reeler
realer
sealer
stealer
steeler
spieler
squealer
wheeler

appealer
concealer
freewheeler
faith healer
four-wheeler
junk dealer
misdealer
paint sealer
revealer
repealer
resealer
scene-stealer
two-wheeler
unpeeler
unsealer

used-car dealer
wheeler-dealer

EL-ur

cellar
dweller
feller
Keller
queller
sheller
smeller
speller
stellar
seller
sweller
teller
tell 'er
weller
yeller

best seller
bank teller
compeller
cliff dweller
cave dweller
dispeller
expeller
exceller
foreteller

impeller
misspeller
ol' yeller
propeller
reteller
reseller
rebeller
storm cellar
wine cellar

cellar dweller
fortuneteller
Helen Keller
interstellar
Rockefeller
story teller
underseller

EL-ur-ē

celery
Ellery

EL-us

Ellis
jealous
smell us
sell us
trellis
tell us
zealous

befell us
compel us
expel us
impel us
propel us
repel us

overjealous
overzealous
show-and-tell us
undersell us

EL-ust
(See EL-ist)

EL-ut

pellet
sell it
smell it
tell it
yell it
zealot

appellate
befell it
compel it
dispel it
expel it
foretell it
impel it
misspell it
retell it
repel it

kiss and tell it
show-and-tell it
undersell it

EL-u-tun

gelatin
skeleton

ELV

delve
shelve
twelve

ELV-ēng

delving
shelving

ELV-us

Elvis
pelvis
shelve us

ELV-ut

shelve it
velvet

ELVZ

delves
elves
selves
shelves

bookshelves
ourselves
themselves
yourselves

ĒL-yu

Celia
feel ya
heal ya
steal ya
wheel ya

Amelia
Cecelia
camellia
Cornelia
conceal ya
Ophelia
reveal ya

hemophilia

EL-yun

hellion

rebellion

ĒLZ

deals
eels
fields
feels
heels

heals
keels
kneels
meals
peels
peals
reels
seals
steals
steels
spiels
squeals
wields
wheels
yields

appeals
big deals
camilles
congeals
conceals
high heels
hot wheels
ideals
misdeals
ordeals
reveals
repeals
reseals
redeals
square meals
square deals
schlemiels
unpeels
unseals

bloodmobiles
bookmobiles
cool one's heels
Christmas seals
dirty deals
double-deals
Ferris wheels
glockenspiels
hell on wheels
Oldsmobiles

paddlewheels
pimpmobiles
spinning wheels
spin one's wheels
set of wheels
training wheels

court of appeals
down at the heels
head over heels

ELZ

bells
belles
cells
dells
dwells
ells
gels
hells
jells
knells
l's
melds
quells
sells
shells
smells
spells
swells
tells
welds
wells
yells

compels
cartels
Cornell's
dispels
expels
excels
foretells
gazelles
hotels
hell's bells

impels
lapels
misspells
motels
noels
oil wells
propels
pastels
retells
Raquel's
resells
rappels
rebels
repels
unshells

bagatelles
caravels
citadels
cockleshells
carousels
chanterelles
diving bells
dinner bells
Dardanelles
infidels
jingle bells
Jezebels
muscatels
magic spells
mademoiselles
oversells
parallels
padded cells
red blood cells
southern belles
tortoise shells
undersells
wedding bells
wishing wells

ĒM

beam
cream
deem

deme
dream
gleam
ream
steam
scheme
seem
seam
scream
stream
team
teem
theme

abeam
airstream
agleam
blaspheme
bloodstream
crossbeam
cold cream
centime
daydream
downstream
drill team
esteem
extreme
home team
high beam
ice cream
inseam
jet stream
moonbeam
midstream
millstream
morpheme
mainstream
pipedream
redeem
regime
sunbeam
supreme
sour cream
track team
tag team

upstream
wet dream
whipped cream

academe
balance beam
baseball team
blow off steam
color scheme
clotted cream
debate team
double-team
football team
let off steam
on the beam
self-esteem
wrinkle cream

broad in the beam
basketball team
expansion team
impossible dream
peaches and cream
pyramid scheme
vanishing cream
visiting team

American Dream

EM

crème
femme
gem
hem
m
phlegm
stem
them

A.M.
ahem
b.m.
condemn
FM
pro tem
pipestem

P.M.
rehem

Bethlehem
diadem
IBM
MGM
requiem
rpm
stratagem
theorem

ad hominem
crème de la crème

Ē-man

free man
heman
G-man
the man

EM-blē

trembly

assembly

EM-bul

tremble

assemble
resemble

reassemble

EM-bur

ember
member

December
dismember
gang member
November
remember
September

burning ember
charter member

EM-bur-ēng

membering

dismembering
remembering

ĒM-ē

beamy
creamy
dreamy
gleamy
Mimi
preemie
steamy
seamy
screamy

daydreamy
sashimi
uncreamy

screaming-meemie(s)

EM-ē

demi
Emmy
semi

EM-e-dē
(See EM-u-dē)

ĒM-en
(See ĒM-un)

ĒM-ēng

beaming
creaming
deeming
dreaming

gleaming
reaming
steaming
scheming
seeming
seaming
screaming
streaming
teaming
teeming

blaspheming
daydreaming
mainstreaming
pipedreaming
redeeming

EM-ēng
Fleming
hemming
lemming
stemming

condemning
rehemming

ĒM-ēng-lē
beamingly
seemingly

ĒM-ē-u

anemia
bulimia
Bohemia
leukemia
uremia

academia

hypoglycemia

pernicious anemia
sickle cell anemia

ĒM-ē-ur

creamier
dreamier
steamier

ĒM-ik

anemic
bulimic
uremic

EM-ik

endemic
polemic
systemic

academic
epidemic

EM-ik-ul
(See EM-uk-ul)

EM-i-nāt
(See EM-u-nāt)

EM-i-nē
(See EM-un-ē)

ĒM-ish

squeamish

extremish

EM-ish

blemish
Flemish

ĒM-ist

extremist
supremest

ĒM-lē

seem!y

extremely
supremely
unseemly

EM-lun

gremlin
Kremlin

ĒM-lus

creamless
dreamless
schemeless
screamless
seamless
streamless
themeless

EM-ni-tē
(See EM-nu-dē)

EM-nu-dē

indemnity
solemnity

double indemnity

ĒM-ō

Nemo
primo

EM-ō

demo
MO
memo

EMP

hemp
kemp
temp

EMP-ō

tempo

contempo
up-tempo

EMPT

dreamt
kempt
tempt

attempt
contempt
exempt
preempt
unkempt
undreamt

tax-exempt

criminal contempt

EMPT-ē

empty
tempty

EMPT-ēng

tempting

attempting
exempting
preempting

EMPT-i-bul

attemptible
contemptible
preemptible

EMP-ur-ur

emperor
temperer

ĒM-u

Lima
prima
Pima
schema

edema
eczema
Fatima

emphysema
Hiroshima
Iwo Jima

EM-u

Emma

dilemma
trilemma

horns of a dilemma

ĒM-u-bul

creamable
dreamable
steamable

redeemable
unseemable

irredeemable

EM-u-dē

remedy

Yosemite

EM-u-kul

chemical

academical
epidemical

ĒM-un

beamin'
creamin'

demon
dreamin'
gleamin'
steamin'
schemin'
screamin'
streamin'
semen
seaman
teamin'
teemin'

redeemin'
speed demon

EM-un

hemmin'
lemon
stemmin'

condemnin'

EM-un-āt

emanate

disseminate

EM-un-ē

Gemini
lemony

anemone
Gethsemane
hegemony

ĒM-ur

beamer
creamer
deemer
dreamer
femur
gleamer
lemur
reamer

steamer
schemer
screamer
streamer

blasphemer
daydreamer
extremer
esteemer
pipedreamer
redeemer
supremer
tramp steamer

Stanley Steamer

EM-ur

hemmer
stemmer
tremor

condemner

ĒM-ur-ē

creamery
schemery

EM-ur-ē

emory
memory

ĒMZ

beams
creams
deems
demes
dreams
gleams
steams
schemes
seems
seams
screams
teams

teems
themes

blasphemes
daydreams
drill teams
esteems
extremes
ice creams
jet streams
moonbeams
morphemes
pipedreams
redeems
regimes
Supremes
track teams
wet dreams

color schemes
double-teams

burst at the seams
impossible dreams
pyramid schemes

EMZ

gems
hems
m's
stems

bm's
condemns
rehems

M&M's
rpm's
stratagems

ĒN

bean
been
clean
dean
green

glean
gene
Jean
keen
lean
lien
mean
mien
preen
queen
seen
scene
screen
spleen
sheen
teen
'tween
wean

between
Bactine
bad scene
canteen
caffeine
come clean
careen
chlorine
codeine
convene
cuisine
colleen
demean
door screen
dentine
dry-clean
drag queen
Darlene
eighteen
Eugene
foreseen
fifteen
fourteen
gangrene
greenbean
hygiene

Irene
Joaquin
Kathleen
latrine
mob scene
machine
marine
morphine
Maxine
May queen
Marlene
nineteen
obscene
on-screen
preteen
prescreen
praline
protein
pea green
prom queen
pristine
ravine
Racine
routine
reclean
scalene
Sistine
silkscreen
sunscreen
sateen
smokescreen
sardine
stringbean
spot-clean
serene
sixteen
subteen
sea green
saline
spring-clean
tureen
thirteen
unseen
umpteen
unclean

unkeen
vitrine
vaccine
wide-screen

Aberdeen
amandine
Augustine
Argentine
Abilene
bowling green
Byzantine
contravene
Constantine
coffee bean
come between
change machine
closet queen
crepe de Chine
Dramamine
evergreen
epicene
fax machine
Florentine
fall between
fairy queen
figurine
get between
gum machine
gabardine
go-between
gasoline
guillotine
Halloween
haute cuisine
harvest queen
intervene
in-between
jellybean
jumping bean
kidney bean
kerosene
kelly green
Josephine
Listerine

libertine
limousine
lean and mean
magazine
Maybelline
make the scene
Marecine
mezzanine
mustard green
movie screen
Nazarene
nectarine
nicotine
never seen
overseen
on the scene
putting green
philistine
peachy-keen
quarantine
reconvene
slot machine
serpentine
sight unseen
seventeen
submarine
squeaky clean
soybean
soup tureen
silver screen
sweet sixteen
sex machine
smithereen(s)
trampoline
tambourine
tourmaline
tangerine
time machine
unforeseen
Vaseline
velveteen
village green
vent one's spleen
wolverine
wintergreen

acetylene
adding machine
amphetamine
aquamarine
carbon 14
elephantine
emerald green
flying machine
God save the queen
internecine
keep one's nose clean
merchant marine
milking machine
nouvelle cuisine
rowing machine
see and be seen
St. Bernadine
sewing machine
tetracycline
U.S. Marine
vending machine
voting machine
washing machine

answering machine
betwixt and between
few and far between

EN

Ben
den
glen
hen
ken
men
n
pen
ten
then
when
wren
yen
Zen

again

amen
Big Ben
Big Ten
bullpen
Cheyenne
cayenne
firemen
he-men
hang ten
Pac Ten
pigpen
peahen
playpen
RN
Sen-Sen
take ten
unpen

Adrienne
ballpoint pen
count to ten
fountain pen
julienne
lion's den
mother hen
now and then
poison pen
supermen
where or when

comedienne
equestrienne
Parisienne
slip of the pen
tragedienne

every now and then
mad as a wet hen
OB-GYN

ENCH

bench
clench
drench
French
quench

stench
trench
wrench
wench

entrench
park bench
retrench
unclench
work bench

monkeywrench
warm the bench

ENCH-ēng

benching
clenching
drenching
quenching
wrenching

entrenching
gut-wrenching
unclenching

ENCH-mun

Frenchman
henchman

ENCH-u

sent ya

absentia
dementia
valencia

in absentia

ENCH-ul
(See EN-shul)

ENCH-un
(See EN-shun)

ENCH-un-ul
(See EN-shun-ul)

ENCH-ur
(See EN-shur)

ENCH-ur-ē
(See EN-shur-ē)

ENCH-ur-sum
(See EN-shur-sum)

ENCH-us

bench us
drench us
quench us

contentious
licentious
pretentious

conscientious
unpretentious

ENCH-us-nus

contentiousness
licentiousness
pretentiousness

conscientiousness
unpretentiousness

ENCH-ū-ul
(See EN-shū-ul)

ĒND

beaned
cleaned
fiend
greened
gleaned
leaned

preened
queened
screened
weaned

archfiend
careened
convened
demeaned
dry-cleaned
dope fiend
machined
prescreened
recleaned
silkscreened
unscreened

contravened
guillotined
intervened
quarantined
reconvened
serpentined
submarined
trampolined

END

bend
blend
end
fend
friend
lend
mend
pend
penned
rend
send
spend
tend
trend
vend
wend
yenned

append

amend
amened
ascend
attend
best friend
boyfriend
befriend
bartend
commend
contend
dead-end
day's end
depend
defend
distend
descend
expend
extend
godsend
girlfriend
intend
impend
kneebend
land's end
loose end
misspend
offend
portend
pretend
rear end
suspend
South Bend
split end
the end
transcend
tail end
tag end
upend
unbend
unpenned
wit's end
year-end

apprehend
bitter end

bosom friend
comprehend
condescend
dividend
end-to-end
family friend
lady friend
man's best friend
on the mend
open-end
overspend
round the bend
recommend
reprehend
stand on end

around the bend
at one's wits' end
fair-weather friend
gentleman friend
hold up one's end
misapprehend
overextend
off the deep end
receiving end
superintend
world without end

END-ē

bendy
trendy
Wendy

modus vivendi

END-ēng

bending
blending
ending
fending
lending
mending
pending
rending

sending
spending
tending
vending
wending

appending
amending
ascending
attending
befriending
bartending
commending
contending
dead-ending
depending
defending
distending
descending
expending
heartrending
intending
impending
misspending
offending
portending
pretending
suspending
transcending
upending
unbending

apprehending
comprehending
condescending
overspending
patent pending
recommending

deficit spending
misapprehending
overextending
superintending
storybook ending

END-en-sē
(See END-un-sē)

END-ent
(See END-unt)

END-id
(See END-ud)

END-ij

spendage

appendage

END-ix

Bendix

appendix

END-lus

bendless
endless
friendless
trendless

END-ō

crescendo
Nintendo

diminuendo

END-u

Brenda

addenda

agenda

hacienda

END-u-bul

bendable
blendable

endable
lendable
mendable
sendable
spendable
wendable

amendable
ascendable
attendable
commendable
dependable
defendable
expendable
extendable
pretendable
suspendable
unpendable
unbendable

recommendable
undependable

END-ud

blended
ended
fended
mended
pended
splendid
tended
vended
wended

appended
amended
ascended
attended
befriended
bartended
commended
contended
dead-ended
depended
defended
distended

descended
expended
extended
intended
impended
offended
portended
pretended
rear-ended
suspended
transcended
upended

apprehended
comprehended
condescended
open-ended
recommended
reprehended

misapprehended
overextended
superintended

END-um

bend 'em
blend 'em
end 'em
lend 'em
mend 'em
penned 'em
send 'em
spend 'em
tend 'em
vend 'em

agendum

apprehend 'em
comprehend 'em
referendum 'em
recommend 'em

overextend 'em

END-un

bendin'
blendin'
endin'
fendin'
lendin'
mendin'
pendin'
rendin'
sendin'
tendon
tendin'
vendin'
wendin'

appendin'
ascendin'
attendin'
befriendin'
bartendin'
commendin'
contendin'
dependin'
defendin'
descendin'
expendin'
extendin'
heartrendin'
intendin'
impendin'
misspendin'
offendin'
pretendin'
suspendin'
transcendin'

apprehendin'
comprehendin'
condescendin'
overspendin'
recommendin'

Achilles' tendon
misapprehendin'
overextendin'
superintendin'

END-uns

pendants

attendance
attendants
ascendance
ascendants
dependence
defendants
descendants
descendence
dependents
resplendence
transcendence

independence

interdependence
superintendents

END-un-sē

tendency

ascendancy
dependency
descendancy

chemical dependency

END-unt

pendant

attendant
ascendant
dependent
defendant
descendant
resplendent
transcendent

co-dependent
co-defendent
independent

interdependent
superintendent

END-ur

bender
blender
ender
fender
gender
lender
mender
render
sender
slender
spender
splendor
tender
vendor
wender

appender
arm bender
amender
ascender
attender
befriender
book lender
big spender
bartender
contender
commender
defender
descender
dead-ender
depender
distender
engender
extender
ear bender
expender
goaltender
intender
misspender
mind bender
offender
portender
pretender
suspender

surrender
tail-ender
transcender
upender
unbender
weekender

apprehender
big-time spender
comprehender
condescender
elbow-bender
first offender
fender bender
legal tender
moneylender
recommender
sex offender

misapprehender
overextender
public defender

unconditional
    surrender

END-ur-ēng

rendering
tendering

engendering

END-ur-īz

slenderize
tenderize

END-ur-lē

slenderly
tenderly

END-ur-nus

slenderness
tenderness

END-us

bend us
blend us
end us
mend us
send us
tend us

attend us
befriend us
commend us
defend us
extend us
horrendous
offend us
suspend us
stupendous
transcend us
tremendous
upend us

apprehend us
comprehend us
recommend us

overextend us
superintend us

ĒNDZ
(See ĒNZ)

ENDZ
(See ENZ)

ĒN-ē

blini
beanie
eeny
genie
Jeanie
meany
nene
queenie
teeny

wienie

bikini
Bellini
Houdini
linguine
martini
Puccini
wahine
zucchini

eeny meeny
fettuccine
Mussolini
scaloppine
Toscanini
tortellini
tetrazzini
teeny weeny
taglierini

EN-ē

any
benny
Denny
Jenny
Kenny
many
penny

antennae
Jack Benny
not any
pinch-penny

Henny Penny
J. C. Penney
lucky penny
nota bene
pretty penny

ĒN-ē-ens
(See ĒN-ē-uns)

ĒN-ē-ent
(See ĒN-ē-unt)

EN-e-mē
(See EN-u-mē)

ĒN-ēng

beaning
cleaning
greening
gleaning
leaning
meaning
preening
screening
weaning

careening
convening
demeaning
dry-cleaning
recleaning
well-meaning

contravening
intervening
quarantining
reconvening

EN-ēng

penning
yenning

ĒN-est
(See ĒN-ust)

ĒN-ē-u

Armenia
gardenia

ĒN-ē-ul

genial
lenial
menial
venial

congenial
ungenial

EN-ē-ul

biennial
centennial
millenial
perennial

bicentennial

quadricentennial

ĒN-ē-uns

lenience

convenience

ĒN-ē-unt

lenient

convenient

inconvenient

ĒN-ē-us

genius

ingenious

homogeneous

ĒN-ēz

blinis
beanies
genies
meanies
nenes
wienies

bikinis
martinis
wahines

EN-ēz

bennies
Denny's
pennies

ĒNG

bing
bring
cling
ding
fling
king
ping
ring
sing
sting
sling
spring
string
swing
thing
wing
wring
zing

arm sling
bullring
brass ring
Beijing
bee sting
class ring
Chungking
drug ring
drawstring
earring
first-string
G-string
ginseng
hamstring
hairspring
key ring
kite string
left wing
mainspring

Nanking
offspring
plaything
porch swing
Palm Spring(s)
something
sure thing
shoestring
Sing Sing
theft ring
upswing
wingding
wellspring

à la king
apron string
anything
buck and wing
bathtub ring
boxing ring
center ring
chicken wing
ding-a-ling
diamond ring
everything
innerspring
in full swing
not a thing
napkin ring
onion ring
on the wing
pinkie ring
rites of spring
static cling
signet ring
second-string
teething ring
wedding ring

ass in a sling
do one's own thing
engagement ring
familiar ring
ring-a-ding-ding
under one's wing
whole 'nother thing

harbinger-of-spring
puppet on a string

throw one's hat in the
   ring

ĒNG-dum

dinged 'em
kingdom
kinged 'em
zinged 'em

United Kingdom

ĒNG-ē

clingy
dinghy
pingy
stingy
swingy
springy
zingy

ĒNG-ēng

bringing
clinging
dinging
flinging
kinging
pinging
ringing
singing
stinging
slinging
springing
stringing
swinging
winging
wringing
zinging

hamstringing
mud-slinging

upbringing

ding-a-linging

ĒNG-ē-nus

clinginess
springiness
stringiness

ĒNG-lē

kingly
singly

ĒNG-lēng

jingling
mingling
Ringling
shingling
singling
tingling

commingling

intermingling

ĒNG-lish

English
tinglish

ĒNG-ō

bingo
dingo
gringo
jingo
lingo
Ringo

flamingo
Mandingo

beach blanket bingo

ENGTH

length
strength

at length
brute stength
full-length
full strength

tower of stength

go to any length

ENGTH-un

lengthen
strengthen

ĒNG-ul

bingle
Engel
jingle
mingle
single
shingle
swingle
tingle

atingle
commingle
Kriss Kringle

intermingle
swinging single

hang up one's shingle

ĒNG-ur

bring 'er
clinger
dinger
flinger
finger
linger
pinger
ringer

singer
stinger
slinger
springer
swinger
stringer
winger
wringer
zinger

bee stinger
bellringer
dead-ringer
folk singer
gunslinger
Goldfinger
humdinger
hand wringer
hashslinger
left-winger
mud slinger
malinger
ring finger
right-winger
torch singer
wingdinger

butterfinger(s)
ladyfinger
sticky finger(s)
snap one's finger
trigger finger

madrigal singer
not lift a finger
slip through one's
    finger(s)

wrap around one's
    little finger

ĒNG-ur-ēng

fingering
lingering

malingering

ĒNGZ

bings
brings
clings
dings
flings
kings
pings
rings
sings
stings
slings
springs
strings
swings
things
wings
wrings
zings

arm slings
box springs
bee stings
class rings
drug rings
drawstrings
earrings
hamstrings
hear things
heartstrings
key rings
kite strings
mainsprings
no strings
playthings
porch swings
pursestrings
Palm Springs
pull strings
shoestrings
theft rings
upswings
wingdings

apron strings

bathtub rings
center rings
chicken wings
ding-a-lings
diamond rings
king of kings
wedding rings
water wings

one of those things

Colorado Springs
in the swim of things

ĒN-ik

scenic

schizophrenic

EN-ik

eugenic
hygienic

allergenic
biogenic
ecumenic
Panhellenic
photogenic
schizophrenic

hypoallergenic

EN-im
(See EN-um)

ĒN-is
(See ĒN-us)

EN-is
(See EN-us)

EN-ish

hennish
tennish

replenish

ĒN-ist
(See ĒN-ust)

EN-i-sun
(See EN-u-sun)

EN-it-ē
(See EN-ud-ē)

ĒN-ix

Phoenix

schizophrenics

EN-ix

Lennox

hygienics

calisthenics
schizophrenics

ENJ

avenge
revenge

Stonehenge

Montezuma's revenge

ĒNK

brink
blink
chink
clink
dink
drink

fink
inc.
ink
kink
link
mink
pink
plink
rink
sink
stink
slink
shrink
twink
think
wink
zinc

Brink's, Inc.
cuff link
chain-link
golf link
hoodwink
hot pink
in sync
lipsync
methink(s)
mixed drink
preshrink
ratfink
rethink
soft drink

bobolink
Humperdinck
in the pink
interlink
in the drink
in a wink
kitchen sink
missing link
out of sync
on the blink
on the brink
pen and ink
rinky dink

roller rink
skating rink
shocking pink
tiddlywink(s)
take a drink
tickled pink

back from the brink
no food or drink

ĒNK-ē

blinky
clinky
dinky
finky
inky
kinky
pinkie
rinky
stinky
slinky
Twinkie
winky

Helsinki

rinky dinky

ĒNK-ēng

blinking
clinking
drinking
finking
inking
kinking
linking
pinking
plinking
sinking
stinking
slinking
shrinking
thinking
winking

hoodwinking

lipsyncing
preshrinking
ratfinking
rethinking
unthinking

interlinking
wishful thinking

**ĒNK-et
(See ĒNK-ut)**

ĒNK-lē

pinkly
twinkly

distinctly
instinctly
succinctly

indistinctly

ĒNK-lēng

crinkling
inkling
sprinkling
tinkling
twinkling
wrinkling

ĒNK-lur

crinkler
sprinkler
tinkler
twinkler
wrinkler
Winkler

ĒNK-ō

pinko
stinko

**ĒNKS
(See ĒNX)**

ĒNK-shun

distinction
extinction

ĒNKT

blinked
clinked
finked
inked
kinked
linked
pinked
slinked
winked

distinct
extinct
hoodwinked
instinct
precinct
succinct

indistinct
interlinked

ĒNKT-iv

distinctive
instinctive

**ĒNKT-lē
(See ĒNK-lē)**

ĒNKT-ur

inked 'er
linked 'er
sphincter

distincter
succincter

interlinked 'er

ĒNK-u-bul

blinkable
clinkable
drinkable
linkable
sinkable
shrinkable
thinkable

hoodwinkable
unthinkable
unsinkable

ĒNK-ul

crinkle
inkle
sprinkle
tinkle
twinkle
wrinkle

periwinkle
Rip Van Winkle

ĒNK-un

blinkin'
clinkin'
drinkin'
finkin'
Jenkin(s)
kinkin'
Lincoln
linkin'
pinkin'
plinkin'
sinkin'
stinkin'
slinkin'
shrinkin'
thinkin'
winkin'

hoodwinkin'
lpsyncin'
ratfinkin'

ĒNK-ur

blinker
clinker
drinker
finker
inker
kinker
linker
pinker
sinker
stinker
slinker
shrinker
tinker
thinker
winker

free thinker
fast drinker
headshrinker
hoodwinker
lipsyncer
nondrinker
preshrinker
ratfinker
rethinker

interlinker
social drinker
tiddlywinker

hook, line, and sinker

ĒNK-ut

blink it
clink it
drink it
ink it
kink it
link it
pink it
sink it
shrink it
trinket
think it

wink it

lipsync it
preshrink it
rethink it

interlink it

ĒN-nus

cleanness
greenness
keenness
leanness
meanness

ĒN-ō

keno
Reno
vino

Aquino
bambino
cioppino
casino
Latino
merino
padrino

Angeleno
cappuccino
El Camino
Filipino
langostino
maraschino
palomino
Valentino

San Bernardino

ENS

bents
cents
dense
dents
fence

gents
hence
pence
rents
sense
Spence
scents
tense
tents
thence
vents
whence

air vents
condense
commence
cements
contents
defense
dispense
descents
extents
expense
foments
ferments
frequents
good sense
horse sense
indents
immense
incense
intense
laments
make sense
nonsense
no sense
offense
pup tents
past tense
pretense
percents
presents
repents
resents
relents

suspense
sixth sense
two cents

common sense
chain-link fence
consequence
circumvents
compliments
complements
circus tents
discontents
evidence
future tense
frankincense
false pretense
hypertense
implements
in a sense
malcontents
no nonsense
on the fence
picket fence
present tense
recompense
represents
self-defense

biblical sense
civil defense
dollars and cents
not worth two cents
over the fence
sit on the fence

national defense
truth or
    consequence(s)

out-of-pocket expense

ĒNS-ē

eensy
teensy

eensy-weensy

ENS-ēng

fencing
sensing
tensing

condensing
commencing
defensing
dispensing
incensing

recompensing

EN-shul

credential
essential
potential
prudential
sequential
tangential
torrential

confidential
consequential
deferential
differential
existential
incremental
influential
inessential
penitential
providential
presidential
preferential
quintessential
referential
residential
reverential
unessential

inconsequential

EN-shun

mention
pension

tension

attention
ascension
abstention
contention
convention
detention
descension
dimension
declension
dissension
distension
extension
indention
intention
invention
prevention
pretension
retension
suspension
subvention
unmention(ed)

apprehension
circumvention
comprehension
condescension
hypertension
inattention
in contention
intervention
not to mention
rapt attention
reprehension
three dimension
unconvention(al)

anal retention
bone of contention
misapprehension
ounce of prevention
retirement pension

honorable mention

EN-shun-ēng

mentining
pensioning

EN-shun-u-bul

mentionable
pensionable

unmentionable

EN-shun-ul

conventional
dimensional
intentional

three-dimensional
unconventional
unintentional

EN-shur

censure
clencher
drencher
denture
Frencher
quencher
venture

adventure
entrencher
fist clencher
gut-wrencher
indenture
joint venture
teeth clencher
unclencher

misadventure

EN-shurd

censured
ventured

indentured

EN-shur-ē

century

penitentiary

plenipotentiary

EN-shur-ēng

censuring
venturing

indenturing

EN-shur-sum

censure some
venturesome

adventuresome
indenture some

EN-shus
(See ENCH-us)

EN-shus-nus
(See ENCH-us-nus)

EN-shū-ul

sensual

accentual
consensual
eventual

ENS-i-bul
(See ENS-u-bul)

ENS-ik-ul
(See ENS-uk-ul)

ENS-il
(See ENS-ul)

ENS-it-ē
(See ENS-ud-ē)

ENS-iv

pensive

condensive
defensive
expensive
extensive
intensive
ostensive
offensive

apprehensive
comprehensive
hypertensive
inexpensive
recompensive
reprehensive
unoffensive

incomprehensive
labor-intensive

ENS-iv-lē

pensively

defensively
expensively
extensively
intensively
offensively

apprehensively
comprehensively
inexpensively

ENS-lus

senseless

defenseless
knock senseless
offenseless
suspenseless

ENST

fenced
sensed
tensed

against
condensed
commenced
defensed
dispensed
incensed
offensed

evidenced
recompensed

ENS-u-blē

sensibly

defensibly
ostensibly

reprehensibly

incomprehensibly

ENS-u-bul

fenceable
sensible
tensable

condensible
commenceable
defensible
dispensable
insensible
nonsensible
ostensible
unsensible

comprehensible
indefensible
indispensable
recompensable
reprehensible

incomprehensible
irreprehensible

ENS-ud-ē

density
tensity

intensity
immensity
propensity
hypertensity

ENS-uk-ul

sensical

forensical
nonsensical

ENS-ul

pencil
stencil

blue pencil
prehensile
red pencil
utensil

ENS-ur

censor
denser
fencer
Spencer
sensor
tensor
tenser

condenser
commencer
dispenser
incenser
immenser
intenser
resents 'er

recompense 'er

represents 'er
supplements 'er

ENS-ur-ē

sensory

compensary
dispensary

ENS-ur-ut

censor it

commensurate

ENS-us

census
fence us
rents us
sense us
tense us

consensus
condense us
cements us
incense us
presents us
resents us

ENS-uz

fences
senses
tenses

condenses
commences
defenses
dispenses
expenses
incenses
offenses
pretenses

consequences
mend one's fences

recompenses

business expenses
come to one's senses

truth or consequences

ENT

bent
cent
dent
gent
lent
Lent
meant
pent
rent
sent
scent
spent
tent
vent
went

airvent
assent
augment
cement
consent
content
descent
dement
dissent
event
extent
for rent
foment
frequent
ferment
hellbent
indent
invent
intent
ill-spent
lament
misspent

pup tent
percent
prevent
present
repent
resent
relent
torment
unbent
unspent
well spent

came and went
circumvent
consequent
compliment
complement
circus tent
discontent
Efferdent
evident
field event
heart's content
heaven sent
implement
malcontent
make a dent
Pepsodent
represent
underwent

age of consent
blessed event
experiment
misrepresent
nonresident
not one red cent

advice and consent
in any event
one hundred per cent
to one's heart's content

ENT-ē

plenty
twenty

aplenty
al dente
La Puente

cognoscenti
horn of plenty
roaring twentie(s)
twenty-twenty

ENT-ēng

denting
renting
scenting
tenting
venting

assenting
augmenting
cementing
consenting
dissenting
fomenting
frequenting
fermenting
indenting
inventing
lamenting
preventing
presenting
repenting
resenting
relenting
tormenting

circumventing
complimenting
complementing
implementing
representing
unrelenting

experimenting
misrepresenting

ENT-ens
(See ENT-uns)

ENT-ful

scentful

contentful
eventful
inventful
repentful
relentful
resentful
tormentful

uneventful

ENT-ik-ul
(See ENT-uk-ul)

ENT-il
(See ENT-ul)

ENT-is
(See ENT-us)

ENT-ist

dentist

adventist
apprenticed
contentest
intentest
repentist
relentist
tormentist

ENT-it-ē
(See ENT-ud-ē)

ENT-iv

attentive
augmentive
dementive
incentive
inventive

lamentive
preventive
retentive
repentive
relentive
tormentive

circumventive
implementive
represive
unrepentive

experimentive

ENT-lē

Bentley
gently

contently
intently

consequently
discontently
evidently

ENT-lus

dentless
scentless
tentless
ventless

eventless
relentless

ENT-ment

contentment
presentment
resentment
relentment

discontentment
malcontentment

ENT-ō

cento
lento

memento
pimento
Sorrento

Sacramento

ENT-rē

entry
gentry
sentry

reentry

element'ry
landed gentry
point of entry

ENT-rik

centric

concentric
eccentric

heliocentric

ENT-rik-ul

centrical
ventricle

concentrical
eccentrical

ENTS
(See ENS)

ENT-u

yenta

magenta
placenta

Oscar de la Renta

ENT-ub-ul

dentable
rentable

tentable
ventable

assentable
accentable
augmentable
cementable
dementable
dissentable
frequentable
fermentable
indentable
inventable
lamentable
preventable
presentable
repentable

circumventable
complimentable
complementable
documentable
implementable
representable
unpresentable

experimentable

ENT-ud

dented
rented
scented
tented
vented

assented
augmented
cemented
consented
contented
demented
dissented
fomented
fermented
indented
invented

lamented
prevented
presented
repented
resented
relented

circumvented
complimented
complemented
discontented
implemented
malcontented
represented
supplemented

experimented
misrepresented

ENT-ud-ē

entity

identity
nonentity

ENT-uk-ul

tentacle

authentical
identical

ENT-ul

dental
gentle
lentil
mental
rental
Yentl

fragmental
fermental
judgmental
parental
placental
repental

regental
segmental
ungentle

accidental
continental
complemental
compartmental
departmental
detrimental
documental
elemental
fundamental
governmental
incremental
instrumental
implemental
incidental
monumental
occidental
oriental
ornamental
regimental
sacramental
sentimental
supplemental
summer rental
transcendental
temperamental

coincidental
developmental
experimental
environmental
temperamental
unsentimental

intercontinental
interdepartmental

ENT-ul-ē

mentally

parentally

accidentally

departmentally
detrimentally
fundamentally
governmentally
incrementally
instrumentally
incidentally
monumentally
sentimentally
temperamentally

coincidentally
experimentally
environmentally
temperamentally
unsentimentally

ENT-ul-ust

gentlest
mentalist
fundamentalist
instrumentalist
sentimentalist
transcendentalist

coincidentalest
environmentalist

ENT-um

bent 'em
dent 'em
lent 'em
rent 'em
sent 'em
spent 'em

augment 'em
cement 'em
frequent 'em
ferment 'em
indent 'em
invent 'em
lament 'em
momentum
misspent 'em

prevent 'em
present 'em
resent 'em
torment 'em

ENT-uns

sentence

repentence
relentence

ENT-ur

center
denter
enter
mentor
renter
sent 'er
tenter
venter

ascenter
cementer
dissenter
descenter
dead center
frequenter
fermenter
indenter
inventor
lamenter
nerve center
off center
on center
presenter
percenter
reenter
repenter
resenter
relenter
tormentor
trade center

civic center
circumventer

complimenter
complementer
control center
documenter
do not enter
epicenter
front and center
implementor
left-of-center
representor
supplementer
shopping center
ten-percenter
trauma center
unrelenter

misrepresenter
medical center

ENT-urd

centered
entered

reentered
self-centered

ENT-ur-ē

alimentary
complimentary
complementary
documentary
elementary
parliamentary
rudimentary
supplementary

ENT-ur-ēng

centering
entering

ENT-us

bent us
dent us

lent us
meant us
rent us
spent us
sent us

apprentice
cement us
ferment us
invent us
momentous
prevent us
portentous
present us
resent us
torment us

circumvent us
heaven sent us
represent us

misrepresent us
non compos mentis

ENT-ust
(See ENT-ist)

EN-tu-tiv

tentative

augmentative
preventative

argumentative
representative

misrepresentative

ĒN-u

Gina
Lena
Nina
Tina

arena
Athena

czarina
cantina
Christina
farina
galena
Georgina
hyena
Latina
Medina
marina
novena
patina
Purina
subpoena
tsarina

Argentina
ballerina
Catalina
concertina
Magdalena
ocarina
Pasadena
Wilhemina

laughing hyena

prima ballerina

EN-u

henna

antenna
sienna
Vienna

EN-ū

menu
pen you
then you
venue

unpen you

change of venue

ĒN-u-bul

cleanable
screenable
weanable

amenable
convenable
dry-cleanable
uncleanable

intervenable
quarantinable
reconvenable

EN-u-bul

pennable
tenable

untenable
unpennable

EN-ud-ē

Kennedy

amenity
obscenity
serenity

EN-ud-ur

senator

progenitor

ĒN-ul

penal
renal
venal

adrenal

EN-um

denim
pen 'em
venom

blue denim
snake venom
unpen 'em

EN-um-ē

denimy
enemy
ten o' me
venomy

EN-uns

pennants
penance
tenants

lieutenants

EN-unt

pennant
tenant

lieutenant

ĒN-ur

cleaner
greener
gleaner
keener
leaner
meaner
preener
screener
teener
wiener
weaner

convener
careener
demeanor
dry cleaner
housecleaner
obscener
pipe cleaner
prescreener

routiner
steam cleaner
spot-cleaner
serener
street cleaner
uncleaner
unkeener

contravener
grass is greener
intervener
misdemeanor
quarantiner
reconvener
trampoliner
vacuum cleaner
window cleaner

take to the cleaner(s)

EN-ur

Jenner
penner
tenner
tenor
yenner

EN-ur-āt

generate
venerate

degenerate
regenerate

ĒN-ur-ē

beanery
greenery
scenery

machinery

EN-ur-ē

plenary

centenary

EN-ur-jē
(See IN-ur-jē)

ĒN-us

clean us
Enos
freeness
genus
penis
queen us
seen us
screen us
Venus
wean us

between us
convene us
demean us
Salinas

come between us
intravenous
never seen us
overseen us
quarantine us

EN-us

Dennis
menace
pen us
tennis
Venice

unpen us

table tennis

ĒN-ust

cleanest
greenest
keenest
leanest
meanest

hygienist

machinist
obscenest
routinest
serenest
uncleanest

EN-u-sun

Tennyson
venison

EN-ut

Bennett
pen it
senate
tenet

U.S. Senate

EN-ut-ur
(See EN-ud-ur)

EN-ū-us

strenuous
tenuous

ingenuous

disingenuous

ĒNX

brinks
Brink's
blinks
chinks
clinks
drinks
dinks
finks
inks
jinx
kinks
links
lynx

minks
minx
pinks
rinks
sinks
sphinx
stinks
slinks
shrinks
thinks
twinks
winks
zincs

cuff links
golf links
hoodwinks
high jinks
larynx
lipsyncs
methinks
mixed drinks
preshrinks
rethinks
ratfinks
soft drinks

bobolinks
forty winks
interlinks
kitchen sinks
missing links
skating rinks
tiddlywinks

ĒN-yō

niño

El Niño

jalapeño

EN-yū
(See EN-ū)

ĒN-yu

niña

seen ya

gardenia

schizophrenia

ĒN-yus
(See ĒN-ē-us)

EN-yū-us
(See EN-ū-us)

ĒNZ

beans
cleans
deans
fiends
greens
gleans
genes
jeans
leans
liens
means
miens
preens
queens
scenes
screens
spleens
teens
weans

bluejeans
baked beans
canteens
careens
convenes
cuisines
colleens
demeans

dry-cleans
drag queens
greenbeans
Irene's
latrines
mob scenes
machines
marines
prescreens
ravines
racines
routines
recleans
sunscreens
sateens
smokescreens
sardines
stringbeans
spot-cleans
spring-cleans
tureens
vitrines
vaccines

by all means
bowling greens
contravenes
can of beans
coffee beans
chili beans
closet queens
full of beans
fax machines
fairy queens
figurines
guillotines
hill of beans
intervenes
jellybeans
jumping beans
kidney beans
limousines
libertines
magazines
mezzanines

New Orleans
Nazarenes
nectarines
Philippines
putting greens
philistines
quarantines
reconvenes
slot machines
serpentines
spill the beans
submarines
soybeans
sex machines
smithereens
trampolines
tambourines
tangerines
wolverines
ways and means

adding machines
amphetamines
aquamarines
behind the scenes
flying machines
merchant marines
milking machines
washing machines

ENZ

bends
blends
cleanse
dens
ends
fends
friends
glens
hens
kens
lends
lens
mends
pens

rends
sends
spends
tens
tends
trends
vends
wrens
wends
yens

appends
amends
ascends
attends
amens
best friends
boyfriends
bartends
befriends
commends
contends
dead-ends
depends
defends
distends
descends
expends
extends
girlfriends
godsends
intends
impends
kneebends
loose ends
misspends
offends
portends
pretends
pigpens
playpens
peahens
rear ends
suspends
transcends

upends
unpens
unbends
zoom lens

apprehends
at loose ends
bosom friends
camera lens
contact lens
comprehends
condescends
dividends
fountain pens
lions' dens
lady friends
make amends
mother hens
odds and ends
overspends
poison pens
recommends
reprehends

comediennes
equestriennes
fair-weather friends
Mercedez-Benz
misapprehends
overextends
Parisiennes
superintends
tragediennes

OB-GYNs
telephoto lens

ENZ-ē

frenzy

McKenzie

ENZ-u

cadenza
credenza

influenza

ENZ-ur

bends 'er
blends 'er
cleanser
ends 'er
sends 'er
spends 'er
tends 'er

attends 'er
befriends 'er
commends 'er
defends 'er
extends 'er
offends 'er
suspends 'er
transcends 'er

apprehends 'er
comprehends 'er
recommends 'er

overextends 'er
superintends 'er

Ē-ō

Cleo
frío
Leo
río
trio
Theo

con brio

Galileo

Ē-on

be on
eon
freon
Leon
neon
pee on
peon

ski on

agree on

disagree on

ĒP

beep
bleep
cheap
cheep
creep
deep
feep
heap
jeep
keep
leap
neap
peep
reap
seep
steep
sheep
sleep
sweep
veep
weep

asleep
black sheep
Bo Peep
broad sweep
clean sweep
deep sleep
dirt cheap
dog-cheap
housekeep
junkheap
knee-deep
mine sweep
scrapheap
skin-deep
shopkeep
timekeep
upsweep

upkeep
waist-deep

ankle-deep
beauty sleep
chimneysweep
flying leap
lover's leap
oversleep
police sweep
put to sleep
quantum leap
sound asleep
twilight sleep

make one's flesh creep
read 'em and weep
top of the heap

EP

hep
pep
prep
rep
step
Shep
strep
schlep
yep

bicep
doorstep
footstep
false step
first step
goose step
half-step
in step
misstep
sidestep
two-step

overstep

EP-chū-ul

conceptual
perceptual

ĒP-ē

creepy
cheapie
seepy
sleepy
tepee
weepy

EP-ē

peppy
preppie
schleppy

**ĒP-en
(See ĒP-un)**

ĒP-ēng

beeping
bleeping
cheeping
creeping
heaping
keeping
leaping
peeping
reaping
seeping
steeping
sleeping
sweeping
weeping

housekeeping
in keeping
safekeeping
shopkeeping
timekeeping

oversleeping

EP-ēng

pepping
prepping
repping
stepping
schlepping

misstepping
sidestepping

ĒP-ē-nus

creepiness
seepiness
sleepiness
weepiness

**EP-id
(See EP-ud)**

**ĒP-in
(See ĒP-un)**

ĒPS

beeps
bleeps
cheeps
creeps
heaps
jeeps
keeps
leaps
peeps
reaps
seeps
sleeps
sweeps
veeps
weeps

for keeps
housekeeps
junkheaps

flying leaps
oversleeps
play for keeps

EPS

peps
preps
reps
steps
streps
schleps
yeps

accepts

intercepts
oversteps

EP-shun

conception
deception
exception
inception
perception
reception

contraception
depth perception
interception
misconception
preconception
sense perception
take exception

wedding reception
without exception

Immaculate
  Conception
sensory perception

EP-shun-ul

conceptional
exceptional

EPS-us

peps us
preps us

accepts us
prolepsis

EPT

crept
kept
leapt
pepped
prepped
slept
schlepped
stepped
swept
wept

accept
adept
concept
except
goose-stepped
inept
misstepped
precept
rainswept
sidestepped
unkept
unswept
upswept
windswept

contracept
intercept
overslept
overstepped

EPT-i-bul
(See EPT-u-bul)

EPT-ik

peptic
skeptic
septic

aseptic
dyspeptic

antiseptic
epileptic

EPT-ik-ul

skeptical

aseptical
receptacle

antiseptical

EPT-iv

deceptive
perceptive
receptive
susceptive

contraceptive
interceptive
imperceptive

oral contraceptive

EPTS
(See EPS)

EPT-u-bul

acceptable
perceptible
susceptible

imperceptible

EPT-ur

kept 'er
prepped 'er

scepter
swept 'er

accept 'er
adepter
inepter
sidestepped 'er

interceptor

EP-ud

tepid
decrepit
intrepid

ĒP-ul

people
steeple

boat people
church steeple

chosen people
we the people

ĒP-un

beepin'
bleepin'
cheapen
cheepin'
creepin'
deepen
heapin'
leapin'
peepin'
reapin'
seepin'
sleepin'
sweepin'
steepen
weepin'

housekeepin'
minesweepin'
safekeepin'

shopkeepin'

oversleepin'

EP-un

peppin'
preppin'
steppin'
schleppin'
weapon

goose-steppin'
misssteppin'
sidesteppin'
two-steppin'

deadly weapon
oversteppin'

ĒP-un-ēng

cheapening
deepening
steepening

ĒP-ur

beeper
bleeper
creeper
cheaper
deeper
heaper
keeper
leaper
peeper
reaper
seeper
steeper
sleeper
sweeper
weeper

bee keeper
doorkeeper
grim reaper
gate keeper

goalkeeper
housekeeper
innkeeper
minesweeper
sound sleeper
shopkeeper
timekeeper
zookeeper

carpet sweeper
oversleeper
record keeper

EP-ur

hepper
leper
pepper
prepper
stepper

green pepper
goose-stepper
high-stepper
sidestepper
red pepper

cayenne pepper
overstepper
red-hot pepper
salt and pepper

EP-urd

leopard
peppered
shepherd

German shepherd
salt-and-peppered

EP-ur-ub-ul

reparable
separable

irreparable
inseparable

EP-ur-us

leperous
pepper us

obstreperous

ĒR

beer
bier
blear
clear
cheer
dear
deer
drear
ear
fear
gear
hear
here
jeer
leer
mere
mirror
near
peer
pier
queer
rear
seer
sere
sear
sheer
sphere
shear
steer
spear
smear
sneer
schmear
tear
tier
veer
we're

year

amir
adhere
arrear
all clear
appear
austere
besmear
brassiere
bum steer
career
cashier
cashmere
cohere
dog-ear
draft beer
empire
endear
emir
frontier
first gear
fakir
high gear
hear! hear!
headgear
inhere
King Lear
leap year
last year
light-year
mid-year
new year
near beer
next year
off year
premier
pierced ear
Pap smear
root beer
reindeer
revere
severe
stripped gear
sincere

Shakespeare
steer clear
Tangier
tin ear
unclear
voir dire
veneer
Zaire

auctioneer
atmosphere
bombardier
boutonniere
buccaneer
brigadier
commandeer
coast is clear
crystal-clear
chiffonnier
cavalier
chandelier
chanticleer
disappear
domineer
ear-to-ear
financier
free and clear
far and near
gondolier
gadgeteer
grenadier
ginger beer
hemisphere
interfere
in arrear(s)
in the clear
inner ear
insincere
jardiniere
lavaliere
loud and clear
lend an ear
landing gear
lunar year

musketeer
mouseketeer
mountaineer
mutineer
Mt. Rainier
nowhere near
never fear
overhear
out of fear
overseer
play by ear
Paul Revere
pioneer
persevere
pamphleteer
privateer
profiteer
racketeer
rearview mirror
reappear
souvenir
scrutineer
stratosphere
to the rear
volunteer
vintage year
world premier
yesteryear

avec plaisir
bring up the rear
cauliflower ear
cry in one's beer
calendar year
charioteer
election year
Happy New Year
see one's way clear
up to one's ear(s)

academic year
blow it out your ear

ĒRD

beard
cheered

cleared
eared
feared
geared
jeered
leered
neared
peered
reared
sheared
speared
sneered
smeared
seared
steered
tiered
teared
veered
weird

adhered
appeared
besmeared
Bluebeard
Blackbeard
brassiered
cashiered
dog-eared
endeared
graybeard
inhered
lop-eared
premiered
revered
two-tiered
uncleared
veneered

auctioneered
commandeered
disappeared
domineered
engineered
interfered
persevered
pioneered

racketeered
reappeared
volunteered

ĒR-ē

bleary
cheery
Cleary
dearie
dreary
eerie
jeery
leery
query
smeary
sneery
teary
theory
weary

inquiry
unweary
unleery
war-weary

big bang theory
Einstein's theory
hara-kiri

trickle-down theory
Timothy Leary

ĒR-ēd

queried
theoried
wearied

ĒR-ē-ēng

querying
wearying

ĒR-en-ēz
(See ĒR-un-ēz)

ĒR-ēng

clearing
fearing
hearing
jeering
leering
nearing
peering
shearing
steering
spearing
smearing
sneering
tearing
tiering
veering

adhering
appearing
besmearing
cohering
dog-earing
endearing
inhering
premiering
revering
veneering

auctioneering
buccaneering
disappearing
domineering
engineering
hard of hearing
interfering
mutineering
overhearing
pioneering
persevering
profiteering
racketeering
reappearing
volunteering

electioneering

Congressional
  Hearing

ĒR-ē-nus

bleariness
cheeriness
dreariness
eeriness
leeriness
teariness
weariness

ĒR-est
(See ĒR-ust)

ĒR-ē-sum

drearisome
query some
wearisome

ĒR-ē-u

Syria

Algeria
bacteria
diphtheria
hysteria
Iberia
Liberia
Nigeria
Siberia
wisteria

cafeteria
mass hysteria

ĒR-ē-ud

myriad
period

ĒR-ē-ul

cereal
serial

arterial
bacterial
ethereal
empyreal
funereal
imperial
material
venereal

immaterial
managerial
raw material

ĒR-ē-ul-iz-um

etherealism
imperialism
materialism

ĒR-ē-um

query 'em
weary 'em

anthurium
delirium
imperium

ĒR-ē-un

queryin'
Syrian
wearyin'

Algerian
criterion
Iberian
Liberian
Nigerian
Siberian

Presbyterian

ĒR-ē-ur

blearier
cheerier
drearier

eerier
leerier
sneerier
smearier
tearier
wearier

anterior
exterior
inferior
interior
posterior
superior
ulterior

Lake Superior

ĒR-ē-us

query us
serious
weary us

delirious
imperious
mysterious
unserious

deleterious

ĒR-ē-ust

bleariest
cheeriest
dreariest
eeriest
leeriest
sneeriest

ĒR-ēz

Ceres
dearies
queries
series
theories
wearies

inquiries
World Series

ĒR-ful

cheerful
earful
fearful
jeerful
sneerful
tearful

brassiereful
unfearful
untearful
uncheerful

ĒR-ij

peerage
steerage

ĒR-ik

lyric

empiric
satiric

atmospheric
esoteric
exoteric
panegyric

ĒR-i-kul
(See ĒR-u-kul)

ĒR-i-sist
(See ĒR-u-sist)

ĒR-ist
(See ĒR-ust)

ĒR-it
(See ĒR-ut)

ĒR-lē

clearly
dearly
queerly
yearly

austerely
severely
sincerely
unclearly

cavalierly
insincerely

ĒR-lus

cheerless
fearless
peerless
spearless
tearless

brassiereless
careerless

ĒR-nus

clearness
dearness
queerness
sheerness

austereness
severeness
sincereness

ĒR-ō

hero
Nero
zero

ground zero
subzero
Shapiro
war hero

below zero

ĒRS

fierce
pierce

ĒRS-um

cheer some
fearsome
hear some
jeer some
near some
smear some

ĒR-u

era
lira
Vera

chimera
Madeira

aloe vera

ĒR-u-kul

lyrical
miracle
spherical

chimerical
empirical
satirical

ĒR-um

clear 'em
cheer 'em
fear 'em
hear 'em
jeer 'em
near 'em
sear 'em
steer 'em
spear 'em
serum
smear 'em

blood serum
endear 'em
premier 'em
revere 'em
truth serum

commandeer 'em
engineer 'em
never fear 'em
overhear 'em
pioneer 'em
volunteer 'em

ĒR-u-mid

here amid
pyramid

ĒR-un-ēz

Pyrenees
tyrannies

ĒR-uns

clearance

adherence
appearance
coherence
inherence

disappearance
domineerance
interference
incoherence
perseverance
reappearance

ĒR-unt

adherent
coherent
inherent

perseverant

ĒR-up

clear up
cheer up
gear up
syrup
smear up
stirrup
tear up
we're up

ĒR-ur

clearer
cheerer
dearer
fearer
hearer
jeerer
leerer
mirror
nearer
peerer
queerer
searer
sheerer
shearer
steerer
spearer
sneerer
smearer
veerer

adherer
austerer
severer
sincerer
unclearer

disappearer
domineerer
interferer
insincerer
overhearer
perseverer
rearview mirror
reappearer

ĒR-u-sist

lyricist

empiricist

ĒR-ust

clearest
dearest
lyrist
merest
nearest
queerest
sheerest

austerest
severest
sincerest
unclearest

Mommy Dearest

ĒR-ut

clear it
cheer it
fear it
hear it
jeer it
near it
spirit
sear it
steer it
spear it
smear it
veer it

besmear it
endear it
free spirit
high spirit
revere it
team spirit
veneer it

auctioneer it
domineer it

evil spirit
engineer it
Holy Spirit
never fear it
overhear it
pioneer it
volunteer it

ĒRZ

beers
biers
clears
cheers
dears
deers
ears
fears
gears
hears
jeers
leers
nears
peers
piers
rears
seers
sears
spheres
shears
Sears
steers
spears
smears
sneers
schmears
tears
tiers
veers
years

all ears
adheres
Algiers
arrears
appears

besmears
brassieres
careers
cashiers
dog-ears
endears
emirs
frontiers
inheres
premiers
reveres
stripped gears
veneers

auctioneers
bombardiers
buccaneers
commandeers
chandeliers
chanticleers
disappears
engineers
financiers
gondoliers
interferes
musketeers
mouseketeers
mountaineers
mutineers
overhears
overseers
pioneers
perseveres
profiteers
racketeers
rabbit ears
reappears
souvenirs
vale of tears
volunteers
yesteryears

blood, sweat, and
    tears
crocodile tears
fall on deaf ears

up to one's ears

wet behind the ears

ĒS

crease
cease
fleece
grease
Greece
geese
lease
Nice
niece
piece
peace
Weiss

apiece
cassis
caprice
cerise
Cochise
cassis
Clarisse
decrease
decease
for lease
far piece
grandniece
hairpiece
increase
lendlease
Matisse
mouthpiece
Maurice
make peace
obese
police
release
surcease
sublease
showpiece
timepiece
two-piece

valise
wild geese
world peace

bits and piece(s)
centerpiece
dove of peace
elbow grease
frontispiece
go to piece(s)
Golden Fleece
hold one's peace
keep the peace
mantelpiece
masterpiece
microfiche
piece by piece
predecease
prerelease
press release
speak one's piece
time-release

all in one piece
companion piece
gaggle of geese
period piece
secret police

conversation piece
justice of the peace

ES

bless
Bess
chess
cress
dress
'fess
guess
less
mess
press
s
stress
tress

Tess
yes

address
assess
abscess
access
b.s.
bench-press
caress
confess
compress
depress
digress
duress
distress
egress
excess
express
full dress
finesse
free press
headdress
housedress
ingress
impress
Loch Ness
largess
mixed bless(ing)
noblesse
oppress
outguess
obsess
profess
P.S.
progress
possess
regress
recess
redress
repress
sundress
suppress
success
transgress

unless
undress

acquiesce
air express
baroness
CBS
cocktail dress
coalesce
convalesce
decompress
D.D.S.
dispossess
evening dress
effervesce
formal dress
fancy dress
flower press
full-court press
garlic press
granny dress
IRS
in excess
L.D.S.
more or less
nonetheless
nothing less
not care less
overdress
overstress
printing press
party dress
repossess
reassess
retrogress
s.o.s.
second-guess
under stress
UPS
underdress
watercress
wedding dress

anyone's guess
change of address
christening dress

dress for success
direct address
form of address
farewell address
howling success
keynote address
nevertheless
permanent press
pony express
under duress

anybody's guess
freedom of the press
Gettysburg Address
ladder of success

American Express
Associated Press

ES-chul

bestial

celestial
incestual

ES-chun

question

congestion
digestion
ingestion
moot question
suggestion

beg the question
beyond question
chest congestion
decongestion
indigestion
move the question
pop the question
Twenty Question(s)

autosuggestion
out of the question

traffic congestion

acid indigestion

ES-chū-us
(See EST-ū-us)

ĒS-ē

D.C.
fleecy
greasy
Nisei
_sí sí_

Assisi
FCC

AC/DC

ES-ē

dressy
Jessie
lessee
messy

undressy
unmessy

ES-en
(See ES-un)

ĒS-ēng

creasing
ceasing
fleecing
greasing
leasing
piecing

decreasing
increasing
policing
releasing
subleasing

predeceasing
prereleasing
time-releasing

ES-ēng

blessing
dressing
guessing
messing
pressing
stressing

addressing
assessing
abscessing
accessing
b.s.ing
benchpressing
caressing
confessing
compressing
depressing
digressing
distressing
expressing
finessing
impressing
mixed blessing
oppressing
outguessing
obsessing
professing
progressing
possessing
regressing
recessing
repressing
suppressing
transgressing
undressing

acquiescing
coalescing
convalescing
decompressing

dispossessing
effervescing
overdressing
overstressing
repossessing
reassessing
retrogressing
underdressing
window dressing

ES-ens
(See ES-uns)

ĒS-en-sē
(See ĒS-un-sē)

ĒS-ent
(See ĒS-unt)

ES-ent
(See ES-unt)

ES-ents
(See ES-uns)

ĒS-ēz

feces
he sees
species
she sees
we seize

ES-ful

stressful

accessful
distressful
expressful
oppressful
repressful
successful

ĒSH

leash
quiche

baksheesh
corniche
dog leash
hashish
rime riche
unleash

microfiche
nouveau riche

ESH

flesh
fresh
mesh
thresh

afresh
enmesh
gooseflesh
horseflesh
refresh

Bangladesh
dairy fresh
in the flesh
press the flesh

ĒSH-ē

chi-chi
he/she
Nishi
specie
Vichy

ĒSH-ē-āt

appreciate
depreciate
initiate

ESH-ēng

meshing
threshing

enmeshing
refreshing

ĒSH-u

geisha
Mischa

Alicia
Lucretia

ĒSH-un

Grecian
leashin'

completion
deletion
depletion
excretion
secretion
unleashin'
Venetian

incompletion

ESH-un

cession
freshen
Hessian
meshin'
session

accession
aggression
bull session
concession
confession
compression
depression
discretion
digression
expression

enmeshin'
impression
jam session
obsession
oppression
possession
procession
progression
profession
regression
refreshen
recession
rap session
repression
secession
succession
suppression
transgression

false impression
intercession
indiscretion
lame-duck session
retrogression
repossession
summer session
self-expression
take possession
use discretion

hang-dog expression
learned profession
make an impression
plenary session

executive session
under the impression
world's oldest
    profession

ESH-un-ist

impressionist
recessionist
secessionist

ESH-un-ul

confessional
congressional
discretional
impressional
processional
progressional
professional
recessional

unprofessional

paraprofessional
semiprofessional

ESH-ur

Cheshire
fresher
mesher
pressure
thresher

air pressure
blood pressure
enmesher
peer pressure
refresher
wheat thresher

ĒSH-us

leash us
specious

capricious
facetious
unleash us

ESH-us

precious

enmesh us
refresh us

semiprecious

ES-i-bul
(See ES-u-bul)

ES-ij

dressage
message
presage

get the message

ES-i-mul
(See ES-u-mul)

ĒS-is
(See ĒS-us)

ĒS-iv

adhesive
cohesive

ES-iv

aggressive
accessive
depressive
digressive
excessive
expressive
impressive
oppressive
obsessive
progressive
possessive
processive
regressive
recessive
repressive
suppressive
successive

decompressive
repossessive
reassessive

manic-depressive
passive-aggressive

ES-iv-nus

aggressiveness
excessiveness
expressiveness
oppressiveness
obsessiveness
progressiveness
repressiveness

ESK

desk

burlesque
front desk
grotesque

arabesque
copy desk
city desk
humoresque
picturesque
Romanesque
statuesque

ESK-ō

fresco

alfresco

ES-lē

Leslie
Nestle
Presley
Wesley

ES-lēng

nestling
wrestling

ES-lur

nestler
wrestler

ĒS-lus

ceaseless
creaseless
greaseless

ES-lus

chestless
dressless
guestless
restless
stressless
testless

ES-ment

assessment
impressment
oppressment
repressment
suppressment

reassessment

ES-ō

bless so
dress so
guess so
mess so
press so
stress so

address so
caress so
confess so
depress so
digress so
distress so
espresso
impress so
I guess so

oppress so
profess so
suppress so

ES-pit
(See ES-put)

ES-put

despot
respite

ĒST

beast
creased
ceased
east
feast
fleeced
greased
least
leased
pieced
priest
yeast

at least
artiste
batiste
decreased
deceased
Far East
increased
Mideast
northeast
Near East
policed
released
subleased
southeast
ungreased

hartebeest
king of beast(s)
Middle East

wildebeest

last but not least
mark of the beast
to say the least

beauty and the beast

EST

best
breast
blest
blessed
chest
crest
dressed
EST
fest
guessed
guest
jest
lest
messed
nest
pest
pressed
quest
rest
stressed
test
tressed
vest
wrest
west
zest

at best
arrest
abreast
armrest
attest
addressed
assessed
abscessed
accessed
behest

bequest
beau geste
backrest
best dressed
bird nest
blood test
bed rest
congest
confessed
contest
Celeste
compressed
conquest
caressed
crow's nest
digest
divest
detest
depressed
digressed
distressed
expressed
finessed
far west
footrest
funfest
gabfest
go west
hope chest
headrest
houseguest
hard-pressed
incest
inquest
infest
invest
ingest
impressed
ice chest
in jest
life vest
midwest
Mae West
molest
next best

northwest
oppressed
obsessed
outguessed
out west
protest
patch test
professed
possessed
processed
progressed
request
rat nest
recessed
repressed
suggest
screen test
suppressed
stress test
southwest
songfest
slugfest
transgressed
Trieste
talkfest
unpressed
undressed
unrest
unstressed
unguessed
war chest
Wild West
well-dressed

acid test
acquiesced
all the rest
beauty rest
beat one's breast
Budapest
by request
Bucharest
cedar chest
chicken breast
come to rest

driver's test
day of rest
decompressed
decongest
dispossessed
empty nest
effervesced
for the best
false arrest
hairy chest
hornet's nest
house arrest
ink blot test
last request
lay to rest
level best
litmus test
manifest
overdressed
readdressed
repossessed
reassessed
Rorschach test
self-addressed
second best
self-possessed
treasure chest
unimpressed
unpossessed
unassessed
unsuppressed

aptitude test
bulletproof vest
close to the vest
feather one's nest
medicine chest
overnight guest
pregnancy test
permanent-pressed
put to the test
under arrest
Wasserman test

citizen's arrest
cardiac arrest

Community Chest
comparison test

EST-ē

chesty
pesty
testy
teste(s)
zesty

EST-ed
(See EST-ud)

EST-ēng

besting
cresting
guesting
jesting
nesting
resting
testing
wresting

arresting
bequesting
congesting
contesting
digesting
divesting
detesting
infesting
investing
ingesting
molesting
protesting
requesting
suggesting

decongesting
manifesting

comparison testing

EST-ful

festful
jestful
restful
zestful

suggestful

EST-i-bul
(See EST-u-bul)

EST-ik

domestic
majestic

EST-in
(See EST-un)

EST-iv

festive
restive

arrestive
attestive
contestive
congestive
digestive
detestive
divestive
ingestive
molestive
protestive
suggestive

ĒST-lē

beastly
leastly
priestly

EST-lur
(See ES-lur)

EST-lus
(See ES-lus)

EST-ō

pesto
zesto

Modesto

manifesto

EST-rē-un

equestrian
pedestrian

EST-rul

ancestral
orchestral

EST-u

Vesta

fiesta
siesta

EST-u-bul

testable

arrestable
attestable
bequestable
congestable
comestible
contestable
digestible
divestible
detestable
infestable
ingestible
molestable
protestable
requestable

suggestible

manifestable

EST-ud

bested
crested
quested
jested
nested
quested
rested
tested
vested
wrested

arrested
attested
congested
contested
digested
divested
detested
infested
invested
ingested
molested
protested
requested
suggested

barrel-chested
double-breasted
decongested
manifested

EST-ul

pestle
Vestal

EST-un

bestin'
destine
guestin'

Heston
jestin'
questin'
restin'
testin'
Weston

arrestin'
attestin'
bequestin'
clandestine
congestin'
digestin'
divestin'
detestin'
infestin'
intestine
investin'
ingestin'
molestin'
protestin'
predestine
requestin'
suggestin'

EST-unt

arrestant
congestant
contestant

decongestant

beauty contestant

ĒST-ur

creased 'er
Easter
fleeced 'er
greased 'er
keister
leased 'er
meester

decreased 'er
increased 'er

policed 'er
released 'er

EST-ur

best 'er
Chester
Esther
fester
Hester
jester
Lester
nester
Nestor
pester
rester
tester

ancestor
arrester
attester
addressed 'er
congester
contester
court jester
caressed 'er
depressed 'er
detester
infestor
divestor
investor
ingester
molestor
protestor
semester
sequester
trimester
taste tester

polyester

EST-ur-ēng

festering
gesturing

pestering

sequestering

ĒST-us

fleeced us
priestess

decreased us
increased us
policed us
released us

EST-us

best us
blessed us
dressed us
Festus
guessed us
messed us
pressed us
rest us
stressed us
test us

arrest us
asbestos
addressed us
assessed us
accessed us
congest us
compressed us
caressed us
detest us
depressed us
distressed us
finessed us
impressed us
molest us
oppressed us
outguessed us
possessed us
request us
repressed us

suggest us
suppressed us

EST-ū-us

incestuous
tempestuous

ĒS-u

Lisa
Pisa
visa

Louisa
Teresa

Mona Lisa

ES-u

contessa
Odessa
Vanessa

ĒS-u-bul

creasable
fleeceable
greasable
leasable
pieceable
peaceable

decreasable
increasable
releasable

ES-u-bul

blessable
dressable
guessable
messable
pressable
stressable

addressable

assessable
accessible
caressable
confessable
compressible
depressable
digressible
distressable
expressible
finessible
impressible
oppressible
possessable
repressible
suppressible
transgressible

inaccessible
inexpressible
irrepressible
repossessible
reassessible

ES-ul

nestle
pestle
trestle
vessel
wrestle

arm wrestle
blood vessel

ES-u-mul

decimal

infinitessimal

ĒS-un

creasin'
ceasin'
fleecin'
Gleason
greasin'

leasin'
piecin'

decreasin'
increasin'
lendleasin'
policin'
releasin'
subleasin'

internecine
predeceasin'
prereleasin'

ES-un

blessin'
dressin'
guessin'
lesson
lessen
messin'
pressin'
stressin'

abscessin'
caressin'
confessin'
compressin'
depressin'
digressin'
distressin'
expressin'
finessin'
impressin'
oppressin'
professin'
possessin'
processin'
regressin'
recessin'
suppressin'
undressin'

learn one's lesson
object lesson

Smith and Wesson

delicatessen

ES-uns

crescents
essence

depressants
fluorescence
oppressants
quintessence
quiescence
senescence
tumescence

acquiescence
adolescence
convalescence
effervescence
iridescence
luminescence
obsolescence
phosphorescence

ĒS-un-sē

decency
recency

indecency

ĒS-unt

decent
recent

indecent
unrecent

ES-unt

crescent

candescent
depressant
fluorescent
incessant

oppressant
quiescent
tumescent

adolescent
acquiescent
convalescent
effervescent
evanescent
incandescent
iridescent
juvenescent
obsolescent
phosphorescent

antidepressant

ĒS-unt-lē

decently
recently

indecently

ĒS-ur

ceaser
creaser
fleecer
greaser
leaser
piecer

decreaser
increaser
lendleaser
obeser
policer
releaser
surceaser
subleaser
two-piecer

prereleaser
predeceaser

ES-ur

blesser
dresser
guesser
lesser
messer
presser
stressor
yessir

aggressor
addressor
assessor
accessor
b.s. 'er
benchpresser
cross-dresser
caresser
confessor
compressor
depressor
digresser
distresser
expressor
finesser
hairdresser
impresser
oppressor
outguesser
obsessor
processor
professor
progresser
possessor
regressor
redresser
suppressor
successor
transgressor
undresser

acquiescer
coalescer
convalescer
decompressor

dispossessor
food processor
fancy dresser
overdresser
predecessor
repossessor
reassessor
second-guesser
tongue depressor
underdresser
word processor

father confessor

ES-ur-ē

accessory

possessory

ĒS-us

fleece us
grease us
lease us
thesis

decrease us
increase us
police us
prosthesis
release us

anamnesis
Dionysus
predecease us
senior thesis

ĒT

beet
beat
bleat
cheat
Crete
cleat
eat
feet

feat
fete
fleet
greet
heat
meet
mete
meat
neat
pleat
Pete
peat
seat
sheet
skeet
sleet
street
suite
sweet
treat
tweet
teat
wheat

aesthete
athlete
backseat
bedsheet
back street
browbeat
buckwheat
compete
clipsheet
cold feet
complete
conceit
concrete
canned heat
car seat
crow's feet
deceit
dead heat
discrete
deplete
defeat

deepseat(ed)
Dutch treat
delete
deadbeat
drumbeat
discreet
dopesheet
downbeat
entreat
elite
excrete
effete
escheat
front seat
fact sheet
flat feet
hot seat
heartbeat
hoofbeat
jump seat
lunchmeat
loveseat
Main Street
mistreat
mesquite
mincemeat
maltreat
newsbeat
off-beat
petite
prosit
pommes frites
proof sheet
poop sheet
repeat
replete
retreat
receipt
reheat
reseat
rap sheet
secrete
sweetmeat
swapmeet
short-sheet

side street
smear-sheet
spreadsheet
steam heat
trackmeet
tout de suite
time sheet
upbeat
unseat
unsweet
white heat
Wall Street

aquavit
body heat
bucketseat
balance sheet
bittersweet
cellulite
city street
catbird seat
county seat
driver's seat
easy street
hotel suite
have a seat
indiscrete
incomplete
make ends meet
overeat
overheat
one-way street
parakeet
potty seat
piece of meat
prickly heat
rumbleseat
ringside seat
senate seat
scandal sheet
sugar sweet
short and sweet
shredded wheat
sneaky pete
stocking feet

swindle sheet
trick or treat
toilet seat
two left feet
tally sheet
window seat

beat a retreat
bicycle seat
bon appétit
Dunn and Bradstreet
honeymoon suite
land on one's feet
pickled pigs' feet
red as a beet
set in concrete
Sesame Street

for the love of pete

ET

bet
debt
fret
get
jet
let
met
Met(s)
net
pet
set
stet
sweat
threat
vet
wet
whet
yet

abet
all wet
all set
as yet
brunette
beget

brochette
bedwet
bad debt
briquette
beset
baguette
Corvette
cadet
coquette
croquette
cold sweat
chubbette
death threat
dead set
deepset
dinette
dragnet
duet
forget
fanjet
gazette
Gillette
hair net
headset
in debt
Jeanette
jet set
kismet
lorgnette
layette
mind-set
not yet
nymphet
no sweat
octet
offset
Paulette
quartet
quintet
reset
regret
roulette
rosette
sublet
smart set

septet
sunset
side bet
sextet
Tibet
toilette
typeset
teaset
thickset
upset
unmet
valet
vignette

alphabet
amulet
Antoinette
bassinet
bachelorette
bayonet
Bernadette
better yet
coronet
calumet
castanet
clarinet
cigarette
crêpe suzette
diaper set
dripping wet
dinette set
epithet
heavyset
hedge a bet
Juliet
Lafayette
majorette
minaret
minuet
matching set
martinet
novelette
out of debt
place a bet
pirouette

rivulet
serviette
silhouette
super jet
safety net
string quartet
statuette
sobriquet
suffragette
Soviet
triple threat
turbojet
teacher's pet
vinaigrette
wringing wet

Erector Set
marionette
mosquito net
national debt
Russian roulette

audio cassette
forgive and forget
hail fellow well met
video cassette

Romeo and Juliet

ETCH
(See ECH)

ĒT-ē
(See ĒD-ē)

ET-ē
(See ED-ē)

ĒT-ed
(See ĒD-ud)

ET-ed
(See ED-ud)

ĒT-en
(See ĒT-un)

ET-en
(See ET-un)

ĒT-ēng
(See ĒD-ēng)

ET-ēng
(See ED-ēng)

ĒT-ens

be tense
free tents
me tense
pretense
retents
we tense

ĒT-ē-nus
(See ĒD-ē-nus)

ET-ē-nus
(See ED-ē-nus)

ĒT-est
(See ĒD-ust)

ET-ful

fretful

forgetful
regretful

ĒTH

heath
Keith
'neath

sheath
teeth
wreath

beneath
bequeath
buck teeth
eye teeth
false teeth

Christmas wreath
grit one's teeth
underneath

ETH

breath
death

bad breath
Macbeth

baby's-breath
catch one's breath
cause of death
hold one's breath
kiss of death
living death
out of breath
put to death
short of breath
save one's breath
starve to death
shibboleth
sudden death
take a breath
talk to death
wrongful death

Elizabeth
in the same breath
scared half to death
tickled to death
under one's breath

accidental death
take away one's breath

matter of life and
  death

ĒTHE

breathe
sheathe
seethe
teethe
wreathe

bequeath
unsheathe

ĒTHE-en
(See ĒTHE-un)

ĒTHE-ēng

breathing
seething
teething

bequeathing
unsheathing

ĒTHE-un

breathin'
heathen
seethin'
teethin'

ĒTHE-ur

breather
either
neither
seether
teether

bequeather
unsheather

heavy breather

ETHE-ur

feather
heather
leather
nether
tether
weather
whether

bellwether
foul weather
fairweather
together
untether

altogether
change of weather
get-together
patent leather
stormy weather
tar and feather

birds of a feather
get it together
hellbent for leather
light as a feather
under the weather

get one's act together
in the altogether
pull oneself together

put two and two
  together

ETHE-ur-ē

feathery
leathery
weathery

ETHE-ur-ēng

feathering
tethering
weathering

ETHE-urz

feathers
heathers
leathers
tethers
weathers

horsefeathers
pinfeathers
untethers

ĒTH-ul

lethal

bequeathal

ETH-ul

Bethel
Ethel
methyl

ĒT-id
(See ĒD-ud)

ET-ik
(See ED-ik)

ET-i-ket
(See ED-i-kut)

ET-i-kul
(See ED-i-kul)

ET-i-lē
(See ED-u-lē)

ĒT-in
(See ĒT-un)

ET-ish
(See ED-ish)

ĒT-ist
(See ĒD-ust)

ET-i-sun
(See ED-is-un)

ET-it
(See ED-ut)

ET-i-tiv
(See ED-u-tiv)

ET-i-tur
(See ED-u-tur)

ET-lur
(See ED-lur)

ĒT-nus

fleetness
neatness
sweetness

completeness
concreteness
discreteness
discreetness
eliteness
effeteness
petiteness
upbeatness

incompleteness

ĒT-ō
(See ĒD-ō)

ET-ō
(See ED-ō)

ET-rik

metric

obstetric
symmetric

asymmetric
diametric
geometric
isometric

ET-sō

fret so
mezzo
sweat so

intermezzo

ET-sum

bet some
et some
get some
gets 'em
jetsam
lets 'em
met some
pets 'em
wets 'em

ĒT-u
(See ĒD-u)

ET-u
(See ED-u)

ET-ub-ul
(See ED-ub-ul)

ĒT-ud
(See ĒD-ud)

ET-ud
(See ED-ud)

ĒT-ul
(See ĒD-ul)

ET-ul
(See ED-ul)

ET-ul-sum
(See ED-ul-sum)

ĒT-um
(See ĒD-um)

ĒT-un

beaten
bleatin'
cheatin'
cretin
eaten
fetin'
fleetin'
greetin'
heatin'
meetin'
neaten
pleatin'
seatin'
sweeten
treatin'
wheaten

browbeaten
competin'
completin'
depletin'
defeatin'
deletin'
entreatin'
excretin'

moth-eaten
mistreatin'
repeatin'
retreatin'
secretin'
unseatin'
uneaten
unbeaten

overeaten
overheatin'
trick-or-treatin'
weatherbeaten

ET-un

bettin'
frettin'
gettin'
jettin'
lettin'
nettin'
pettin'
settin'
sweatin'
threaten
wettin'
whettin'

abettin'
begettin'
bedwettin'
besettin'
forgettin'
offsettin'
resettin'
regrettin'
sublettin'
Tibetan
upsettin'

pirouettin'

ET-un-us

bettin' us
frettin' us

gettin' us
lettin' us
nettin' us
pettin' us
sweatin' us
threaten us
tetanus
wettin' us

ĒT-ur
(See ĒD-ur)

ET-ur
(See ED-ur)

ĒT-ur-ē
(See ĒD-ur-ē)

ĒT-ur-ēng
(See ĒD-ur-ēng)

ET-ur-ēng
(See ED-ur-ēng)

ET-ur-it
(See ED-ur-ut)

ET-ur-un
(See ED-ur-un)

ET-ur-ut
(See ED-ur-ut)

ĒT-us
(See ĒD-us)

ET-us
(See ED-us)

ĒT-us-uz
(See ĒD-us-uz)

ET-u-tiv
(See ED-u-tiv)

ET-u-tur
(See ED-u-tur)

Ē-u

Leah
mia
via

Bahia
Crimea
Garcia
idea
Judea
Korea
Maria
Medea
sangria
Sophia
tortilla
urea

bright idea
cara mía
diarrhea
galleria
gonorrhea
panacea
pizzeria
pyorrhea
ratafia

Ave Maria
Cassiopeia

onomatopoeia

Ē-u-bul

freeable
fleeable
kneeable
seeable
skiable

agreeable
decreeable
foreseeable

disagreeable
guaranteeable
unforeseeable

Ē-u-dē

deity

homogeneity

Ē-ul-ist

realist

idealist
surrealist

Ē-ul-iz-um

realism

idealism
surrealism

Ē-ul-tē

fealty
realty

Ē-um

be 'em
free 'em
flee 'em
see 'em
tree 'em

foresee 'em

lyceum
museum
per diem

art museum
athenaeum
coliseum
mausoleum
oversee 'em
referee 'em
third-degree 'em
wax museum

Ē-un

bein'
fleein'
freein'
kneein'
paean
peein'
skiin'
seein'
treein'

Aegean
Crimean
McKeehan
plebeian

Caribbean
disagreein'
European
guaranteein'
overseein'
refereein'

epicurean

Indo-European

Ē-ur

keyer
fleer
freer
peer
seer

carefreer
sightseer

disagreer
guaranteer
overseer

Ē-ut

be it
flee it
fiat
see it
ski it

decree it
foresee it

guarantee it
oversee it
referee it

ĒV

cleave
eave
eve
grieve
heave
leave
peeve
sleeve
Steve
thieve(s)
weave
we've

achieve
aggrieve
believe
bereave
conceive
deceive
endive
naive
pet peeve
perceive

qui vive
receive
relieve
reprieve
retrieve
reweave
shirtsleeve
sick leave
shore leave
upheave

by-your-leave
basketweave
Christmas Eve
disbelieve
interweave
love and leave
misconceive
make believe
New Year's Eve
preconceive
take one's leave
Tel Aviv

Adam and Eve
ace up one's sleeve
laugh up one's sleeve
overachieve
on the *qui vive*
recitative
underachieve

absent without leave
maternity leave

wear one's heart on
   one's sleeve

EV

Bev
rev

Kiev

EV-ē

bevy
Chevy

heavy
levee
levy

top-heavy

hot and heavy

ĒV-ē-āt

deviate

abbreviate
alleviate

EV-el
(See EV-ul)

ĒV-en
(See ĒV-un)

EV-en
(See EV-un)

ĒV-ēng

cleaving
grieving
heaving
leaving
peeving
weaving

achieving
aggrieving
believing
bereaving
conceiving
deceiving
perceiving
receiving
relieving
retrieving
reweaving

disbelieving

interweaving
misconceiving
preconceiving

overachieving
underachieving

EV-enth
(See EV-unth)

ĒV-ē-us

devious
previous

mischievious [*sic*]

ĒV-il
(See ĒV-ul)

EV-il
(See ĒV-ul)

ĒV-ish

peevish

naivish

EV-it-ē
(See EV-ud-ē)

ĒV-ment

achievement
bereavement

overachievement
underachievement

EV-o-lunt
(See EV-u-lunt)

ĒV-u

diva
Eva
viva

Geneva

ĒV-ub-ul

grievable
heavable
leavable
peevable

achievable
believable
conceivable
deceivable
perceivable
receivable
relievable
reprievable
retrievable

inconceivable
irretrievable
interweavable
make-believable

accounts receivable

EV-ud-ē

brevity
levity

longevity

ĒV-ul

evil
weevil

boll weevil
medieval
primeval
retrieval
upheaval

EV-ul

bevel
devil
level
Neville
revel

bedevil
dishevel
daredevil
eye level
high-level
low-level
sea level
split level
she-devil
top level
unlevel

on the level
raise the devil

go to the devil
poverty level

Tasmanian devil

EV-ul-ēng

beveling
leveling
reveling

bedeviling

EV-ul-rē

devilry
revelry

EV-u-lunt

benevolent
malevolent

ĒV-un

even
grievin'

heavin'
leavin'
peevin'
Steven
thievin'
weavin'

achievin'
break even
believin'
conceivin'
deceivin'
get even
perceivin'
receivin'
relievin'
reprievin'
retrievin'
uneven

disbelievin'
even-steven
misconceivin'
make-believin'

EV-un

Devon
heaven
Kevin
Levin
leaven
seven

eleven
hog heaven
thank heaven

lucky seven
seventh heaven

bundle from heaven
stink to high heaven
7-Eleven

EV-unth

seventh

eleventh

ĒV-ur

beaver
cleaver
fever
griever
heaver
lever
leaver
peever
weaver

achiever
believer
bereaver
conceiver
deceiver
hay fever
meat cleaver
naiver
perceiver
reliever
receiver
repriever
retriever
reweaver
swamp fever
spring fever
upheaver

basketweaver
cantilever
cabin fever
disbeliever
eager beaver
interweaver
misconceiver
make-believer
nonbeliever
preconceiver
reachiever

scarlet fever
wide receiver
yellow fever

golden retriever
overachiever
Potomac fever
underachiever

EV-ur

clever
ever
lever
never
sever
Trevor

endeavor
forever
however
whenever
wherever
whatever
whichever
whoever
whomever

howsoever
last forever
whomsoever
whatsoever
wheresoever
whosoever

ĒV-ur-ē

fevery
thievery

EV-ur-ē

every
reverie

EV-ur-ēng

levering
severing

endeavoring

EV-ur-ens
(See EV-ur-uns)

EV-ur-est
(See EV-ur-ust)

EV-ur-ij

beverage
leverage
severage

EV-ur-uns

reverence
severance

irreverence

EV-ur-ust

cleverest
Everest

ĒV-us

grievous
grieve us
leave us
peeve us

aggrieve us
believe us
deceive us
perceive us
receive us
relieve us
retrieve us
upheave us

Ē-wā

freeway
leeway
seaway
the way
we weigh

Ē-wē

kiwi
peewee

ĒX

beaks
cheeks
creaks
creeks
dekes
eeks
ekes
freaks
geeks
Greeks
leaks
leeks
peeks
peaks
piques
reeks
seeks
speaks
squeaks
streaks
sheiks
tweaks
weeks
wreaks

bespeaks
boutiques
critiques
misspeaks
pipsqueaks
reseeks
techniques

EX

Czechs
checks
decks
ex
flex
flecks
hex
hecks
necks
pecks
Rex
specks
sex
sects
treks
vex
wrecks
x

annex
affects
apex
bisects
blank checks
Brand X
bedecks
bad checks
bounced checks
convex
complex
collects
connects
corrects
cross-checks
defects
directs
dissects
deflects
detects
duplex
ejects
erects
effects
elects

expects
fly specks
fair sex
goosenecks
henpecks
index
infects
insects
inflects
inspects
injects
Kleenex
latex
marked decks
neglects
objects
perfects
perplex
projects
protects
prospects
poopdecks
rechecks
respects
rejects
reflex
rednecks
reflects
roughnecks
rainchecks
suspects
shipwrecks
selects
spot-checks
subjects
safe sex
simplex
train wrecks
tape decks
vertex
vortex

architects
break their necks

birth defects
clear the decks
circumflex
cashier's checks
disinfects
dialects
doublechecks
disconnects
fairer sex
genuflects
hunts and pecks
incorrects
introspects
intersects
intellects
interjects
leathernecks
LAX
misdirects
oral sex
retrospects
resurrects
rubbernecks
rubber checks
reelects
redirects
reconnects
sound effects
stronger sex
save their necks
total wrecks
unisex
unconnects
weaker sex

certified checks
overprotects
promenade decks
pay one's respects
religious sects
special effects

personal effects
security checks

EX-ē

hexy
prexy
sexy
vexy

apoplexy

EX-ēng

exing
hexing
vexing

annexing
indexing
perplexing

EX-ē-u

dyslexia

anorexia

**EX-i-bul
(See EX-u-bul)**

EX-ik

dyslexic

anorexic

**EX-it
(See EX-ut)**

**EX-it-ē
(See EX-ud-ē)**

EXT

flexed
hexed
next
sexed

text
vexed

annexed
context
indexed
pretext
perplexed
reflexed

oversexed
undersexed
unisexed

EX-ub-ul

flexible
hexable
vexable

annexable
indexable
inflexible
perplexable

EX-ud-ē

complexity
duplexity
perplexity

EX-us

checks us
decks us
necks us
nexus
plexus
pecks us
Texas
vex us

annex us
affects us
Alexis
bisects us
collects us

connects us
corrects us
cross-checks us
directs us
dissects us
deflects us
detects us
ejects us
elects us
expects us
henpecks us
infects us
inspects us
injects us
neglects us
perfects us
perplex us
projects us
protects us
respects us
reflects us
suspects us
selects us
subjects us

disinfects us
disrespects us
disconnects us
intersects us
interjects us
misdirects us
reconnects us
resurrects us
reelects us
redirects us
solar plexus
unconnects us

overprotects us

EX-ut

checks it
decks it
exit
flex it

hex it
necks it
pecks it
wrecks it

annex it
affects it
bisects it
collects it
connects it
corrects it
cross-checks it
directs it
dissects it
deflects it
detects it
ejects it
erects it
effects it
elects it
expects it
fire exit
infects it
index it
inspects it
injects it
neglects it
no exit
perfects it
projects it
protects it
respects it
rechecks it
rejects it
reflects it
suspects it
spot-checks it
selects it

disinfects it
doublechecks it
disconnects it
intersects it
interjects it
misdirects it
reconnects it

resurrects it
reelects it
redirects it

overprotects it

emergency exit

EX-ut-ē
(See EX-ud-ē)

EX-ū-ul

sexual

asexual
bisexual
effectual
transsexual

homosexual
intellectual
ineffectual

heterosexual

closet homosexual
pseudo intellectual

EX-uz

exes
flexes
hexes
sexes
vexes
x's

annexes
duplexes
indexes
perplexes
reflexes

ĒZ

b's
bees
bries

breeze
c's
cheese
d's
e's
ease
fees
flees
frees
fleas
frieze
freeze
g's
geez
grease
he's
jeez
keys
knees
leas
ouis
p's
pleas
peas
pees
please
quays
seas
seize
sees
sprees
shes
skis
sleaze
sneeze
tease
t's
teas
tees
tweeze
thees
these
trees
threes
v's

wheeze
z's

at ease
appease
agrees
blue cheese
big cheese
Belize
cerise
Chinese
chemise
capiz
cream cheese
displease
disease
deep freeze
degrees
decrees
foresees
goatees
high teas
herpes
high seas
knock-knees
latchkeys
Louise
marquees
M.D.'s
main squeeze
passkeys
queen bees
sea breeze
settees
Seabees
sweet peas
tehees
tepees
TVs
TDs
trustees
trapeze
unfreeze
wee wees
whoopees

ABCs
addressees
Androcles
assignees
absentees
antifreeze
bumblebees
black-eyed peas
Balinese
bat the breeze
Brooklynese
by degrees
Cantonese
Celebes
cottage cheese
chickadees
chimpanzees
Cyclades
Christmas trees
disagrees
dungarees
devotees
fricassees
filigrees
finder's fees
family trees
guarantees
gum disease
garnishees
honeybees
Hercules
indices
ill at ease
if you please
jamborees
jubilees
Japanese
knobby knees
licensees
Lebanese
legalese
maître d's
minor keys
nominees
nth degrees

oversees
overseas
on one's knees
Ph.D.'s
pedigrees
peonies
Pyrenees
Pekingese
pretty please
refugees
repartees
referees
Siamese
shopping sprees
shoot the breeze
Socrates
Seven Seas
third degrees
Viennese
water skis

academese
archdiocese
Diogenes
Florida Keys
Hippocrates
isosceles
kissing disease
on bended knees
parentheses
RSVP's
Vietnamese

EZ

fez
prez
says

Cortez
Inez
Suez
who says

Alvarez
Simon says

ĒZD

breezed
eased
pleased
seized
sneezed
teased
tweezed
wheezed

appeased
displeased
diseased

ĒZ-ē

breezy
cheesy
easy
queasy
sleazy
sneezy
wheezy

Parcheesi
play kneesie(s)
speakeasy
uneasy
unbreezy
Zambezi

free and easy
over easy

**ĒZ-el
(See ĒZ-ul)**

ĒZ-ēng

breezing
easing
freezing
pleasing
seizing
sneezing
teasing

wheezing

appeasing
displeasing
unfreezing

EZ-ent
(See EZ-unt)

ĒZ-ē-nus

breeziness
easiness
queasiness
wheeziness

uneasiness

ĒZ-ē-um

elysium
magnesium

ĒZH-u

flees ya
freeze ya
please ya
seize ya
tease ya

amnesia
displease ya
Rhodesia
Tunisia
unfreeze ya

analgesia
aphrodesia
anesthesia
Indonesia
Micronesia
Polynesia

anaphrodesia
Milk of Magnesia

ĒZH-un

lesion

adhesion
artesian
cohesion
Parisian
Rhodesian
Tunisian

Indonesian
Polynesian

ĒZH-ur

leisure
seizure

at your leisure
search and seizure

EZH-ur

leisure
measure
pleasure
treasure

ĒZ-i-bul
(See ĒZ-u-bul)

EZ-i-dens

hesitance
presidents
residence
residents

nonresidents

EZ-i-dunt

hesitant
president
resident

nonresident
vice president

EZ-i-tuns
(See EZ-i-dens)

EZ-i-tunt
(See EZ-i-dunt)

ĒZ-mō

lo mismo
machismo

ĒZ-u

Liza
Pisa
visa

Louisa

Mona Lisa

ĒZ-u-bul

easable
freezable
feasible
pleasable
sneezable
squeezable
seizable
teasable
tweezable
wheezable

appeasable
displeasable
diseasable
reprisable
unfreezable

ĒZ-ul

diesel
easel
measle(s)
weasel

ĒZ-un

breezin'
easin'
freezin'
pleasin'
reason
season
seizin'
sneezin'
squeezin'
treason
teasin'
tweezin'
wheezin'

appeasin'
displeasin'
high treason

out of season
stand to reason

no rhyme or reason

ĒZ-un-ēng

reasoning
seasoning

EZ-uns

presence
pheasants
peasants
presents

omnipresence

EZ-unt

pheasant
peasant
pleasant
present

unpleasant

everpresent

for the present
omnipresent

ĒZ-un-u-bul

reasonable
seasonable
treasonable

unreasonable

ĒZ-ur

Caesar
easer
freezer
frees 'er
geezer
greaser
pleaser
please 'er
seizer
seize 'er
sneezer
squeezer
squeeze 'er
tweezer(s)
wheezer

appeaser
appease 'er
displeaser
displease 'er
deep freezer
ol' geezer

guarantees 'er
pretty pleaser

Nebuchadnezzar

ĒZ-us

ease us
frees us
freeze us
Jesus
knees us

please us
sees us
squeeze us
seize us
tease us

appease us
bejesus
displease us
deep-freeze us

exegesis

I SOUNDS

Ī

aye
by
bye
buy
cry
dry
die
dye
eye
fie
fly
fry
guy
high
hi
I
i
lie
lye
my
nigh
pi
pie
pry
ply
rye

sly
spry
sigh
sty
shy
sky
spy
tie
Thai
thigh
try
thy
vie
why
wye
wry
y

aye aye
ally
ace high
awry
apply
bye-bye
bonzai
blow-dry
belie
bull's-eye

black tie
barfly
blowfly
blue sky
bird's-eye
bone-dry
bow tie
black eye
buckeye
cacti
comply
deep-fry
decry
drip dry
defy
deny
draw nigh
deadeye
espy
far cry
firefly
fall guy
fly high
French fry
fisheye
fish fry
good-bye
gadfly

GI
glass eye
get by
gun-shy
hereby
horsefly
housefly
Hi-Y
hogtie
hi-fi
imply
July
knee-high
lanai
mud pie
mai tai
magpie
mind's eye
Masai
medfly
necktie
nearby
outcry
pigsty
Popeye
pinkeye
porkpie
quasi
red-eye
rabbi
reply
rely
run by
spin dry
Shanghai
sci-fi
standby
sky-high
supply
shoofly
small fry
sneak by
slip by
shuteye
thereby

tongue-tie
thigh-high
two-ply
tie-dye
untie
Versailles
whereby
white-tie
war cry
well-nigh
wise guy

alibi
Alpha Chi
alkali
apple pie
all-time high
Alpha Phi
amplify
beddy-bye
butterfly
bluetail fly
battle cry
bald-faced lie
beautify
beady eye
by and by
certify
camera-shy
calcify
counterspy
crucify
classify
clarify
codify
cutie pie
cherry pie
do or die
deify
dignify
dragonfly
evil eye
eagle eye
edify
eye-to-eye

FBI
falsify
fortify
flying high
gratify
Gemini
glorify
high and dry
hue and cry
hook and eye
hushaby
horrify
humble pie
justify
lullaby
live a lie
Lorelei
liquefy
mortify
misapply
mollify
mystify
modify
Mordecai
Molokai
multiply
magnify
mummify
metrify
notify
naked eye
nullify
occupy
on the sly
ossify
overbuy
overlie
petrify
pizza pie
private eye
pacify
purify
putrefy
passerby
power supply

Paraguay
qualify
quantify
right-to-die
rectify
ramify
ratify
rarefy
rockaby
reapply
sanctify
signify
stupefy
satisfy
samurai
seeing eye
Sigma Chi
simplify
specify
shoo-fly pie
tigereye
terrify
testify
typify
tsetse fly
underlie
Uruguay
UPI
unify
up and die
underbuy
vilify
verify
what a guy
you and I

beatify
chicken pot pie
catch someone's eye
declassify
demystify
disqualify
dissatisfy
electrify
easy as pie

exemplify
electric eye
eat humble pie
Eskimo Pie
Fourth of July
intensify
indemnify
in short supply
identify
in a pig's eye
little white lie
mud in your eye
Mr. Nice Guy
not bat an eye
natural high
never say die
old college try
pie in the sky
personify
preoccupy
refortify
see eye-to-eye
solidify
vox populi
wink of an eye

apple of one's eye
an eye for an eye
Alpha Delta Pi
artificial high
bigger fish to fry
catcher in the rye
corpus delicti
easy on the eye
Treaty of Versailles

Ī-ad

dryad
triad

ĪB

bribe
gibe
jibe

scribe
tribe
vibe(s)

ascribe
bad vibe(s)
conscribe
describe
imbibe
inscribe
prescribe
proscribe
subscribe
transcribe

circumscribe
diatribe
resubscribe

Indian tribe
oversubscribe

IB

bib
crib
dib(s)
fib
glib
jib
lib
mib
nib
rib
sib
squib

ad lib
corncrib
his nib(s)
her nib(s)
prime rib
sparerib

Adam's rib
baby bib
women's lib

ĪB-el
(See ĪB-ul)

ĪB-ēng

bribing
gibing
jibing

ascribing
conscribing
describing
imbibing
inscribing
prescribing
proscribing
subscribing
transcribing

circumscribing
resubscribing

oversubscribing

IB-ēng

cribbing
fibbing
ribbing

ad-libbing

IB-et
(See IB-ut)

IB-ē-u

Libya
tibia

IB-ē-un

Libyan

amphibian
Caribbean

IB-it
(See IB-ut)

IB-it-iv
(See IB-ud-iv)

IB-its
(See IB-uts)

IB-lē

dribbly
glibly
nibbly
quibbly
scribbly

IB-lēng

dribbling
nibbling
quibbling
sibling
scribbling

double dribbling

Ī-bol

eyeball
fly ball
highball
I bawl
my ball

eyeball-to-eyeball

Ī-bold

eyeballed
piebald

IB-rē-um

Librium

equilibrium

ĪB-u-bul

bribable
jibable

ascribable
conscribable
describable
inscribable
prescribable
proscribable
subscribable
transcribable

circumscribable
indescribable

IB-ud-iv

exhibitive
inhibitive
prohibitive

IB-ū-dur

attributor
contributor
distributor

ĪB-ul

Bible
libel
tribal

IB-ul

dibble
dribble
fribble
kibble
nibble
quibble
Sibyl
scribble

double dribble

IB-uld

dribbled
kibbled
nibbled
quibbled
ribald
scribbled

IB-un

fibbin'
gibbon
ribbon
ribbin'

blue ribbon

ĪB-ur

briber
bribe 'er
fiber
jiber
Schreiber
Tiber

ascriber
describer
imbiber
inscriber
prescriber
proscriber
subscriber
transcriber

circumscriber
resuscriber

IB-ur

cribber
fibber
glibber
gibber
libber
ribber

ad-libber

women's libber

IB-ur-dē

liberty

at liberty

flibbertigibbety

ĪB-ur-ē

bribery
jibery

IB-ur-tē
(See IB-ur-dē)

IB-ūt

tribute

attribute
contribute
distribute

IB-ut

fib it

ad-lib it
adhibit
exhibit
inhibit
prohibit

flibbertigibbet
people's exhibit

IB-uts

kibitz

exhibits
inhibits
prohibits

uninhibits

flibbertigibbets

IB-ut-ud

exhibited
inhibited
prohibited

uninhibited

IB-ū-tur
(See IB-ū-dur)

IB-yūt
(See IB-ūt)

ICH

bitch
ditch
glitch
hitch
itch
niche
pitch
rich
stitch
switch
snitch
twitch
witch
which

bewitch
chain stitch
enrich
eye twitch
high pitch
Ipswich
jock itch
last ditch
light switch
rich bitch
restitch

unhitch

bait-and-switch
cable-stitch
dimmer switch
fever pitch
filthy rich
masterswitch
perfect pitch
superrich
strike it rich

Halloween witch
son-of-a-bitch
seven-year itch
without a hitch

asleep at the switch

ICH-ē

bitchy
itchy
twitchy
witchy

ICH-en
(See ICH-un)

ICH-ēng

bitching
ditching
hitching
itching
pitching
stitching
switching
snitching
twitching

bewitching
enriching
restitching
unhitching

cable-stitching

ICH-ē-nus

bitchiness
itchiness
twitchiness

ICH-ment

bewitchment
enrichment

ICH-un

bitchen
bitchin'
ditchin'
hitchin'
itchin'
kitchen
pitchin'
richen
stitchin'
switchin'
snitchin'
twitchin'

bewitchin'
enrichen
restitchin'
soup kitchen
unhitchin'

ICH-ur

bitcher
ditcher
hitcher
itcher
pitcher
richer
stitcher
switcher
snitcher
twitcher

bewitcher
enricher

ICH-ur-ē

stitchery
snitchery
twitchery
witchery

ICH-uz

bitches
britches
ditches
glitches
hitches
itches
niches
pitches
riches
stitches
switches
snitches
twitches
witches

bewitches
enriches
in stitches
rich bitches
restitches
unhitches

from rags to riches

ĪD

bride
bide
chide
clyde
cried
died
dyed
dried
eyed
fried
guide
glide

hide
Ide(s)
lied
pride
pried
plied
ride
side
slide
snide
stride
sighed
shied
spied
tide
tied
tried
vied
wide

allied
aye-ayed
aside
abide
astride
applied
backslide
backside
beside
black-eyed
blue-eyed
brown-eyed
bedside
broadside
blindside
bright-eyed
bromide
belied
bug-eyed
collide
cockeyed
confide
chloride
cross-eyed
complied

child bride
cowhide
divide
decide
deride
decried
defied
denied
drip-dried
dry-eyed
deep-fried
downside
elide
espied
ebb tide
fireside
free ride
freeze-dried
flip side
fisheyed
false pride
green-eyed
hillside
horsehide
high tide
hogtied
hawkeyed
inside
implied
joyride
landslide
lakeside
low tide
misguide
mud slide
outride
outside
oxhide
on side
offside
poolside
preside
pie-eyed
provide
reside

red tide
roadside
red-eyed
rawhide
replied
relied
riptide
ringside
seaside
stateside
sulfide
subside
spin-dried
sun-dried
supplied
shanghaied
stir-fried
statewide
snowslide
sloe-eyed
tongue-tied
topside
take side(s)
tour guide
untied
untried
worldwide
wall-eyed
wayside
wide-eyed
yuletide

amplified
alongside
alibied
bleary-eyed
beautified
beady-eyed
brush aside
buggy ride
bona fide
coincide
cut and dried
cyanide
chicken-fried

citywide
crucified
clarified
codified
certified
calcified
classified
countryside
dignified
demandside
distaff side
dewy-eyed
deified
edified
eventide
eagle-eyed
evil-eyed
fratricide
freedom ride
far and wide
falsified
fortified
fungicide
gratified
glassy-eyed
genocide
glorified
homicide
horrified
herbicide
horseback ride
hit one's stride
Ironside(s)
justified
joyride
liquefied
misallied
matricide
mortified
mollified
mystified
magnified
mummified
modified
multiplied

misapplied
mountainside
nationwide
nullified
notified
override
occupied
ossified
oceanside
on the side
other side
patricide
pesticide
petrified
pacified
purified
prophesied
putrefied
qualified
quantified
riverside
ratified
regicide
reapplied
rarefied
rectified
ramified
rockabyed
subdivide
sissified
share a ride
suicide
slip and slide
sanctified
stupefied
side-by-side
signified
satisfied
step aside
simplified
specified
set aside
spermicide
starry-eyed
supply-side

terrified
TV Guide
take in stride
thumb a ride
testified
typified
travel guide
teary-eyed
turn the tide
up and died
unified
underside
vilified
verified
wave aside

disqualified
dissatisfied
deep down inside
declassified
electrified
exemplified
fit to be tied
formaldehyde
here comes the bride
infanticide
intensified
insecticide
identified
indemnified
Jekyll and Hyde
mail-order bride
personified
preoccupied
refortified
self-satisfied
solidified
tyrannicide
take for a ride
thorn in one's side
tan someone's hide
unsatisfied
unoccupied
unverified

along for the ride

father of the bride
mother of the bride
overqualified
roller-coaster ride

continental divide

ID

bid
did
grid
hid
id
kid
lid
mid
quid
rid
Sid
skid
slid
squid

amid
backslid
eyelid
forbid
high bid
hybrid
low bid
Madrid
nonskid
outbid
outdid
rebid
redid
undid
whiz kid

Captain Kidd
flip one's lid
highest bid
katydid
lowest bid
on the skid(s)
overbid

overdid
pyramid
toilet lid
underbid

Billy the Kid

ĪD-ē

didie
flighty
Friday
Heidi
ID
mighty
nightie
tidy
whitey

almighty
all righty
gal Friday
Good Friday
untidy

Aphrodite
high and mighty

ID-ē

bitty
biddy
city
ditty
flitty
giddy
gritty
kitty
kiddie
middy
nitty
pretty
pity
shitty
slitty
titty
witty

committee
fun city
fat city
self-pity
tent city

itty-bitty
inner city
Kansas City
nitty-gritty
sitting pretty
Salt Lake City
Walter Mitty

Atlantic City
Mexico City

Oklahoma City
Ways and Means
   Committee

ĪD-en
(See ĪD-un)

ID-en
(See ID-un)

ĪD-ēng

biting
biding
citing
chiding
fighting
guiding
gliding
hiding
knighting
lighting
riding
righting
sighting
siding
spiting
sliding

slighting
striding
tiding
writing

abiding
bullfighting
backbiting
backsliding
broadsiding
cockfighting
colliding
confiding
delighting
dividing
deriding
deciding
exciting
eliding
fistfighting
floodlighting
gang fighting
ghostwriting
gunfighting
highlighting
handwriting
igniting
infighting
inviting
inciting
indicting
joyriding
landsliding
moonlighting
misguiding
outriding
prizefighting
presiding
providing
reciting
residing
smooth riding
subsiding
spotlighting
skywriting

speedwriting
track lighting
typewriting
uniting

coinciding
copyrighting
disuniting
dynamiting
extraditing
expediting
horseback riding
law-abiding
overriding
proselyting
peroxiding
pillow fighting
reconditing
reuniting
subdividing
uninviting
underwriting

ID-ēng

bidding
fitting
flitting
gritting
gridding
getting
hitting
kidding
knitting
pitting
quitting
ridding
sitting
skidding
splitting
spitting
slitting
twitting

admitting
acquitting

befitting
bullshitting
committing
earsplitting
emitting
forbidding
formfitting
forgetting
hard-hitting
hairsplitting
house-sitting
hand-knitting
loose-fitting
no kidding
outfitting
outbidding
outwitting
omitting
permitting
pinch-hitting
rebidding
remitting
refitting
sidesplitting
submitting
switch-hitting
transmitting
tightfitting
unfitting
unwitting

benefitting
counterfeiting
do one's bidding
manumitting
overbidding
readmitting
recommitting
resubmitting
unremitting
underbidding

overcommitting
stick to one's knitting

ID-ē-u

Lydia

perfidia

ID-ē-um

idiom
pity 'em

cymbidium

ID-ē-un

Gideon
prettyin'
pityin'

meridian

postmeridian

ID-ē-nus

biddiness
flittiness
giddiness
grittiness
prettiness
shittiness
wittiness

ID-ē-ur

flittier
giddier
grittier
prettier
pitier
shittier
Whittier
wittier

ID-ē-us

giddy us
hideous
piteous

pity us
pretty us
witty us

fastidious
invidious
insidious
perfidious

ID-ē-ust

flittiest
giddiest
grittiest
prettiest
shittiest
wittiest

itty-bittiest

ID-ē-ut

idiot
pity it

ID-if-ī
(See ID-uf-ī)

ID-i-gā-shun

litigation
mitigation

ID-ik

critic

acidic
arthritic
Semitic

analytic
armchair critic
catalytic
drama critic
diacritic
movie critic

paralytic
parasitic

anti-Semitic

ID-ik-ul

critical

juridical
political

analytical
apolitical
catalytical
diacritical
hypocritical
parasitical

ĪD-il
(See ĪD-ul)

ID-ish

British
flittish
kiddish
skittish
Yiddish

ID-i-siz-um

criticism
witticism

ID-it-ē
(See ID-ud-ē)

IDJ
(See IJ)

ĪD-lē

idly
snidely

widely

cockeyedly

ID-lē

diddly
piddly

ĪD-lēng

bridling
idling
sidling
titling

entitling

ID-lēng

diddling
fiddling
middling
piddling
riddling
twiddling
whittling

belittling

fair to middling

ID-nē

kidney
mid-knee
Sydney

ĪD-nus

snideness
wideness

wide-eyedness

ĪD-ō

dido
Fido

my dough
pie dough
right-o

Hokkaido

ID-ō

ditto
kiddo
widow

black widow
golf widow

Ī-drāt

dehydrate

carbohydrate

IDST

didst
midst

amidst

ĪD-u

Ida

Oneida

ĪD-u-bul

bitable
citable
fightable
guidable
hidable
lightable
ridable
rightable
slidable
sightable
writable

abidable

dividable
delightable
decidable
excitable
highlightable
ignitable
incitable
indictable
recitable
unitable
unguidable

copyrightable
expeditable
subdividable
reunitable

ID-u-bul

biddable
gettable
hittable
kiddable
knittable
quittable
splittable

admittable
acquittable
committable
forbiddable
forgettable
outbiddable
outfittable
permittable
remittable
submittable
transmittable
unsplittable

counterfeitable
readmittable

ĪD-ud

bided
cited

chided
glided
guided
knighted
lighted
prided
righted
sided
slighted
sighted
spited
tided

alighted
abided
broadsided
collided
confided
divided
decided
derided
delighted
excited
elided
far-sighted
foresighted
floodlighted
highlighted
ignited
invited
incited
indicted
lopsided
misguided
moonlighted
near-sighted
one-sided
presided
provided
resided
recited
requited
shortsighted
spotlighted
surfeited

subsided
united
uprighted

copyrighted
coincided
dynamited
extradited
expedited
many-sided
peroxided
proselyted
reunited
subdivided
unrequited
undecided
undersided.

ID-ud

fitted
flitted
gritted
kidded
knitted
lidded
mitted
pitted
ridded
skidded
slitted
twitted
witted

admitted
acquitted
befitted
bullshitted
committed
dimwitted
emitted
hand-knitted
half-witted
nitwitted
outfitted
outwitted

omitted
permitted
remitted
refitted
submitted
transmitted
tightfitted
unfitted

benefited
counterfeited
manumitted
noncommitted
pyramided
readmitted
resubmitted
recommitted
unpermitted

ID-ud-ē

quiddity

acidity
cupidity
fluidity
frigidity
flaccidity
humidity
lucidity
liquidity
morbidity
rapidity
rigidity
stupidity
solidity
timidity
validity

ID-uf-ī

acidify
humidify
solidify

ĪD-ul

bridal
bridle
bride'll
guide'll
idle
idyll
idol
sidle
tidal
title
vital

entitle
mistitle
retitle
recital
requital
subtitle
unbridle

fratricidal
fungicidal
germicidal
herbicidal
homicidal
movie idol
royal title
suicidal

matinee idol

ID-ul

brittle
diddle
fiddle
griddle
little
middle
piddle
riddle
skittle
spittle
tittle
twiddle

victual(s)
whittle

acquittal
belittle
committal
git-fiddle
hospital
lickspittle
remittal
transmittal

Chicken Little
noncommittal
pancake griddle
peanut brittle
second fiddle
taradiddle

around the middle
fit as a fiddle
hi-diddle-diddle
little by little
play second fiddle

ID-ul-ē

diddely
giddily
Italy
tiddely
wittily

ĪD-um

bite 'em
chide 'em
eyed 'em
fight 'em
guide 'em
hide 'em
item
knight 'em
light 'em
plied 'em
ride 'em
sight 'em

spite 'em
slight 'em
smite 'em
tied 'em
tried 'em
write 'em

abide 'em
beside 'em
delight 'em
divide 'em
defied 'em
denied 'em
hot item
highlight 'em
inside 'em
incite 'em
line item
misguide 'em
provide 'em
recite 'em
spotlight 'em

ad infinitum

ID-um-ē

bit o' me
rid o' me

epitome

ĪD-un

bidin'
chidin'
Dryden
guidin'
glidin'
hidin'
ridin'
sidin'
slidin'
stridin'
tidin'
widen

abidin'

backslidin'
broadsidin'
collidin'
decidin'
joyridin'
deridin'
misguidin'
outridin'
presidin'
providin'
Poseidon
residin'
subsidin'

coincidin'
overridin'
subdividin'

slippin' and slidin'

ID-un

biddin'
bidden
hidden
kiddin'
ridden
riddin'
swidden
skiddin'

bedridden
forbidden
hagridden
outbidden
outbiddin'
rebidden
rebiddin'
unbidden

overridden

ĪD-uns

guidance

abidance

misguidance
subsidence

ĪD-unt

strident
Trident

ĪD-ur

biter
brighter
bider
cider
chider
dried 'er
eider
eyed 'er
fighter
guide 'er
guider
glider
hide 'er
knight 'er
lighter
pried 'er
plied 'er
rider
sighter
spider
Snyder
spiter
slighter
slight 'er
slider
smite 'er
snider
Schneider
strider
tighter
triter
tied 'er
tried 'er
wider
writer
whiter

alighter
abider
astride 'er
backslider
beside 'er
broadsider
contriter
collider
confider
crime-fighter
delighter
delight 'er
divider
decider
defied 'er
denied 'er
elider
firefighter
ghostwriter
ghost rider
highlighter
hang glider
hard cider
insider
inciter
indicter
lamplighter
moonlighter
misguider
misguide 'er
nail biter
outsider
one-nighter
provider
presider
resider
reciter
rough rider
spotlighter
sky writer
seasider
songwriter
subsider
speech writer
typewriter

uprighter
uptighter

apple cider
bareback rider
coincider
freedom fighter
freedom rider
horseback rider
letter writer
overrider
room divider
slip and slider

black widow spider
center divider
mystery writer

ID-ur

bidder
bitter
critter
flitter
fritter
glitter
get 'er
gritter
hitter
jitter
knitter
kidder
litter
pitter
quitter
ridder
sitter
spitter
shitter
slitter
skidder
splitter
skitter
titter
twitter

admitter

acquitter
aglitter
atwitter
bullshitter
consider
corn fritter
clutch hitter
committer
embitter
emitter
forbidder
fence-sitter
hairsplitter
high bidder
low bidder
misfitter
no-hitter
outbidder
outfitter
outwitter
omitter
pinch hitter
permitter
pipe fitter
rebidder
remitter
refitter
rail-splitter
submitter
sidesplitter
transmitter
unfitter
undid 'er

baby-sitter
home-run hitter
kitty litter
orn'ry critter
overbidder
reconsider
underbidder

pick of the litter

designated hitter

ID-ur-āt

iterate
obliterate

ĪD-ur-ē

cidery
nitery
spidery

ID-ur-ē

bittery
flittery
glittery
jittery
pittery
skittery
tittery
twittery

ID-ur-ēng

flittering
frittering
glittering
littering
pittering
skittering
tittering
twittering

considering
embittering

reconsidering

ID-ur-ul

clitoral
literal

ID-ur-us

clitoris
titter us
embitter us

ID-ur-ut

literate
titter it

considerate
illiterate

inconsiderate

ĪD-us

bite us
cite us
chide us
eyed us
fight us
guide us
hide us
knight us
Midas
right us
situs
sight us
spite us
slight us
tried us
write us

arthritis
abide us
bursitis
bronchitis
cystitis
delight us
despite us
excite us
gastritis
ignite us
invite us
incite us
indict us
neuritis
phlebitis
St. Vitus
unite us

dynamite us

dermatitis
extradite us
expedite us
hepatitis
laryngitis
meningitis
reunite us
tonsillitis
tendinitis
underwrite us

appendicitis
conjunctivitis
peritonitis

poliomyelitis

ID-u-siz-um
(See ID-i-siz-um)

ID-ut-ē
(See ID-ud-ē)

ID-ū-ul

assidual
decidual
residual

individual

ID-ū-us

assiduous
deciduous

ĪD-u-wā

bite away
chide away
cried away
died away
guide away
hideaway
lied away
pried away

ride away
right away
right o' way
slide away
stride away
shied away
tried a way

Ī-ēng

buying
crying
drying
dying
eyeing
flying
frying
lying
prying
plying
sighing
spying
tying
trying
vying

applying
blow-drying
belying
complying
deep-frying
decrying
drip-drying
defying
denying
espying
hogtying
implying
replying
relying
supplying
untying

amplifying
beautifying
certifying

calcifying
crucifying
classifying
clarifying
codifying
deifying
dignifying
edifying
falsifying
fortifying
gratifying
glorifying
horrifying
justifying
mortifying
misapplying
mollifying
mystifying
modifying
multiplying
magnifying
mummifying
notifying
nullifying
occupying
ossifying
overbuying
petrifying
pacifying
purifying
putrefying
qualifying
rectifying
ramifying
ratifying
reapplying
sanctifying
signifying
stupefying
satisfying
simplifying
specifying
terrifying
testifying
typifying

underlying
unifying
underbuying
vilifying
verifying

beatifying
declassifying
demystifying
disqualifying
dissatisfying
electrifying
exemplifying
intensifying
indemnifying
identifying
personifying
preoccupying
refortifying
solidifying

Ī-ens
(See Ī-uns)

Ī-ent
(See Ī-unt)

Ī-et
(See Ī-ut)

Ī-et-ē
(See Ī-ud-ē)

ĪF

fife
knife
life
rife
strife
wife

dog's life
ex-wife

fishwife
good life
housewife
high life
jackknife
love life
low-life
midwife
midlife
nightlife
pro life
pen knife
still life
shelf life
true-life
wildlife

afterlife
carving knife
man and wife
pocketknife
right to life
take to wife
way of life

common-law wife
husband and wife
larger-than-life
new lease on life
not on your life

IF

cliff
dif
if
jiff
miff
riff
skiff
sniff
stiff
tiff
whiff

bored stiff
midriff

Radcliffe
scared stiff
what if

frozen stiff
handkerchief
hieroglyph
in a jiff
neckerchief
what's the dif?
working stiff

IF-ē

iffy
jiffy
miffy
spiffy
sniffy
whiffy

in a jiffy

ĪF-el
(See ĪF-ul)

ĪF-en
(See ĪF-un)

IF-en
(See IF-un)

ĪF-ēng

knifing

jackknifing
midwifing

IF-ēng

miffing
sniffing
stiffing

tiffing
whiffing

IF-ik

horrific
pacific
prolific
Pacific
specific
terrific
unific

blue Pacific
beatific
calorific
honorific
hieroglyphic
scientific
saporific
soporific
unspecific

species-specific
unscientific

ĪF-lēng

rifling
stifling
trifling

IF-lēng

piffling
riffling
sniffling

ĪF-lus

knifeless
lifeless
strifeless
wifeless

IF-lus

driftless
giftless
riffless
shiftless
sniffless
whiffless

IFS

cliffs
drifts
gifts
ifs
jiffs
miffs
riffs
rifts
skiffs
stiffs
shifts
sifts
tiffs
whiffs

airlifts
face-lifts
spendthrifts
snowdrifts
shoplifts
ski lifts
uplifts

handkerchiefs
working stiffs

IFT

drift
gift
grift
lift
miffed
rift
swift
shift

sift
sniffed
shrift
stiffed
tiffed
thrift
whiffed

airlift
adrift
chairlift
day shift
face-lift
forklift
gear shift
makeshift
night shift
spendthrift
swing shift
split shift
short shrift
snowdrift
shoplift
stick shift
ski lift
uplift

birthday gift
graveyard shift
get the drift
sure and swift

continental shift

IFT-ē

fifty
nifty
shifty
swifty
thrifty

unthrifty

fifty-fifty

IFT-ēng

drifting
lifting
rifting
shifting
sifting

shoplifting
uplifting
weightlifting

IFT-lus
(See IF-lus)

IFTS
(See IFS)

IFT-ur

drifter
lifter
miffed 'er
snifter
swifter
shifter
sifter
stiffed 'er
sniffed 'er
whiffed 'er

airlifter
flour sifter
forklifter
shoplifter
uplifter
weightlifter

brandy snifter

ĪF-ul

die full
eyeful
Eiffel
rifle

stifle
spryful
trifle

IF-ul

piffle
riffle
skiffle
sniffle

ĪF-un

hyphen
knifin'
syphon

IF-un

miffin'
sniffin'
stiffen
stiffin'
tiffin'
whiffin'

IF-un-ē

Tiffany

Epiphany
polyphony

ĪF-ur

cipher
fifer
knifer
lifer
rifer

decipher
encipher
jackknifer
pro lifer

IF-ur

differ
miff 'er
sniffer
stiffer
tiffer
whiffer

IF-ur-us

coniferous
melliferous
odiferous
proliferous
splendiferous
saliferous
stelliferous
vociferous

ĪF-us

Dreyfuss
knife us
typhus

IG

big
brig
cig
dig
fig
frig
gig
jig
mig
pig
prig
rig
sprig
swig
trig
twig
wig
Whig

zig

bigwig
oil rig
renege
shindig
talk big

care a fig
dance a jig
flip one's wig
guinea pig
make it big
whirligig

chauvinist pig
thingamajig

IG-ē

biggie
ciggy
piggy
twiggy

IG-ēng

digging
frigging
jigging
rigging
swigging

reneging

Ī-glas

eyeglass
spyglass
my glass

IG-lē

giggly
jiggly
squiggly
wiggly
Wrigley

wriggly

piggly wiggly

IG-lēng

giggling
jiggling
niggling
sniggling
squiggling
wiggling
wriggling

IG-lur

giggler
jiggler
niggler
squiggler
wiggler
wriggler

IG-mē

dig me
pygmy
rig me

IG-ment

figment
pigment

IG-mu

sigma
stigma

enigma

IG-nē-us

igneous
ligneous

**IG-ni-fi
(See IG-nu-fi)**

IG-nu-fi

dignify
signify

IG-nunt

benignant
indignant
malignant

IG-ul

giggle
jiggle
niggle
sniggle
squiggle
wiggle
wriggle

IG-um-ē

bigamy
big o' me
trigamy

polygamy

make a pig o' me

IG-u-mist

bigamist

polygamist

ĪG-ur

Geiger
tiger

Braunschweiger

paper tiger

IG-ur

bigger
chigger

digger
figger
frigger
jigger
rigor
rigger
snigger
swigger
trigger
vigor

ditchdigger
doo-jigger
gravedigger
gold digger
hair trigger
outrigger

whiskey jigger
vim and vigor

quick on the trigger
thingamajigger

IG-urd

figgered
niggard
sniggered
swiggered
triggered

IG-ur-ēng

figgering
sniggering
triggering

IG-ur-us

figger us
rigorous
trigger us
vigorous

IG-ut

bigot
dig it
frigate
pig it
rig it
spigot
swig it

IG-ū-us

ambiguous
contiguous

Ī-īd

dry-eyed
pie-eyed

IJ

bridge
fridge
midge
ridge
smidge

abridge
drawbridge
footbridge
refrig
toll bridge

burn one's bridge(s)

IJ-en
(See IJ-un)

IJ-et
(See IJ-ut)

IJ-id

frigid
rigid

IJ-in
(See IJ-un)

IJ-i-nul

original

aboriginal

IJ-it
(See IJ-ut)

IJ-ud
(See IJ-id)

IJ-un

bridgin'
pigeon
pidgin
smidgen
widgeon

abridgin'
clay pigeon
religion
stool pigeon

carrier pigeon
old-time religion

freedom of religion

IJ-un-us

bridgin' us

indigenous

IJ-ur-unt

belligerent
refrigerant

IJ-us

bridge us

litigious

prodigious
prestigious
religious

sacrilegious
irreligious

IJ-ut

bridge it
Bridget
digit
fidget
Gidget
midget

abridge it

double digit

IJ-ū-ul
(See ID-ū-ul)

IJ-ū-us
(See ID-ū-us)

ĪK

bike
dike
hike
Ike
like
mike
pike
psych
shrike
spike
strike
tyke
trike

alike
childlike
catlike
dislike

dreamlike
first strike
godlike
hitchhike
Klondike
lifelike
on strike
outpsych
Third Reich
turnpike
unlike
Van Dyke
warlike

down the pike
go on strike
hunger strike
look-alike
Lucky Strike
ladylike
motorbike
sportsmanlike
sid-down strike
sound alike
tandem bike
take a hike
unalike
wildcat strike

IK

brick
chick
click
crick
dick
flick
hick
kick
lick
nick
pick
prick
Rick
quick
sic

sick
Schick
stick
slick
shtick
tick
tic
trick
thick
wick

airsick
beatnick
big stick
bootlick
broomstick
chopstick
cowlick
Chap Stick
card trick
dik-dik
drop kick
dipstick
drumstick
goldbrick
heartsick
handpick
homesick
hat trick
ice pick
joystick
lipstick
lovesick
nitpick
oil slick
pinprick
place-kick
quick kick
quick trick
rope trick
rainslick
seasick
slapstick
salt lick
St. Nick

sidekick
skin flick
toothpick
triptych
top kick
yardstick

bailiwick
Bolshevik
bone to pick
candlewick
candlestick
dirty trick
double-quick
fiddlestick
finger prick
hockey stick
heretic
lunatic
Moby Dick
nervous tic
politic
pogo stick
Reykjavík
ricky-tick
swizzle stick
waterpick
walking stick

cut to the quick
impolitic
licorice stick
lay it on thick

body politic
short end of the stick

IK-chur

picture
stricture

get the picture
motion picture

ĪK-ē

Mikie
Nike
psyche
spiky

IK-ē

chickie
cliquey
chickee
dickey
gicky
hickey
icky
kicky
mickey
Nicky
picky
quickie
sticky
sickie
tricky
Vicki

doohickey
lime rickey

IK-en
(See IK-un)

IK-en-ēng
(See IK-un-ēng)

ĪK-ēng

biking
hiking
liking
psyching
spiking
striking
Viking

disliking

hitchhiking
outpsyching

motorbiking

IK-ēng

clicking
flicking
kicking
licking
nicking
picking
pricking
sticking
ticking
tricking

ass-kicking
drop-kicking
goldbricking
handpicking
nonsticking
place-kicking
slim picking(s)

finger-licking
take a licking

alive and kicking

IK-et
(See IK-ut)

IK-et-ē
(See IK-ud-ē)

IK-lē

prickly
quickly
sickly
slickly
tickly
thickly

IK-lēng

pickling
prickling
tickling
trickling

bicycling

IK-nus

quickness
sickness
slickness
thickness

ĪKS
(See ĪX)

IKS
(See IX)

IK-sē
(See IX-ē)

IK-shun

diction
fiction
friction
striction

addiction
affliction
constriction
conviction
depiction
eviction
infliction
nonfiction
prediction
restriction

benediction
contradiction

crucifixion
dereliction
drug addiction
interdiction
jurisdiction
prediliction
proper diction
science fiction
valediction

IK-shun-ul

fictional
frictional

jurisdictional

IK-sur
(See IX-ur)

IKT

bricked
clicked
flicked
kicked
licked
nicked
picked
pricked
slicked
strict
ticked
tricked

addict
afflict
conflict
constrict
convict
depict
evict
handpicked
inflict
nitpicked
picnicked

predict
restrict
rain-slicked

contradict
derelict
interdict
overstrict

eggs Benedict

IKT-ēng

addicting
afflicting
conflicting
constricting
convicting
depicting
evicting
inflicting
predicting
restricting

contradicting

IK-tim
(See IK-tum)

IK-tiv

addictive
afflictive
conflictive
constrictive
restrictive
vindictive

contradictive
nonrestrictive

IKTS
(See IX)

IKT-u-bul

addictable
constrictable
convictable
depictable
evictable
inflictable
predictable
restrictable

contradictable
unpredictable

IKT-um

dictum
kicked 'em
licked 'em
picked 'em
tricked 'em
victim

afflict 'em
constrict 'em
convict 'em
depict 'em
evict 'em
handpicked 'em
predict 'em
restrict 'em

contradict 'em

IKT-ur

kicked 'er
licked 'er
picked 'er
pricked 'er
Richter
stricter
tricked 'er
victor

addictor
afflictor
conflictor

constrictor
convictor
depictor
evictor
handpicked 'er
inflictor
predictor
restricter

contradictor

boa constrictor

IKT-ur-ē

victory

benedictory
contradictory
moral victory

ĪK-u

mica
pica

Formica

balalaika

ĪK-u-bul

hikable
likable
spikable
strikable

dislikable
outpsychable
unlikable

IK-u-bul

flickable
kickable
lickable
nickable
prickable
stickable

trickable

applicable
despicable
explicable
handpickable

inexplicable

IK-ud-ē

chickadee
rickety

persnickety

ĪK-ul

cycle
Michael

Carmichael
life cycle
recycle

motorcycle
unicycle

IK-ul

brickle
chicle
fickle
nickel
pickle
prickle
sickle
tickle
trickle

bicycle
big nickel
dill pickle
icicle
popsicle
plug nickel
vehicle

butter brickle

in a pickle
motorcycle
pumpernickel

hammer and sickle

IK-ū-lur

funicular
navicular
particular
vehicular
ventricular

perpendicular

IK-ū-lus

meticulous
ridiculous

IK-um

click 'em
flick 'em
kick 'em
lick 'em
nick 'em
pick 'em
prick 'em
sic 'em
stickum
stick 'em
trick 'em

IK-un

chicken
clickin'
dicken(s)
Dicken(s)
flickin'
kickin'
lickin'
quicken
sicken
stricken

slickin'
stickin'
thicken
trickin'

grief-stricken
love-stricken
nitpickin'
spring chicken
unthicken

cotton pickin'
panic stricken
rubber chicken
terror-stricken

poverty-stricken

IK-un-ēng

quickening
sickening
thickening

IK-up

brick up
flick up
hiccup
kick up
lick up
nick up
pickup
prick up
stick up
slick up

ĪK-ur

biker
hiker
like 'er
piker
spiker
striker

disliker
hitchhiker

outpsych 'er
unlike 'er

hungerstriker

IK-ur

bicker
clicker
dicker
flicker
kicker
licker
liquor
nicker
picker
pricker
quicker
sicker
sticker
slicker
ticker
tricker
thicker
vicar
wicker

ass kicker
bootlicker
drop kicker
goldbricker
heartsicker
homesicker
hard liquor
lovesicker
nitpicker
nose picker
picnicker
place kicker
potlicker
rain slicker
seasicker

bumper sticker
city slicker
cotton picker

cherry picker
garage clicker

IK-ur-ē

bickery
chicory
dickory
flickery
hickory
liquory
stickery
slickery
trickery

Terpsichore

hickory dickory

IK-ur-ēng

bickering
dickering
flickering

ĪK-us

ficus
like us
psych us
strike us
dislike us
outpsych us
unlike us

IK-ut

cricket
flick it
kick it
lick it
nick it
prick it
picket
pick it
ricket(s)
stick it

ticket
thicket
wicket

dropkick it
handpick it
meal ticket
not cricket
placekick it

parking ticket
sticky wicket

lottery ticket

IK-ut-ē
(See IK-ud-ē)

IK-ut-ēng

picketing
ticketing

IK-uts

crickets
pickets
rickets
tickets
thickets
wickets

IK-wi-dē

antiquity
iniquity
ubiquity

IK-wi-tē
(See IK-wi-dē)

IK-yū-lur
(See IK-ū-lur)

ĪL
(See also Ī-ul)

aisle
bile
chil'
dial
file
faille
guile
I'll
isle
mile
Nile
pile
rile
style
stile
smile
tile
trial
vile
while
wile

argyle
agile
awhile
beguile
Carlisle
card file
compile
cross-file
defile
erstwhile
exile
freestyle
gentile
hostile
high style
hair style
in style
lifestyle
last mile
meanwhile
mobile

misfile
nail file
on file
old style
puerile
profile
revile
restyle
reptile
servile
stockpile
senile
slush pile
sandpile
turnstile
woodpile
worthwhile

Anglophile
arctophile
after while
country mile
Cajun style
crocodile
cramp one's style
crack a smile
domicile
down the aisle
family style
Francophile
for a while
infantile
in a while
juvenile
letter file
latest style
mercantile
out of style
peristyle
rank and file
reconcile
single file
unworthwhile
wedding aisle
worth one's while

western style
xenophile

bibliophile
circular file
Emerald Isle
fingernail file
go out of style
mile after mile
nautical mile
once in a while

go the extra mile
in a little while
lay 'em in the aisle(s)

every once in a while

IL

bill
chill
dill
drill
frill
fill
gill
grill
hill
ill
Jill
kill
mill
nil
pill
Phil
quill
rill
still
shrill
sill
spill
swill
shill
skill
till
thrill

twill
'twill
trill
will

at will
anthill
boot hill
be still
boat drill
Brazil
Churchill
distill
downhill
dullsville
freewill
fire drill
fulfill
gin mill
gristmill
goodwill
handbill
instill
ill will
keep still
landfill
mixed grill
molehill
Nashville
Nob Hill
oil spill
pep pill
playbill
quadrille
refill
standstill
sawmill
show bill
splitsville
treadmill
top bill
true bill
until
uphill
vaudeville

windmill

bitter pill
bar and grill
Benadryl
cut and fill
chlorophyll
codicil
coupe de ville
daffodil
degree mill
diet pill
dollar bill
dressed to kill
fit to kill
fill the bill
game of skill
G.I. Bill
Jack and Jill
Jacksonville
Louisville
lumbermill
laetrile
mercantile
mercy kill(ing)
overkill
on the pill
pen and quill
peppermill
rumor mill
shoot to kill
sleeping pill
take a pill
through the mill
windowsill
whippoorwill
water pill

barbecue grill
Beverly Hill(s)
battle of will(s)
Buffalo Bill
Capitol Hill
diploma mill
grist for the mill
king of the hill

license to kill
over the hill
run-of-the-mill
stewed to the gill(s)
two-dollar bill
Treasury bill
vitamin pill

Cecil B. DeMille
green around the
   gill(s)

IL-burt

filbert
Gilbert

ILCH

filch
milch
zilch

ĪLD

aisled
child
dialed
filed
mild
piled
riled
styled
smiled
tiled
whiled
wild

brainchild
beguiled
compiled
cross-filed
defiled
exiled
flower child
godchild
hogwild

lovechild
misfiled
moonchild
misdialed
man-child
reviled
restyled
run wild
Rothschild
self-styled
stepchild
stockpiled
with child

in the wild
Oscar Wilde
reconciled

call of the wild

ILD

build
billed
chilled
dilled
drilled
frilled
filled
guild
gild
grilled
killed
milled
stilled
spilled
shilled
skilled
swilled
tilled
thrilled
trilled
willed

distilled
fulfilled
instilled

ill-willed
rebuild
refilled
strong-willed
treadmilled
unskilled
unfilled
weak-willed

overkilled
overbuild
unfulfilled

ILD-ēng

building
gilding

ĪLD-ish

childish
mildish
wildish

ĪLD-lē

mildly
wildly

ILD-ū

mildew
still do
will do

ĪLD-ur

filed 'er
milder
riled 'er
wilder

defiled 'er
exiled 'er

reconciled 'er

ILD-ur

builder
billed 'er
drilled 'er
filled 'er
gilder
grilled 'er
killed 'er
stilled 'er
thrilled 'er

bewilder
fulfilled 'er
shipbuilder

ĪLD-ust

mildest
wildest

ĪLDZ
(See ĪLZ)

ILDZ
(See ILZ)

Ī-lē

dryly
highly
shyly
smiley
slyly
wryly
Wiley
wily

life of Riley

IL-ē

billy
Billie
chili
Chile

chilly
dilly
filly
frilly
hilly
lily
Millie
silly
shrilly
Tillie
willy

Antille(s)
Achille(s)
Chantilly
hillbilly
unfrilly
unchilly

Easter lily
gild the lily
Piccadilly
piccalilli
silly billy
water lily
willy nilly

gilding the lily

IL-ē-ā-dur

affiliator
conciliator
humiliator

IL-ē-ak

hemophiliac
sacroiliac

IL-ē-āt

affiliate
conciliate
humiliate

IL-ē-ā-tur
(See IL-ē-ā-dur)

ĪL-ēng

dialing
filing
piling
riling
styling
smiling
tiling
wiling

beguiling
compiling
defiling
exiling
misfiling
profiling
reviling
restyling
stockpiling

IL-ēng

billing
Billing(s)
chilling
drilling
filling
grilling
killing
milling
schilling
spilling
swilling
shilling
thrilling
trilling
willing

distilling
fulfilling
God willing
instilling
oil drilling
refilling
top billing
unwilling

mercy killing
self-fulfilling

IL-ē-nus

chilliness
frilliness
silliness

ĪL-et
(See ĪL-ut)

IL-et
(See IL-ut)

IL-ē-un
(See also IL-yun)

Castillian
Churchillian
reptilian
Sicilian
vermillion

IL-ē-unt
(See IL-yunt)

IL-ē-ur

chillier
frillier
hillier
sillier

familiar

unfamiliar

IL-ē-us

bilious
silly us

punctilious

supercilious

IL-ēz

chilis
dillies
fillies
Gillies
lilies
Millie's
willies

Antilles
Achilles
hillbillies

Easter lilies

IL-ful

sylphful
skillful
willful

IL-i-grē
(See IL-u-grē)

IL-ij

pillage
spillage
tillage
village

IL-ik

acrylic
idyllic
umbilic

imbecilic

IL-in
(See IL-un)

ĪL-ist

stylist
vilest

Ī-līt

highlight
I light
my light
skylight
twilight

IL-i-tāt

militate

debilitate
facilitate

rehabilitate

IL-it-ē
(See IL-ud-ē)

ILK

bilk
ilk
milk
silk

corn silk
spilt milk

buttermilk
hit the silk
Liebfraumilch
malted milk
soft as silk

cry over spilt milk

ILK-ē

milky
silky

Wendell Willkie

ILK-ēng

bilking
milking

ILK-un

bilkin'
milkin'
silken

IL-nus

chillness
illness
stillness
shrillness

ĪL-ō

buy low
fly low
high-low
lie low
silo
Shiloh

Venus de Milo

IL-ō

billow
pillow
still low
willow

armadillo
Amarillo
peccadillo
pussy willow
weeping willow

IL-ō-ē

billowy
pillowy
willowy

ĪL-on

nylon
pylon

pile on
smile on

ILT

built
guilt
gilt
hilt
jilt
kilt
lilt
quilt
silt
spilt
stilt
tilt
wilt

atilt
full tilt
hand-quilt
rebuilt
unspilt
unbuilt
well built

crazy quilt
custom-built
do not tilt
jerry-built
out of guilt
patchwork quilt
to the hilt
Vanderbilt

ILT-ē

guilty
lilty
quilty
silty
tilty
wilty

not guilty

ILT-ēng

jilting
lilting
quilting
tilting
wilting

ILT-un

Hilton
liltin'
stilton
tiltin'
wiltin'

ILT-ur

built 'er
filter
jilter
kilter
philter
quilter
spilt 'er
tilter
wilter

hand-quilter
rebuilt 'er

out of kilter

cigarette filter

IL-u

villa

Attila
axilla
chinchilla
cedilla
flotilla
gorilla
guerrilla
manilla
maxilla

megillah
Manila
Priscilla
scintilla
vanilla

sarsaparilla

urban guerrilla

ĪL-ub-ul

dialable
filable
pilable
rilable
stylable
tilable

compilable
defilable
exilable
profilable

reconcilable

irreconcilable

IL-ub-ul

billable
chillable
drillable
fillable
grillable
killable
syllable
spillable
swillable
thrillable
tillable
willable

distillable
fulfillable
instillable
refillable
unfillable

IL-u-dē

agility
ability
civility
docility
facility
fertility
fragility
futility
gentility
hostility
humility
mobility
nobility
senility
servility
sterility
stability
tranquillity
utility
virility

audibility
affability
changeability
capability
credibility
disability
durability
flexibility
fallibility
feasibility
gullibility
inability
infertility
imbecility
instability
liability
plausibility
possibility
probability
sensibility
tangibility
versatility
visibility

viability
workability

accessibility
adaptability
accountability
acceptability
absorbability
admissibility
affordability
alterability
amiability
amicability
applicability
approachability
availability
compatibility
desirability
dependability
incredibility
impossibility
infallibility
inflexibility
insensibility
intangibility
malleability
public utility
responsibility
upward mobility

incompatibility
inevitability
inelegibility

IL-u-grē

filligree
still agree
will agree

ĪL-um

dial 'em
file 'em
pile 'em
rile 'em

style 'em

asylum
beguile 'em
compile 'em
defile 'em
exile 'em
misfile 'em
misdial 'em
revile 'em
restyle 'em
stockpile 'em

reconcile 'em

insane asylum

political asylum

IL-un

billin'
chillin'
drillin'
Dillon
fillin'
grillin'
killin'
millin'
spillin'
swillin'
thrillin'
trillin'
villain
willin'

distillin'
fulfillin'
instillin'
refillin'

Ampicillin
overkillin'
penicillin

ĪL-und

highland
island

Thailand

Long Island
Rhode Island

ĪL-und-ur

highlander
islander

IL-un-us

billin' us
chillin' us
drillin' us
fillin' us
grillin' us
killin' us
thrillin' us
villainous
villainess
willin' us

fulfillin' us

ĪL-ur

dialer
filer
miler
piler
riler
styler
smiler
Tyler
tiler
viler

beguiler
compiler
defiler
exiler
hair styler
misfiler
misdialer
profiler
reviler

restyler
stockpiler

letter filer
reconciler
rank-and-filer

IL-ur

biller
chiller
driller
filler
griller
iller
killer
miller
pillar
stiller
shriller
spiller
swiller
tiller
thriller
triller
willer

distiller
fulfiller
instiller
man killer
painkiller
refiller
stone pillar

chiller-diller
caterpillar
killer-diller
lady-killer
overkiller
Phyllis Diller

IL-ur-ē

Hilary
pillory

auxiliary

ancillary
artillery
distillery

IL-us

bill us
chill us
drill us
fill us
grill us
kill us
Phyllis
thrill us
Willis
will us

fulfill us

amaryllis

ĪL-ut

dial it
file it
eyelet
pilot
pile it
rile it
style it
tile it

beguile it
co-pilot
compile it
cross-file it
defile it
exile it
misfile it
misdial it
profile it
revile it
restyle it
stockpile it
test pilot

gyropilot

reconcile it

automatic pilot

IL-ut

billet
bill it
chill it
drill it
fill it
fillet
grill it
kill it
skillet
swill it
thrill it
will it

distill it
instill it
refill it

IL-u-tāt
(See IL-i-tāt)

IL-u-tōr-ē

dilatory

depilatory

IL-yun

billion
million
skillion
trillion
zillion

Brazilian
Castilian
civilian
cotillion
Churchillian
pavilion
quadrillion

reptilian
septillion
Sicilian
sextillion
tourbillion
vermilion

Maximilian

one in a million

IL-yunt

brilliant

resilient

IL-yur
(See IL-ē-ur)

IL-yus
(See IL-ē-us)

ĪLZ

aisles
child's
dials
files
guiles
isles
miles
piles
riles
styles
stiles
smiles
tiles
trials
wilds
wiles

beguiles
compiles
cross-files
defiles

exiles
hair styles
lifestyles
misfiles
profiles
reviles
restyles
reptiles
stockpiles
sandpiles
turnstiles
woodpiles

crocodiles
domiciles
Francophiles
in the wilds
juveniles
reconciles
xenophiles

bibliophiles
nautical miles

lay 'em in the aisles

ILZ

bills
builds
chills
drills
frills
fills
gills
gilds
grills
hills
ills
kills
mills
pills
Phils
quills
rills
stills
sills

spills
swills
shills
skills
thrills
trills
wills

anthills
boat drills
Catskills
distills
fire drills
fulfills
gin mills
handbills
instills
no frills
oil spills
pep pills
rebuilds
refills
sawmills
treadmills
true bills
windmills

coupe de villes
daffodils
degree mills
diet pills
dollar bills
lumbermills
overbuilds
overkills
sleeping pills
whippoorwills

Beverly Hills
battle of wills
stewed to the gills
vitamin pills

green around the gills

ĪM

chime
crime
clime
climb
dime
grime
I'm
lime
mime
prime
rhyme
rime
slime
time
thyme

bigtime
bedtime
daytime
enzyme
full-time
hard time
high time
halftime
ill-time(d)
keep time
kill time
lifetime
lead time
lunchtime
meantime
make time
mark time
nighttime
naptime
noontime
old-time
playtime
pastime
prime time
post time
part-time
peacetime
ragtime

sublime
showtime
springtime
sometime
sack time
small-time
tell time
two-time
waltz time
well-time(d)
wartime
war crime

anytime
aforetime
beforetime
Christmastime
curtain time
dinnertime
double-time
doorbell chime
every time
equal time
Father Time
five and dime
Guggenheim
high old time
in good time
in no time
maritime
mountain climb
Miller time
nick of time
one thin dime
one more time
overtime
play for time
pantomime
summertime
suppertime
stitch in time
take one's time
wintertime

all in good time
every time

from time to time
many a time
nursery rhyme
nickel-and-dime
one at a time
partners in crime
stop on a dime
time after time

ahead of one's time
daylight savings time
once upon a time
once in a lifetime

IM

brim
dim
grim
him
hymn
Jim
Kim
limb
prim
rim
slim
skim
swim
Tim
trim
vim
whim

horn-rim(med)
prelim

autonym
acronym
antonym
cherubim
homonym
pseudonym
synonym
seraphim
sink or swim

fill to the rim
out on a limb
tear limb from limb

IMB-ō

bimbo
kimbo
limbo

akimbo
in limbo

IM-bul

cymbal
nimble
symbol
thimble
timbale

sex symbol

phallic symbol
status symbol

IMB-ur

limber
timbre
timber

IMB-ur-lē

Kimberly
limberly

IMD

brimmed
dimmed
rimmed
slimmed
skimmed
trimmed

horn-rimmed

ĪM-ē

by me
blimey
buy me
eye me
fly me
fry me
grimy
limey
ply me
rhymy
rimy
stymie
slimy
spry me
shy me
sly me
spy me
tie me
try me
why me

defy me
deny me
hogtie me
run by me
stand by me
sneak by me
slip by me
untie me

alibi me
beautify me
crucify me
classify me
fortify me
gratify me
glorify me
horrify me
justify me
mortify me
mystify me
notify me
nullify me
petrify me

pacify me
qualify me
satisfy me
specify me
terrify me
vilify me

declassify me
disqualify me
dissatisfy me
electrify me
identify me
personify me
preoccupy me
refortify me

IM-ē

gimme
jimmy
shimmy

**ĪM-en
(See ĪM-un)**

**IM-en
(See IM-un)**

ĪM-ēng

chiming
climbing
miming
priming
rhyming
timing

two-timing

IM-ēng

brimming
dimming
rimming
slimming
skimming

swimming
trimming

ĪM-ē-nus

griminess
liminess
sliminess

**IM-est
(See IM-ust)**

**IM-e-trē
(See IM-u-trē)**

**IM-e-tur
(See IM-u-dur)**

IM-ē-un

jimmyin'
Simian
Simeon
shimmyin'

IMF

lymph
nymph

IM-ij

image
scrimmage

football scrimmage
spitting image

IM-ik

gimmick
mimic

bulimic

IM-ik-rē

gimmickry
mimicry

**IM-il-ē
(See IM-ul-ē)**

**IM-in-āt
(See IM-un-āt)**

**IM-in-ul
(See IM-un-ul)**

**IM-it
(See IM-ut)**

IM-i-tā-shun

imitation
limitation

**IM-it-ē
(See IM-ud-ē)**

ĪM-lē

timely

sublimely
untimely

IM-lē

dimly
grimly
primly
slimly

IM-nus

dimness
grimness
primness

slimness
trimness

IMP

blimp
crimp
chimp
gimp
imp
limp
pimp
primp
simp
shrimp
skimp
wimp

IMP-ē

blimpy
gimpy
shrimpy
skimpy
wimpy

IMP-ēng

crimping
limping
pimping
primping
skimping

IMP-lē

crimply
dimply
limply
pimply
simply

IMP-lēng

crimpling
dimpling
rimpling

IMPS

blimps
crimps
chimps
glimpse
imps
limps
pimps
primps
simps
shrimps
skimps
wimps

IMP-tum

crimped 'em
pimped 'em
symptom

IMP-ul

crimple
dimple
pimple
rimple
simple
wimple

goose pimple

plain and simple

IMP-ur

crimper
gimper
limper
primper
pimper
simper
skimper
whimper

IMP-ur-ēng

simpering
whimpering

IM-ud-ē

proximity

anonymity
equanimity
magnanimity
inanimity

IM-ud-ur

limiter
scimitar

perimeter

IM-uk
(See IM-ik)

IM-uk-rē
(See IM-ik-rē)

IM-ūl-āt

simulate
stimulate

IM-ul-ē

simile

facsimile

IM-ū-lunt

simulant
stimulant

ĪM-un

chimin'
climbin'

hymen
mimin'
primin'
rhymin'
Simon
timin'
Wyman

two-timin'

pantomimin'
Simple Simon

nickel-and-dimin'

IM-un

brimmin'
dimmin'
lemon
rimmin'
skimmin'
slimmin'
Simmon(s)
swimmin'
trimmin'
women

persimmon

men and women

IM-un-āt

discriminate
eliminate
recriminate

IM-un-ul

criminal
women'll

subliminal

ĪM-ur

chimer
climber

mimer
primer
rhymer
timer

Alzheimer(s)
egg timer
old-timer
sublimer

mountain climber
Oppenheimer
pantomimer
social climber
wisenheimer

IM-ur

dimmer
grimmer
glimmer
primmer
primer
rimmer
simmer
shimmer
slimmer
skimmer
swimmer
trimmer

light dimmer
tree trimmer

IM-ur-ēng

glimmering
simmering
shimmering

IM-us

dim us
grimace
slim us
trim us

ĪM-ust

I must
primest
rhymist

sublimest

pantomimist

IM-ust

dimmest
grimaced
grimmest
primmest
slimmest
trimmest

ĪM-ut

climate
climb it
prime it
rhyme it
time it

IM-ut

dim it
limit
rim it
skim it
slim it
swim it
trim it

speed limit
untrim it

go the limit
three-mile limit

IM-ut-ē
(See IM-ud-ē)

IM-u-trē

symmetry
trim a tree

asymmetry

IM-u-tur
(See IM-u-dur)

IM-utz

limits
Nimitz

IM-yū-lāt
(See IM-ū-lāt)

ĪMZ

chimes
crimes
climes
climbs
dimes
limes
mimes
primes
rhymes
times

bedtimes
enzymes
hard times
lifetimes
lunchtimes
naptimes
pastimes
two-times
windchimes
war crimes

betweentimes
oftentimes
pantomimes
party times

behind the times
nursery rhymes

IMZ

brims
dims
hymns
Jim's
limbs
rims
slims
skims
swims
trims
whims

prelims

acronyms
antonyms
cherubims
homonyms
pseudonyms
synonyms
seraphims
sinks or swims

IM-zē

flimsy
whimsy

ĪN

brine
dine
fine
Klein
line
mine
nine
pine
Rhine
spine
stein
sine

sign
shine
swine
shrine
tine
thine
twine
vine
whine
wine

all mine
A-line
assign
align
alpine
airline
beeline
bloodline
back nine
Bernstein
bustline
benign
byline
bovine
baseline
clothesline
canine
chow line
cloud nine
coastline
combine
confine
consign
co-sign
carbine
coal mine
cruiseline
decline
divine
define
design
deadline
dateline
Einstein

equine
enshrine
entwine
front nine
feline
fine line
frown line
front line
food line
fish line
goal line
gold mine
guideline
grapevine
high sign
headline
hemline
hot line
hard line
hairline
incline
lifeline
laugh line
land mine
moonshine
main line
malign
May wine
neckline
opine
outline
outshine
old-line
on-line
pipeline
punch line
plumb line
phone line
peace sign
quinine
red wine
recline
refine
resign

redline
Rhine wine
sunshine
stag line
stop sign
supine
strychnine
sideline
skyline
streamline
shoeshine
sun sign
salt mine
turbine
trunk line
tow line
white wine

alkaline
asinine
aquiline
Auld Lang Syne
bottom line
by design
borderline
calamine
conga line
countersign
credit line
concubine
county line
columbine
color line
clinging vine
checkout line
disentwine
down the line
disincline
draw the line
drop a line
danger sign
dotted line
dollar sign
Frankenstein

form a line
first in line
fishing line
finish line
free-throw line
fall in line
firing line
hold the line
intertwine
iodine
knotty pine
leonine
Liechtenstein
monkeyshine
out of line
on the line
porcupine
Palestine
picket line
private line
party line
redesign
rain or shine
realign
rise and shine
royal line
storyline
same old line
shipping line
scrimmage line
saturnine
turpentine
traffic fine
timberline
toe the line
undermine
underline
unrefine(d)
undersign
vintage wine
valentine
wine and dine
wait in line
water sign

warning sign
yours and mine

above the line
assembly line
end of the line
electric line
fifty-yard line
receiving line
top-of-the-line
victory sign

lay it on the line
Mason-Dixon line

where the sun doesn't
   shine

IN

bin
been
chin
din
fin
Flynn
gin
grin
in
inn
kin
men
pin
sin
shin
skin
spin
tin
thin
twin
win
yin

all in
aspen
akin
agrin

again
begin
built-in
butt in
bearskin
Berlin
buckskin
break-in
blend in
cash in
close-in
chin-chin
check-in
coonskin
chagrin
cave-in
come in
Corryn
do in
drive-in
dig in
din-din
foreskin
give in
herein
hairpin
has-been
he-men
hang in
hat pin
horn in
kingpin
kidskin
live-in
linchpin
moleskin
move in
no-win
pigskin
run-in
shut-in
straight pin
shoo-in
stickpin
snakeskin

sidespin
sit-in
sealskin
swimfin
stand-in
sharkskin
sheepskin
tailspin
trade-in
thick skin
therein
turn in
tune in
trash bin
thin skin
topspin
unpin
wherein
within
weigh in
write-in
wear thin
walk-in

born again
bowling pin
bobbypin
bathtub gin
discipline
deadly sin
double chin
Gunga Din
Ho Chi Minh
in a spin
kith and kin
live in sin
Lohengrin
lapel pin
loony bin
might have been
mandolin
mortal sin
Mickey Finn
muffin tin
muscle in

next of kin
onionskin
on the chin
on-again
off-again
peregrine
play to win
paraffin
paper-thin
pull the pin
rolling pin
Rin Tin Tin
safety pin
save one's skin
swearing-in
shirttail kin
thick or thin
three wise men
underpin
ultrathin
violin
wafer-thin

fraternal twin
guilty as sin
Holiday Inn
now and again
neat as a pin
over again
Rumpelstiltskin
self-discipline
Siamese twin
time and again
through thick and thin
ugly as sin
under one's skin

Huckleberry Finn
identical twin
original sin
take it on the chin
time and time again

INCH

cinch
clinch

finch
flinch
inch
lynch
pinch
squinch
winch

bullfinch
goldfinch
unflinch(ing)

in a clinch
in a pinch
in the clinch(es)
inch by inch
lead-pipe cinch
Merrill Lynch
penny-pinch

not give an inch

INCH-ē

cinchy
pinchy

da Vinci

INCH-ēng

cinching
clinching
flinching
inching
lynching
pinching

unflinching

penny-pinching

INCH-ur

cincher
clincher
flincher
incher
lyncher

pincher

waist cincher

penny-pincher

ĪND

bind
blind
dined
fined
find
grind
hind
kind
lined
mined
mind
pined
rind
signed
twined
wined
wind
whined

assigned
A-lined
aligned
behind
broadmind(ed)
consigned
confined
combined
co-signed
declined
duck blind
divined
defined
designed
entwined
enshrined
fact-find
fault-find
headlined
inclined

mankind
maligned
moonshined
opined
outlined
reclined
redlined
remind
refined
resigned
snow-blind
self-wind
sidelined
streamlined
unwind
unbind
unkind

bacon rind
blow one's mind
bump and grind
color-blind
change of mind
call to mind
cross one's mind
countersigned
disentwined
disinclined
fall behind
frame of mind
humankind
intertwined
in a bind
keep in mind
lemon rind
mastermind
never mind
overwind
one-track mind
open mind
on one's mind
peace of mind
redesigned
realigned
speak one's mind

undermined
unrefined
underlined
womankind
wined and dined

boggle the mind
come from behind
four of a kind
legally blind
marrying kind
make up one's mind
one of a kind
out of one's mind
presence of mind
piece of one's mind
two of a kind
Venetian blind

IND

chinned
grinned
pinned
sinned
skinned
thinned
wind

abscind
break wind
chagrined
downwind
headwind
rescind
thick-skinned
tradewind
tailwind
thin-skinned
unpinned
whirlwind
woodwind

bag of wind
double-chinned
disciplined
second wind

underpinned

gone with the wind

three sheets to the
     wind

IND-ē

Cindy
Indy
lindy
windy

ĪND-ed
(See ĪND-ud)

IND-ed
(See IND-ud)

ĪND-ēng

binding
blinding
minding
winding

reminding
self-winding
unwinding
unbinding

masterminding
overwinding

IND-ēng

winding

abscinding
rescinding

IND-i-kāt

indicate
syndicate

vindicate

contraindicate

ĪND-lē

blindly
kindly

unkindly

IND-lē

dwindly
Lindley
spindly

IND-lēng

dwindling
kindling
pindling
swindling

rekindling

ĪND-nus

blindness
kindness

night blindness
snowblindness
unkindness

colorblindness

ĪND-ud

blinded
minded

broadminded
reminded

masterminded

IND-ud

winded

abscinded

longwinded
rescinded

IND-ul

bindle
dwindle
kindle
swindle
spindle

rekindle

ĪND-ur

binder
blinder
dined 'er
fined 'er
finder
grinder
kinder
minder
signed 'er
wined 'er
winder

assigned 'er
behind 'er
bookbinder
confined 'er
designed 'er
entwined 'er
faultfinder
meat grinder
maligned 'er
pathfinder
reminder
range finder
rewinder
sidelined 'er
self-winder
sidewinder
spellbinder
unwinder
unkinder

unbinder
view finder

bump-and-grinder
coffee grinder
masterminder
minute minder
overwinder
organ grinder
undermined 'er
wined and dined 'er

IND-ur

cinder
hinder
pinned 'er
tinder

rescinder
unpinned 'er

disciplined 'er

ĪN-ē

briny
heinie
piny
spiny
shiny
signee
tiny
twiny
viny
whiny

IN-ē

any
guinea
Ginny
many
Minnie
mini
ninny
shinny

skinny
tinny
whinny

New Guinea

ignominy
micromini
Ol' Virginny
one too many

IN-en
(See IN-un)

ĪN-ēng

dining
fining
mining
pining
signing
shining
twining
vining
whining
wining

assigning
aligning
combining
confining
consigning
co-signing
declining
divining
defining
designing
enshrining
headlining
inclining
maligning
opining
outlining
outshining
reclining
refining

resigning
redlining
sidelining
streamlining

countersigning
disentwining
disinclining
intertwining
redesigning
realigning
undermining
underlining

wining and dining

interior designing

IN-ēng

chinning
grinning
inning
pinning
sinning
skinning
thinning
winning

beginning
ninth inning
unpinning

disciplining
underpinning

I-nes
(See I-nus)

IN-et
(See IN-ut)

IN-ē-u
(See IN-yu)

IN-ē-ul

lineal
pineal

IN-ē-um

delphinium

condominium

IN-ē-un

Finian
shinnyin'
whinnyin'

Darwinian
Justinian
Virginian

Carolinian
West Virginian

ĪN-ē-ur

brinier
spinier
shinier
vinier

IN-ē-ur

linear
shinnier
skinnier
tinnier

IN-ful

binful
been full
grinful
sinful

ING
(See ĒNG)

ĪN-ī

Illini
Mt. Sinai

Cedars-Sinai

IN-ik

cynic
clinic

IN-i-kul
(See In-u-kul)

ĪN-ish

chinnish
finish
Finnish
thinnish
tinnish

diminish
refinish

photo finish

IN-ish-ēng

finishing

diminishing
refinishing

IN-ist
(See IN-ust)

IN-ist-ur

minister
sinister

administer
prime minister

IN-it-ē
(See IN-ud-ē)

IN-i-tiv
(See IN-u-div)

INJ

binge
cringe
dinge
fringe
hinge
singe
tinge
twinge

impinge
infringe
syringe
unhinge

lunatic fringe

INJ-ē

bingy
dingy
fringy
mingy
stingy

INJ-ēng

binging
cringing
fringing
hinging
singeing
twinging
impinging
infringing
unhinging

INJ-in
(See INJ-un)

INJ-ment

impingement
infringement

INJ-un

bingin'
cringin'
engine
hingin'
singein'
twingin'

impingin'
infringin'
steam engine
unhingin'

Honest Injun

INJ-unt

stringent

astringent
contingent

INJ-ur

binger
cringer
ginger
hinger
injure
singer
twinger .

impinger
infringer
unhinger

INK
(See ĒNK)

IN-kum

income
men come

ĪN-lē

finely
finally

benignly
divinely
felinely
supinely

asininely
superfinely
saturninely

IN-lē

Finley
spindly
thinly

McKinley

IN-lund

Finland
inland

ĪN-lus

spineless
signless
vineless
wineless

sunshineless
skylineless

IN-lus

chinless
ginless
grinless

ĪN-ment

assignment
alignment
confinement
consignment

entwinement
enshrinement
malignment
refinement

realignment

solitary confinement

ĪN-ō

rhino
wino

albino

IN-ō

minnow
winnow

INS

blintze
chintz
dints
flints
glints
hints
lints
mints
mince
prints
prince
quince
quints
rinse
sprints
stints
since
tints
wince

blueprints
cheese blintz
crown prince
convince
evince

footprints
handprints
hair rinse
imprints
misprints
reprints
skinflints
spearmints
shin splints
voice prints

dinner mints
ever since
fingerprints
fairy prince
peppermints

INS-ē

chintzy
quinsy
Quincy

INS-ēng

mincing
rinsing
wincing

convincing
evincing

INS-i-bul
(See INS-u-bul)

INS-i-dens

incidence

coincidence

INS-ik

extrinsic
intrinsic

INST

minced
rinsed
winced

against
convinced
evinced

INST-ur

rinsed 'er
spinster

against 'er
convinced 'er
Westminster

INS-u-bul

rinsable
winceable

convinceable
invincible

INS-u-duns
(See INS-i-dens)

INS-ul-ur

insular

peninsular

INS-um

been some
chin some
grin some
in some
pin some
sin some
spin some
thin some
winsome
win some

begin some
within some

INT

dint
flint
glint
hint
lint
mint
print
quint
stint
splint
squint
sprint
tint
blueprint
fine print
footprint
handprint
imprint
misprint
newsprint
reprint
skinflint
small print
spearmint
varmint
fingerprint
out-of-print
peppermint
U.S. Mint

INT-ē

glinty
linty
minty
squinty

INT-ēng

glinting
hinting

minting
printing
splinting
squinting
sprinting
tinting

imprinting
misprinting
reprinting

fingerprinting

INTH

plinth

absinthe
Corinth

hyacinth
labyrinth

INT-ij

mintage
vintage

INT-ō

pinto
Shinto

San Jacinto

INT-rē

entry
wintry

INTS
(See INS)

INTS-ē
(See INS-ē)

INT-u-bul

hintable
mintable
printable
tintable

unprintable

INT-un

glintin'
hintin'
mintin'
printin'
squintin'
sprintin'
tintin'
Vinton

badminton
blueprintin'
imprintin'
misprintin'
reprintin'

fingerprintin'

INT-ur

enter
hinter
minter
printer
splinter
squinter
sprinter
tinter
winter

blueprinter
imprinter
misprinter
midwinter
reprinter

dead of winter
do not enter
fingerprinter

IN-tur-ēng

entering
splintering
wintering

IN-tur-um

enter 'em
interim
splinter 'em

IN-ū

been you
in you
pin you
sinew
spin you
win you

continue
within you

discontinue

ĪN-u

China
Dinah
myna

angina
vagina

Indochina

North Carolina
South Carolina

ĪN-u-bul

finable
minable
signable
shinable

assignable
combinable

confinable
declinable
definable
designable
entwinable
enshrinable
malignable
outlinable
outshinable
reclinable
refinable

disentwinable
intertwinable
indefinable
redesignable
realignable
underminable
unassignable

IN-u-bul

pinnable
skinnable
spinnable
winnable

beginnable

disciplinable

IN-u-dē

finity
trinity

affinity
divinity
infinity
vicinity
virginity

asininity
femininity
masculinity

IN-u-div

definitive
infinitive

split infinitive

IN-uk
(See IN-ik)

IN-u-kul

binnacle
clinical
cynical
pinnacle

ĪN-ul

final
rhinal
spinal
vinyl

semifinal
Smart and Final

ĪN-ul-ē

finally
spinally
whinily

IN-u-mu

cinema
enema

IN-un

chinnin'
grinnin'
linen
pinnin'
sinnin'
spinnin'
skinnin'

winnin'

beginnin'
McKinnon
unpinnin'

disciplinin'
underpinnin'

air one's dirty linen

ĪN-ur

diner
finer
liner
miner
minor
piner
Reiner
signer
shiner
Shriner
twiner
whiner

A-liner
assigner
aligner
airliner
beeliner
benigner
baseliner
combiner
check signer
confiner
consignor
co-signer
coal miner
cruiseliner
decliner
diviner
definer
designer
enshriner
eyeliner
entwiner

gold miner
headliner
incliner
jetliner
moonshiner
maligner
opiner
outliner
outshiner
one-liner
recliner
refiner
resigner
sideliner
supiner
shoeshiner
shelf liner
streamliner

Asia Minor
asininer
countersigner
disentwiner
forty-niner
hair designer
intertwiner
ocean liner
redesigner
realigner
rise-and-shiner
undersigner
Ursa Minor
underminer
underliner
wine-and-diner

luxury liner

IN-ur

chinner
dinner
grinner
inner
pinner
sinner

skinner
spinner
thinner
winner

born winner
Berliner
beginner
mule skinner
paint thinner
prizewinner
tailspinner
unpinner

after dinner
born againer
discipliner
TV dinner
underpinner

ĪN-ur-ē

binary
dinery
finery
vinery
winery

refinery

IN-ur-jē

energy
synergy

asynergy

Ī-nus

dryness
dine us
fine us
highness
Linus
minus
nighness
spryness
shyness

slyness
sinus
sign us

assign us
Aquinas
align us
combine us
confine us
decline us
design us
define us
enshrine us
entwine us
malign us
outshine us
red-eyeness
refine us
sideline us
streamline us
your highness

disentwine us
intertwine us
plus or minus
redesign us
undermine us
wine and dine us

ĪN-ust

finest

divinest

asininest

IN-ust

thinnest

violinist

IN-ut

been it
chin it
in it

minute
pin it
skin it
spin it
spinnet
win it

begin it
has been it
last minute
one minute
unpin it
within it

discipline it
in a minute
just a minute
might have been it
play to win it
underpin it

up-to-the-minute

IN-u-tē
(See IN-u-dē)

IN-ū-us

sinuous

continuous

discontinue us

IN-yū
(See IN-ū)

IN-yu

been ya
in ya
win ya
zinnia

Sardinia
Virginia

West Virginia

IN-yun

minion
pinion

dominion
opinion
Virginian

Old Dominion
rack and pinion
West Virginian

public opinion

IN-yū-us
(See IN-ū-us)

ĪNZ

binds
dines
blinds
fines
finds
grinds
Heinz
kinds
lines
mines
minds
pines
rinds
spines
steins
signs
shines
shrines
tines
twines
vines
whines
winds
wines

all kinds
assigns

aligns
airlines
behinds
bloodlines
bustlines
bylines
canines
combines
confines
consigns
co-signs
coal mines
cruiselines
declines
divines
defines
designs
deadlines
enshrines
entwines
felines
faultfinds
fine lines
guidelines
headlines
hemlines
hairlines
inclines
lifelines
land mines
maligns
necklines
opines
outlines
outshines
pipelines
punch lines
reclines
reminds
refines
resigns
redlines
sidelines
skylines
streamlines

shoeshines
unwinds

countersigns
concubines
columbines
color lines
clinging vines
disentwines
danger signs
intertwines
masterminds
monkeyshines
overwinds
porcupines
picket lines
redesigns
realigns
storylines
undermines
underlines
vital signs
valentines
wines and dines
warning signs

dressed to the nines
read between the lines

INZ

bins
chins
fins
gins
grins
inns
pins
sins
shins
skins
spins
tins
twins
winds
wins

begins
built-ins
bearskins
drive-ins
hairpins
run-ins
rescinds
shut-ins
shoo-ins
sit-ins
swimfins
stand-ins
sheepskins
trade-ins
tradewinds
tailwinds
unpins
whirlwinds
woodwinds

bobby pins
disciplines
double chins
loony bins
might-have-beens
mandolins
Mickey Finns
peregrines
violins

fraternal twins
Holiday Inns
Siamese twins

seven deadly sins

Ī-ō

bio
I owe
my, oh

Ohio
Tamayo

Ī-on

cry on
die on
fly on
high on
ion
lie on
nigh on
spy on
tie on
try on

rely on

keep an eye on
malathion

Ī-ō-wu

Iowa
Kiowa

ĪP

gripe
hype
pipe
ripe
stripe
swipe
snipe
tripe
type
wipe

blood type
blowpipe
bagpipe
drain pipe
hand-wipe
pitch pipe
pinstripe
peace pipe
retype
sideswipe
stovepipe

tintype
tailpipe
unripe
windpipe

archetype
guttersnipe
Handi Wipe
linotype
overripe
prototype
stenotype
teletype
underripe
waterpipe
yellow stripe

daguerreotype
electrotype
media hype
stereotype

IP

blip
chip
clip
dip
drip
flip
grip
grippe
gyp
hip
lip
nip
pip
quip
rip
sip
skip
scrip
slip
strip
ship
snip

tip

trip

whip

zip

airstrip

airship

bean dip

blue chip

bullwhip

catnip

cowslip

cow chip

courtship

cruise ship

deanship

drag strip

equip

fat lip

film clip

field trip

flagship

friendship

guilt trip

horsewhip

hot tip

hairclip

hardship

harelip

handgrip

half-slip

head trip

jump ship

judgeship

kinship

lordship

let slip

midship

outstrip

pink slip

power trip

Q-Tip

round trip

roach clip

steamship

spaceship

sheepdip

sideslip

side trip

township

troopship

unzip

warship

wingtip

authorship

brinkmanship

business trip

battleship

bite one's lip

censorship

crack the whip

curl one's lip

chairmanship

chocolate chip

comic strip

chips and dip

chancellorship

comradeship

craftsmanship

clipper ship

double-dip

ego trip

fellowship

fingertip

filter tip

Gaza Strip

give the slip

gamesmanship

horsemanship

internship

ladyship

lose one's grip

leadership

landing strip

microchip

membership

overtip

ownership

paper clip

pistol-whip

partnership

penmanship

poker chip

pillow slip

pirate ship

party whip

rocket ship

salesmanship

showmanship

silvertip

scholarship

stewardship

sponsorship

sportsmanship

statesmanship

seamanship

skinny-dip

Sunset Strip

trusteeship

take a dip

take a sip

underslip

undertip

weatherstrip

acquaintanceship

apprenticeship

button one's lip

bargaining chip

citizenship

computer chip

championship

companionship

dictatorship

Freudian slip

guardianship

good sportsmanship

one-upmanship

potato chip

partisanship

postnasal drip

run a tight ship

shoot from the hip

stiff upper lip

your ladyship

distributorship

IP-ē

bippy
blippy
chippy
dippy
drippy
flippy
hippie
lippy
nippy
quippy
skippy
snippy
tippy
yippie
yippee
zippy

catnippy
Xanthippe

Mississippi

ĪP-ēng

griping
hyping
piping
swiping
sniping
striping
typing
wiping

retyping
sideswiping

IP-ēng

blipping
chipping
clipping
dipping

dripping
flipping
gripping
gypping
nipping
quipping
ripping
sipping
skipping
slipping
stripping
shipping
snipping
tipping
tripping
whipping
zipping

equipping
horsewhipping
outstripping
unzipping

overtipping
pistol-whipping
undertipping

newspaper clipping

IP-ē-nus

dippiness
drippiness
hippiness
nippiness
snippiness
yippiness

IP-et
(See IP-ut)

IP-et-ē
(See IP-ud-ē)

IP-ē-unt

insipient
incipient
percipient
recipient

IP-ij

clippage
rippage
shippage
slippage

ĪP-ist
(See ĪP-ust)

IP-it-ē
(See IP-ud-ē)

IP-lēng

crippling
Kipling
rippling
stripling
stippling
tippling
tripling

IP-let
(See IP-lut)

IP-lur

crippler
rippler
tippler
tripler
stippler

IP-lut

driplet
riplet
triplet

IP-ment

shipment

equipment

ĪP-ō

hypo

typo

IP-on

clip-on
drip on
Nippon
sip on
skip on
slip on
snip on
tip on
trip on

ĪPS

gripes
hypes
pipes
stripes
swipes
snipes
types
wipes

blowpipes
bagpipes
drain pipes
pitchpipes
retypes
sideswipes
tailpipes
windpipes

archetypes
guttersnipes
Handiwipes
prototypes
Stars and Stripes

IPS

blips
chips
clips
dips
drips
flips
grips
gyps
hips
lips
nips
pips
quips
rips
sips
skips
slips
strips
ships
snips
tips
trips
whips
zips

airships
bean dips
blue chips
catnips
chapped lips
courtships
cowslips
cow chips
cruise ships
equips
eclipse
fat lips
field trips
friendships
flagships
hot lips
horsewhips
hardships
harelips

handgrips
kinships
lordships
outstrips
parsnips
Q-tips
read lips
steamships
sheepdips
townships
unzips
warships
worships
wingtips

amidships
business trips
battleships
comic strips
censorships
chocolate chips
chips and dips
ego trips
fellowships
fingertips
fish and chips
filter tips
internships
ladyships
lick one's lips
landing strips
memberships
microchips
ownerships
overtips
paper clips
partnerships
pistol whips
poker chips
pillow slips
scholarships
smack one's lips
swivel-hips
sponsorships
trusteeships

underslips
undertips
weatherstrips

apocalypse
acquaintanceships
apprenticeships
citizenships
computer chips
championships
dictatorships
Freudian slips
guardianships
lunar eclipse
potato chips
postnasal drips
stiff upper lips
solar eclipse

IPS-ē

gypsy
tipsy

Poughkeepsie

IP-shun

ascription
conniption
conscription
description
Egyptian
inscription
prescription
proscription
subscription
transcription

circumscription
resubscription

oversubscription

IP-sō

ipso
quip so

slip so
tip so

calypso

IP-stik

dip stick
lipstick

IP-stur

hipster
tipster

ĪPT

griped
hyped
piped
striped
sniped
swiped
typed
wiped

retyped
sideswiped

stereotyped

IPT

blipped
clipped
chipped
crypt
dipped
dripped
flipped
gypped
gripped
lipped
nipped
quipped
ripped
script
slipped

sipped
snipped
skipped
shipped
stripped
tipped
tripped
whipped
zipped

big-hipped
conscript
equipped
fat-lipped
harelipped
hand-dipped
horsewhipped
outstripped
postscript
tight-lipped
transcript
unzipped
unclipped

filter-tipped
movie script
manuscript
nondescript
overtipped
pussy-whipped
pistol-whipped
undertipped
weatherstripped

IPT-ik

cryptic
stypic

elliptic

apocalyptic

IPT-iv

ascriptive
descriptive

inscriptive
prescriptive
proscriptive
subscriptive
transcriptive

nondescriptive

IPT-us

clipped us
gypped us
gripped us
script us
slipped us
skipped us
shipped us
stripped us
tipped us
tripped us
whipped us

equipped us
unzipped us

eucalyptus
overtipped us
pistol-whipped us
undertipped us

IP-ud-ē

bippity
clippety
hippity
snippety

serendipity

IP-ul

cripple
nipple
ripple
tipple
triple

IP-ūl-āt

stipulate

manipulate

ĪP-und

ripened
stipend

ĪP-ur

diaper
griper
hyper
kiper
piper
riper
swiper
sniper
typer
viper
wiper

bagpiper
pied piper
retyper
sideswiper
sandpiper

windshield wiper

stereotyper

IP-ur

clipper
chipper
dipper
dripper
flipper
gripper
kipper
nipper
quipper
ripper
sipper

skipper
slipper
shipper
stripper
tipper
tripper
whipper
yipper
zipper

Big Dipper
equipper
glass slipper
horsewhipper
hairclipper
house slipper
outstripper
unzipper
Yom Kippur

bedroom slipper
double-dipper
Jack the Ripper
little nipper
Little Dipper
overtipper
pistol-whipper
undertipper

ĪP-ust

ripest
typist

unripest

IP-ut

chip it
clip it
dip it
flip it
grip it
nip it
rip it
sip it
snippet

skip it
slip it
strip it
snip it
tip it
trip it
whippet
whip it
zip it

IP-yū-lāt
(See IP-ū-lāt)

ĪR
(See also Ī-ur)

byre
choir
dire
fire
hire
ire
lyre
mire
pyre
quire
spire
sire
squire
tire
wire

afire
acquire
attire
admire
aspire
barbed wire
brush fire
bonfire
backfire
conspire
catch fire
ceasefire
church choir

campfire
crossfire
desire
dog-tire(d)
esquire
expire
entire
flat tire
foxfire
for hire
haywire
hellfire
high wire
hang fire
hotwire
inspire
inquire
live wire
misfire
McGuire
on fire
perspire
quagmire
respire
rewire
require
retire
rehire
sapphire
satire
spitfire
spare tire
snow tire
shellfire
surefire
tripwire
transpire
umpire
vampire
wildfire

ball of fire
line of fire
overtire
play with fire

reacquire
rapid-fire
set on fire
sick and tire(d)
trial by fire
under fire
uninspire
underwire

down to the wire
funeral pyre
ready, aim, fire
under the wire

ĪRD

fired
hired
ired
mired
spired
sired
squired
tired
wired

acquired
attired
admired
aspired
conspired
desired
dog-tired
expired
hotwired
inspired
inquired
misfired
perspired
rewired
required
rehired
transpired
umpired

overtired
reacquired

sick and tired
uninspired
undesired

ĪR-ē
(See Ī-ur-ē)

ĪR-en
(See ĪR-un)

ĪR-ēng

firing
hiring
miring
siring
squiring
tiring
wiring

acquiring
admiring
aspiring
backfiring
conspiring
desiring
expiring
hot wiring
inspiring
inquiring
misfiring
perspiring
respiring
rewiring
requiring
retiring
rehiring
transpiring
umpiring

awe-inspiring
overtiring
reacquiring
uninspiring
underwiring

ĪR-is
(See ĪR-us)

ĪR-ish

Irish
mirish
wirish

ĪR-lus

tireless
wireless

ĪR-ment

acquirement
requirement
retirement

Ī-rō

Cairo
gyro
I row
my row
pyro
tyro

ĪR-sum

fire some
hire some
tiresome
wire some

acquire some
admire some
desire some
require some
retire some

ĪR-u

Ira
Myra
Elvira

ĪR-u-bul

firable
hirable
squirable
tirable
wirable

acquirable
aspirable
conspirable
desirable
expirable
inspirable
inquirable
perspirable
rewirable
requirable
retirable
rehirable
untirable

reacquirable
uninspirable
undesirable

ĪR-ul

spiral
viral

ĪR-un

Byron
firin'
hirin'
Myron
mirin'
siren
squirin'
tirin'
wirin'

environ

ĪR-unz

sirens

environs

ĪR-ur

direr
firer
hirer
sirer
squirer
tirer
wirer

acquirer
admirer
aspirer
conspirer
desire 'er
inspirer
inquirer

ĪR-us

fire us
hire us
iris
mire us
sire us
tire us
virus
wire us

acquire us
admire us
desire us
desirous
inspire us
papyrus
require us
retire us
rehire us

Buenos Aires
overtire us
uninspire us

ĪS

dice
ice
lice
mice
nice
price
rice
slice
splice
spice
twice
thrice
vice

advice
allspice
concise
crushed ice
deice
device
dry ice
entice
head lice
list price
no dice
on ice
precise
preslice
suffice
shoot dice
sale price
think twice
wild rice

asking price
awful nice
block of ice
break the ice
edelweiss
imprecise
loaded dice
merchandise
overprice
on thin ice

once or twice
paradise
sacrifice
sticker price
three blind mice
underprice

at any price
fool's paradise
fair market price
legal advice
self-sacrifice
sugar and spice
sensing device
skate on thin ice

bird of paradise
supreme sacrifice

IS

bliss
Chris
hiss
kiss
miss
piss
priss
Swiss
sis
this

amiss
abyss
dismiss
French-kiss
hear this
near miss
remiss

candy kiss
hit or miss
wedded bliss

ISC-ō
(See ISK-ō)

ĪS-ē

dicey
icy
licey
pricey
spicy

unspicy

nicey-nicey

IS-ē

hissy
kissy
missy
prissy
sissy

kissy-kissy
reminiscy

IS-en
(See IS-un)

ĪS-ēng

icing
pricing
ricing
slicing
splicing

deicing
enticing
preslicing
sufficing

overpricing
sacrificing
underpricing

self-sacrificing

IS-ēng

hissing
kissing

missing
pissing
prissing

dismissing

ĪS-ē-ur

dicier
icier
pricier
spicier

ĪS-ēz

crises
high seas
high C's
my seas
Pisces

IS-ēz

missies
sissies

Ulysses

kissy-kissies

ISH

dish
fish
pish
squish
splish
swish
wish

cold fish
death wish
goldfish
kingfish
main dish
queer fish
side dish

birthday wish

chafing dish
jellyfish
make a wish

drink like a fish

fine kettle of fish

ISH-ē

fishy
swishy
splishy
squishy
wishy

ISH-ē-āt

vitiate

initiate
officiate
propriate

ISH-ēng

dishing
fishing
squishing
swishing
wishing

gone fishing
spearfishing

ISH-en-sē
(See ISH-un-sē)

ISH-ent
(See ISH-unt)

ISH-ful

dishful
wishful

ISH-ū

issue
kiss you
miss you
tissue

back issue
dismiss you
dead issue
first issue
scar tissue

force the issue
toilet tissue

ISH-u

Tricia

Leticia
militia
Patricia

ISH-ul

initial
judicial
official

artificial
beneficial
prejudicial
superficial
sacrificial
unofficial

ISH-un

dishin'
fishin'
mission
Titian
wishin'

audition
ambition
admission
addition

attrition
beautician
clinician
commission
contrition
cognition
condition
emission
edition
fruition
gone fishin'
ignition
logician
musician
magician
munition
nutrition
optician
omission
permission
Phoenician
position
patrician
partition
perdition
petition
physician
rendition
remission
sedition
submission
suspicion
technician
tradition
Tahitian
tactician
transition
transmission
tuition
Venetian
volition

air-condition
apparition
apposition

acquisition
admonition
ammunition
abolition
cosmetician
competition
coalition
composition
dietician
disposition
definition
demolition
deposition
extradition
erudition
exhibition
expedition
exposition
electrician
free admission
first edition
good condition
intermission
intuition
inquisition
imposition
inhibition
in addition
manumission
mint condition
malnutrition
obstetrician
preposition
premonition
prohibition
politician
proposition
pole position
readmission
requisition
recondition
recognition
repetition
supposition
superstition

statistician

A–1 condition
arithmetician
academician
dialectician
decomposition
fetal position
juxtaposition
lotus position
mathematician
out of commission
out of condition
pediatrician
predisposition
theoretician

delicate condition
female intuition
fishing expedition
limited edition
unfair competition

ISH-un-ēng

auditioning
conditioning
commissioning
positioning
petitioning
partitioning
transitioning

air-conditioning
impositioning
requisitioning
reconditioning

juxtapositioning

ISH-un-ist

nutritionist

abolitionist
exhibitionist
prohibitionist

ISH-un-sē

deficiency
efficiency
omnisciency
sufficiency

inefficiency
insufficiency
self-sufficiency

ISH-unt

deficient
efficient
omniscient
sufficient

inefficient
insufficient
self-sufficient

ISH-un-ul

additional
conditional
nutritional
traditional
transitional
volitional

compositional
prepositional
unconditional

ISH-un-ur

auditioner
commissioner
conditioner
positioner
parishioner
petitioner
practitioner

air conditioner
hair conditioner

ISH-ur

disher
fissure
fisher
squisher
swisher
wisher

kingfisher
well-wisher

ISH-us

dish us
squish us
vicious
wish us

ambitious
auspicious
capricious
delicious
fictitious
factitious
judicious
malicious
nutritious
officious
propitious
pernicious
seditious
suspicious

avaricious
expeditious
inauspicious
impropitious
injudicious
repetitious
superstitious
surreptitious

ISH-us-lē

viciously

ambitiously

auspiciously
capriciously
deliciously
fictitiously
judiciously
maliciously
nutritiously
officiously
propitiously
suspiciously

avariciously
expeditiously
inauspiciously
repetitiously
surreptitiously

ISH-yū
(See ISH-ū)

IS-ib-ul
(See IS-ub-ul)

ĪS-ik-ul

bicycle
icycle
tricycle

IS-il
(See IS-ul)

IS-i-mō

altissimo
fortissimo

pianissimo

generalissimo

IS-i-pāt

dissipate

anticipate

ĪS-is
(See ĪS-us)

IS-it

hiss it
kiss it
licit
miss it

dismiss it
elicit
explicit
is this it?
implicit
illicit
solicit

inexplicit

IS-it-ē
(See IS-ud-ē)

IS-it-ēng
(See IS-ud-ēng)

IS-i-tus
(See IS-u-dus)

ĪS-iv

divisive
decisive
derisive
incisive

IS-iv

missive

admissive
divisive
permissive
remissive

submissive
transmissive

ISK

brisk
bisque
disk
disc
frisk
risk
tsk
whisk

high risk
slipped disk
tsk tsk

asterisk
compact disk
floppy disk
obelisk
solar disk
tamarisk

ISK-ē

frisky
risky
whiskey

unfrisky
unrisky

Irish whiskey

ISK-ēng

frisking
risking
tsking
whisking

ISK-et
(See ISK-ut)

ISK-it
(See ISK-ut)

ISK-ō

cisco
Crisco
disco
Frisco

Nabisco

San Francisco

ISK-ownt

discount
miscount

ISK-un

friskin'
riskin'

Franciscan

San Franciscan

ISK-ur

brisker
frisker
risker
whisker

by a whisker

ISK-us

discus
frisk us
risk us

hibiscus

ISK-ut

biscuit
brisket
frisk it
risk it

ĪS-lē

nicely

concisely
precisely

imprecisely

IS-lē

bristly
gristly

IS-lēng

bristling
whistling

ĪS-lus

iceless
miceless
priceless
spiceless
viceless

IS-lus

kissless
listless

ISM
(See IZ-um)

IS-mus

Christmas
isthmus

ISP

crisp
lisp
wisp

burn to a crisp
will o' the wisp

ISP-ē

crispy
lispy
wispy

ISP-ēng

crisping
lisping

ISP-ur

crisper
lisper
whisper

ĪST

Christ
diced
heist
iced
priced
riced
sliced
spliced
spiced
tryst

deiced
enticed
high-priced
sufficed
sale priced

Antichrist
before Christ
Church of Christ
Jesus Christ
overpriced
pull a heist
poltergeist
sacrificed
secret tryst
underpriced

IST

cyst
fist
gist
grist
hissed
kissed
list
Liszt
missed
mist
pissed
prissed
tryst
twist
wrist
whist

arm-twist
assist
blacklist
checklist
close-fist(ed)
consist
dean's list
desist
dismissed
enlist
exist
guest list
hit list
just missed
limp wrist
persist
price list
resist
subsist
shit list
tongue twist
two-fist(ed)
untwist
unlist(ed)

Bolshevist

Christmas list
co-exist
mailing list
preexist
reminisced
shake one's fist
shopping list
waiting list

cease and desist
enemy list
grocery list
hand over fist
most-wanted list
slap on the wrist

ĪST-ē

feisty
iced tea

IST-ē

Christy
misty
twisty

IST-em
(See IST-um)

IST-ēn

Christine
pristine
Sistine

ĪST-ēng

heisting
trysting

IST-ēng

listing
misting
twisting

assisting
blacklisting
consisting
desisting
enlisting
existing
insisting
persisting
resisting
subsisting
untwisting

co-existing
pre-existing

multiple listing

IST-ens
(See IST-uns)

IST-ent
(See IST-unt)

IST-ful

fistful
listful
wistful

insistful
persistful
resistful

IST-i-bul
(See IST-u-bul)

IST-ik

cystic
mystic

artistic
ballistic
holistic
heuristic

linguistic
logistic
sadistic
sophistic
stylistic
statistic
simplistic

atavistic
atheistic
altruistic
agonistic
casuistic
communistic
futuristic
fatalistic
masochistic
optimistic
pluralistic
pantheistic
realistic
syllogistic

antagonistic
anachronistic
animalistic
characteristic
idealistic
opportunistic
ritualistic
surrealistic
unrealistic
vital statistic

IST-ik-ul

mystical

artistical
logistical
linguistical
statistical

egotistical

antagonistical
characteristical

IST-lē
(See IS-lē)

IST-lēng
(See IS-lēng)

IST-u-bul

listable
twistable

blacklistable
enlistable
resistible
untwistable

irresistible

IST-ud

listed
misted
twisted

assisted
blacklisted
close-fisted
consisted
desisted
enlisted
existed
insisted
persisted
resisted
subsisted
two-fisted
unlisted
untwisted

co-existed
preexisted

IST-ul

Bristol
crystal
pistol

cap pistol
lead crystal

hot as a pistol

IST-um

hissed 'em
kissed 'em
missed 'em
list 'em
system
twist 'em

assist 'em
dismissed 'em
enlist 'em
just missed 'em
resist 'em
untwist 'em

buddy system
legal system
merit system
preexist 'em

IST-us

distance

assistance
consistence
existence
insistence
long-distance
persistence
resistance
subsistence

co-existence
go the distance
inconsistence
keep one's distance
shouting distance

passive resistance

IST-unt

distant

assistant
consistent
existent
insistent
persistent
resistant
subsistent

co-existent
equidistant
inconsistent

tamper-resistant

IST-unt-lē

distantly

consistently
insistently
persistently

inconsistently

ĪST-ur

heist 'er
iced 'er
priced 'er
spiced 'er
shyster
sliced 'er

enticed 'er
schlockmeister

burgermeister
overpriced 'er
sacrificed 'er

IST-ur

blister
hissed 'er
kissed 'er
lister

mister
missed 'er
pissed 'er
sister
twister

arm-twister
assister
blacklister
big sister
dismissed 'er
desister
enlister
insister
just missed 'er
persister
resister
sob sister
stepsister
subsister
transistor
tongue twister
weak sister

co-exister
fever blister

cease-and-desister

IST-ur-ē

blistery
history
mystery

IST-ur-ēng

blistering
sistering

IS-u-bul

kissable
miscible

admissible
dismissible
omissible

permissible
remissible
submissible

inadmissible

IS-ud-ē

complicity
duplicity
ethnicity
felicity
lubricity
plasticity
publicity
simplicity
toxicity

authenticity
domesticity
elasticity
electricity
eccentricity
multiplicity
specificity

egocentricity

IS-ud-ēng

eliciting
soliciting

IS-u-dus

felicitous
solicitous

IS-ul

Bissell
bristle
gristle
missal
missile
thistle
this'll
whistle

abyssal
cruise missile
dismissal
epistle
train whistle
wolf whistle

blow the whistle
guided missile
wet one's whistle

clean as a whistle

IS-ul-ē

bristly
gristly
prissily
Sicily

ĪS-um

buy some
dice 'em
die some
ice 'em
price 'em
sigh some
slice 'em
splice 'em

ĪS-un

bison
dicin'
icin'
pricin'
slicin'
splicin'
spicin'
Tyson

enticin'
sufficin'

overpricin'
sacrificin'

streptomycin
underpricin'

IS-un

christen
glisten
hissin'
kissin'
listen
missin'
prissin'

dismissin'
French kissin'

look and listen
reminiscin'

IS-un-ēng

christening
glistening
listening

ĪS-ur

dicer
icer
nicer
pricer
slicer
splicer
spicer

conciser
deicer
enticer
preciser

overpricer
sacrificer

self-sacrificer

IS-ur

hisser
kisser

misser
pisser
prisser

ass-kisser
dismisser
French-kisser

reminiscer

ĪS-us

crisis
Isis
ice us
price us

entice us
suffice us

mid-life crisis
sacrifice us

IS-us

hiss us
kiss us
miss us
piss us

dismiss us
narcissus

IS-ut

hiss it
kiss it
licit
miss it

dismiss it
elicit
explicit
is this it?
implicit
illicit
solicit

IS-ut-ē
(See IS-ud-ē)

IS-ut-us
(See IS-ud-us)

IS-uz

hisses
kisses
misses
Mrs.
pisses
prisses

abysses
dismisses
French-kisses
near misses

ĪT

bite
byte
bright
blight
cite
Dwight
fight
fright
flight
height
kite
knight
light
mite
might
night
plight
quite
right
rite
site
sight
spite

slight
sleight
sprite
smite
tight
trite
write
wight
white

airtight
all-night
alight
all right
backbite
bombsight
bug bite
bullfight
birthright
catfight
contrite
crash site
cockfight
daylight
downright
delight
despite
dog fight
eyesight
excite
foresight
forthright
frostbite
firelight
finite
fortnight
Fulbright
flashlight
footlight
fistfight
floodlight
gaslight
good night
green light
gang fight

graphite
ghostwrite
gun fight
hindsight
highlight
headlight
handwrite
heat light
ignite
in-flight
insight
invite
incite
indict
last night
lamplight
lucite
limelight
lovelight
late-night
midnight
moonlight
mike fright
Miss Right
not quite
night-light
outright
off-white
playwright
prizefight
polite
penlight
porchlight
red light
recite
requite
skylight
sunlight
stoplight
searchlight
streetlight
spotlight
sit tight
Snow White
Semite

snakebite
starlight
skintight
skywrite
stage fright
strobe light
tonight
top flight
take flight
Twelfth Night
termite
typewrite
twilight
torchlight
twinight
taillight
unite
upright
uptight
white knight

at first sight
appetite
black and white
broad daylight
bring to light
candlelight
charter flight
cellulite
copyright
civil right
come to light
day and night
divine right
disunite
dynamite
erudite
extradite
expedite
featherlight
fly-by-night
Fahrenheit
flight-or-fright
gesundheit
honor bright

Inner Light
Israelite
impolite
in the right
know by sight
legal right
lily-white
Mr. Right
malachite
Muscovite
neophyte
not quite right
neon light
oversight
overbite
overnight
out-of-sight
overheight
pearly white
parasite
plebiscite
pilot light
proselyte
pillow fight
recondite
Rainbow Brite
reunite
stalactite
see the light
shining light
satellite
stalagmite
second sight
spend the night
signal light
serve one right
socialite
transvestite
take a bite
traffic light
tripartite
underwrite
watertight
wedding night
yellow light

bit of all right
dawn's early light
electrolyte
go fly a kite
high as a kite
hermaphrodite
indirect light
infrared light
love at first sight
meteorite
natural light
out like a light
opening night
starlight, starbright
sweetness and light
tomorrow night
Turkish delight

by cover of night
higher than a kite
idiot's delight
lady-of-the-night
middle of the night
supersonic flight

straighten up and fly
    right
ultraviolet light

IT

bit
chit
fit
flit
grit
git
get
hit
it
kit
knit
lit
mitt
nit
pit

quit
sit
skit
Schmidt
snit
split
spit
slit
shit
tit
twit
wit
whit
writ
zit

armpit
admit
alit
acquit
befit
base hit
bullshit
commit
close-knit
cockpit
dimwit
emit
forget
hot tip
horseshit
hairsplit
hand-knit
half-wit
legit
lamplit
moonlit
misfit
mess kit
nitwit
outfit
op. cit.
obit
outwit
omit

permit
pinch-hit
press kit
remit
refit
sunlit
smash hit
submit
starlit
Sanskrit
sandpit
snake pit
switch-hit
tool kit
to wit
transmit
true grit
tight fit
tar pit
two-bit
tight-knit
unfit
unsplit
witnit

bit by bit
benefit
baby-sit
caffeine fit
counterfeit
catcher's mitt
do one's bit
double-knit
doctor kit
every bit
first-aid kit
hypocrite
have a fit
illegit
manumit
Messerschmitt
perfect fit
passion pit
readmit
resubmit

recommit
repair kit
shoe-shine kit
sewing kit
throw a fit

bottomless pit
banana split
champ at the bit
conniption fit
lickety-split
overcommit

emergency kit

ITCH
(See ICH)

ĪT-ē
(See ĪD-ē)

IT-ē
(See ID-ē)

ĪT-em
(See ĪD-um)

ĪT-en
(See ĪT-un)

IT-en
(See IT-un)

ĪT-en-ēng
(See ĪT-un-ēng)

ĪT-ēng
(See ĪD-ēng)

IT-ēng
(See ID-ēng)

IT-ē-us
(See ID-ē-us)

IT-ē-ust
(See ID-ē-ust)

ĪT-ful

frightful
rightful
spiteful

contriteful
delightful
exciteful
insightful
inciteful

ITH

kith
myth
pith
smith
with

blacksmith
forthwith
goldsmith
gunsmith
herewith
locksmith
live with
therewith

coppersmith
monolith
metalsmith
over with
silversmith
shibboleth
walk off with

on a par with
paleolith

over and done with

ITH-ē

pithy
smithy

ĪTHE

blithe
lithe
scythe
tithe
writhe

ITHE-ur

blither
dither
hither
slither
thither
whither
wither
zither

come hither

in a dither

hither and thither

ITHE-ur-ēng

blithering
slithering
withering

ITH-ik

mythic

Neolithic

Paleolithic

IT-i-gā-shun
(See ID-i-gā-shun)

IT-ik
(See ID-ik)

IT-i-kul
(See ID-i-kul)

ĪT-is
(See ĪD-us)

IT-ish
(See ID-ish)

IT-i-siz-um
(See ID-i-siz-um)

ĪT-lē

brightly
lightly
nightly
rightly
slightly
spritely
tritely
tightly

contritely
forthrightly
fortnightly
finitely
politely
unsightly

eruditely
impolitely

once-over-lightly

IT-lēng

chittling
whittling

belittling

ĪT-lus

biteless
fightless

flightless
sightless

contriteless

IT-lus

hitless
spitless
shitless
witless
zitless

scared shitless

ĪT-ment

excitement
incitement
indictment

IT-nē

jitney
Mt. Whitney

ĪT-nēng

bright'ning
fright'ning
height'ning
lightning
tight'ning
whit'ning

enlight'ning
greased lightning
white lightning

ĪT-nur

brightener
frightener
heightener
lightener
tightener
whitener

ĪT-nus

brightness
lightness
rightness
tightness
triteness
whiteness

politeness

eruditeness

ĪT-nus

fitness
witness

eye witness

Jehovah's Witness
physical fitness

ĪT-ō
(See ĪD-ō)

IT-ō
(See ID-ō)

ĪT-of

bite off
fight off
light off
night off
right off
write-off

ĪTS

bites
bytes
blights
fights
flights
heights
kites

knights
lights
mites
nights
plights
rights
rites
sites
sights
spites
slights
sprites
smites
writes

alights
bombsights
bug bites
bullfights
cat fights
crash sites
delights
excites
flashlights
footlights
fistfights
gay rights
gang fights
ghostwrites
highlights
headlights
ignites
insights
invites
incites
indicts
last rites
night-lights
playwrights
prizefights
recites
skylights
stoplights
searchlights
streetlights

states' rights
snakebites
skywrites
termites
typewrites
torchlights
unites
white knights

Bill of Rights
Brooklyn Heights
copyrights
civil rights
dead to rights
disunites
dynamites
equal rights
extradites
expedites
Israelites
Muscovites
neophytes
Northern Lights
oversights
overbites
parasites
plebiscites
proselytes
pillowfights
recondites
reunites
squatter's rights
satellites
socialites
transvestites
underwrites
women's rights

animal rights
meteorites
Turkish delights

ITS

blitz
bits

chits
ditz
fritz
fits
flits
grits
gets
hits
its
kits
knits
mitts
nits
pits
quits
ritz
sits
skits
snits
splits
spits
slits
shits
spritz
spitz
tits
twits
wits
writs
zits

armpits
admits
acquits
befits
base hits
bullshits
commits
cockpits
dimwits
emits
four bits
forgets
housesits
hot tips

hand-knits
halfwits
misfits
mess kits
nitwits
outfits
outwits
omits
permits
pinch hits
remits
refits
smash hits
submits
tool kits
transmits
tidbits
tight fits
tar pits
two-bits
the pits

Biarritz
baby-sits
call it quits
caffeine fits
counterfeits
catchers' mitts
first-aid kits
Horowitz
hypocrites
manumits
on the fritz
readmits
resubmits
recommits
slivovitz

banana splits
hominy grits
put on the ritz

ITS-ē

bitsy
ditzy

Fritzi
glitzy
itsy
Mitzi
ritzy

itsy-bitsy

ITS-ēng

blitzing
spritzing

ĪT-ud
(See ĪD-ud)

IT-ud
(See ID-ud)

ĪT-ul
(See ĪD-ul)

IT-ul
(See ID-ul)

IT-ul-ē
(See ID-ul-ē)

ĪT-um
(See ĪD-um)

IT-um-ē
(See ID-um-ē)

ĪT-un

bitin'
brighten
Brighton
citin'
fightin'
frighten

heighten
lighten
sightin'
spitin'
slightin'
Titan
Triton
tighten
writin'
whiten

enlighten

IT-un

Britain
Briton
bitten
flittin'
fitten
grittin'
hittin'
kitten
knittin'
mitten
quittin'
smitten
sittin'
splittin'
spittin'
written

admittin'
acquittin'
befittin'
bullshittin'
forgettin'
flea-bitten
frostbitten
Great Britain
handwritten
outwittin'
permittin'
rewritten
remittin'
sex kitten

submittin'
sidesplittin'
typewritten
transmittin'
tight fittin'
unwritten

benefittin'
baby-sittin'
manumittin'
readmittin'
recommittin'
underwritten

IT-un-ē

Brittany
kitteny
litany

ĪT-un-ēng

brightening
frightening
heightening
lightening
tightening
whitening

enlightening

IT-uns

pittance

admittance
remittance
transmittance

no admittance
readmittance

ĪT-un-ur
(See ĪT-nur)

ĪT-up

get-up
hit up
lit up
sit-up
spit-up
split-up

ĪT-ur
(See ĪD-ur)

IT-ur
(See ID-ur)

IT-ur-āt
(See ID-ur-āt)

ĪT-ur-ē
(See ID-ur-ē)

IT-ur-ē
(See ID-ur-ē)

IT-ur-ēng
(See ID-ur-ēng)

IT-ur-ul
(See ID-ur-ul)

IT-ur-us
(See ID-ur-us)

IT-ur-ut
(See ID-ur-ut)

ĪT-us
(See ĪD-us)

ĪT-u-wā
(See ĪD-u-wā)

Ī-u

via

Josiah
Messiah
pariah

Jeremiah
jambalaya
Nehemiah
Zachariah

Ī-ub-ul

dryable
friable
eyeable
liable
pliable
pryable
sighable
tieable
tryable
viable

compliable
defiable
deniable
reliable

certifiable
clarifiable
dignifiable
falsifiable
fortifiable
justifiable
modifiable
unreliable
undeniable
verifiable

Ī-ud-ē

piety

anxiety
impiety
propriety
society
sobriety
variety

high society
impropriety
insobriety
notoriety

café society
garden variety

Ī-ud-ur

dieter
quieter
rioter

proprietor

Ī-uk-ul

maniacal
zodiacal

Ī-ul
(See also ĪL)

dial
trial
viol
vial

bass viol
denial
field trial
mistrial
misdial
on trial
pretrial
retrial

sundial

self-denial

Ī-ul-āt

violate

annihilate

Ī-un

Brian
buyin'
cryin'
dyin'
eyein'
flyin'
fryin'
ion
lyin'
lion
pryin'
plyin'
Ryan
sighin'
scion
spyin'
tyin'
tryin'
vyin'
Zion

applyin'
belyin'
complyin'
decryin'
drip-dryin'
defyin'
denyin'
espyin'
Hawaiian
implyin'
outlyin'
Orion
O'Brien
replyin'

relyin'
sea lion
supplyin'
untyin'

dandelion

Ī-uns

clients
giants
science

affiance
alliance
appliance
compliance
defiance
reliance

Christian Science
exact science
in defiance
misalliance
noncompliance
nonalliance
pseudoscience
self-reliance

letters and science

Ī-unt

Bryant
client
giant
pliant
riant

compliant
defiant
reliant

self-reliant

Ī-ur
(See also ĪR)

briar

buyer
choir
crier
drier
dyer
eyer
flier
friar
fryer
higher
liar
nigher
plier(s)
prior
pryer
plyer
shyer
sigher
slyer
spryer
spyer
trier
tyer
vier
wrier

applier
belier
clothes dryer
church choir
complier
defier
denier
hair dryer
high flyer
implier
outcrier
replier
relier
sweetbrier
supplier
town crier
untier

alibier
amplifier

beautifier
certifier
calcifier
crucifier
classifier
clarifier
codifier
deifier
dignifier
edifier
falsifier
fortifier
gratifier
glorifier
horrifier
identifier
intensifier
justifier
liquefier
mystifier
mortifier
magnifier
modifier
multiplier
mollifier
nullifier
notifier
occupier
purifier
petrifier
putrefier
pacifier
prophesier
qualifier
quantifier
ratifier
rectifier
specifier
sanctifier
stupefier
speechifier
satisfier
simplifier
signifier
terrifier

testifier
unifier
verifier
vilifier
versifier

declassifier
disqualifier
electrifier
intensifier
identifier
personifier
solidifier

Ī-ur-ē

diary
fiery
miry
priory
wiry

inquiry

Ī-urn

iron
I earn

andiron
cast iron
environ(s)
gridiron
pump iron

curling iron

Ī-us

buy us
bias
dry us
eye us
fly us
fry us
nigh us
ply us
pious

shy us
try us
tie us
why us?

belie us
come by us
decry us
defy us
deny us
Elias
espy us
hogtie us
Matthias
nearby us
Pope Pius
run by us
stand by us
supply us
sneak by us
slip by us
Tobias
untie us
unbias(ed)
unpious

beautify us
crucify us
certify us
classify us
fortify us
gratify us
glorify us
horrify us
justify us
mortify us
mollify us
mystify us
modify us
mummify us
notify us
nullify us
on the bias
occupy us
petrify us
pacify us

purify us
qualify us
racial bias
stupefy us
satisfy us
specify us
terrify us
typify us
unify us

declassify us
disqualify us
dissatisfy us
electrify us
exemplify us
identify us
personify us
preoccupy us
refortify us
solidify us

Ī-ust

biased
driest
highest
slyest
spryest
shyest
wryest

unbiased

Ī-ut

by it
buy it
diet
eye it
fiat
fly it
fry it
quiet
riot
spy it
tie it

try it
Wyatt

apply it
belie it
be quiet
crash diet
disquiet
decry it
defy it
deny it
espy it
hogtie it
imply it
run riot
supply it
unquiet

Ī-u-tē
(See Ī-u-dē)

Ī-uth

lieth

Goliath

Ī-u-trē

podiatry
psychiatry

Ī-u-tur
(See Ī-u-dur)

Ī-u-tus

quiet us
riotous

disquiet us

ĪV

chive
dive

drive
five
hive
I've
jive
knive(s)
live
strive
skive
thrive
wive(s)

alive
arrive
archive
beehive
connive
crash-dive
contrive
derive
deprive
endive
high five
high dive
hang five
line drive
nosedive
pile drive
revive
survive
skydive
swan dive
St. Ive(s)
skin-dive
take five
test drive

deep-sea dive
five-by-five
nine-to-five
overdrive
skin alive
take a dive

hip to the jive

Currier and Ive(s)

IV

give
live
shiv
sieve

forgive
misgive
outlive
relive
what give(s)?

live and let live

ĪV-ē

IV
ivy
jivey

halls of ivy
poison ivy

IV-ē

civvie(s)
divvy
privy
skivvy

IV-el
(See IV-ul)

ĪV-en
(See ĪV-un)

IV-en
(See IV-un)

ĪV-ēng

diving
driving
jiving
striving

thriving

arriving
conniving
crash-diving
contriving
drunk driving
deriving
depriving
nosediving
reviving
surviving
skydiving
skin diving

IV-ēng

giving
living

clean living
forgiving
lawgiving
misgiving
outliving
reliving
Thanksgiving

cost of living
make a living
unforgiving

IV-et
(See IV-ut)

IV-ē-u

trivia

Bolivia
Olivia

IV-ē-ul

trivial

convivial

IV-ē-un

divvyin'
Vivian

Bolivian
oblivion

IV-ē-us

divvy us
privy us

lascivious
oblivious

IV-id
(See IV-ud)

IV-il
(See IV-ul)

IV-it-ē
(See IV-ud-ē)

ĪV-u

Godiva
saliva

ĪV-u-bul

drivable
jivable
thrivable

contrivable
deprivable
revivable
survivable

IV-u-bul

givable
livable

forgivable
relivable

unforgivable

IV-ud

livid
vivid

IV-ud-ē

activity
acclivity
captivity
declivity
festivity
lascivity
nativity
proclivity

creativity
conductivity
collectivity
exclusivity
inactivity
objectivity
productivity
relativity
sensitivity
subjectivity

insensitivity

radioactivity

ĪV-ul

rival

archival
archrival
arrival
contrival
deprival
revival
survival

old-time revival

IV-ul

civil
drivel
snivel
swivel
shrivel

uncivil

IV-ul-ēng

sniveling
swiveling
shriveling

ĪV-un

divin'
drivin'
Ivan
jivin'
liven
strivin'
thrivin'

arrivin'
connivin'
contrivin'
derivin'
deprivin'
enliven
nosedivin'
revivin'
survivin'
skydivin'
test drivin'

IV-un

driven
given
livin'
striven

forgiven
God-given
misgivin'

outlivin'
relivin'

powerdriven

ĪV-uns

connivance
contrivance

ĪV-ur

diver
driver
fiver
jiver
striver
thriver

aliver
arriver
cabdriver
conniver
contriver
depriver
deriver
drunk driver
nosediver
pearl diver
piledriver
reviver
race driver
survivor
skydiver
swandiver
screwdiver
slave driver
truckdriver

hit-and-run driver

IV-ur

flivver
giver
liver
quiver

river
shiver
sliver

aquiver
calf's liver
caregiver
chopped liver
deliver
downriver
East River
forgiver
high liver
lawgiver
outlive 'er
upriver

lily-liver
up the river

chopped chicken liver
Indian giver
sell down the river

ĪV-ur-ē

ivory
wivery

connivery

IV-ur-ē

livery
quivery
shivery
slivery

delivery

IV-ur-ēng

quivering
shivering
slivering

delivering

IV-ur-us

carnivorous
deliver us
herbivorous
omnivorous

ĪV-ut

drive it
jive it
private

derive it
deprive it
revive it
survive it

IV-ut

civet
divot
give it
live it
rivet
trivet

forgive it
misgive it
outlive it
relive it

IV-ut-ē
(See IV-ud-ē)

Ī-wā

byway
highway
my way
shy way
sly way

ĪX

bikes
dikes

hikes
likes
mikes
pikes
spikes
strikes
tykes
trikes

dislikes
hitchhikes
outpsychs
three strikes
turnpikes

hungerstrikes
Lucky Strikes
motorbikes

IX

bricks
chicks
clicks
cricks
dicks
fix
flicks
hicks
kicks
licks
mix
nix
nicks
picks
pricks
pix
pics
sticks
sics
six
Styx
slicks
ticks
tics
tricks

wicks

admix
affix
broomsticks
conflicts
card tricks
chopsticks
cake mix
drumsticks
depicts
deep-six
evicts
goldbricks
handpicks
icepicks
lipsticks
matchsticks
nitpicks
oil slicks
predicts
pinpricks
quick fix
restricts
rope tricks
toothpicks
transfix
unclicks

bag of tricks
Bolsheviks
Beatrix
crucifix
candlesticks
candlewicks
contradicts
dirty tricks
fiddlesticks
get one's kicks
hit the bricks
in a fix
intermix
interdicts
Mocha Mix
nervous ticks
politics

pogo sticks
pick-up-sticks
ton of bricks
walking sticks

executrix

Spirit of '76

IX-chur

fixture
mixture

admixture
light fixture

IX-ē

Dixie
pixie
Trixie

whistling Dixie

**IX-en
(See IX-un)**

IX-ēng

fixing
mixing
nixing

admixing
affixing
deep-sixing
transfixing

intermixing

**IX-it
(See IX-ut)**

**IX-shun
(See IK-shun)**

IXT

fixed
mixed
nixed

affixed
admixed
betwixt
deep-sixed
transfixed

intermixed

IX-un

Dixon
fixin'
mixin'
nixin'
Nixon
vixen

affixin'
deep-sixin'
transfixin'

intermixin'

IX-ur

clicks 'er
fixer
flicks 'er
kicks 'er
licks 'er
mixer
nixer
nicks 'er
picks 'er
pricks 'er
sticks 'er
ticks 'er
tricks 'er

affixer
elixir
evicts 'er

hand mixer
prefixer
restricts 'er
suffixer
transfixer

contradicts 'er
cement mixer
intermixer
party mixer

IX-ut

fix it
flicks it
kicks it
licks it
mix it
nix it
nicks it
picks it
pricks it
sticks it
slicks it

affix it
deep-six it
handpicks it
nitpicks it
prefix it
transfix it

ipse dixit
intermix it
Mr. Fix-it

ĪZ

bys
buys
cries
dies
dyes
dries
eyes
flies
fries

guise
guys
highs
lies
lyes
plies
pies
prize
pries
rise
ryes
sties
sighs
shies
spies
size
skies
ties
tries
thighs
vies
vise
whys
wise

advise
assize
arise
apprise
applies
allies
baptize
bye-byes
blue skies
belies
capsize
comprise
chastise
clockwise
complies
crosswise
despise
door prize
deep-fries
decries

defies
demise
denies
disguise
devise
drip-dries
excise
edgewise
espies
franchise
fireflies
first prize
French fries
four-eyes
good-byes
get wise
gadflies
high-rise
hi-fis
implies
incise
Julys
king-size
likewise
life-size
lengthwise
Levi's
leastwise
moonrise
make eyes
magpies
mud pies
neckties
outcries
outsize
pigsties
pintsize
queen-size
revise
red eyes
relies
reprise
replies
remise
sunrise

surprise
surmise
spin-dries
standbys
supplies
sheep's eyes
snake eyes
time flies
unwise
unties
wiseguys
widthwise

atomize
authorize
activize
amortize
analyze
advertise
agonize
apple pies
aggrandize
amplifies
alibis
bastardize
battle cries
bald-faced lies
brutalize
butterflies
beautifies
burglarize
booby prize
circumcise
canonize
cauterize
civilize
climatize
centralize
communize
crucifies
colonize
compromise
close your eyes
criticize
crystallize

clarifies
codifies
certifies
calcifies
classifies
dramatize
deifies
dragonflies
eagle eyes
energize
equalize
eulogize
evil eyes
edifies
emphasize
enterprise
enfranchise
exorcise
exercise
fertilize
feast one's eyes
formalize
fraternize
fantasize
falsifies
fortifies
fossilize
feminize
family ties
gratifies
goo-goo eyes
glorifies
galvanize
Geminis
humanize
hypnotize
horrifies
harmonize
idolize
ill-advise(d)
improvise
immunize
jeopardize
justifies
liquefies

lullabies
legalize
localize
legal-size
mortifies
misapplies
mollifies
magnetize
mystifies
mechanize
modifies
magnifies
memorize
mummifies
minimize
modernize
moralize
mesmerize
motorize
mobilize
mercerize
multiplies
nasalize
nullifies
neutralize
notarize
notifies
Nobel Prize
overbuys
ostracize
otherwise
oxidize
organize
occupies
oversize
paralyze
past your eyes
private eyes
penalize
pack of lies
pluralize
publicize
patronize
pasteurize
plagiarize

petrifies
pacifies
purifies
polarize
qualifies
quantifies
recognize
realize
rectifies
rhapsodize
ratifies
ramifies
summarize
sanctifies
stupefies
satisfies
simplifies
scandalize
specifies
supervise
satirize
sensitize
sermonize
synchronize
sterilize
stigmatize
scrutinize
socialize
subsidize
Sanforize
specialize
signifies
standardize
stabilize
sympathize
symbolize
terrorize
take the prize
tyrannize
tiger eyes
theorize
tenderize
tranquilize
traumatize
temporize

tantalize
televise
terrifies
typifies
utilize
ups and dies
underlies
unifies
undersize
urbanize
vilifies
verifies
vitalize
vocalize
vulgarize
verbalize
victimize
vaporize
womanize
westernize
weather-wise
well-advise(d)
worldly wise

as the crow flies
actualize
allegorize
alphabetize
apologize
acclimatize
antagonize
capitalize
cut down to size
chicken pot pies
characterize
commercialize
cannibalize
categorize
contrariwise
counterclockwise
decentralize
dehumanize
deodorize
disenfranchise
declassifies

demobilize
demystifies
democratize
demoralize
devitalize
dichotomize
disorganize
disqualifies
dissatisfies
economize
evade your eyes
extemporize
electric eyes
electrifies
epitomize
exemplifies
familiarize
free enterprise
federalize
fanaticize
family ties
hypothesize
idealize
immortalize
italicize
intensifies
identifies
imdemnifies
liberalize
little white lies
legitimize
militarize
monopolize
nationalize
natural highs
naturalize
open one's eyes
Olympic-size
philosophize
preoccupies
Pulitzer Prize
personifies
popularize
revitalize
refortifies

regularize
rationalize
romanticize
reorganize
ritualize
secularize
sight for sore eyes
sensualize
soliloquize
systematize
solidifies
theologize
take by surprise
try on for size
ventriloquize
visualize
word to the wise

Americanize
artificial highs
consolation prize
continental rise
departmentalize
economy-size
legitimatize
materialize
memorialize
particularize
professionalize
private enterprise
psychoanalyze
revolutionize
spiritualize
universalize

editorialize
institutionalize
internationalize

IZ

biz
fizz
frizz
his
is

Liz
Ms.
quiz
tizz
'tis
whiz

as is
gin fizz
gee whiz
pop quiz
showbiz

ĪZD

prized
sized

advised
assized
apprised
baptized
capsized
comprised
chastised
despised
disguised
devised
franchised
outsized
pint-sized
revised
surprised
surmised

authorized
amortized
analyzed
advertised
agonized
aggrandized
brutalized
burglarized
circumcised
canonized
cauterized
civilized

climatized
centralized
colonized
compromised
criticized
crystallized
dramatized
energized
equalized
eulogized
emphasized
exorcised
exercised
fertilized
formalized
fraternized
fantasized
feminized
galvanized
humanized
hypnotized
harmonized
idolized
ill-advised
improvised
immunized
jeopardized
legalized
localized
magnetized
mechanized
memorized
minimized
modernized
moralized
mesmerized
motorized
mobilized
mercerized
nasalized
neutralized
notarized
ostracized
oxidized
organized

oversized
paralyzed
penalized
pluralized
publicized
patronized
pasteurized
plagiarized
polarized
recognized
realized
rhapsodized
summarized
scandalized
supervised
satirized
sensitized
sermonized
synchronized
sterilized
stigmatized
scrutinized
socialized
subsidized
Sanforized
specialized
standardized
stabilized
sympathized
symbolized
terrorized
tyrannized
theorized
tenderized
tranquilized
traumatized
temporized
tantalized
televised
utilized
undersized
urbanized
vitalized
vocalized
vulgarized

verbalized
victimized
vaporized
westernized
well-advised

as advertised
actualized
allegorized
alphabetized
apologized
acclimatized
antagonized
capitalized
characterized
categorized
decentralized
dehumanized
deodorized
disenfranchised
demobilized
democratized
demoralized
devitalized
dichotomized
disorganized
economized
extemporized
epitomized
familiarized
federalized
fanaticized
hypothesized
idealized
immortalized
italicized
liberalized
legitimized
militarized
monopolized
nationalized
philosophized
popularized
revitalized
regularized

rationalized
romanticized
reorganized
secularized
sensualized
soliloquized
systematized
theologized
visualized

Americanized
departmentalized
legitimatized
materialized
memorialized
particularized
professionalized
psychoanalyzed
revolutionized
spiritualized

editorialized
institutionalized

IZD

fizzed
frizzed
quizzed
whizzed

IZ-ē

busy
dizzy
fizzy
frizzy
is he?
tizzy
'tis he
whizzy

tin Lizzie

IZ-el
(See IZ-ul)

IZ-en
(See IZ-un)

ĪZ-ēng

prizing
rising
sizing

advising
assizing
arising
apprising
baptizing
capsizing
comprising
chastising
despising
disguising
devising
excising
franchising
revising
reprising
surprising
surmising

authorizing
amortizing
analyzing
advertising
agonizing
aggrandizing
brutalizing
burglarizing
circumcising
canonizing
cauterizing
civilizing
centralizing
colonizing
compromising
criticizing
crystallizing
dramatizing
energizing

equalizing
eulogizing
emphasizing
enterprising
enfranchising
exorcising
exercising
fertilizing
formalizing
fraternizing
fantasizing
fossilizing
feminizing
galvanizing
humanizing
hypnotizing
harmonizing
idolizing
improvising
immunizing
jeopardizing
legalizing
localizing
merchandising
magnetizing
mechanizing
memorizing
minimizing
modernizing
moralizing
mesmerizing
motorizing
mobilizing
neutralizing
notarizing
ostracizing
organizing
paralyzing
penalizing
pluralizing
publicizing
patronizing
pasteurizing
plagiarizing
polarizing

recognizing
realizing
summarizing
scandalizing
supervising
satirizing
sensitizing
sermonizing
synchronizing
sterilizing
stigmatizing
scrutinizing
socializing
subsidizing
Sanforizing
specializing
standardizing
stabilizing
sympathizing
symbolizing
terrorizing
tyrannizing
theorizing
tenderizing
tranquilizing
traumatizing
temporizing
tantalizing
televising
utilizing
urbanizing
vitalizing
vocalizing
verbalizing
victimizing
womanizing

alphabetizing
apologizing
acclimatizing
antagonizing
capitalizing
characterizing
commercializing
categorizing

decentralizing
dehumanizing
deodorizing
demobilizing
democratizing
demoralizing
devitalizing
economizing
extemporizing
epitomizing
familiarizing
hypothesizing
idealizing
immortalizing
italicizing
legitimizing
militarizing
monopolizing
nationalizing
naturalizing
philosophizing
popularizing
revitalizing
rationalizing
romanticizing
reorganizing
ritualizing
systematizing
visualizing

materializing
memorializing
professionalizing
psychoanalyzing
revolutionizing

editorializing
institutionalizing

IZ-ēng

fizzing
frizzing
quizzing
whizzing

IZH-un

vision

collision
concision
derision
decision
division
envision
elision
incision
Parisian
provision
precision
revision

circumcision
double vision
field of vision
indecision
line of vision
long division
supervision
split decision
subdivision
television
tunnel vision

landmark decision

IZH-un-ul

visional

divisional
provisional
revisional

IZ-i-bul
(See IZ-u-bul)

IZ-i-kul
(See IZ-u-kul)

IZ-il-ē

busily
dizzily
frizzily
fizzily

IZ-it
(See IZ-ut)

IZ-it-iv
(See IZ-ud-iv)

IZ-it-ur
(See IZ-ud-ur)

ĪZ-krak

buys crack
guys crack
wisecrack

IZ-lē

drizzly
fizzly
grizzly
grisly
sizzly

IZ-lēng

drizzling
fizzling
quisling
sizzling

IZM
(See IZ-um)

ĪZ-ment

guisement

advisement

assizement
apprisement
baptizement
chastisement
devisement
franchisement
revisement

aggrandizement
advertisement
enfranchisement

disenfranchisement
under advisement

IZ-mul

dismal

abysmal

ĪZ-ō

proviso

Valparaiso

ĪZ-u-bul

prizeable
sizeable

advisable
assizable
capsizable
despisable
disguisable
devisable
franchisable
revisable
surprisable
surmisable

analyzable
advertisable
civilizable
colonizable
compromisable
dramatizable

energizable
exorcisable
hypnotizable
immunizable
memorizable
minimizable
modernizable
ostracizable
paralyzable
publicizable
patronizable
polarizable
realizable
recognizable
summarizable
satirizable
sensitizable
sterilizable
subsidizable
standardizable
terrorizable
televisable

antagonizable
visualizable

IZ-u-bul

frizzable
fizzable
risible
quizzable
visible

divisible
invisible

indivisible

IZ-u-div

acquisitive
inquisitive

IZ-u-dur

visitor

acquisitor

exquisiter
inquisitor

IZ-u-kul

physical
quizzical

ĪZ-ul

arisal
apprisal
despisal
revisal
reprisal
surmisal

IZ-ul

chisel
drizzle
fizzle
frizzle
grizzle
sizzle
swizzle

IZ-um

Chisholm
fizz 'em
frizz 'em
ism
prism
quiz 'em
schism

baptism
deism
fascism
racism
sophism
seism
simplism
truism
theism

altruism
anarchism
aneurysm
aphorism
atavism
atheism
activism
animism
barbarism
botulism
chauvinism
catechism
cynicism
cataclysm
centralism
criticism
cretinism
communism
despotism
Darwinism
dualism
dogmatism
egotism
exorcism
extremism
embolism
euphemism
formalism
heroism
humanism
hedonism
hypnotism
idealism
Judaism
journalism
modernism
monoism
magnetism
mannerism
moralism
mechanism
mesmerism
mysticism
me-too-ism
masochism

nepotism
narcissism
nihilism
optimism
ostracism
organism
old-boyism
pacifism
paganism
plagiarism
pantheism
pessimism
pugilism
pragmatism
rheumatism
realism
stigmatism
skepticism
stoicism
syllogism
symbolism
socialism
synchronism
solecism
spoonerism
solipsism
terrorism
tokenism
vandalism
vulgarism
voyeurism
witticism

astigmatism
antagonism
alcoholism
anachronism
animalism
amateurism
capitalism
cannibalism
conservatism
commercialism
Catholicism
consumerism

determinism
evangelism
eroticism
fanaticism
favoritism
federalism
hyperbolism
imperialism
impressionism
liberalism
militarism
metabolism
male chauvinism
opportunism
polytheism
Puritanism
patriotism
parallelism
paternalism
provincialism
rationalism
romanticism
recidivism
somnambulism
separatism
volunteerism
ventriloquism

Americanism
abolitionism
anti-Semitism
agrarianism
colloquialism
colonialism
defense mechanism
exhibitionism
irrationalism
imperialism
industrialism
Mohammedanism
microorganism
materialism
professionalism
sensationalism
spiritualism

sadomasochism

animal magnetism
individualism
indeterminism
vegetarianism

humanitarianism

disestablishmentarianism

ĪZ-un

prizin'
risin'
sizin'

advisin'
arisin'
apprisin'
assizin'
baptizin'
capsizin'
comprisin'
chastisin'
despisin'
disguisin'
devisin'
excisin'
franchisin'
horizon
revisin'
reprisin'
sun risin'
surprisin'
surmisin'
uprisin'

IZ-un

fizzin'
frizzin'
hisn
mizzen
prison
quizzin'
risen

whizzin'
wizen

arisen
imprison

IZ-un-ur

prisoner
quizzin' 'er
wizener

imprison 'er

ĪZ-ur

buys 'er
dyes 'er
eyes 'er
flies 'er
geyser
kaiser
miser
plies 'er
prize 'er
riser
sizer
ties 'er
tries 'er
visor
wiser

advisor
ariser
apprizer
applies 'er
baptizer
capsize 'er
chastiser
divisor
defies 'er
denies 'er
disguiser
despiser
deviser
franchiser
incisor

reviser
surpriser
surmiser
sun visor

atomizer
activizer
amortizer
analyzer
appetizer
advertiser
aggrandizer
authorize 'er
brutalizer
beautifies 'er
canonize 'er
cauterize 'er
civilizer
crucifies 'er
colonizer
compromise 'er
classifies 'er
circumciser
centralizer
communizer
dramatizer
exorciser
enfranchiser
eulogize 'er
equalizer
energizer
emphasizer
enterpriser
exerciser
formalizer
fertilizer
fortifies 'er
feminizer
fraternizer
fantasizer
gratifies 'er
glorifies 'er
galvanizer
humanizer
horrifies 'er

harmonizer
hypnotizer
idolize 'er
improviser
immunizer
jeopardize 'er
justifies 'er
legalizer
mortifies 'er
mollifies 'er
magnetizer
mystifies 'er
mechanizer
modifies 'er
magnifies 'er
memorizer
minimizer
moralizer
modernizer
mesmerizer
motorizer
mobilizer
nullifies 'er
neutralizer
notifies 'er
organizer
ostracizer
penalize 'er
petrifies 'er
paralyzer
publicizer
patronizer
pasteurizer
plagiarizer
qualifies 'er
recognize 'er
summarizer
stupefies 'er
satisfies 'er
scandalize 'er
sterilizer
stigmatizer
scrutinize 'er
subsidizer
sympathizer

symbolizer
supervisor
sensitizer
socializer
Sanforizer
specializer
synthesizer
tenderizer
terrifies 'er
typifies 'er
terrorizer
tranquilizer
traumatizer
tantalizer
televisor
utilizer
vitalizer
victimize 'er
vaporizer
womanizer

apologizer
acclimatizer
antagonizer
capitalizer
characterize 'er
categorizer
demobilizer
disenfranchiser
demoralizer
disqualifies 'er
dissatisfies 'er
decentralizer
deodorizer
electrifies 'er
economizer
epitomizer
fanaticizer
hypothesizer
idealizer
identifies 'er
immortalizer
monopolizer
nationalizer
preoccupies 'er

personifies 'er
popularizer
refortifies 'er
reorganizer
revitalizer
rationalizer
romanticizer

legitimatizer
psychoanalyzer

IZ-ur

fizzer
frizzer
quizzer
scissor(s)
whizzer

IZ-urd

blizzard
gizzard
lizard
scissored
vizard
wizard

lounge lizard

ĪZ-ur-ē

advisory
provisory

supervisory

IZ-ut

fizz it
frizz it
is it?
visit

exquisite
revisit

IZ-u-tiv
(See IZ-u-div)

IZ-u-tur
(See IZ-u-dur)

O SOUNDS

Ō

	owe	although
	pro	bandeau
bow	Poe	Bordeaux
beau	roe	bateau
blow	row	*bon mot*
crow	Rho	below
dough	sew	bestow
doe	so	Cousteau
faux	sol	*chapeau*
floe	sow	château
flow	stow	*cachepot*
foe	sloe	CO
fro	show	crossbow
go	slow	cash flow
grow	snow	deathblow
glow	schmo	death row
ho	toe	*de trop*
hoe	throw	eat crow
Joe	though	forego
know	tow	freak show
lo	whoa	flambeau
low	woe	floorshow
mot	yo	free flow
Moe		golf pro
mow	ago	game show
no	all show	gung ho
o	all-pro	go-go
oh	aglow	heigh-ho

heave-ho
hello
hum ho
ice floe
info
in tow
Jim Crow
John Doe
Jane Doe
KO
Kwang-Chow
light show
low blow
lie low
longbow
Monroe
moon glow
no show
no-no
nouveau
no-go
outflow
old crow
outgrow
oxbow
outgo
peep show
pueblo
quiz show
rainbow
Rousseau
road show
scarecrow
so-so
say-so
stone's throw
shad roe
skid row
sideshow
sourdough
ski tow
tent show
Thoreau
talk show
tiptoe

van Gogh
yo-yo
you know

all for show
afterglow
Alamo
apropos
art nouveau
best in show
BTO
Buffalo
blow by blow
body blow
crowning blow
calico
CIO
cookie dough
cupid's bow
CEO
dynamo
daddy-o
do-si-do
ebb and flow
even so
even though
fatal blow
fall below
friend or foe
fashion show
gigolo
go below
haricot
hammertoe
high and low
hammerthrow
heel-and-toe
in the know
Ivanhoe
Idaho
Jericho
Jackie O
Kokomo
long ago
Mexico

Mary Jo
mistletoe
minstrel show
Navajo
overflow
overgrow
overthrow
oleo
Ohio
on the go
on tiptoe
olio
one-man show
Oreo
puppet show
piccolo
pompano
portico
Pimlico
picture show
peridot
quid pro quo
Romeo
rodeo
radio
ratio
right-to-know
run the show
SRO
status quo
strike a blow
steal the show
Scorpio
stop the show
so-and-so
stop and go
studio
stereo
semipro
send below
Sloppy Joe
tally ho
TKO
talent show
tippytoe

tic tac toe
Tokyo
to and fro
tale of woe
TV show
toe-to-toe
touch and go
undertow
undergo
underthrow
vertigo
video
white as snow
Wild West show
yes and no
years ago

from the word go
Geronimo
get-up-and-go
go with the flow
hard row to hoe
in utero
medicine show
new-fallen snow
New Mexico
portfolio
Pinocchio
pistachio
punctilio
politico
pay as you go
raring to go
radicchio
ready to go
ready, set, go
silencio
star of the show
whether or no

dog-and-pony show
ex officio
Michaelangelo
pianissimo

generalissimo

pure as the driven
  snow

eeny meeny miny mo

O

aah
ah
awe
blah
baa
bah
bra
caw
chaw
craw
claw
daw
draw
flaw
fa
gnaw
hah
jaw
law
la
ma
naw
paw
pa
raw
rah
saw
schwa
Shaw
straw
spa
shah
slaw
trois
thaw
tau
taw
yah

ah hah
buzz saw
by-law
bourgeois
bear claw
Crenshaw
case law
chainsaw
Choctaw
cha-cha
coleslaw
cat's-paw
éclat
faux pas
foresaw
foie gras
guffaw
gewgaw
grandma
grandpa
ga-ga
glass jaw
ha-ha
hee-haw
hoopla
hurrah
hacksaw
health spa
hawkshaw
in-law
in awe
jackdaw
jigsaw
lockjaw
last straw
leash law
lynchlaw
moola
macaw
outlaw
oompah
old saw
outdraw
power saw
patois

pooh-bah
pshaw
quickdraw
rickshaw
ripsaw
southpaw
seesaw
state law
scrimshaw
sang-froid
ta-ta
tah-dah
Utah
voilà
wah-wah
Warsaw
withdraw

Arkansas
blah, blah, blah
Bogota
baklava
baccarat
brouhaha
canon law
coup d'état
common law
Chickasaw
Chippewa
court of law
civil law
five-card draw
hem and haw
in the raw
la de da
last hurrah
lower jaw
Mardi Gras
moussaka
Mackinac
martial law
Murphy's Law
ma-and-pa
nursing bra
oversaw

oompah-pah
overawe
overdraw
ooh and aah
Omaha
Panama
padded bra
peau de soie
petits pois
qué será
sunshine law
tra la la
training bra
Wichita

above the law
brother-in-law
comsi comsa
father-in-law
federal law
hip hip hurrah
luck of the draw
lay down the law
ménage à trois
Minnie Ha Ha
mother-in-law
quick on the draw
stick in one's craw
sister-in-law
unwritten law

attorney-at-law
long arm of the law
letter of the law
pâté de foie gras
qué será, será

ŌB

globe
Job
lobe
probe
robe
strobe

bathrobe

choir robe
disrobe
earlobe
lap robe
moon probe
microbe
space probe
wardrobe

claustrophobe

bibliophobe

OB

bob
blob
cob
daub
fob
gob
glob
job
knob
lob
mob
rob
sob
slob
snob
swab
squab
throb

athrob
boob job
bag job
corncob
con job
doorknob
fat slob
hobnob
heartthrob
kabob
nabob
nose job
odd-job

snowjob
watch fob

cottonswab
inside job
on-the-job
pull a job
put-up job
reverse snob
shish kebab

corn on the cob
rough as a cob
thingamabob
yessireebob

lie down on the job

ŌB-ē

Gobi
hobie
no bee
obi

Jacoby
Nairobi

OB-ē

bobby
hobby
knobby
lobby
snobby
swabby
slobby

kohlrabi

Hammurabi
Watanabe

OB-ē-ist

hobbyist
knobbiest
lobbyist

snobbiest
slobbiest

ŌB-ēng

probing
robing

disrobing

OB-ēng

bobbing
daubing
lobbing
mobbing
robbing
sobbing
swabbing
throbbing

hobnobbing

ŌB-ē-u

phobia

acrophobia
claustrophobia
homophobia
hydrophobia
technophobia
xenophobia

agoraphobia

ŌB-ik

phobic

aerobic

acrophobic
claustrophobic
homophobic

agoraphobic

ŌB-il
(See ŌB-ul)

OB-in
(See OB-un)

OB-ish

blobbish
slobbish
snobbish
throbbish

OB-lēng

bobbling
gobbling
hobbling
squabbling
wobbling

OB-lin
(See OB-lun)

OB-lō

Pablo
sob low

Diablo

OB-lun

bobblin'
goblin
gobblin'
hobblin'
squabblin'
wobblin'

hobgoblin

OB-lur

bobbler
cobbler
gobbler
hobbler
squabbler

wobbler

cherry cobbler
turkey gobbler

ŌB-ō

hobo
lobo
no beau
no bow
oboe
slow beau

OB-ōn

jawbone
sawbone(s)

OB-ru

sabra

macabre

candleabra

OB-stur

lobster
mobster
sobster

OB-ub-ul

bobbable
daubable
probable
robbable
swabbable

improbable

ŌB-ul

global
mobile
Mobil
noble

Sobel

Chernobyl
ennoble
ignoble
immobile

OB-ul

bauble
bobble
cobble
gobble
hobble
squabble
wobble

collywobble(s)

OB-un

bobbin
bobbin'
dobbin
lobbin'
mobbin'
robin
robbin'
sobbin'
swabbin'
throbbin'

hobnobbin'
round robin

Baskin-Robbin(s)

ŌB-ur

prober
rober
sober

cold sober
disrober
October

OB-ur

bobber
clobber
dauber
jobber
lobber
mobber
mob 'er
robber
rob 'er
sobber
slobber
swabber
throbber

graverobber
hobnobber
heartthrobber
macabre

cradle robber
cops and robber(s)

OB-ur-ē

robbery
snobbery
slobbery

highway robbery

OB-ur-ēng

clobbering
slobbering

ŌB-ust

no bust
robust

ŌCH

broach
coach
poach
roach

approach
cockroach
encroach
reproach
stagecoach

self-reproach

OCH

blotch
botch
crotch
klatsch
notch
Scotch
splotch
swatch
watch

birdwatch
debauch
deathwatch
hopscotch
nightwatch
stopwatch
topnotch
weight-watch
wristwatch

coffee klatsch
pocket watch

OCH-ē

bocce
blotchy
splotchy

hibachi

ŌCH-ēng

broaching
coaching
poaching

approaching

encroaching
reproaching

OCH-ēng

botching
blotching
notching
splotching
watching

birdwatching
debauching
weight-watching

OCH-ō

macho
nacho

gazpacho

ŌCH-u-bul

broachable
coachable
poachable

approachable
reproachable

unapproachable

ŌCH-ur

coach 'er
poacher

approach 'er

OCH-ur

botcher
notcher
splotcher
watcher

bird watcher
clock watcher

debaucher
girl watcher
hopscotcher
weight-watcher

ŌD

bode
bowed
code
crowed
flowed
goad
glowed
hoed
load
lode
lowed
mowed
mode
node
ode
owed
ohed
Rhode(s)
rowed
road
rode
strode
sowed
sewed
stowed
Spode
showed
slowed
snowed
toed
towed
toad

abode
bestowed
back road
corrode
caseload
crossroad

commode
carload
dress code
decode
erode
explode
forebode
freeload
hoptoad
high road
implode
lymph node
Morse Code
no-noed
outmode
payload
planeload
railroad
shipload
tiptoed
truckload
toll road
unload
workload
zip code

à la mode
buffaloed
Comstock Lode
episode
ebbed and flowed
electrode
hammertoed
hit the road
mother lode
open road
overload
overrode
overflowed
pigeon-toed
penal code

area code
carry the load
one for the road
middle of the road

OD

awed
bahed
broad
bod
cawed
Claude
clawed
clod
cod
flawed
fraud
gnawed
God
hod
jawed
laud
mod
nod
odd
plod
pawed
pod
prod
quad
rod
sawed
scrod
sod
squad
shod
Todd
trod
wad

abroad
applaud
ah-hahed
bipod
bomb squad
Cape Cod
defraud
death squad
downtrod
facade

faux pased
goon squad
Greek god
hot-rod
hurrahed
maraud
outlawed
pea pod
roughshod
roulade
ramrod
slipshod
seesawed
spit-wad
slack-jawed
tightwad
tripod
tin god
thank God
unwad
unshod
untrod
ungod(ly)
unflawed
vice squad

Axelrod
act of God
bunco squad
cattle prod
demigod
fishing rod
firing squad
go with God
give the nod
goldenrod
house of God
hemmed and hawed
la-de-dahed
lightning rod
Lamb of God
land of Nod
monkeypod
oompah-pahed
overawed

ohed and ahed
riot squad
promenade
shoot one's wad
tra-la-lahed
traverse rod
wrath of God

divining rod
Marquis de Sade
Scheherazade
so help me God

by guess and by God

ŌD-ē

bloaty
brodie
Cody
doty
Dodie
floaty
OD
roadie
toady
throaty

coyote
Capote
Quixote

OD-ē

Audi
blotty
bawdy
body
clotty
cloddy
dotty
gaudy
haughty
knotty
naughty
ploddy
potty

spotty
shoddy
snotty
Scottie
Saudi
squatty
toddy
thoughty

chapati
cum laude
embody
gelati
homebody
hot toddy
karate
nobody
somebody
wide body

antibody
able body
anybody
busybody
ev'rybody
glitterati
manicotti
student body
training potty

everybody
heavenly body
illiterati
illuminati
magna cum laude
summa cum laude

OD-ed
(See ŌD-ud)

ŌD-ēd

pottied

embodied
full-bodied

OD-ed
(See OD-ud)

ŌD-el
(See ŌD-ul)

OD-el
(See OD-ul)

OD-en
(See OD-un)

ŌD-ēng

boating
boding
bloating
coding
coating
doting
floating
goading
gloating
loading
noting
quoting
toting
voting

connoting
corroding
devoting
decoding
demoting
denoting
eroding
emoting
exploding
foreboding
misquoting
outvoting
promoting
unloading

color coding
overloading

OD-ēng

blotting
clotting
dotting
jotting
knotting
lauding
nodding
potting
plotting
plodding
rotting
spotting
squatting
swatting
trodding
wadding
yachting

applauding
allotting
boycotting
defrauding
globe-trotting
hot-rodding
marauding
ramrodding
unwadding

promenading

OD-ē-nus

bawdiness
gaudiness
naughtiness
spottiness
shoddiness
snottiness
squattiness

OD-ē-ō

audio
patio

**OD-es
(See OD-us)**

**OD-es-ē
(See OD-us-ē)**

**OD-est
(See OD-ust)**

ŌD-ē-um

odium
podium
sodium
rhodium

ŌD-ē-un

toadyin'

custodian
Cambodian

nickelodeon

ŌD-ē-us

odious

commodious
melodious

**OD-i-bul
(See OD-u-bul)**

**OD-i-fi
(See OD-u-fi)**

OD-ij

cottage
wattage

OD-ik

otic

aquatic
biotic
chaotic
despotic
exotic
erotic
hypnotic
methodic
melodic
neurotic
narcotic
psychotic
quixotic
seismotic
spasmodic

aeronautic
idiotic
periodic
patriotic
semiotic
symbiotic
unexotic
unerotic

antibiotic
antispasmotic
macrobiotic

OD-i-kul

nautical
otical

exotical
erotical
despotical
hypnotical
melodical

methodical
seismotical
spasmodical

aeronautical
idiotical
periodical

OD-i-lē
(See OD-u-lē)

OD-is
(See OD-us)

OD-is-ē
(See OD-us-ē)

OD-ish

moddish
oddish
Scottish

OD-it
(See OD-ut)

OD-it-ē
(See OD-ut-ē)

OD-i-tōr-ē
(See OD-u-tōr-ē)

ŌD-iv

dotive
motive
notive
votive

connotive
demotive
emotive

automotive
locomotive

ulterior motive

ODJ
(See OJ)

OD-lē

broadly
godly
oddly

slipshodly
ungodly

ŌD-lēng
(See ŌD-ul-ēng)

OD-lēng
(See OD-ul-ēng)

OD-lin
(See OD-lun)

OD-lun

bottlin'
coddlin'
dawdlin'
modelin'
maudlin
swaddlin'
toddlin'
waddlin'

remodelin'

mollycoddlin'

OD-lur

bottler
coddler

dawdler
modeler
toddler
twaddler
waddler

mollycoddler

ŌD-ō

dodo
no dough
photo
sotto

DeSoto
Kyoto
risotto
Wirephoto

Matsumoto
telephoto

dead as a dodo

OD-ō

auto
blotto
grotto
lotto
motto
Otto
Prado

bravado
Delgado
mulatto
Mikado
potato
staccato
tomato
vibrato

avocado
Alvarado
Colorado
Coronado

desperado
Eldorado
obligato
pizzicato

amontillado
inamorato

aficionado
incommunicado

Ō-down

flow down
hoedown
go down
lowdown
sew down
showdown
slowdown

OD-rē

Audrey
bawdry
cadre
padre
tawdry

compadre

ŌD-u

coda
quota
soda

club soda
cream soda
iota
pagoda
ricotta
Toyota

baking soda
ice cream soda
Minnesota
North Dakota

root-beer soda
Scotch and soda
Sarasota
South Dakota

bicarbonate of soda

OD-u

gotta
oughta
whatta

armada
airmada
cantata
Carlotta
cicada
errata
Estrada
Granada
pro rata
piccata
piñata
ramada
regatta
sonata
tostada
Zapata

Ensenada
enchilada
terra cotta
veal piccata

carne asada
inamorata
persona grata
piña colada

aficionada
persona non grata
the whole enchilada

ŌD-u-bul

floatable
goadable

loadable
notable
potable
quotable
totable
votable

corrodable
demotable
denotable
decodable
erodable
explodable
misquotable
promotable
unquotable
unnotable
unloadable

OD-u-bul

audible
laudable
plottable
proddable
spottable

applaudable
defraudable
inaudible
unwadable

ŌD-ud

boded
boated
bloated
coded
coated
doted
floated
goaded
gloated
loaded
moded
noted

quoted
toted
voted

connoted
corroded
devoted
denoted
decoded
emoted
eroded
exploded
misquoted
outmoded
outvoted
promoted
unloaded

overloaded
sugar-coated

OD-ud

clotted
dotted
knotted
lauded
nodded
plodded
podded
prodded
potted
plotted
rotted
spotted
slotted
squatted
swatted
sodded
trotted
wadded

allotted
applauded
carotid
marauded
ramrodded

unwadded

polka-dotted
promenaded
turkey-trotted

OD-u-fī

codify
modify

**OD-u-kul
(See OD-i-kul)**

ŌD-ul

modal
nodal
total
yodel

subtotal
teetotal

anecdotal
sacerdotal

OD-ūl

module
nodule
odd yule

OD-ul

bottle
coddle
caudle
dawdle
glottal
model
mottle
swaddle
toddle
throttle
twaddle
waddle

Coke bottle
duck waddle
floor model
full throttle
remodel
role model
scale model

Aristotle
airplane model
baby bottle
fashion model
hit the bottle
mollycoddle
water bottle
working model

hot-water bottle
Iztaccihuatl

OD-u-lē

bodily
bawdily
gaudily
haughtily
naughtily
spottily
shoddily
snottily

ŌD-ul-ēng

totaling
yodeling

OD-ul-ēng

bottling
coddling
dawdling
modeling
swaddling
toddling
throttling
waddling

remodeling
mollycoddling

OD-ul-us

bottle us
coddle us
nautilus
throttle us

ŌD-um

bloat 'em
bowed 'em
coat 'em
code 'em
float 'em
goad 'em
hoed 'em
load 'em
mowed 'em
note 'em
owed 'em
quote 'em
rode 'em
sowed 'em
scrotum
sewed 'em
showed 'em
snowed 'em
towed 'em
tote 'em
totem
vote 'em
wrote 'em

corrode 'em
demote 'em
erode 'em
explode 'em
factotum
misquote 'em
outmode 'em
outvote 'em
promote 'em
unload 'em

OD-um

autumn
awed 'em
brought 'em
bottom
bought 'em
clawed 'em
caught 'em
dot 'em
flawed 'em
fought 'em
gnawed 'em
got 'em
laud 'em
pot 'em
prod 'em
pawed 'em
rot 'em
shot 'em
spot 'em
sawed 'em
sought 'em
swat 'em
Sodom
taught 'em
trod 'em
wad 'em

applaud 'em
defraud 'em
forgot 'em
false bottom
hit bottom
hurrahed 'em
rock bottom
unwad 'em

Foggy Bottom
overawed 'em

OD-um-ē

autumny
bottomy
lotta me
notta me

odd o' me
sodomy

dichotomy
lobotomy

tracheotomy

OD-un

Aden
laudin'
noddin'
ploddin'
proddin'
sodden
trodden
waddin'

applaudin'
defraudin'
downtrodden
hot-roddin'
maraudin'
unwaddin'
untrodden

ŌD-ur

boater
bloater
coder
doter
floater
goader
gloater
loader
motor
noter
odor
oater
quoter
rotor
Schroeder
toter
voter
wrote 'er

corroder
connoter
demoter
denoter
decoder
emoter
exploder
eroder
freeloader
misquoter
promoter
remoter
reloader
unloader

overloader

absentee voter

OD-ur

awed 'er
brought 'er
blotter
broader
caught 'er
cotter
clotter
daughter
dotter
fodder
fought 'er
got 'er
hotter
jotter
knotter
lauder
modder
nodder
otter
odder
plodder
plotter
potter
prodder
rotter

slaughter
swatter
spotter
squatter
solder
shodder
trodder
tauter
trotter
taught 'er
totter
water
wadder
yachter

applauder
allotter
bathwater
breakwater
backwater
bilge water
bloodshotter
Clearwater
defrauder
dishwater
dogtrotter
distraughter
fox-trotter
fly swatter
floodwater
firewater
globetrotter
hot-rodder
hot water
ink blotter
ice water
jerkwater
manslaughter
marauder
ramrodder
rosewater
rainwater
salt water
sea otter
step-daughter

spring water
still water
tread water
tap water
unwadder

above water
alma mater
bread and water
bottled water
cannon fodder
drink of water
fire and water
holy water
in hot water
promenader
teeter-totter
turkey-trotter
toilet water
underwater
walk on water

dead in the water
fish out of water

come hell or high
water

ŌD-ur-ē

coterie
notary
odory
rotary
votary

OD-ur-ē

dottery
lottery
pottery
tottery
watery

camaraderie

OD-ur-ēng

doddering
daughtering
pottering
slaughtering
soldering
watering

mouth-watering

ŌD-ur-īz

motorize
notarize
note 'er eyes
odorize
voter ayes

deodorize
promote 'er eyes

OD-ur-īz

blot 'er eyes
cauterize
clawed 'er eyes
dot 'er i's
got 'er eyes
sought 'er eyes

OD-ur-ut

bought 'er it
moderate
slaughter it
taught 'er it
water it

immoderate

ŌD-us

bloat us
coat us
goad us
lotus
load us

modus
note us
owed us
quote us
rowed us
rode us
showed us
slowed us
towed us
wrote us

demote us
denote us
erode us
misquote us
outmode us
outvote us
promote us
unload us

OD-us

bodice
bought us
brought us
caught us
fought us
goddess
glottis
got us
prod us
sought us
spot us
shot us
swat us
taught us

sex goddess

epiglottis

OD-us-ē

goddessy
odyssey

geodesy

OD-ust

hottest
modest
oddest
sawdust
tautest

distraughtest
immodest
maraudist
slipshoddest

OD-ut

audit
awed it
blot it
bought it
brought it
clawed it
caught it
dot it
flawed it
fought it
got it
laud it
plaudit
pawed it
prod it
pot it
sawed it
spot it
shot it
swat it
taught it
thought it

allot it
applaud it
forgot it
outlawed it
unwad it

overawed it
overshot it

OD-ut-ē

oddity

commodity

OD-u-tōr-ē

auditory

laudatory

OD-wā

Broadway

flawed way

mod way

odd way

off-Broadway

slipshod way

unflawed way

Ō-ē
(See also ŌĒ)

bowie

blowy

Chloe

doughy

glowy

Joey

showy

snowy

ŌĒ
(See also Ō-ē)

boy

buoy

cloy

coy

goy

joy

ploy

poi

Roy

soy

toy

Troy

ahoy

annoy

bok choy

boy toy

destroy

deploy

enjoy

employ

Hanoi

killjoy

Kilroy

lifebuoy

oh boy

Savoy

Tolstoi

unshowy

viceroy

attaboy

altar boy

corduroy

fair-haired boy

good ole boy

hoi polloi

Iroquois

Illinois

overjoy

mama's boy

Peck's Bad Boy

pride and joy

redeploy

real McCoy

ship ahoy

Tinkertoy

unemploy

viceroy

water boy

whipping boy

Helen of Troy

the real McCoy

mama's little boy

ŌĒD

buoyed

cloyed

Freud

Floyd

Lloyd

ployed

toyed

void

android

annoyed

alloyed

avoid

crapoid

decoyed

deployed

devoid

destroyed

enjoyed

employed

keloid

Negroid

schizoid

thyroid

typhoid

tabloid

asteroid

adenoid

arachnoid

alkaloid

anthropoid

celluloid

cretinoid

hemorrhoid

mongoloid

null and void

overjoyed

Polaroid

paranoid

rheumatoid

redeployed

self-employed

trapezoid
unemployed

ŌĒD-ēng

voiding

avoiding
exploiting
keloiding

ŌĒD-ud

voided

avoided
exploited
keloided

ŌĒD-ur

goiter
loiter
moider
voider

avoider
adroiter
devoider
destroyed 'er
exploiter
embroider
employed 'er

overjoyed 'er
reconnoiter

ŌĒD-ur-ēng

loitering
moidering

embroidering
no loitering
reconnoitering

ŌĒD-us

buoyed us
coitus

annoyed us
avoid us
deployed us
destroyed us
enjoyed us
exploit us
employed us

overjoyed us

ŌĒ-ēng

buoying
cloying
toying

annoying
destroying
deploying
enjoying
employing

redeploying

ŌĒK

stoic

heroic

ŌĒL

boil
broil
coil
Doyle
foil
Hoyle
loyal
oil
roil
royal
soil
spoil
toil

airfoil
coal oil

crude oil
despoil
disloyal
embroil
gargoyle
hard-boil
recoil
soft-boil
strike oil
tinfoil
topsoil
turmoil
uncoil
unspoil

baby oil
boil in oil
battle royal
castor oil
disembroil
hydrofoil
olive oil
Standard Oil

cod-liver oil

aluminum foil
according to Hoyle
burn the midnight oil

ŌĒLD

boiled
broiled
coiled
foiled
oiled
roiled
soiled
spoiled
toiled

despoiled
embroiled
hard-boiled
parboiled
recoiled

uncoiled
unspoiled
well-oiled

disembroiled

ŌĒL-ē

boily
doily
oily
spoily

ŌĒL-ēng

boiling
broiling
coiling
foiling
oiling
roiling
soiling
spoiling
toiling

despoiling
embroiling
recoiling
uncoiling

ŌĒL-et
(See ŌĒL-ut)

ŌĒL-ist
(See ŌĒL-ust)

ŌĒL-tē

loyalty
royalty

disloyalty

ŌĒL-ur

boiler
broiler

coiler
foiler
loyaler
oiler
royaler
soiler
spoiler
toiler

despoiler
disloyaler
embroiler
potboiler
recoiler

ŌĒL-ust

loyalist
loyalest
royalist
royalest

ŌĒL-ut

boil it
broil it
coil it
foil it
oil it
spoil it
soil it
toilet

hard-boil it

ŌĒ-ment

deployment
enjoyment
employment

redeployment
unemployment

ŌĒN

coin
groin

join
loin

adjoin
conjoin
disjoin
Des Moines
enjoin
purloin
rejoin
sirloin

flip a coin
tenderloin

ŌĒND

coined
joined

adjoined
conjoined
disjoined
enjoined
purloined
rejoined

Ō-ēng

bowing
blowing
Boeing
crowing
flowing
going
growing
glowing
hoeing
knowing
lowing
mowing
owing
rowing
sewing
sowing
stowing
showing

snowing
toeing
throwing
towing

all-knowing
bestowing
churchgoing
foregoing
flamethrowing
free-flowing
fast growing
mind-blowing
outflowing
outgoing
ongoing
stonethrowing
tiptoeing

easygoing
overflowing
overthrowing
partygoing
rodeoing
tippytoeing
undergoing

O-ēng

aahing
awing
bahing
cawing
chawing
clawing
drawing
gnawing
jawing
pawing
rahing
sawing
thawing

cha-chaing
guffawing
hurrahing
hee-hawing

outlawing
oompahing
outdrawing
pshawing
seesawing
withdrawing

overawing
overdrawing

hip-hip-hurrahing

ŌĒNT

joint
point

anoint
appoint
ballpoint
bluepoint
beer joint
clip joint
checkpoint
disjoint
dew point
gyp joint
high point
match point
midpoint
pinpoint
strip joint
viewpoint
West Point

at gunpoint
at sword's point
Brownie point(s)
boiling point
breaking point
counterpoint
disappoint
focal point
needlepoint
out of joint
petit point
reappoint

starting point
to the point
turning point
vantage point

break-even point
decimal point
get to the point
jumping-off point
nose out of joint

exclamation point

ŌĒNT-ed
(See ŌĒNT-ud)

ŌĒNT-ēng

pointing

anointing
appointing
pinpointing

disappointing
needlepointing
reappointing

ŌĒNT-ment

ointment

appointment
disjointment

disappointment
reappointment

fly in the ointment

ŌĒNT-ud

jointed
pointed

appointed
disjointed
loose-jointed
pinpointed

disappointed
double-jointed
needlepointed
reappointed

ŌĒS

choice
Joyce
voice

by choice
free choice
first choice
invoice
last choice
no choice
one voice
prochoice
rejoice
Rolls-Royce
turquoise

dealer's choice
still, small voice

multiple choice

ŌĒS-ēng

voicing

invoicing
rejoicing

ŌĒST

foist
hoist
moist
voiced

invoiced
rejoiced
unmoist
unvoiced

ŌĒST-ēng

foisting
hoisting

ŌĒST-ur

cloister
hoister
moister
oyster
roister

ŌĒST-ur-us

boisterous
cloister us
roisterous

ŌĒ-sum

joysome
noisome

annoy some
enjoy some
employ some

ŌĒT

Hoyt

adroit
Detroit
exploit

maladroit

Ō-et
(See Ō-ut)

ŌĒT-ēng
(See ŌĒD-ēng)

ŌĒT-ur
(See ŌĒD-ur)

ŌĒT-ur-ēng
(See ŌĒD-ur-ēng)

ŌĒT-us
(See ŌĒD-us)

ŌĒ-u
(See ŌĒ-yu)

ŌĒ-ul
(See ŌĒL)

ŌĒ-uns

buoyance

annoyance
clairvoyance
flamboyance

ŌĒ-unt

buoyant

clairvoyant
flamboyant

ŌĒ-ur

Boyer
cloyer
coyer
showier
snowier
voyeur

annoyer
destroyer
deployer
enjoy 'er
employer

ŌĒ-us

joyous

annoy us
destroy us
deploy us
enjoy us
employ us

unemploy us

ŌĒ-yu

buoy ya
Goya

annoy ya
destroy ya
enjoy ya
employ ya
La Jolla
Montoya
Sequoia

overjoy ya
paranoia
redeploy ya
unemploy ya

ŌĒ-yur
(See ŌĒ-ur)

ŌĒZ

buoys
boys
joys
noise
poise
ploys
toys

annoys
cowboys
convoys
decoys
doughboys

destroys
deploys
enjoys
employs
envoys
killjoys
playboys
schoolboys
turquoise
tomboys
viceroys

counterpoise
equipoise
overjoys
redeploys
traffic noise
Tinkertoys
water boys
whipping boys

avoirdupois

ŌĒZ-ē

Boise
noisy

turquoisy

ŌĒZ-un

noisin'
poison
poisin'

ŌF

loaf
oaf

OF

boff
coif
cough
doff
golf

off
prof
quaff
scoff
soph
trough

blast-off
brush-off
Bake-Off
cutoff
castoff
dummkopf
day off
goof-off
hands off
kickoff
kiss-off
Khrushchev
lift-off
layoff
payoff
playoff
runoff
ripoff
show-off
standoff
send-off
spin-off
take-off
tip-off
trade-off
turn-off
tee off
well-off
write-off

better off
Gorbachev
hit it off
laugh it off
on and off
smoker's cough
stroganoff
whooping cough
water trough

Baryshnikov
blow the lid off
beat the socks off

miniature golf

ŌF-ē

low fee
no fee
pro fee
Sophie
trophy

OF-ē

coffee
scoffy
toffee

OF-el
(See OF-ul)

OF-en
(See OF-un)

OF-ēng

coughing
coifing
doffing
golfing
offing
scoffing

in the offing

OF-en-ur
(See OF-un-ur)

OF-et
(See OF-ut)

OF-ik

apostrophic
catastrophic
philosophic

OF-in
(See OF-un)

OF-is
(See OF-us)

OF-ish

crawfish

standoffish

OF-it
(See OF-ut)

OFT

coiffed
coughed
doffed
loft
oft
quaffed
soft
scoffed
waft

aloft
hayloft

OFT-ē

lofty
softy

OFT-en
(See OFT-un)

OFT-un

loftin'
often
waftin'

OF-ul

awful
lawful
waffle

falafel
god-awful
unlawful

OF-un

coughin'
coffin
doffin'
often
scoffin'
soften

every so often

OF-un-ē

cacophony
Christophany

OF-un-ur

oftener
scoffin' er
softener

OF-un-us

soften us
scoffin' us

cacophonous

ŌF-ur

chauffeur
gofer

gopher
loafer
shofar

penny loafer

OF-ur

boffer
cougher
coif 'er
coffer
doffer
offer
off 'er
proffer
quaffer
scoffer

make an offer

ŌF-ur-ēng

chauffeuring
goferring

OF-ur-ēng

offering
proffering

OF-us

coif us
office
off us
scoff us

OF-ut

off it
profit
prophet
scoff it

nonprofit

ŌG

brogue
rogue
vogue

OG

bog
cog
clog
dog
fog
frog
flog
glogg
grog
hog
jog
log
nog
Prague
schlag
tog

agog
bird dog
befog
backlog
bulldog
bullfrog
defog
dense fog
eggnog
groundhog
guard dog
hedgehog
hangdog
leapfrog
prologue
road hog
red-dog
ship's log
top dog
unclog
warthog

watchdog
whole-hog
yule log

analog
catalog
chili dog
dialogue
dog-eat-dog
demagogue
epilogue
go whole hog
monologue
navy grog
polliwog
pedagogue
pea-soup fog
pettifog
synagogue
salty dog
travelogue
underdog
waterlog

beware of dog
card catalog
go to the dog(s)
put on the dog
rain cats and dog(s)
sleep like a log
Seeing-Eye dog

live high on the hog

ŌG-ē

bogy
bogey
dogie
fogy
Hoagy
stogy
shogi
Yogi

Muskogee
old fogy

OG-ē

boggy
cloggy
doggie
foggy
froggy
groggy
hoggy
smoggy
soggy

OG-ēng

bogging
clogging
dogging
fogging
flogging
hogging
jogging
logging

befogging
bulldogging
defogging
hotdogging
unclogging

cataloging
waterlogging

OG-in
(See OG-un)

ŌG-ish

roguish
voguish

OG-lēng

boggling
joggling
ogling

hornswoggling
mind-boggling

ŌG-ō

logo
no go
slow go

OG-ō

Chicago
Iago
Zhivago

Santiago

OG-ruf-ē

biography
cartography
cosmography
cryptography
cacography
demography
geography
lithography
orthography
photography
pornography
stenography
typography
topography

bibliography
choreography
lexicography
oceanography
physiography

autobiography
cinematography

OG-ruf-ur

biographer
cartographer
lithographer
pornographer
photographer
stenographer

topographer

bibliographer
choreographer

ŌG-u

toga
yoga

Calistoga
Saratoga

Ticonderoga

OG-u-div
(See OG-u-tiv)

ŌG-ul

mogul
ogle
Vogel

OG-ul

boggle
goggle
joggle
ogle
toggle

boondoggle
hornswoggle

OG-u-mē

hog o' me

monogamy

ŌG-un

hogan
Logan
slogan

OG-un

cloggin'
doggin'
foggin'
floggin'
hoggin'
joggin'
loggin'
noggin

bulldoggin'
defoggin'
leapfroggin'
toboggan
uncloggin'

cataloguin'

OG-ur

augur
bogger
clogger
dogger
fogger
flogger
hogger
jogger
logger

bulldogger
befogger
defogger
leapfrogger
unclogger

cataloguer
pettifogger

memory jogger

OG-ur-ē

augury
doggery
toggery

pettifoggery

OG-ur-ul

doggerel

inaugural

OG-ust

August

demagoguist
monologuist

OG-u-tiv

derogative
prerogative

interrogative

OG-u-tōr-ē

derogatory

interrogatory

OJ
(See also OJH)

dodge
Hadj
Hodge
lodge

barrage
corsage
collage
dislodge
garage
hodgepodge
mirage
montage
massage
ski lodge

bon voyage
camouflage
decoupage
entourage

fuselage
hunting lodge
sabotage
Travelodge
wrist corsage

espionage

OJ-ē

stodgy

demagogy
pedagogy

OJ-en-ē
(See OJ-un-ē)

OJ-ēng

dodging
lodging

dislodging
massaging

camouflaging
sabotaging

ŌJH

loge

Limoges

OJH

barrage
corsage
fromage
garage
massage
montage
mirage
potage
triage

abatage

bon voyage
camouflage
entourage
decoupage
decolletage
sabotage

OJ-ik

logic
stodgic

pathologic

OJ-ik-ul

logical

illogical

analogical
astrological
biological
cosmological
chronological
geological
mythological
neurological
pathological
psychological
theological
technological
tautological
zoological

archeological
anthropological
climatological
etymological
entomological
genealogical
gynocological
ideological
meteorological
sociological
physiological
toxicological

OJ-un-ē

progeny

misogeny
monogyny

OJ-ur

codger
dodger
lodger
Roger

barrager
dislodger
massager
Will Roger(s)

camouflager
Jolly Roger
sabotage 'er

ŌK

bloke
broke
coke
Coke
choke
cloak
croak
folk
joke
oak
oke
poke
soak
spoke
stoke
stroke
smoke
sloke
toque
woke
yolk
yoke

awoke
baroque
bad joke
backstroke
breaststroke
bespoke
convoke
cowpoke
chain-smoke
dead broke
downstroke
evoke
egg yolk
flat broke
go broke
housebroke
heatstroke
invoke
in-joke
kinfolk
misspoke
menfolk
provoke
revoke
slowpoke
sunstroke
showfolk
sidestroke
stone-broke
townsfolk
unyoke
uncloak

artichoke
countryfolk
cloud of smoke
Diet Coke
dirty joke
go for broke
Holyoke
holy smoke
just plain folk(s)
masterstroke
okey-doke
puff of smoke

poison oak
running joke
womenfolk

go up in smoke
practical joke
pig in a poke

OK
(See also OLK)

ach
auk
block
Bach
chock
cock
chalk
clock
crock
dawk
doc
dock
flock
frock
gawk
grok
hawk
hock
Jacques
jock
knock
lock
loch
mock
Mach
pock
rock
roc
smock
sock
stock
shock
stalk
squawk
schlock

talk
walk
wok

ad hoc
armlock
backtalk
Bangkok
boardwalk
beanstalk
bedrock
cellblock
catwalk
crosswalk
cornstalk
cakewalk
car lock
cold-cock
chalk talk
duckwalk
dry dock
deadlock
defrock
flintlock
fast-talk
girltalk
gridlock
gamecock
Hitchcock
hemlock
hard rock
hamhock
headlock
Iraq
in stock
jaywalk
jayhawk
jive talk
knock-knock
livestock
Mohawk
o'clock
outtalk
outwalk
pep talk

punk rock
padlock
peacock
post doc
roadblock
Rorshach
restock
sidewalk
sweet talk
spacewalk
shamrock
Sherlock
shellshock
shoptalk
sleepwalk
small talk
sales talk
sunblock
shylock
speed walk
smooth-talk
tick-tock
take stock
time clock
unlock
Van Gogh
woodblock
windsock
woodcock
warlock
wedlock

Antioch
auction block
aftershock
alarm clock
acid rock
baby talk
blue-chip stock
butcher block
chicken hawk
cuckoo clock
culture shock
chopping block
double-talk

eagle hawk
future shock
hammerlock
hollyhock
interlock
John Hancock
Little Rock
laughingstock
mental block
nature walk
overstock
out of stock
open stock
on the block
pillow talk
park and lock
poppycock
round-the-clock
shuttlecock
stumbling block
saddle block
summer stock
starting block
tomahawk
tic-a-lock
table talk
take a walk
writer's block
weathercock

around-the-clock
coquilles St. Jacques
capital stock
cock of the walk
digital clock
electric shock
grandfather's clock
hard as a rock

chip off the old block
new kid on the block
security lock

biological clock

ŌK-ē

croaky
cokie
gnocchi
hokey
Okie
poky
smoky

Old Smokey

hokey-pokey
okey-dokey

OK-ē

cocky
chalky
gawky
gnocchi
hockey
jockey
rocky
stocky
squawky
sake
talkie

disc jockey
desk jockey
field hockey
ice hockey
Milwaukee
rumaki
souvlaki

Jabberwocky
Nagasaki
shiitake
sukiyaki
teriyaki
walkie-talkie

ŌK-el
(See ŌK-ul)

ŌK-en
(See ŌK-un)

ŌK-ēng

choking
croaking
joking
poking
soaking
stoking
stroking
smoking

convoking
chain-smoking
evoking
invoking
no smoking
provoking
revoking
unyoking

OK-ēng

blocking
clocking
docking
flocking
gawking
knocking
locking
mocking
pocking
rocking
smocking
socking
stocking
shocking
stalking
squawking
talking
walking

cakewalking
deadlocking

defrocking
fast-talking
gridlocking
jaywalking
outtalking
outwalking
padlocking
restocking
spacewalking
sweet-talking
silk stocking
sleepwalking
speed-walking
smooth-talking
tick-tocking
unlocking

body stocking
double-talking
interlocking
overstocking
pillow-talking
tic-a-locking

OK-ē-nus

cockiness
chalkiness
gawkiness
rockiness
stockiness
squawkiness
talkiness

ŌK-ē-ō

Tokyo

Pinocchio

OK-et
(See OK-ut)

ŌK-ē-ul

baroquial
parochial

ŌK-ē-ur

hokier
pokier
smokier

OK-ēz

jockeys
Rockies
talkies

disc jockeys

OK-ī

cockeye
hawkeye

streptococci

OK-i-lē
(See OK-u-lē)

OK-nē

cockney
knock-knee

ŌK-ō

cocoa
loco
poco
Yoko

rococo

barococo

poco a poco

OK-ō

socko
taco

Morocco
sirocco

OK-ri-sē
(See OK-ru-sē)

OK-ru-sē

autocracy
androcracy
bureaucracy
democracy
hypocrisy
monocracy
plutocracy
theocracy
technocracy
timocracy

aristocracy
mediocracy

OK-ru-tēz

Socrates

Hippocrates

mediocrities

ŌKS
(See ŌX)

OKS
(See OX)

OK-shun

auction

concoction

OK-shus
(See OX-yus)

OKS-ik
(See OX-ik)

ŌKT

choked
cloaked
croaked
joked
poked
soaked
stoked
stroked
smoked

convoked
chain-smoked
evoked
invoked
provoked
revoked

OKT

blocked
chocked
chalked
cocked
clocked
crocked
docked
flocked
frocked
gawked
hocked
knocked
locked
mocked
rocked
pocked
socked
stalked
stocked
shocked
smocked
squawked
talked
walked

concoct

deadlocked
defrocked
half-cocked
jaywalked
landlocked
outtalked
padlocked
restocked
shellshocked
sweet-talked
tick-tocked
unfrocked
unlocked

baby-talked
double-talked
interlocked
overstocked
pillow-talked

OKT-ur

blocked 'er
cocked 'er
clocked 'er
doctor
docked 'er
hocked 'er
knocked 'er
locked 'er
mocked 'er
proctor
socked 'er
stalked 'er
shocked 'er
walked 'er

concocter
outtalked 'er
sweet-talked 'er
unfrocked 'er
witch doctor

ŌK-u

coca
mocha

polka

Almond Roca
carioca
tapioca

ŌK-ul

focal
local
vocal
yokel

bifocal
trifocal

local yokel

OK-ul

cockle

debacle

OK-u-lē

broccoli
cockily
gawkily
rockily

OK-ū-lur

jocular
ocular

binocular

ŌK-um

broke 'em
choke 'em
croak 'em
hokum
joke 'em
poke 'em
soak 'em
stroke 'em

smoke 'em
woke 'em

ŌK-un

broken
chokin'
croakin'
jokin'
oaken
pokin'
spoken
strokin'
token
woken

awoken
bus token
bespoken
chain-smokin'
evokin'
Hoboken
housebroken
heartbroken
invokin'
love token
misspoken
outspoken
plainspoken
provokin'
revokin'
soft-spoken
unspoken
unbroken
well-spoken

by the same token

OK-up

chalk up
knock up
lockup
stock up
talk up
walk-up

ŌK-ur

broker
choker
croaker
joker
ocher
poker
stoker
stroker
smoker
soaker
woke 'er

awoke 'er
chain-smoker
convoker
evoker
fire stoker
invoker
nonsmoker
provoker
powerbroker
pawn broker
pearl choker
revoker
stockbroker
strip poker

mediocre
red-hot poker

OK-ur

blocker
cocker
clocker
chalker
crocker
docker
flocker
frocker
gawker
hawker
knocker
locker
mocker

rocker
socker
soccer
stalker
shocker
stocker
smocker
squawker
snocker
talker
walker

defrocker
door knocker
fast talker
floorwalker
footlocker
jaywalker
men's locker
night stalker
outtalker
padlocker
sweet-talker
sunblocker
smooth-talker
sleepwalker
streetwalker
unlocker
unblocker

beta blocker
double-talker
interlocker
Knickerbocker
off one's rocker
pillow talker
tic-a-locker
tightrope walker

OK-ur-ē

crockery
mockery

ŌK-us

broke us
crocus
choke us
croak us
focus
hocus
joke us
locus
poke us
soak us
stroke us
smoke us
woke us

awoke us
in focus
provoke us

hocus-pocus
out of focus

OK-us

block us
Bacchus
caucus
coccus
clock us
dock us
knock us
mock us
rock us
raucous
sock us
shock us
stalk us
walk us

Caracas
defrock us
landlock us
maracas
padlock us
sweet-talk us
unlock us

streptococcus
staphylococcus

political caucus

ŌK-ust

focused
locust

OK-ut

block it
Crockett
clock it
docket
dock it
hawk it
hock it
knock it
locket
lock it
mock it
pocket
rocket
rock it
socket
sprocket
sock it
shock it
stock it
walk it

air pocket
back pocket
deep pocket(s)
don't knock it
eye socket
hip pocket
light socket
padlock it
pickpocket
restock it
skyrocket
sweet-talk it
unlock it

vest pocket
watch pocket

booster rocket
line one's pocket(s)
on the docket
overstock it
out-of-pocket
park and lock it

hole in one's pocket

OK-ut-iv

talkative

evocative
provocative
revocative
untalkative

OK-ū-us

nocuous

innocuous

OK-wu

aqua

Chautauqua

OK-wurd

awkward
mock word
shock word

OK-yū-lur
(See OK-ū-lur)

ŌL

boll
bowl
cole
coal

dole
droll
foal
goal
hole
Joel
knoll
kohl
Lowell
mole
poll
pole
roll
role
stroll
soul
Seoul
sole
shoal
stole
skoal
scroll
toll
troll
whole

armhole
bridge toll
black hole
bedroll
bankroll
beanpole
condole
control
console
Creole
charcoal
cajole
Dust Bowl
drum roll
enscroll
enroll
extol
egg roll
fishbowl

foxhole
fur stole
field goal
flagpole
hellhole
half-sole
insole
keyhole
knothole
loophole
light pole
logroll
Maypole
manhole
mudhole
North Pole
parole
pothole
punch bowl
patrol
porthole
peephole
pinhole
payroll
rathole
Rose Bowl
resole
steamroll
straw poll
South Pole
sinkhole
tadpole
unroll
washbowl

aureole
arms control
as a whole
barber pole
barrel roll
buttonhole
birth control
casserole
census poll
camisole

crowd control
cubbyhole
cruise control
Dr. Scholl
Dead Sea Scroll(s)
Español
fishing pole
finger bowl
fishin' hole
flood control
Gallup poll
goldfish bowl
ground control
heart and soul
Interpol
jelly roll
leading role
lose control
Musterole
metropole
money roll
Nat King Cole
nineteenth hole
on a roll
on the dole
on the whole
Old King Cole
pigeonhole
protocol
pest control
rigmarole
rock and roll
rabbit hole
self-control
Seminole
shore patrol
sugar bowl
Super Bowl
starring role
swimming hole
Tootsie Roll
totem pole
take its toll
take control
toilet bowl

title role
water hole

ace in the hole
bladder control
body and soul
Costa del Sol
disease control
filet of sole
Hollywood Bowl
magnetic pole
out of control
overcontrol
remote control
telephone pole
traffic control
under control
watering hole

air-traffic control
quality control
rake over the coal(s)
shake, rattle and roll
utility pole

committee of the
    whole

low man on the totem
    pole

OL

all
awl
ball
bawl
brawl
call
crawl
doll
drawl
fall
gall
hall
haul
loll

moll
maul
pall
Paul
stall
shawl
scrawl
sprawl
Saul
small
squall
tall
trawl
wall
yawl
y'all

atoll
AWOL
appall
air ball
at all
befall
beer hall
blackball
baseball
Bacall
beanball
bird call
banal
cornball
Chagall
cue ball
close call
cure-all
crank call
Clairol
catcall
cabal
catchall
downfall
dance hall
DeGaulle
enthrall
eightball

end-all
eyeball
fuzzball
forestall
free-fall
fire wall
fly ball
fireball
football
footfall
foul ball
Great Wall
goofball
gumball
gun moll
golf ball
highball
house call
hairball
hard ball
handball
install
jump ball
long haul
last call
landfall
Lysol
miscall
meatball
mess hall
nightfall
Nepal
name-call
oddball
on call
pitfall
pratfall
phone call
prayer shawl
pinball
play ball
pool hall
pall-mall
recall
rainfall

rag doll
roll call
spitball
speedball
seawall
short haul
snowfall
snowball
screwball
scuzzball
St. Paul
softball
stonewall
Sioux Fall(s)
sick call
tell all
toll call
town hall
U-Haul
windfall
whitewall
will-call
wolf call
Warhol
you-all

aerosol
above all
alcohol
after all
all in all
billiard ball
Barbie doll
beck and call
Berlin Wall
butterball
basketball
baby doll
bowling ball
Billyball
cannonball
caterwaul
come to call
carryall
cattle call

curtain call
cotton ball
crystal ball
city hall
climb the wall
collect call
coverall
disenthrall
distress call
down the hall
end it all
folderol
free-for-all
fancy ball
Geritol
gangster's moll
have a ball
judgment call
know it all
Kewpie doll
knuckleball
living doll
local call
Leventhal
music hall
matzo ball
Montreal
nature's call
overhaul
off-the-wall
obscene call
overall
on the ball
overcall
one and all
parasol
port of call
popcorn ball
paper doll
protocol
Provençale
pro football
return call
study hall
shopping mall

Senegal
Southern drawl
Seconal
still and all
Tylenol
tether ball
Taj Mahal
touch football
ten feet tall
tennis ball
volleyball
wake-up call
Wailing Wall
waterfall
wherewithal
wall-to-wall

clarion call
carry the ball
cholesterol
courtesy call
Carnegie Hall
drive up the wall
debutante ball
go to the wall
hole in the wall
justice for all
long-distance call
make one's skin crawl
Niagara Fall(s)
Neanderthal
once and for all
push to the wall
Tammany Hall

Australian crawl
be-all and end-all
behind the eight ball
community hall
go over the wall
over the long haul
phenobarbital
rubbing alcohol
up against the wall
writing on the wall

rob Peter to pay Paul

ŌLD

bold
bowled
cold
doled
fold
foaled
gold
hold
holed
mold
mould
old
polled
rolled
scold
sold
strolled
told
trolled
tolled

all told
age-old
arm hold
behold
blindfold
billfold
controlled
cajoled
catch cold
condoled
consoled
choke hold
enfold
extolled
enscrolled
enrolled
foothold
foretold
freehold
fanfold
fool's gold
handhold
household

head cold
half-soled
ice-cold
leasehold
out cold
prefold
paroled
patrolled
retold
remold
resoled
resold
spun gold
stronghold
steamrolled
twofold
threshold
toehold
twice-told
tenfold
untold
unrolled
unfold
uphold
unmold
unsold
white gold
withhold

buttonholed
big and bold
catch a cold
centerfold
common cold
days of old
fluff and fold
grab a hold
good as gold
heart of gold
hot and cold
hundredfold
Jell-O mold
liquid gold
marigold
manifold

overbold
oversold
pure as gold
pigeonholed
pot of gold
rock-and-rolled
self-controlled
solid gold
stranglehold
thousandfold
uncontrolled
undersold

blow hot and cold
climate controlled
lo and behold
out in the cold
overcontrolled

accordion-fold
to have and to hold
worth one's weight in
  gold

OLD

balled
bald
bawled
brawled
called
crawled
dolled
drawled
galled
hauled
lolled
mauled
palled
stalled
scrawled
sprawled
squalled
scald
trawled
walled

appalled
blackballed
enthralled
eyeballed
forestalled
installed
miscalled
recalled
snowballed
so-called
stonewalled
uncalled
whitewalled

caterwauled
overhauled
unenthralled
unrecalled

ŌLD-ē

Goldie
moldy
oldie

golden oldie

OLD-ē

baldie

Vivaldi

Garibaldi

ŌLD-en
(See ŌLD-un)

ŌLD-ēng

folding
holding
molding
scolding

beholding
blindfolding

enfolding
handholding
prefolding
remolding
unfolding
upholding
unmolding
withholding

OLD-ēng

balding
scalding

ŌLD-un

golden
holdin'
olden

beholden
blindfoldin'
enfoldin'
embolden
handholdin'

OLD-un

baldin'
Mauldin
scaldin'
Walden

ŌLD-ur

bolder
boulder
colder
folder
holder
molder
older
shoulder
scolder
smolder
told 'er

blindfolder
beholder
cardholder
controlled 'er
cajoled 'er
cold shoulder
consoled 'er
enfolder
extolled 'er
enrolled 'er
freeholder
householder
leaseholder
landholder
potholder
paroled 'er
rub shoulder(s)
soft shoulder
shareholder
unfolder
upholder
withholder

head and shoulder(s)
officeholder

bigger and bolder
chip on one's shoulder
manila folder
policy holder
straight from the
    shoulder
shoulder-to-shoulder

cry on someone's
    shoulder

OLD-ur

alder
balder
balled 'er
called 'er
galled 'er
mauled 'er
scalder

appalled 'er
blackballed 'er
enthralled 'er
eyeballed 'er
recalled 'er

ŌLD-ur-ēng

shouldering
smoldering

ŌL-ē

drolly
Foley
goalie
holy
holey
joli
solely
slowly
scrolly
shoaly
wholly

cannoli
enrollee
parolee
unholy

guacamole
holy moly
ravioli
roly-poly

OL-ē

Ali
Bali
collie
crawly
colly
dolly
Dali
drawly
folly
golly

holly
jolly
Molly
Ollie
Polly
Raleigh
squally
scrawly
sprawly
trolley
volley
Wally

Bengali
by golly
finale
loblolly
Somali
Svengali
tamale

creepy-crawly
grand finale
get one's jollie(s)
hot tamale
Hello Dolly
Mexicali
melancholy
off one's trolley

by guess and by golly

OL-ej
(See OL-ij)

OL-em
(See OL-um)

ŌL-en
(See ŌL-un)

OL-en
(See OL-un)

ŌL-ēng

bowling
doling
polling
rolling
strolling
trolling

bankrolling
condoling
controlling
consoling
cajoling

enscrolling
enrolling
extolling
logrolling
paroling
resoling
steamrolling
unrolling

buttonholing
pigeonholing
rock-and-rolling

overcontrolling

OL-ēng

balling
bawling
brawling
calling
crawling
drawling
falling
galling
hauling
lolling
mauling
palling
stalling
scrawling
sprawling

squalling
trawling

appalling
befalling
blackballing
birdcalling
catcalling
enthralling
eyeballing
forestalling
free-falling
installing
miscalling
pratfalling
recalling
snowballing
stonewalling

Avon calling
caterwauling
disenthralling
overhauling
overcalling

ŌL-ē-ō

folio
olio
oleo
polio

portfolio

**OL-es
(See OL-us)**

**OL-et
(See OL-ut)**

ŌL-ē-u

magnolia
Mongolia

Anatolia

OL-ē-u

Somalia

inter alia
melancholia

ŌL-ē-um

linoleum
petroleum

ŌL-ē-un

Mongolian
Napoleon
simoleon
Tyrolean

Anatolian

OLF

golf
Rolf

Adolph

ŌL-ful

doleful
soulful

ŌL-gu

Olga
Volga

**OL-id
(See OL-ud)**

**OL-i-fi
(See OL-u-fi)**

OL-ij

college
haulage

knowledge

acknowledge
foreknowledge

carnal knowledge
junior college

OL-ik

colic
folic
frolic
Gaulic
rollick

bucolic
carbolic
hydraulic
systolic
symbolic

alcoholic
apostolic
chocoholic
diabolic
diastolic
foodaholic
fun and frolic
metabolic
melancholic
sleepaholic
vitriolic
workaholic

OL-ik-il

follicle
symbolical

diabolical
hyperbolical

**OL-ip
(See OL-up)**

ŌL-ish

drollish
Polish

OL-ish

dollish
polish
smallish
tallish

abolish
demolish
repolish

apple-polish
spit-and-polish

OL-ish-ēng

polishing

abolishing
demolishing
repolishing

OL-it
(See OL-ut)

OL-it-ē
(See OL-ud-ē)

ŌL-jur

Bolger
Folger(s)
soldier

ŌLK
(See ŌK)

OLK
(See also OK)

balk
caulk

chalk
stalk
talk
walk

backtalk
boardwalk
beanstalk
catwalk
crosswalk
cornstalk
chalk talk
duckwalk
fast-talk
jaywalk
jive talk
outtalk
outwalk
pep talk
side walk
sweet-talk
spacewalk
shoptalk
sleepwalk
small talk
sales talk
speed walk
smooth talk

baby talk
double-talk
Jonas Salk
nature walk
pillow talk

cock of the walk

OLK-ēng
(See also OK-ēng)

balking
caulking
stalking
walking

OLK-un

Balkan
balkin'
caulkin'
stalkin'
walkin'

OLK-ur
(See also OK-ur)

balker
chalker
stalker
talker
walker

deerstalker
floorwalker
jaywalker
night stalker
sweet-talker
smooth-talker
sleepwalker
streetwalker

baby-talker
double-talker
tightrope walker

OLM
(See also OM)

alm
balm
calm
palm
psalm
qualm

becalm
date palm
embalm
keep calm
napalm
uncalm

itchy palm

Twenty-third Psalm

OLM-ē
(See OM-ē)

OLM-ēng
(See also OM-ēng)

calming
palming

becalming
embalming

OLM-ist
(See OM-ist)

OLM-ur
(See OM-ur)

ŌL-ō

bolo
polo
solo

water polo

OL-ō

follow
hollow
swallow
wallow

Apollo

hard to swallow
São Paulo

OL-ō-ēng

following
hollowing

swallowing
wallowing

OL-ō-jē
(See OL-u-jē)

OL-ō-jist
(See OL-u-jist)

OL-ō-ur

follower
hollower
swallower
wallower

sword-swallower

OL-owt

all out
bawl out
call out
crawl out
fallout
haul out
stall out
sprawl out

ŌLS

bolts
colts
dolts
jolts
molts

deadbolts
revolts
unbolts

lightning bolts
nuts and bolts

OLS

false
faults
halts
malts
schmaltz
salts
vaults
waltz

asphalts
assaults
bank vaults
cobalts
defaults
exalts
pole-vaults
true-false

double faults
Epsom salts
somersaults
smelling salts
true or false

Viennese waltz

OLS-ē

falsy
schmaltzy

ŌLS-tur

bolster
holster
oldster
pollster

gun holster
upholster

OLS-u

balsa
salsa

ŌLS-um

bowl some
Folsom
poll some
roll some
stroll some
stole some
wholesome

ŌLT

bolt
colt
dolt
jolt
molt

deadbolt
revolt
unbolt

lightning bolt

OLT

fault
halt
malt
salt
vault

at fault
asphalt
assault
bank vault
cobalt
default
exalt
find fault
gevalt
gestalt
no fault
pole-vault
rock salt

by default
double fault

earthquake fault
grain of salt
pinch of salt
somersault
to a fault
worth one's salt

San Andreas Fault

aggravated assault

OLT-ē

faulty
halty
malty
salty

ŌLT-en
(See ŌLT-un)

ŌLT-ēng

bolting
jolting
molting

revolting
unbolting

OLT-ēng

faulting
halting
salting
vaulting

assaulting
defaulting
exalting
pole vaulting

somersaulting

ŌLTS
(See ŌLS)

OLTS
(See OLS)

ŌLT-un

boltin'
Colton
joltin'
molten

revoltin'
unboltin'

OLT-un

Dalton
faultin'
haltin'
saltin'
vaultin'
Walton

OLT-ur

altar
alter
falter
faulter
halter
palter
salter
vaulter
Walter

assaulter
defaulter
exalter
Gibraltar
pole-vaulter

somersaulter

Rock of Gibraltar

OLT-urd

altered
faltered

haltered

unaltered

OLT-ur-ēng

altering
faltering

ŌL-u

cola
Lola
Nola

Angola
buffola
Crayola
crapola
corolla
drugola
floppola
gayola
Loyola
payola
plugola
Shinola
Victrola
viola

ayatollah
areola
Coca-Cola
Española
gladiola
Gorgonzola
Pepsi-Cola
Pensacola
roseola

OL-u

Allah
challah
gala
Paula

Chapala

chuckwalla
impala
koala
Marsala
Valhalla

Guatemala
Walla Walla

ŌL-u-bul

pollable
rollable
strollable

bankrollable
consolable
controllable
enrollable
extollable
parolable
patrollable
resolable
unrollable

uncontrollable

OL-u-bul

ballable
callable
haulable
maulable
stallable
scrawlable
trawlable

enthrallable
forestallable
installable
miscallable
recallable

OL-ud

solid
stolid
squalid

OL-ud-ē

jollity
polity
quality

equality
frivolity

inequality

OL-u-fi

mollify
qualify

disqualify

OL-u-jē

astrology
apology
anthology
biology
cartology
chronology
cacology
cosmology
ecology
geology
graphology
gemology
gastrology
histology
mythology
neurology
oncology
ontology
penology
phrenology
proctology
psychology
pathology
phonology
philology
photology
scatology

seismology
technology
tautology
theology
toxology
urology
zoology

anthropology
archeology
cosmetology
cardiology
climatology
criminology
dermatology
entomology
etymology
eschatology
Egyptology
gynecology
hematology
hepatology
immunology
ichthyology
ideology
lexicology
ophthalmology
ornithology
pharmacology
pantheology
physiology
piscatology
phraseology
radiology
scientology
sociology
toxicology
terminology

bacteriology
endocrinology
kinesiology
meteorology
microbiology
paleontology
psychopathology

universology

anesthesiology
epidemiology
gastroenterology

OL-u-jist

apologist
astrologist
anthologist
biologist
cosmologist
chronologist
geologist
mythologist
neurologist
oncologist
phrenologist
pathologist
psychologist
philologist
seismologist
theologist
technologist
urologist
zoologist

archeologist
anthropologist
cardiologist
dermatologist
etymologist
Egyptologist
gynecologist
hematologist
ideologist
ichthyologist
immunologist
lexicologist
ornithologist
ophthalmologist
physiologist
phraseologist
radiologist
sociologist

toxicologist

bacteriologist
meteorologist
paleontologist

anesthesiologist
epidemiologist
gastroenterologist

OL-u-jur

astrologer
anthologer
acknowledger
geologer
chronologer

OL-uk
(See OL-ik)

OL-um

ball 'em
call 'em
column
gall 'em
haul 'em
maul 'em
slalom
stall 'em
solemn

appall 'em
befall 'em
enthrall 'em
eyeball 'em
fifth column
forestall 'em
install 'em
miscall 'em
recall 'em

overhaul 'em
spinal column

ŌL-un

bowlin'
colon
dolin'
Nolan
pollin'
rollin'
stolen
strollin'
swollen

condolin'
controlin'
consolin'
enrollin'
extollin'
parolin'
resolin'
unrollin'

spastic colon
semicolon

OL-un

bawlin'
brawlin'
callin'
Collin(s)
crawlin'
drawlin'
fallen
gallin'
haulin'
lollin'
maulin'
pollen
Stalin
stallin'
squallin'

appallin'
befallen
blackballin'
crestfallen
downfallen

enthrallin'
eyeballin'
free-fallin'
installin'
miscallin'
name callin'
recallin'
stonewallin'

OL-un-dur

colander
Hollander

OL-up

all up
ball up
call up
crawl up
doll up
dollop
haul up
polyp
scallop
trollop
wallop
wall up

ŌL-ur

bowler
choler
dolor
droller
molar
polar
poller
roller
stroller
stole 'er
scroller
solar
troller
volar
wholer

condoler
controller
consoler
comptroller
cajoler
enroller
extoller
high roller
hair roller
lawn bowler
log roller
paroler
patroller
resoler
steamroller
unroller

air controller
buttonholer
can't control 'er
holy roller
rock-and-roller

OL-ur

bawler
baller
brawler
caller
collar
crawler
choler
dollar
drawler
faller
galler
holler
hauler
loller
mauler
Mahler
staller
scholar
scrawler
sprawler
smaller

squalor
taller
trawler
waller

appaller
befall 'er
blue-collar
blackballer
bird caller
catcaller
choke collar
dog collar
enthraller
eyeballer
forestaller
free-faller
flea collar
half-dollar
installer
miscaller
name-caller
pratfaller
phone caller
recaller
Rhodes scholar
spitballer
speedballer
snowballer
top dollar
white-collar

creepy crawler
caterwauler
Fulbright scholar
hoot and holler
million-dollar
overhauler
obscene caller

almighty dollar
buttoned-down collar
flotation collar

bet one's bottom
   dollar

hot under the collar
ring around the collar

OL-urd

collard
collared
hollered

OL-ur-ēng

collaring
hollering

ŌL-us

poll us
solace
stole us

control us
console us
enroll us
extol us
Margolis
parole us

OL-us

aweless
braless
call us
clawless
flawless
haul us
jawless
lawless
maul us
pawless
stall us
solace
Wallace

appall us
befall us
Cornwallis
enthrall us

forestall us
install us
recall us

OL-ut

ball it
call it
drawl it
haul it
maul it
stall it
wallet

befall it
blackball it
enthrall it
eyeball it
forestall it
install it
miscall it
recall it

whatchamacallit

**OL-ut-ē
(See OL-ud-ē)**

OLV

solve

absolve
dissolve
evolve
involve
resolve
revolve
unsolve(d)

unresolve(d)

OLV-ēng

solving

absolving

dissolving
evolving
involving
resolving
revolving

problem solving

OLV-u-bul

solvable

absolvable
dissolvable
resolvable
unsolvable

unresolvable

OL-vur

solver

absolver
dissolver
evolver
involve 'er
resolver
revolver

ŌL-yu
(See ŌL-ē-u)

ŌLZ

bowls
bolls
doles
foals
goals
holes
knolls
moles
Olds
polls
poles
rolls

roles
strolls
souls
soles
shoals
skoals
scrolls
tolls
trolls

condoles
controls
consoles
cajoles
enscrolls
enrolls
extols
field goals
paroles
patrols
resoles
straw polls
soup bowls
unrolls

buttonholes
casseroles
camisoles
cubbyholes
Dead Sea Scrolls
fishing poles
finger bowls
jelly rolls
leading roles
metropoles
pigeonholes
Tootsie Rolls
totem poles
toilet bowls

overcontrols
telephone poles

rake over the coals

OLZ

awls
balls
bawls
brawls
calls
crawls
dolls
drawls
falls
galls
halls
hauls
lolls
molls
mauls
palls
Paul's
stalls
shawls
scrawls
sprawls
squalls
trawls
walls
yawls

appalls
befalls
close calls
crank calls
catcalls
enthralls
forestalls
fly balls
gun molls
ground balls
golf balls
house calls
installs
miscalls
recalls
rag dolls
short hauls
Sioux Falls

toll calls
U-Hauls
wolf calls

Barbie dolls
butterballs
base on balls
bowling balls
cannonballs
caterwauls
curtain calls
coveralls
disenthralls
judgment calls
Kewpie dolls
knuckleballs
music halls
matzo balls
overhauls
obscene calls
overalls
overcalls
parasols
paperdolls
shopping malls
Southern drawls
waterfalls

debutante balls
Niagara Falls

OL-zē

ballsy
palsy

ŌM

chrome
comb
dome
foam
gnome
home
loam

ohm
pome
poem
Rome
roam
tome

at home
afoam
coxcomb
down home
rest home
syndrome
sea foam
strike home
Stockholm

Astrodome
broken home
catacomb
chromosome
doubledome
fine-tooth comb
foster home
gastronome
honeycomb
home sweet home
hippodrome
model home
metronome
mobile home
monochrome
nursing home
palindrome
pleasure dome
shaving foam
stay-at-home
Superdome
Teapot Dome

Mercurochrome
no place like home
X chromosome
Y chromosome

OM
(See also OLM)

bomb
calm
Guam
glom
mom
prom
palm
tom

A-bomb
aplomb
Bernbaum
dive-bomb
date palm
embalm
fire bomb
mesdames
napalm
noncom
pompom
sitcom
tom-tom
time bomb
wigwam

grease one's palm
intercom
Notre Dame
peeping Tom
supermom
senior prom
Tannenbaum
Vietnam

atomic bomb
grease someone's palm
nuclear bomb

ŌMB
(See ŌM)

OMB
(See OM)

OM-bat

combat
wombat

OM-bē

zombie

Abercromby

OM-bō

combo
mambo

OM-bul

wamble

ensemble

ŌMD

chromed
combed
domed
foamed
roamed

honeycombed

OMD

bombed
calmed
glommed
palmed

embalmed

ŌM-ē

foamy
grow me
homey

know me
oh me
owe me
roamy
row me
sew me
snow me
show me
slow me
throw me

below me
Naomi
outgrow me

overthrow me

OM-ē

balmy
bomb me
commie
calm me
mommy
swami
Tommy

embalm me
pastrami
salami
tsunami
tatami

origami

OM-e-dē
(See OM-u-dē)

ŌM-en
(See ŌM-un)

OM-en
(See OM-un)

ŌM-ēng

chroming
combing
foaming
gloaming
homing
roaming

honeycombing

OM-ēng

bombing
calming
palming
tomming

embalming

waterbombing

OM-en-ul
(See OM-in-ul)

ŌM-ē-nus

foaminess
hominess

OM-et
(See OM-ut)

OM-et-rē
(See OM-ut-rē)

OM-et-ur
(See OM-ud-ur)

ŌM-ē-um

chromium

encomium

OM-ik

comic

atomic

astronomic
anatomic
economic
gastronomic
palindromic
stand-up comic

OM-i-kul
(See OM-u-kul)

OM-i-lē
(See OM-u-lē)

OM-in-ā-shun

domination
nomination

abomination
denomination

OM-in-āt

dominate
nominate

abominate
denominate

OM-in-ē

hominy
nominee

OM-in-ul

nominal

abdominal
phenomenal

OM-in-uns

dominance
prominence

abominance
predominance

OM-in-us

bombin' us
calmin' us
ominous

abdominous

OM-is
(See OM-us)

OM-ist

calmest
palmist
promised

OM-it
(See OM-ut)

OM-i-tē
(See OM-u-dē)

ŌM-ō

bromo
Como
homo
promo

major-domo

OMP

chomp
clomp
comp
pomp

romp
stomp
swamp
tromp
whomp

OMP-lus

swampless

accomplice

OMPT

chomped
clomped
comped
prompt
romped
stomped
swamped
tromped
whomped

unprompt

OMPT-ur

comped 'er
prompter
stomped 'er
swamped 'er

TelePrompTer

OMP-um

chomp 'em
comp 'em
stomp 'em
swamp 'em
tromp 'em
whomp 'em
wampum

OMP-ur

comp 'er
chomper

romper
swamp 'er
stomper
tromp 'er

OMP-us

comp us
pompous
stomp us
swamp us
tromp us
wampus
whomp us

catawampus

ŌM-u

coma
chroma
Roma

aroma
diploma
glaucoma
narcoma
Paloma
Sonoma
Tacoma

Alta Loma
carcinoma
hematoma
in a coma
Oklahoma
tokonoma

OM-u

amah
Brahma
comma
drama
llama
lama
mama

Rama
trauma

Bahama(s)
big mama
pajama(s)

cinerama
docudrama
diorama
Dalai Lama
futurama
melodrama
psychodrama
Yokohama

OM-u-bul

bombable
calmable
palmable

embalmable

OM-u-dē

comity
comedy
vomity

OM-u-dur

barometer
chronometer
fathometer
hydrometer
kilometer
odometer
speedometer
tachometer
thermometer

alcoholometer

OM-uk
(See OM-ik)

OM-u-kul

comical

atomical

anatomical
astronomical
economical
gastronomical

uneconomical

OM-u-lē

homily

anomaly

ŌM-un

bowman
combin'
foamin'
gloamin'
omen
Roman
roamin'
showman
yeoman

abdomen
cognomen

Abominable Snowman

OM-un

bombin'
Brahman
common
calmin'
palmin'
shaman

embalmin'
fire bombin'
Top Ramen
uncommon

have in common
Tutankhamon

OM-un-ē
(See OM-in-ē)

OM-un-ul
(See OM-in-ul)

OM-un-us
(See OM-in-us)

ŌM-ur

comber
foamer
homer
roamer

beachcomber
misnomer
shalomer

grandslam homer

OM-ur

bomber
calmer
palmer

becalmer
dive bomber
embalmer
mad bomber
napalmer

OM-ur-ut

agglomerate
conglomerate

OM-us

bomb us
calm us

promise
shamus
Thomas

embalm us
St. Thomas

breach of promise
doubting Thomas

lick and a promise

OM-ut

bomb it
calm it
comet
grommet
palm it
vomit

embalm it
firebomb it

Halley's comet

OM-ut-rē

geometry
optometry

trigonometry

OM-ut-ur
(See OM-ud-ur)

ŌN

bone
blown
cone
crone
clone
drone
flown
groan
grown
hone

Joan
known
loan
lone
moan
mown
own
pone
prone
phone
roan
sewn
Sloan
scone
stone
shown
shone
sown
tone
thrown
throne
zone

alone
atone
bemoan
backbone
birthstone
brownstone
brimstone
blouson
breastbone
bloodstone
cyclone
cheekbone
cologne
corn-pone
condone
car phone
car loan
curbstone
disown
dethrone
dial tone
debone

enthrone
end zone
flagstone
freestone
full-blown
full-grown
flintstone
Firestone
fish bone
gallstone
garçon
gemstone
grindstone
homegrown
headphone
high-flown
half-grown
hailstone
headstone
home loan
high tone
hambone
hormone
ingrown
intone
jawbone
keystone
limestone
large-bone(d)
Malone
millstone
moonstone
milestone
new-mown
nose cone
ozone
outshone
postpone
pine cone
pay phone
rhinestone
Ramon
raw bone
Simone
Sno-Kone

sandstone
sawbone(s)
soupbone
strike zone
shinbone
trombone
tombstone
touchstone
tailbone
T-bone
time zone
touch-tone
unknown
unshown
unsewn
ungrown
unblown
unthrown
unsown
whalebone
wishbone
whetstone
well-known
windblown
war zone

anklebone
acetone
all alone
baritone
buffer zone
Blarney stone
crazy bone
carved in stone
collarbone
champignon
chaperon
corazón
cherrystone
combat zone
cortisone
cornerstone
cobblestone
dictaphone
doggie bone

funny bone
frigid zone
gramophone
grunt and groan
herringbone
hold one's own
ice cream cone
knucklebone
kidney stone
little known
lazybone(s)
loading zone
megaphone
monotone
moan and groan
microphone
methadone
neutral zone
overgrown
on one's own
overthrown
overtone
overblown
rolling stone
roll-your-own
stand alone
sousaphone
saxophone
stepping-stone
silicone
telephone
torrid zone
taxi zone
twilight zone
unbeknown
undertone
xylophone
Yellowstone

accident-prone
cast the first stone
cellular phone
Dom Pérignon
extension phone
eau de Cologne

fire and brimstone
go it alone
hospital zone
mind of one's own
no parking zone
sine qua non
savings and loan
testosterone
Temperate Zone

come into one's own
let well enough alone
Moët & Chandon
Ponce de León
semiprecious stone

ON

brawn
Bonn
con
dawn
drawn
don
fawn
gone
john
Kahn
lawn
on
pawn
prawn
Ron
swan
spawn
Vaughn
wan
yawn
yon

add on
anon
Antoine
bon-bon
begone
bring on

Bataan
baton
chiffon
come on
count on
coupon
clip-on
Cézanne
Ceylon
catch on
Canton
dacron
doggone
dream on
Don Juan
Dear John
ex-con
élan
go on
g'wan
hereon
hang on
Iran
long gone
move on
Milan
odds-on
pecan
proton
python
predawn
run-on
right on
Sorbonne
San Juan
Szechwan
salon
Saigon
Tehran
turn on
Tucson
Taiwan
undrawn
upon
won ton

withdrawn
walk-on
Yukon
Yvonne

Amazon
Al-Anon
Avalon
autobahn
Audubon
Babylon
cyclotron
carillon
carry on
call upon
cabochon
crack of dawn
decathlon
echelon
early on
fall back on
goings-on
Genghis Khan
get it on
hanger-on
hereupon
hair salon
hexagon
halcyon
Kublai Khan
keep tabs on
lexicon
Lebanon
liaison
leprechaun
Mazatlán
marathon
mamasan
octagon
on and on
off and on
overdrawn
paragon
papasan
parthenon

pentagon
parmesan
polygon
pro and con
put upon
pour it on
silicon
tarragon
thereupon
talkathon
tie one on
undergone
whereupon
walkathon
woebegone

automaton
Azerbaijan
beauty salon
chateaubriand
depend upon
hither and yon
par avion
phenomenon
Saskatchewan

ONCH

conch
haunch
launch
paunch
staunch

ONCH-ē

paunchy
raunchy

ONCH-ō

honcho
poncho

ONCH-us

conscious
launch us

ŌND

boned
coned
cloned
droned
groaned
honed
loaned
moaned
owned
phoned
stoned
toned
zoned

atoned
bemoaned
condoned
disowned
dethroned
deboned
enthroned
intoned
large-boned
postponed

chaperoned
moaned and groaned
telephoned

OND

bond
blond
blonde
conned
dawned
donned
frond
fond
fawned
pawned
pond
spawned
wand
yawned

abscond
beyond
bail bond
doggoned
despond
fishpond
gourmand
James Bond
junk bond
millpond
palm frond
respond

correspond
liaisoned
magic wand
savings bond
skating pond
tout le monde
vagabond

dishwater blonde
overly fond
strawberry blonde
the great beyond
Treasury bond

OND-ed
(See OND-ud)

OND-ēng

bonding

absconding
responding

corresponding

OND-ent
(See OND-unt)

OND-is
(See OND-us)

OND-lē
(See ON-lē)

OND-nus

blondness
fondness

OND-ō

condo
cuando
mondo
rondo
rondeau

Fernando
glissando
sforzando

OND-rē

laundry
quandary

Chinese laundry
in a quandary

OND-u

Fonda
Honda
ronda
Rhonda
Wanda

Rwanda
Uganda

anaconda

OND-ud

bonded

absconded
responded

corresponded

OND-um

bond 'em
condom
conned 'em
donned 'em
pawned 'em
spawned 'em

beyond 'em

OND-uns

despondence
respondents

correspondence

OND-unt

despondent
respondent

correspondent

OND-ur

bonder
blonder
condor
conned 'er
fawned 'er
fonder
launder
ponder
pawned 'er
spawned 'er
Saunder(s)
squander
wander
yonder

beyond 'er
responder

corresponder
over yonder
wild blue yonder

OND-ur-ē
(See OND-rē)

OND-ur-ēng

laundering
pondering
squandering
wandering

OND-ur-us

launder us
ponderous
squander us

OND-us

bond us
conned us
jaundice

beyond us

ŌN-ē

bony
cony
Coney
crony
groany
moany
phony
pony
stony
Sony
Tony

baloney
Marconi
spumoni
Shoshone
tortoni

abalone
acrimony
antimony

alimony
cannelloni
ceremony
matrimony
macaroni
minestrone
parsimony
pepperoni
polo pony
provolone
palimony
patrimony
rigatoni
sanctimony
Shetland pony
testimony

phony-baloney
zabaglione

holy matrimony

ON-ē

brawny
bonny
Bonnie
Connie
johnny
ranee
scrawny
Swanee
tawny

frangipani
Giovanni
maharanee
Pakistani
stage-door Johnny

Azerbaijani
mulligatawny

ŌN-ēng

boning
coning

cloning
droning
groaning
honing
loaning
moaning
owning
phoning
stoning
toning
zoning

atoning
bemoaning
condoning
disowning
dethroning
deboning
enthroning
intoning
postponing

chaperoning
telephoning

ON-ēng

awning
conning
dawning
donning
fawning
pawning
spawning
yawning

ŌN-ent
(See ŌN-unt)

ON-est
(See ON-ust)

ON-et
(See ON-ut)

ŌN-ē-u
(See ŌN-yu)

ŌN-ē-ul

baronial
colonial

ceremonial
matrimonial
sanctimonial
testimonial

ŌN-ē-um

harmonium
plutonium
zirconium

pandemonium

ŌN-ē-un

phonyin'

Ionian
Jacksonian
Smithsonian
Shoshonean

Babylonian

ŌN-ē-ur

bonier
phonier
stonier

ŌN-ē-us

phony us

baloney us
erroneous
felonious
harmonious

acrimonious
ceremonious

parsimonious
sanctimonious

ONG

bong
dong
Fong
gong
long
prong
song
strong
thong
tong
throng
Wong
wrong

along
belong
ding-dong
daylong
diphthong
erelong
furlong
folk song
go wrong
headlong
headstrong
Hong Kong
hourlong
ice tong
King Kong
lifelong
love song
mah-jongg
oblong
Ping-Pong
prolong
singsong
swan song
so long
sarong
sidelong
two-prong

torch song
theme song
triphthong
yearlong

all night long
all day long
all along
before long
billabong
bump along
come along
come on strong
dinner gong
drinking song
get along
go along
hop-a-long
in the wrong
move along
overlong
run along
right or wrong
sing-along
string along
take-along
tagalong
Vietcong

hammer and tong(s)

ONG-ēng

bonging
donging
gonging
longing
thronging
wronging

belonging
ding-donging
prolonging

ONG-lē

strongly
wrongly

ONG-ō

bongo
Congo

Belgian Congo
chimichango

ONG-u

conga
Tonga

bazonga(s)

ONG-ur

conger
longer
stronger
wronger

ON-ik
(See ON-uk)

ON-iks
(See ON-ix)

ON-ik-u
(See ON-uk-u)

ON-ik-ul
(See ON-uk-ul)

ON-i-mus
(See ON-u-mus)

ON-ish

wannish

admonish
astonish

ON-ish-ment

admonishment
astonishment

ON-ix

chronics
onyx
phonics
tonics

harmonics
Masonics
mnemonics
sardonyx

electronics
gin and tonics
histrionics

supersonics

ONK

bonk
conk
honk
konk
wonk
zonk

chenin blanc

ONK-ē

donkey
honky
konky

honky-tonky

ONK-ēng

bonking
conking
honking
zonking

ONK-ur

bonker(s)
conker
conquer
honker
Yonker(s)

reconquer

divide and conquer

ŌN-lē

lonely
only

not only
unlonely

in name only
one and only
sad and lonely

ON-lē

Conley
fondly
wanly

ŌN-ment

atonement
bemoanment
condonement
dethronement
enthronement
postponement

Day of Atonement

ŌN-ō

Bono
no-no

pro bono

ON-ō

mano
mono

Chicano
paisano
Romano

Capistrano
parmigiano

Americano

ON-ō-mē
(See ON-u-mē)

ONS

aunts
daunts
flaunts
fonts
haunts
jaunts
taunts
sconce
wants

bouffants
détentes
ensconce
nuance
response
savants
séance

ambiance
commandants
confidantes
debutantes
dilettantes
no response
nonchalance
old-maid aunts
renaissance
restaurants

insouciance
par excellence

conditioned response
pièce de résistance

ON-sul

consul
tonsil

ŌN-sum

blown some
flown some
grown some
known some
loan some
lonesome
moan some
own some
phone some
sewn some
stone some
shown some
thrown some

ONS-un

Johnson
Swanson

ensconcin'
Wisconsin

ONS-ur

daunts 'er
haunts 'er
sponsor
taunts 'er
wants 'er

ŌNT

don't
won't

ONT

aunt
daunt
flaunt
font
gaunt
haunt
jaunt
taunt
wont
want

bouffant
détente
DuPont
gallant
piquant
savant
Vermont

commandant
confidante
debutante
dilettante
nonchalant
old-maid aunt
restaurant

ONT-ē

auntie
Dante
flaunty
jaunty
Monte

Chianti

ristorante

Asti spumante

ONT-ēng

daunting
flaunting
haunting

taunting
wanting

ONT-ō

pronto
Tonto

Toronto

Esperanto

ONTS
(See ONS)

ONT-ud

daunted
flaunted
haunted
taunted
wanted

help wanted
most wanted
undaunted

ONT-um

daunt 'em
flaunt 'em
haunt 'em
quantum
taunt 'em
want 'em

ONT-un

dauntin'
flauntin'
jauntin'
hauntin'
tauntin'
wanton
wantin'

ONT-ur

daunt 'er
flaunter
gaunter
haunter
jaunter
saunter
taunter
want 'er

bouffanter
gallanter
piquanter

ONT-us

daunt us
flaunt us
haunt us
Qantas
taunt us
want us

Pocahantas

ŌN-u

Jonah
Kona
krona
Mona
Rona

corona
kimono
Pomona
Verona

Arizona
Barcelona
Desdemona

ON-u

Donna
fauna
Ghana

gonna
sauna
wanna

bwana
Botswana
Chicana
Guiana
gymkhana
iguana
liana
mañana
Madonna
nirvana
piranha
Tijuana

belladonna
Benihana
marijuana
prima donna
Rosh Hashanah

Americana
British Guiana
flora and fauna

ON-uk

chronic
conic
phonic
sonic
tonic

bubonic
bionic
colonic
demonic
euphonic
hedonic
harmonic
ironic
ionic
laconic
moronic
mnemonic

Masonic
Platonic
sardonic
symphonic
Teutonic

catatonic
diatonic
electronic
gin and tonic
histrionic
isotonic
Panasonic
quadraphonic
supersonic
telephonic
ultrasonic

Napoleonic
stereophonic

ON-u-ku

Konica
Hanukkah

harmonica
Veronica

Santa Monica

ON-u-kul

conical
chronicle
monocle

canonical
demonical
iconical
ironical
laconical
mnemonical

histrionical

ŌN-ul

sonal
tonal

zonal

atonal

ON-uld

Donald
Ronald

McDonald

ON-um-ē

astronomy
agronomy
autonomy
economy
gastronomy
synonymy
taxonomy

Deuteronomy

ON-u-mus

anonymous
autonomous
synonymous

Alcoholics Anonymous
Chocoholics
 Anonymous

ON-u-must

agronomist
economist
synonymist

ŌN-unt

component
exponent
opponent
proponent

ŌN-ur

boner
cloner

donor
droner
flown 'er
groaner
honer
known 'er
loaner
loner
moaner
owner
proner
phoner
stoner
shown 'er
toner
thrown 'er
zoner

aloner
atoner
bemoaner
condoner
disowner
dethroner
deboner
intoner
outshone 'er
postponer
part owner

chaperon 'er
overthrown 'er
pull a boner
telephoner

ON-ur

conner
donner
drawn 'er
dawner
fawner
goner
honor
on 'er
pawner

spawner
wanner
yawner

dishonor
O'Connor
time honor(ed)
upon 'er

Afrikaner
do the honor(s)
debt of honor
field of honor
guest of honor
marathoner
maid of honor
on one's honor
place of honor
point of honor
roll of honor
Weimaraner
word of honor

depend upon 'er
matron of honor
Medal of Honor

ŌN-us

bonus
blown us
clone us
flown us
Jonas
known us
loan us
lowness
own us
onus
phone us
stone us
slowness
shown us
thrown us

bemoan us
condone us

disown us
dethrone us
enthrone us
postpone us

ON-us

con us
drawn us
on us

Adonis
doggone us
upon us

ON-ust

honest
wannest

doggonest
dishonest
withdrawnest

woebegonest

ON-ut

bonnet
don it
drawn it
on it
pawn it
sonnet
spawn it

bluebonnet
bank on it
count on it
doggone it
sunbonnet
step on it
upon it
warbonnet

ŌN-yu

blown ya
clone ya

flown ya
known ya
loan ya
own ya
phone ya
shown ya
Sonia
thrown ya

ammonia
begonia
bologna
condone ya
disown ya
dethrone ya
enthrone ya
Estonia
outshone ya
postpone ya
pneumonia
Slavonia

Babylonia
chaperon ya
Caledonia
catatonia
eudemonia
Macedonia
overthrown ya
telephone ya

ON-yu

con ya
drawn ya
on ya
Tanya

cabaña
doggone ya
lasagne
upon ya
withdrawn ya

ŌNZ

bones
cones

clones
drones
groans
hones
Jones
knowns
loans
moans
owns
phones
pones
roans
scones
stones
tones
thrones
zones

atones
bemoans
backbones
birthstones
blousons
bloodstones
brownstones
bare bones
cyclones
cheekbones
colognes
condones
car phones
car loans
curbstones
disowns
dethrones
debones
Dow Jones
enthrones
end zones
flagstones
freestones
fish bones
gallstones
gemstones
grindstones

headphones
home loans
hailstones
headstones
hambones
hormones
intones
jawbones
keystones
limestones
millstones
milestones
nose cones
no bones
postpones
pine cones
pay phones
rhinestones
Sno-Kones
sandstones
sawbones
soup bones
shinbones
trombones
tombstones
touchstones
tailbones
T-bones
thighbones
time zones
unknowns
wishbones
war zones

anklebones
bag of bones
baritones
buffer zones
crazy bones
collarbones
chaperons
cornerstones
cobblestones
Davy Jones
dictaphones

gramophones
grunts and groans
herringbones
ice cream cones
knucklebones
kidney stones
lazybones
loading zones
megaphones
monotones
moans and groans
microphones
neutral zones
overtones
rolling stones
saxophones
skin and bones
stepping-stones
telephones
taxi zones
undertones
xylophones

extension phones
feel in one's bones
no parking zones
savings and loans
skull and crossbones

semiprecious stones

ONZ

bronze
blondes
bonds
cons
dawns
dons
fawns
Fonz
fronds
Hans
johns
lawns
ponds

pawns
prawns
swans
spawns
wands
yawns

absconds
bon-bons
bygones
batons
chiffons
coupons
Don Juans
ex-cons
fishponds
gourmands
icons
junk bonds
long johns
millponds
morons
neutrons
neons
protons
pecans
pythons
responds
salons
walk-ons
won tons

Amazons
autobahns
carillons
corresponds
cyclotrons
decathlons
echelons
hexagons
lexicons
liaisons
leprechauns
magic wands
marathons
octagons

paragons
pentagons
polygons
pros and cons
savings bonds
skating ponds
vagabonds
talkathons
walkathons

automatons
beauty salons
phenomenons
Treasury Bonds

ONZ-ō

Bonzo

Alonzo

ŌP

cope
dope
grope
hope
lope
mope
nope
pope
rope
soap
slope
scope
tope
taupe

Bob Hope
down slope
elope
jump rope
lose hope
last hope
no hope
soft-soap
towrope

tightrope

antipope
antelope
bar of soap
cantaloupe
envelope
gyroscope
give up hope
Great White Hope
horoscope
interlope
isotope
learn the rope(s)
misanthrope
microscope
periscope
ray of hope
stethoscope
seismoscope
spectroscope
telescope

Cape of Good Hope
hope against hope
kaleidoscope

at the end of one's
    rope

OP

bop
cop
crop
clop
chop
drop
fop
flop
glop
hop
lop
mop
pop
prop
plop

sop
slop
shop
stop
strop
swap
top
whop

Aesop
air drop
atop
bus stop
big top
backdrop
bellhop
blacktop
bebop
bar hop
box top
bakeshop
backstop
co-op
chop-chop
carhop
cough drop
closed shop
clip-clop
Cyclop(s)
desktop
doorstop
dust mop
dewdrop
damp-mop
doo-wop
estop
eavesdrop
flip-flop
flattop
flintlock
full stop
gumdrop
hip-hop
headshop
hedgehop

hockshop
hardtop
hilltop
kerplop
milksop
mail drop
malt shop
nonstop
name-drop
on top
outcrop
pawnshop
pit stop
pro shop
pork chop
post-op
rest stop
rooftop
ragmop
raindrop
sharecrop
snowdrop
shortstop
sweatshop
sock hop
schlock shop
stovetop
tiptop
tank top
thrift shop
teardrop
treetop
truck stop
tube top
talk shop
vox pop
wet-mop
wife-swap
workshop

blow one's top
bumper crop
body shop
bunny hop
barbershop

belly flop
born to shop
coffee shop
curly top
carrot-top
grocery shop
glottal stop
keystone cop
knockout drop
lollipop
lindy hop
lemon drop
malaprop
mom and pop
mountaintop
riding crop
reach the top
soda pop
set up shop
table-hop
turboprop
traffic stop
table top
union shop
window-shop
whistle-stop

cream of the crop
karate chop
over the top
sleep like a top

comparison shop

bull in a china shop

ŌP-ē

dopey
gropey
Hopi
mopey
soapy
slopey

OP-ē

copy
choppy
floppy
hoppy
poppy
ploppy
soppy
sloppy

flip-floppy
hard copy
jalopy
recopy
serape
unsloppy

carbon copy

ŌP-en
(See ŌP-un)

ŌP-ēng

coping
doping
groping
hoping
loping
moping
roping
soaping
sloping
scoping

eloping
soft-soaping
interloping

OP-ēng

bopping
copping
cropping
chopping
dropping

flopping
hopping
lopping
mopping
popping
propping
sopping
slopping
shopping
stopping
swapping
topping
whopping

carhopping
clip-clopping
damp-mopping
estopping
ear-popping
eavesdropping
flip-flopping
hip-hopping
heartstopping
kerplopping
name-dropping
outcropping
sharecropping
showstopping
wife-swapping

bunnyhopping
belly-flopping
window-shopping

ŌP-en-ur
(See ŌP-un-ur)

OP-et
(See OP-ut)

ŌP-ē-u

myopia
utopia

cornucopia
Ethiopia

ŌP-ē-un

utopian
Ethiopian

OP-ē-ur

copier
choppier
floppier
soppier
sloppier

photocopier

ŌP-ē-us

copious
dopey us
mopey us
soapy us

OP-ik

topic
tropic

anthropic
myopic
subtopic
subtropic

misanthropic
microscopic
philanthropic
telescopic

heliotropic
kaleidoscopic

OP-ik-ul
(See OP-uk-ul)

ŌP-les
(See ŌP-lus)

OP-les
(See OP-lus)

OP-lur

poplar
toppler

ŌP-lus

hopeless
ropeless
soapless

OP-lus

copless
mopless
topless

OP-o-lis
(See OP-u-lus)

OPS

bops
cops
crops
copse
clops
chops
drops
fops
flops
glops
hops
lops
mops
pops
props
plops
sops
slops
shops
stocks

strops
swaps
schnapps
tops
whops

airdrops
bus stops
big tops
bellhops
barhops
boxtops
co-ops
carhops
coughdrops
Cyclops
doorstops
damp-mops
estops
eyedrops
eavesdrops
flip-flops
flattops
gumdrops
hardtops
name-drops
pawnshops
pitstops
pork chops
rest stops
rooftops
raindrops
sweatshops
sock hops
schlock shops
stovetops
teardrops
treetops
truck stops
workshops

body shops
barbershops
belly flops
coffee shops
glottal stops

keystone cops
knockout drops
lick one's chops
lollipops
lemondrops
malaprops
mountaintops
tablehops
window-shops
whistlestops

OP-sē

dropsy
Flopsy
Mopsy
topsy

autopsy
biopsy

OP-shun

option

adoption

ŌPT

coped
doped
groped
hoped
loped
moped
soaped
sloped
scoped

eloped

OPT

bopped
copped
cropped
chopped
dropped

flopped
hopped
lopped
mopped
opt
popped
propped
plopped
sopped
slopped
stropped
shopped
stopped
swapped
topped
whopped

adopt
bar-hopped
bebopped
clip-clopped
close-cropped
carhopped
dust-mopped
eavesdropped
flip-flopped
kerplopped
name-dropped
sharecropped
uncropped
unstopped
unchopped

belly-flopped
bunny-hopped
lindy-hopped
table-hopped
window-shopped

OPT-ēng

opting

adopting

OPT-ik

coptic
optic

OPT-ur

bopped 'er
copter
chopped 'er
dropped 'er
opter
popped 'er
propped 'er
stopped 'er
swapped 'er
topped 'er
whopped 'er

adopter

helicopter

OP-u-bul

coppable
choppable
droppable
moppable
poppable
stoppable
swappable
toppable

unstoppable

OP-uk
(See OP-ik)

OP-uk-ul

topical
tropical

myopical
subtropical

misanthropical
philanthropical

ŌP-ul

opal

Constantinople

OP-ul

popple
topple

OP-ū-lāt

copulate
populate

OP-ul-ē

choppily
floppily
ploppily
soppily

monopoly

OP-ū-lur

copular
popular

unpopular

OP-u-lus

topple us

acropolis
Christopoulos
metropolis
necropolis

ŌP-un

copin'
dopin'
gropin'
hopin'
lopin'
mopin'

open
ropin'
soapin'
slopin'

elopin'
golf open
jump-ropin'
reopen
soft-soapin'
wide-open

do not open
interlopin'

ŌP-un-ur

dopin' 'er
gropin' 'er
opener
ropin' 'er
soapin' 'er

can opener
eye opener
reopener
soft-soapin' 'er

ŌP-ur

coper
doper
groper
hoper
loper
moper
roper
soaper
sopor

eloper
jump-roper
landloper

interloper

OP-ur

bopper
copper
cropper
chopper
dropper
hopper
mopper
pauper
popper
proper
plopper
shopper
swapper
stopper
topper
whopper

bebopper
clodhopper
corn popper
doorstopper
eyedropper
eye-popper
eavesdropper
flip-flopper
floor mopper
grasshopper
heartstopper
improper
name-dropper
pill popper
sharecropper
show-stopper
woodchopper

belly-flopper
lindy-hopper
popcorn popper
teenybopper
window-shopper

compulsive shopper

knee-high to a
   grasshopper

ŌP-ur-ē

potpourri
popery

OP-ur-ē

coppery
foppery

OP-ur-u-tiv

operative

cooperative
inoperative

ŌP-us

dope us
grope us
opus
rope us
soap us

magnum opus

OP-ut

bop it
crop it
chop it
drop it
hop it
lop it
moppet
mop it
pop it
poppet
prop it
shop it
stop it
swap it
top it
whop it

flip-flop it

OP-yū-lur
(See OP-ū-lur)

ŌR

bore
boar
core
corps
chore
door
drawer
four
for
fore
floor
gore
hoar
lore
more
nor
or
o'er
oar
poor
pore
pour
roar
soar
snore
sore
swore
store
score
shore
spore
Thor
tore
war
wore
whore
yore

adore
at war

afore
abhor
ashore
backdoor
before
bedsore
condor
cash drawer
centaur
cold sore
chain store
cold war
decor
dirt poor
dance floor
deplore
drugstore
downpour
Dutch door
encore
eyesore
explore
fall for
folklore
footsore
forswore
front door
fourscore
flamethrower
galore
heartsore
hard-core
hoped-for
implore
ignore
indoor
iron ore
in for
keep score
mentor
no more
next-door
outdoor
outscore
onshore

offshore
Peace Corps
price war
pray for
postwar
press corps
rapport
restore
repour
sophomore
stage door
seashore
señor
soft-core
top drawer
tie score
top floor
ten-four
trapdoor
threescore
therefore
uproar
wherefore
wild boar
world war
wait for
work for

albacore
army corps
act of war
anymore
all ashore
apple core
antiwar
at death's door
bottom floor
Baltimore
blood and gore
Barrymore
bar the door
cuspidor
corridor
commodore
civil war

carnivore
canker sore
dinosaur
declare war
dresser drawer
discount store
door-to-door
doggie door
evermore
Ecuador
either/or
furthermore
guarantor
heretofore
humidor
have the floor
household chore
hardware store
know the score
lion's roar
matador
metaphor
Marine Corps
man-of-war
mind the store
mirador
nevermore
neither/nor
orator
open door
pinafore
perfect score
paramour
petit four
pompadour
picador
por favor
piscator
reservoir
rich or poor
saddle sore
sliding door
semaphore
Singapore
sophomore

stevedore
signal corps
spoils of war
sycamore
ship-to-shore
state of war
swinging door
take the floor
to die for
troubadour
Trojan War
two-by-four
tug of war
ten-cent store
Theodore
to the core
theretofore
underscore
unwished-for
unhoped-for
unlooked-for
unpaid-for
uncared-for
unasked-for
uncalled-for

Army Air Corps
conservator
conspirator
convenience store
cutting-room floor
department store
esprit de corps
El Salvador
forevermore
grocery store
Korean War
mixed metaphor
row with one oar
revolving door
settle the score
toreador
titanosaur
Vietnam War

five-and-ten-cent store

in on the ground floor
prisoner of war
declaration of war

ŌRB

Forbe(s)
orb

absorb

ŌRB-ut

Corbett
orbit

absorb it

ŌRCH

porch
scorch
torch

blowtorch
back porch
front porch
sun porch

carry a torch
Olympic torch

ŌRCH-ēng

scorching
torching

ŌRCH-un

fortune
scorchin'
torchin'

misfortune

ŌRCH-un-ut

fortunate
scorchin' it

torchin' it

unfortunate

ŌRCH-ur

scorcher
torture
torcher

ŌRCH-urd

orchard
tortured

ŌRD

board
bored
chord
cord
cored
ford
floored
gored
gourd
hoard
Lord
oared
pored
poured
roared
snored
soared
sword
stored
scored
toward
ward
warred
whored

afford
award
accord
aboard
adored

abhorred
backboard
billboard
buckboard
blackboard
chess board
chalkboard
cross sword(s)
Concorde
clipboard
call board
cardboard
deplored
discord
draft board
drainboard
dashboard
dart board
explored
encored
fjord
four-doored
floorboard
headboard
inboard
implored
ignored
keyboard
lost chord
landlord
milord
on-board
outboard
outscored
record
rip cord
restored
reward
skateboard
surfboard
scoreboard
sick ward
springboard
sideboard
shipboard

signboard
seaboard
switchboard
slumlord
two-doored
tackboard
tote board
toward
unpoured
warlord
washboard

all aboard
above board
boogieboard
bed and board
by the board
cutting board
clavichord
checkerboard
drawing board
diving board
harpsichord
ironing board
in accord
ill afford
mortarboard
open-doored
overlord
overboard
off-the-board
paddleboard
room and board
running board
smorgasbord
sounding board
spinal chord
shuffleboard
tape-record
tread the board(s)
untoward
unexplored
unrestored

across the board
bulletin board

emery board
electric cord
extension cord
governing board
go by the board
model T Ford
stiff as a board

chairman of the board
executive board
umbilical cord

Academy Award

ŌRD-ē

Daugherty
forty
Lordy
shorty
sortie
sporty
warty

Top 40

ŌRD-ed
(See ŌRD-ud)

ŌRD-en
(See ŌRD-un)

ŌRD-ēng

boarding
courting
chording
cording
fording
hoarding
sorting
snorting
shorting
sporting
thwarting
warding

assorting
affording
aborting
awarding
according
contorting
cavorting
consorting
comporting
distorting
deporting
exhorting
exporting
extorting
escorting
importing
purporting
retorting
resorting
reporting
rewarding
supporting
skateboarding
surfboarding
transporting

overlording

ŌRD-ē-un

gordian

accordion

ŌRD-id
(See ŌRD-ud)

ŌRD-i-fi
(See ŌRD-u-fi)

ŌRD-in-ut
(See ŌRD-un-ut)

ŌRD-iv

sportive

abortive
contortive
distortive
purportive
supportive

ŌRD-u

sorta

aorta

ŌRD-u-bul

boardable
chordable
courtable
fordable
portable
sortable

affordable
accordable
assortable
abortable
contortable
distortable
deportable
exhortable
extortable
exportable
escortable
importable
purportable
recordable
rewardable
retortable
resortable
reportable
supportable
transportable

insupportable
tape-recordable

ŌRD-ud

boarded
courted
chorded
forded
hoarded
sordid
sorted
sported
warded

assorted
afforded
aborted
awarded
accorded
contorted
cavorted
consorted
distorted
deported
exhorted
extorted
exported
imported
purported
retorted
resorted
reported
recorded
rewarded
supported
transported

unrecorded

ŌRD-u-fi

fortify
mortify

refortify

ŌRD-ul

chortle
chordal

mortal
portal

immortal

portal-to-portal

ŌRD-um

bored 'em
boredom
court 'em
floored 'em
gored 'em
hoard 'em
poured 'em
sort 'em
stored 'em
sport 'em
scored 'em
toward 'em

abort 'em
afford 'em
award 'em
accord 'em
aboard 'em
adored 'em
abhorred 'em
distort 'em
deplored 'em
deport 'em
explored 'em
escort 'em
implored 'em
ignored 'em
import 'em
outscored 'em
postmortem
record 'em
restored 'em
reward 'em
report 'em
support 'em

ŌRD-un

boardin'
cordon
chordin'
fordin'
Gordon
hoardin'
Jordan
warden

affordin'
awardin'
game warden
recordin'
rewardin'
skateboardin'

ŌRD-uns

accordance
concordance
discordance

ŌRD-un-ut

boardin' it
cordon it
ordinate

affordin' it
awardin' it
coordinate
inordinate
recordin' it
rewardin' it
subordinate

insubordinate

ŌRD-ur

border
boarder
chorder
courter
forder
hoarder

mortar
order
porter
quarter
shorter
sorter
thwarter

assorter
aborter
accorder
afforder
awarder
back-order
contorter
court order
close quarter(s)
cavorter
consorter
distorter
deporter
exhorter
escorter
exporter
French Quarter
gag order
headquarter(s)
in order
importer
mail order
retorter
rush order
rewarder
reporter
recorder
ripsnorter
short order
supporter
stop order
transporter
tall order

breakfast order
brick and mortar
bed-and-boarder
call to order

cub reporter
court reporter
custom-order
come to order
flight recorder
in short order
Latin Quarter
law and order
marching order(s)
money order
made-to-order
out of order
pecking order
point of order
rules of order
star reporter
show cause order
tape recorder

apple pie order
Mexican border
pay to the order

athletic supporter
Canadian border
video recorder

ŌRD-ur-ēng

bordering
ordering
portering
quartering

reordering

ŌRD-ur-lē

orderly
quarterly

ŌR-ē

dory
glory
gory
hoary

Laurie
quarry
story
Tory

fish story
John Dory
love story
Maori
one-story
Old Glory
rock quarry
sob story
tall story
two-story
vainglory

allegory
amatory
a priori
auditory
bedtime story
cacciatore
cover story
con amore
category
crematory
De La Torre
dictatory
dilatory
fairy story
horror story
hunky-dory
inventory
laboratory
lavatory
laudatory
morning glory
mandatory
migratory
oratory
purgatory
promontory
promissory
second-story
territory

transitory

accusatory
admonitory
ambulatory
commendatory
circulatory
compensatory
conservatory
cock-and-bull story
derogatory
detective story
depilatory
explanatory
exploratory
inflammatory
laboratory
obligatory
observatory
preparatory
repository
respiratory
regulatory
reformatory
shaggy-dog story

congratulatory
conciliatory
discriminatory
hallucinatory
interlocutory
interrogatory
self-explanatory

ŌR-ēd

gloried
quarried
storied

two-storied

inventoried

ŌR-el
(See ŌR-ul)

ŌR-en
(See ŌR-un)

ŌR-ēng

boring
coring
flooring
goring
oaring
pouring
roaring
snoring
storing
scoring
warring
whoring

adoring
abhorring
deploring
downpouring
encoring
exploring
imploring
ignoring
outscoring
outpouring
restoring
reflooring
riproaring
uproaring

ŌR-ēng-lē

boringly
roaringly

adoringly
riproaringly

ŌR-en-ur
(See ŌR-un-ur)

ŌR-ent
(See ŌR-unt)

ŌR-ē-ō

Oreo

oratorio

ŌR-est
(See ŌR-ust)

ŌR-ē-u

Gloria

euphoria
Pretoria
Victoria

phantasmagoria

ŌR-ē-ul

boreal
oriole

arboreal
censorial
corporeal
memorial
pictorial
raptorial
sartorial
tonsorial
temporeal
tutorial

categorial
dictatorial
equatorial
editorial
promissorial
professorial
senatorial
territorial

accusatorial
supervisorial
time immemorial

ŌR-ē-um

emporium

auditorium
crematorium
inventory 'em
in memoriam
moratorium
sanitorium

ŌR-ē-un

gloryin'
storyin'

censorian
Gregorian
historian
stentorian
Victorian

phantasmagorian
valedictorian

ŌR-ē-us

glorious

censorious
euphorious
inglorious
laborious
notorious
stentorious
uproarious
victorious

inventory us
meritorious
unvictorious

ŌRF

dwarf
wharf

Düsseldorf

ŌRF-un

dwarfin'
orphan

endorphin

ŌRF-us

dwarf us
morphous

amorphous

polymorphous

ŌRG-un

Gorgon
Morgan
organ

guten Morgen

ŌR-ib-ul
(See ŌR-ub-ul)

ŌR-id
(See ŌR-ud)

ŌR-idj
(See ŌR-ij)

ŌR-if-ī

glorify
horrify

ŌR-ij

forage
moorage
porridge
storage

cold storage

ŌR-ik

doric

caloric
euphoric
historic
phosphoric
rhetoric

allegoric
categoric
hydrochloric
metaphoric
meteoric
oratoric
sophomoric
prehistoric
paregoric

phantasmagoric

ŌR-ik-ul
(See ŌR-uk-ul)

ŌR-ist
(See ŌR-ust)

ŌR-it-ē
(See ŌR-ud-ē)

ŌRJ

forge
George
gorge

disgorge
engorge

Valley Forge

ŌRJ-ē

Georgie
orgy

Georgie Porgie

ŌRJ-ur

forger
gorger
ordure

disgorger
engorger

ŌRJ-us

forge us
gorgeous
gorge us

ŌRK

cork
dork
fork
pork
stork
York

New York
pitchfork
salt pork
uncork

blow one's cork
Duke of York
pop one's cork
tuning fork

ŌRK-ē

corky
dorky
Gorki
porky
yorkie

ŌRK-u

Majorca
Minorca

ŌRK-ur

corker
forker
porker

New Yorker
uncorker

ŌRL
(See ŌR-ul)

ŌR-lē

poorly
sorely

ŌRM

dorm
form
norm
storm
swarm
warm

brainstorm
bad form
barnstorm
conform
duststorm
deform
firestorm
free-form
inform
lukewarm
perform
platform
rainstorm
reform
rewarm
snowstorm
sandstorm
transform
tax form
windstorm

co-ed dorm
chloroform
Maidenform
misinform
outperform
order form
proper form
thunderstorm
take by storm
uniform

dance up a storm
ride out the storm

out of uniform

ŌRM-at

doormat
format
floormat

ŌRMD

formed
stormed
swarmed
warmed

brainstormed
conformed
deformed
informed
performed
reformed
rewarmed
transformed

misinformed
outperformed
uninformed
uniformed

ŌRM-ē

bore me
for me
floor me

poor me
swarmy
stormy
tore me

adore me
abhor me
before me
ignore me
live for me
outscore me

ŌRM-ēng

forming
storming
swarming
warming

brainstorming
benchwarming
barnstorming
conforming
deforming
heartwarming
informing
performing
reforming
rewarming
transforming

global warming
habit-forming
misinforming
outperforming
thunderstorming

ŌRM-ist

warmest

conformist
reformist

nonconformist

ŌRM-it-ē
(See ŌRM-ud-ē)

ŌRM-lē

warmly

uniformly

ŌRM-lus

dormless
formless
stormless

ŌRM-ōst

foremost
roar most
snore most
swore most
score most

adore most
abhor most
deplore most
explore most
ignore most

first and foremost

ŌRM-ud-ē

abnormity
conformity
deformity
enormity

nonconformity
uniformity

ŌRM-ul

formal
normal

abnormal
informal
subnormal

above normal
semiformal

ŌRM-ul-īz

formalize
normalize

informalize

ŌRM-un

corpsman
doorman
floorman
foreman
formin'
Mormon
Norman
stormin'
swarmin'
warmin'

brainstormin'
barnstormin'
conformin'
deformin'
heartwarmin'
informin'
jack Mormon
longshoreman
performin'
reformin'
transformin'

habit formin'
jury foreman
misinformin'
outperformin'

ŌRM-uns

dormance

conformance
performance
transformance

ŌRM-unt

dormant

informant

ŌRM-ur

former
stormer
swarmer
warmer

barnstormer
benchwarmer
chairwarmer
conformer
heart-warmer
informer
leg warmer(s)
performer
reformer
transformer

misinformer
outperformer

ŌRM-us

swarm us
storm us
warm us

deform us
enormous
inform us
reform us
transform us

chloroform us
misinform us
outperform us

ŌRM-ust
(See ŌRM-ist)

ŌRM-u-tē
(See ŌRM-u-dē)

ŌRN

born
borne

corn
horn
morn
mourn
porn
sworn
scorn
shorn
torn
thorn
worn
warn

air horn
airborne
adorn
acorn
bullhorn
bighorn
careworn
forsworn
forewarn
firstborn
foghorn
forlorn
freeborn
French horn
greenhorn
highborn
inborn
lovelorn
longhorn
newborn
outworn
popcorn
prewarn
reborn
shopworn
shoehorn
tinhorn
timeworn
untorn
unshorn
unsworn
unborn

well-worn

barleycorn
Capricorn
ear of corn
early morn
flugelhorn
foreign-born
Matterhorn
native born
peppercorn
unicorn
unadorn
weatherworn

around the horn
toot one's own horn

to the manner born

tropic of Capricorn

ŌRN-ē

corny
horny
thorny

ŌRN-ēng

Corning
horning
morning
mourning
scorning
warning

aborning
adorning
flood warning
forewarning
gale warning
good morning

air-raid warning

ŌRN-ful

mournful
scornful
thornful

ŌRN-ur

borne 'er
corner
horner
mourner
sworn 'er
scorner
worn 'er
warner

adorner
cut corner(s)
forewarner
outworn 'er
prewarn 'er

amen-corner
cater-corner(ed)

Little Jack Horner

ŌRN-yu

borne ya
mourn ya
sworn ya
scorn ya
torn ya
worn ya
warn ya

adorn ya
forewarn ya
outworn ya
prewarn ya

California

ŌR-on

moron
more on

pour on
roar on
snore on
swore on
score on

keep score on
make war on

oxymoron

ŌRP

corp
gorp
warp

time warp

ŌRPS

corpse
warps

ŌRP-ur

torpor
warper

ŌRP-us

corpus
porpoise
warp us

habeas corpus

ŌRS

course
coarse
force
horse
hoarse
Morse
Norse
source

air force

brute force
by force
crash course
clotheshorse
concourse
discourse
due course
dark horse
divorce
enforce
endorse
golf course
gift horse
high horse
in force
main course
midcourse
of course
perforce
packhorse
remorse
resource
recourse
racehorse
racecourse
seahorse
sawhorse
strike force
task force
workhorse
warhorse
work force

but of course
choke a horse
charley horse
Crazy Horse
driving force
hobbyhorse
hold your horse(s)
intercourse
in due course
iron horse
labor force
magnum force

police force
quarter horse
rocking horse
reinforce
show of force
stay the course
tour de force
watercourse
wooden horse

beat a dead horse
collision course
grounds for divorce
have intercourse
matter of course
obstacle course
par for the course
refresher course

centrifugal force
correspondence course
cart before the horse

ŌRS-ē

Dorsey
horsey

ŌRS-ēng

coursing
forcing

divorcing
enforcing
endorsing

reinforcing

ŌRS-et
(See ŌRS-ut)

ŌRS-ful

forceful
sourceful

remorseful
resourceful

ŌRSH-um

Florsheim

consortium

ŌRSH-un

portion
torsion

abortion
apportion
contortion
distortion
extortion
proportion

in proportion
reapportion

out of proportion

ŌR-shun-ist

abortionist
contortionist
extortionist

ŌR-si-bul
(See ŌR-su-bul)

ŌRS-ment

enforcement
endorsement

law enforcement
reinforcement

ŌRS-nus

coarseness
hoarseness

ŌRS-ō

more so
torso

abhor so
ignore so

ŌR-su-bul

forcible

divorceable
enforceable
endorsable

ŌR-sul

dorsal
morsel

ŌR-sum

boresome
force 'em
floor some
foursome
gore some
pour some
store some
score some
tore some
wore some

abhor some
divorce 'em
enforce 'em

reinforce 'em

ŌRS-ur

coarser
force 'er
hoarser

discourser
divorce 'er
enforcer

endorser
reinforcer

ŌRS-ut

corset
force it

divorce it
enforce it
endorse it

ŌRT

court
fort
forte
ort
port
quart
sort
snort
short
sport
thwart
torte
tort
wart

assort
abort
airport
backcourt
bad sport
contort
cohort
cavort
consort
cut short
comport
carport
distort
deport
exhort
export
extort

escort
fall short
good sport
high court
hold court
home port
import
in short
moot court
night court
Newport
passport
purport
retort
resort
report
seaport
sell short
Shreveport
support
spoilsport
transport

child support
circuit court
contact sport
center court
day in court
divorce court
davenport
friend at court
heliport
last resort
nonsupport
out-of-court
on report
Rapoport
Supreme Court
small claims court
Sacher torte
traffic court
tennis court
worrywart

contempt of court
kangaroo court

Kennebunkport
laugh out of court
moral support
police escort
spousal support
spectator sport
weather report

make a long story
    short

ŌRT-ē
(See ŌRD-ē)

ŌRT-ed
(See ŌRD-ud)

ŌRT-em
(See ŌRD-um)

ŌRT-en
(See ŌRT-un)

ŌRT-ēng
(See ŌRD-ēng)

ŌRTH

forth
fourth
north
swarth

bring forth
come forth
go forth
henceforth
one-fourth
set forth
thenceforth
up north

and so forth

back and forth
July Fourth

so on and so forth

ŌRTH-ē

Dorothy
swarthy

ŌRT-i-fī
(See ŌRD-u-fī)

ŌRT-ij

portage
shortage

ŌRT-iv
(See ŌRD-iv)

ŌRT-lē

courtly
portly
shortly

ŌRT-ment

assortment
abortment
comportment
deportment
distortment

ŌRTS

courts
forts
orts
ports
quartz
quarts
sorts
snorts
Schwartz

shorts
thwarts
torts
tortes
warts

assorts
all sorts
aborts
airports
bad sports
contorts
cohorts
cavorts
consorts
comports
carports
distorts
deports
exhorts
extorts
exports
escorts
good sports
imports
moot courts
night courts
passports
purports
rose quartz
retorts
resorts
reports
short shorts
seaports
supports
transports

boxer shorts
contact sports
divorce courts
davenports
heliports
last resorts
out of sorts
prince consorts

Sacher tortes
traffic courts
tennis courts
undershorts
worrywarts
water sports

basketball courts
kangaroo courts
spectator sports
weather reports

ŌRT-u
(See ŌRD-u)

ŌRT-u-bul
(See ŌRD-u-bul)

ŌRT-ud
(See ŌRD-ud)

ŌRT-ul
(See ŌRD-ul)

ŌRT-um
(See ŌRD-um)

ŌRT-un

courtin'
Horton
shorten
snortin'
sportin'
thwartin'
Wharton

abortin'
contortin'
cavortin'
distortin'
deportin'
exhortin'

exportin'
extortin'
escortin'
foreshorten
importin'
purportin'
retortin'
resortin'
reportin'
supportin'
transportin'

ŌRT-ur
(See ŌRD-ur)

ŌR-u

aura
Cora
Dora
flora
hora
Laura
Nora
Torah

angora
Aurora
begorra
fedora
menorah
Pandora
señora
Sonora

Bora Bora
Isadora

Sodom and Gomorrah

OR-u
(See ÄR-u)

ŌR-u-bul

horrible
pourable

soarable
storable
scorable

adorable
abhorable
deplorable
explorable
ignorable
outscorable
restorable
unpourable
unscorable

underscorable

ŌR-ud

florid
horrid
torrid

ŌR-ud-ē

authority
majority
minority
priority
sorority
seniority
sonority

port authority

inferiority
moral majority
police authority
simple majority
silent majority
superiority

ŌR-uf-ī
(See ŌR-if-ī)

ŌR-uk
(See ŌR-ik)

ŌR-uk-lē

historically
rhetorically

allegorically
categorically
metaphorically
oratorically

phantasmagorically

ŌR-uk-ul

oracle

historical
rhetorical

allegorical
categorical
metaphorical
oratorical
prehistorical

phantasmagorical

ŌR-ul

coral
choral
floral
laurel
moral
oral
quarrel
sorrel

amoral
immoral
mayoral
pastoral
unmoral

lovers' quarrel
pick a quarrel

ŌR-ul-ē

florally
morally
orally

ŌR-um

bore 'em
for 'em
forum
floor 'em
pour 'em
quorum

adore 'em
abhor 'em
decorum
deplore 'em
explore 'em
implore 'em
outscore 'em

open forum

ŌR-un

borin'
foreign
pourin'
roarin'
soarin'
snorin'
storin'
scorin'
Warren
warrin'

adorin'
abhorin'
deplorin'
explorin'
implorin'
ignorin'
outscorin'
restorin'

riproarin'

oxymoron

ŌR-uns

Florence
Lawrence
torrents
Torrance
warrants

abhorrence

ŌR-unt

torrent
warrant

abhorrent
bench warrant
death warrant
rain torrent
search warrant

ŌR-un-tē

quarantee
warranty

ŌR-un-ur

borin' 'er
coroner
foreigner

adorin' 'er
implorin' 'er
ignorin' 'er

ŌR-us

bore us
Boris
chorus
Doris
for us
Horace

Morris
nor us
or us
o'er us
porous
poor us
score us
tore us

adore us
afore us
abhor us
before us
deplore us
implore us
ignore us
outscore us
restore us
thesaurus

brontosaurus
braunisorous

ŌR-ust

forest
florist
poorest
sorest

ŌR-u-tē
(See ŌR-u-dē)

ŌR-u-tōr-ē

oratory

laboratory

ŌR-wā

doorway
four-way
Norway
poor way

ŌRZ

bores
boars
cores
chores
doors
drawers
floors
gores
oars
pores
pours
roars
soars
snores
sores
stores
scores
shores
spores
wars
whores

adores
abhors
Azores
backdoors
bedsores
condors
centaurs
cold sores
deplores
drugstores
downpours
encores
eyesores
explores
implores
ignores
indoors
mentors
outdoors
outscores
restores
repours

sophomores
Star Wars
trapdoors
uproars
wild boars
world wars

apple cores
cuspidors
corridors
commodores
civil wars
chest of drawers
carnivores
canker sores
dinosaurs
doggie doors
humidors
household chores
matadors
metaphors
orators
on all fours
pinafores
paramours
petit fours
reservoirs
saddle sores
semaphores
sophomores
stevedores
sycamores
swinging doors
troubadours
underscores

conservators
conspirators
department stores
mixed metaphors
toreadors
titanosaurs

ŌS

close
dose

dross
gross

Ambrose
cosmos
dextrose
engross
ethos
glucose
in close
jocose
Laos
lactose
morose
pathos
too close
up close
verbose

adios
bellicose
comatose
diagnose
grandiose
lachrymose
megadose
otiose
overdose
soporose
varicose

OS

boss
cross
dross
floss
gloss
joss
loss
moss
Ross
sauce
toss

across
big boss

Blue Cross
crisscross
emboss
hot sauce
lacrosse
lip gloss
peat moss
ring toss
Red Cross
straw boss
trail boss
tax loss
weight loss

albatross
applesauce
at a loss
cocktail sauce
Charing Cross
cut one's loss(es)
come across
coup de grace
dental floss
double-cross
hit the sauce
hearing loss
run across
soy sauce
Southern Cross
tartar sauce

memory loss
profit and loss
sign of the cross

OS-ē

Aussie
bossy
flossy
glossy
mossy
posse
saucy

ŌS-ē-ā-shun
(See ŌSH-ē-ā-shun)

ŌS-ēng

dosing
grossing

engrossing

diagnosing
overdosing

OS-ēng

bossing
crossing
flossing
glossing
tossing

crisscrossing
embossing

railroad crossing

OS-ē-nus

bossiness
glossiness
mossiness
sauciness

OS-et
(See OS-ut)

OS-ē-ust

bossiest
glossiest
mossiest
sauciest

ŌSH

cloche
gauche

skosh

brioche

OSH

bosh
frosh
gosh
josh
nosh
posh
quash
splosh
squash
swash
slosh
wash

brainwash
backwash
carwash
dishwash
eyewash
goulash
hand wash
hogwash
kibosh
mouthwash
my gosh
panache
whitewash

mackintosh

by guess and by gosh

OSH-ē

sloshy
sploshy
washy

prima facie
Takahashi
wishy-washy

ŌSH-ē-ā-shun

association
negotiation

contract negotiation
guilt by association

OSH-ēng

joshing
quashing
sploshing
swashing
squashing
sloshing
washing

brainwashing
dishwashing
handwashing
whitewashing

ŌSH-un

lotion
motion
notion
ocean
potion

commotion
devotion
demotion
emotion
hand lotion
love potion
promotion
slow motion

forward motion
land o'Goshen
locomotion
make a motion
monkey motion
magic potion
man in motion
Nova Scotian

sleeping potion

Atlantic Ocean
go through the
    motion(s)
Pacific Ocean

perpetual motion

OSH-un

caution
joshin'
sloshin'
squashin'
washin'

brainwashin'
dishwashin'
precaution
rewashin'
whitewashin'

ŌSH-un-ul

motional
notional

commotional
devotional
demotional
emotional
promotional

unemotional

ŌSH-ur

gaucher
kosher

Durocher

OSH-ur

josher
nosher
posher
quasher

splosher
squasher
slosher
washer

dishwasher
whitewasher

ŌSH-us

atrocious
ferocious
precocious

unferocious
unprecocious

supercalifragilistic-
    expialidotious

OSH-us

cautious
josh us
nauseous
splosh us
squash us
wash us

brainwash us
rewash us
incautious
whitewash us

overcautious

OS-ib-ul
(See OS-ub-ul)

OS-ij

crossage
sausage

OS-il
(See OS-ul)

OS-ip
(See OS-up)

ŌS-is
(See ŌS-us)

OS-i-tē
(See OS-u-dē)

ŌS-iv

corrosive
erosive
explosive

OSK

mosque

kiosk

ŌS-lē

closely
grossly

jocosely
morosely
verbosely

ŌS-nus

closeness
grossness

moroseness
verboseness

ŌS-ō

blow so
crow so
grow so
glow so
know so
oh so

so-so

mafioso
virtuoso

affettuoso
capriccioso

OS-ō

basso

crisscross so
Picasso

come across so

OSP-is
(See OSP-us)

OSP-us

auspice
hospice

ŌST

boast
coast
dosed
ghost
grossed
host
most
oast
post
roast
toast

almost
at most
bedpost
compost
engrossed
East Coast
foremost
French toast

glasnost
Gold Coast
goalpost
guest host
guidepost
impost
lamppost
milepost
milktoast
no-host
outpost
outgrossed
pot roast
provost
reposte
seacoast
signpost
topmost
utmost
West Coast

command post
coast-to-coast
diagnosed
furthermost
hitching post
Holy Ghost
innermost
Ivory Coast
northernmost
nethermost
outermost
overdosed
parcel post
southernmost
talk-show host
trading post
uppermost
uttermost
whipping post

standing rib roast
white as a ghost

from pillar to post

OST

bossed
cost
crossed
frost
flossed
glossed
lost
mossed
sauced
tossed

accost
crisscrossed
defrost
exhaust
embossed
get lost
low-cost
star-crossed

double-crossed
holocaust
Pentecost

at any cost
Paradise Lost

keep one's fingers
    crossed

OST-ē

frosty

antipasti

OST-el
(See OST-ul)

ŌST-ēng

boasting
coasting
ghosting
hosting
posting

roasting
toasting

OST-ēng

costing
frosting

accosting
defrosting
exhausting

ŌST-es
(See ŌST-us)

OST-ik

caustic
gnostic

agnostic
acrostic
prognostic

diagnostic

OST-il
(See OST-ul)

ŌST-lē

ghostly
mostly

OST-u

basta
pasta

Acosta
La Costa

antipasta

ŌST-ud

boasted
coasted

ghosted
hosted
posted
roasted
toasted

OST-ud

frosted

accosted
defrosted
exhausted

ŌST-ul

coastal
postal

bicoastal

OST-ul

hostel
hostile

youth hostel

Pentecostal

OST-un

Austin
Boston
costin'
frostin'

accostin'
defrostin'
exhaustin'

ŌST-ur

boaster
coaster
host 'er
poster
roaster
toaster

engrossed 'er
fourposter

diagnosed 'er
roller coaster
turkey roaster

OST-ur

bossed 'er
crossed 'er
cost 'er
foster
froster
Gloucester
lost 'er
roster
tossed 'er

accoster
defroster
exhaust 'er
impostor

double-crossed 'er
snollygoster

OST-ur-us

foster us

preposterous

ŌST-us

dosed us
grossed us
hostess
host us
mostes'
roast us
toast us

engrossed us
outgrossed us

diagnosed us
overdosed us

ŌS-u

rosa

Formosa
mimosa
nervosa
sub rosa

mariposa

anorexia nervosa

OS-u

casa

Hadassah
kielbasa
Mombasa

tabula rasa

ŌS-ub-ul

dosable
grossable

engrossable

diagnosable

OS-ub-ul

bossable
crossable
possible
tossable

crisscrossable
cognoscible
embossable
impossible
uncrossable

Mission Impossible

OS-ud-ē

paucity
raucity

atrocity
ferocity
jocosity
monstrosity
precocity
pomposity
venosity
viscosity
velocity
verbosity
vinosity

animosity
curiosity
grandiosity
generosity
luminosity
preciosity
reciprocity
virtuosity

impetuosity

OS-ul

docile
fossil
glossal
jostle
tossle
wassail

apostle
colossal
old fossil
undocile

OS-u-lot

boss a lot
cross a lot
floss a lot
gloss a lot
ocelot

across a lot
crisscross a lot

emboss a lot

at a loss a lot
come across a lot
double-cross a lot
run across a lot

OS-um

awesome
blossom
boss 'em
cross 'em
floss 'em
gloss 'em
possum
toss 'em

across 'em
crisscross 'em
emboss 'em
opossum
play possum
squash blossom

apple blossom
come across 'em
double-cross 'em
orange blossom
run across 'em

OS-um-ur

awesomer
blossomer
gossamer

OS-up

cross-up
gossip
toss-up

ŌS-ur

closer
doser
grocer

grosser

greengrocer
jocoser
moroser
verboser

diagnoser
overdose 'er

OS-ur

bosser
crosser
Chaucer
flosser
glosser
saucer
tosser

across 'er
crisscrosser
embosser

cup and saucer
double-crosser
flying saucer

ŌS-us

dose us
gnosis
gross us
ptosis

cirrhosis
engross us
hypnosis
neurosis
osmosis
prognosis
psychosis
thrombosis

acidosis
diagnosis
diagnose us
halitosis

overdose us
self-hypnosis
scoliosis
trichinosis

cystic fibrosis
tuberculosis

mononucleosis
osteosclerosis

arteriosclerosis

OS-us

boss us
cross us
toss us

across us
Colossus
proboscis

OS-ut

boss it
cross it
cosset
floss it
faucet
gloss it
toss it

across it
crisscross it
emboss it

come across it
dental-floss it
water faucet

OS-u-tē
(See OS-u-dē)

ŌT

boat
bloat

coat
dote
float
goat
gloat
moat
note
oat
quote
rote
smote
shoat
tote
throat
vote
wrote

afloat
basecoat
C-note
connote
cutthroat
deep throat
devote
dreamboat
demote
denote
emote
footnote
fire boat
gunboat
high note
houseboat
keynote
love note
lifeboat
misquote
outvote
of note
old goat
promote
pound note
powerboat
remote
raincoat

rowboat
rewrote
redcoat
sour note
steamboat
sore throat
slow boat
showboat
sailboat
scapegoat
speedboat
straw vote
strep throat
topcoat
turncoat
tugboat
trenchcoat
U-boat
unquote
voice vote
wild oat(s)

anecdote
all she wrote
antidote
billy goat
creosote
ferryboat
gravy boat
happi coat
locomote
motorboat
miss the boat
nanny goat
overcoat
petticoat
quote/unquote
right to vote
rock the boat
rootbeer float
riverboat
sugarcoat
table d'hôte
underwrote

absentee vote

cut one's own throat
deciding vote
in the same boat
lump in the throat
one man, one vote
popular vote
stick in one's throat
Treasury note
torpedo boat

electoral vote
force down someone's
    throat
jump down someone's
    throat
majority vote
promissory note
unanimous vote

OT

blot
brought
bought
baht
cot
caught
clot
dot
fought
fraught
got
hot
jot
knot
lot
not
naught
ought
pot
plot
rot
sot
Scott
shot
spot

slot
Scot
snot
squat
sought
swat
taught
taut
tot
trot
thought
twat
watt
what
wrought
yacht

allot
à droite
begot
blind spot
bloodshot
bank shot
besot
big shot
bad lot
best shot
boycott
blood clot
blackrot
buckshot
crack shot
cannot
chip shot
crackpot
cheap shot
dogtrot
distraught
dry rot
earshot
foxtrot
flower pot
forgot
French knot
forethought

fleshpot
fat lot
five-spot
fusspot
gunshot
gluepot
grapeshot
hot shot
hot pot
hot spot
handwrought
inkblot
jackpot
job lot
kumquat
loquat
long shot
mug shot
mail slot
mascot
night spot
odd lot
onslaught
pot shot
pump knot
robot
red-hot
store-bought
sunspot
so what?
soft spot
square knot
somewhat
slipknot
smudge pot
snapshot
slingshot
self-taught
sandlot
say what?
stinkpot
ten-spot
topknot
tight spot
teapot

uncaught
upshot
untaught
white-hot
warm spot
whatnot

aquanaut
Argonaut
aeronaut
astronaut
afterthought
apricot
all for naught
boiling hot
booster shot
beauty spot
cosmonaut
caveat
Camelot
coffee pot
counterplot
candid shot
chamber pot
come to naught
diddly-squat
empty lot
flower pot
food for thought
go to pot
granny knot
hot to trot
hatch a plot
Hottentot
hit the spot
Juggernaut
kilowatt
Lancelot
lobster pot
loves me not
liver spot
like a shot
misbegot
melting pot
microdot

megawatt
not so hot
on the dot
overwrought
ocelot
overshot
on the spot
piping hot
polka dot
parting shot
put the shot
polyglot
parking lot
pepper pot
second thought
tommyrot
trouble spot
thanks a lot
tie the knot
turkey trot
take a shot
undershot
Windsor knot

burial plot
by a long shot
forget-me-not
Gordian knot
like it or not
on second thought
overhead shot
some like it hot
sweeten the pot
whether or not
x marks the spot

believe it or not
Johnny-on-the-spot
malice aforethought
not by a long shot

strike while the iron is
    hot

OTCH
(See OCH)

ŌT-ē
(See ŌD-ē)

OT-ē
(See OD-ē)

ŌT-ed
(See ŌD-ud)

OT-ed
(See OD-ud)

OT-ēd
(See OD-ēd)

ŌT-em
(See ŌD-um)

OT-en
(See OT-un)

ŌT-ēng
(See ŌD-ēng)

OT-ēng
(See OD-ēng)

OT-ē-nus
(See OD-ē-nus)

OT-ē-ō
(See OD-ē-ō)

OT-ful

potful
plotful
thoughtful

distraughtful
unthoughtful

ŌTH

both
growth
oath
loath
quoth
troth

outgrowth
regrowth

aftergrowth
overgrowth
take an oath
undergrowth
under oath

loyalty oath

Hippocratic oath
population growth

OTH

broth
cloth
froth
Goth
moth
Roth
sloth
swath
troth

broadcloth
cheesecloth
dust cloth
loincloth

chicken broth
gypsy moth
tablecloth
three-toed sloth

Visigoth

man of the cloth

OTH-ē

brothy
frothy

Chillicothe

ŌTHE

clothe
loathe

betrothe(d)
unclothe

ŌTHE-ēng

clothing
loathing

wolf in sheep's
   clothing

ŌTHE-sum

clothe some
loathesome
loathe some

OTHE-ur

bother
father
pother
rather

godfather
no bother
stepfather

Founding Father(s)

OTHE-urd

bothered
fathered

hot and bothered

OTHE-ur-ēng

bothering
fathering

OTHE-ur-sum

bothersome
bother some
father some

OT-ij
(See OD-ij)

OT-ik
(See OD-ik)

OT-i-kul
(See OD-i-kul)

OT-i-lē
(See OD-u-lē)

OT-ish
(See OD-ish)

ŌT-iv
(See ŌD-iv)

OT-lē

hotly
motley
tautly

OT-lus

dotless
knotless
plotless
potless
spotless
thoughtless

ŌT-ō
(See ŌD-ō)

OT-ō
(See OD-ō)

ŌT-on

dote on
float on
proton
photon
vote on
wrote on

ŌTS

boats
bloats
coats
dotes
floats
goats
moats
notes
oats
quotes
shoats
totes
throats
votes

C-notes
connotes
cutthroats
devotes
dreamboats
demotes
denotes
emotes
footnotes
houseboats
in quotes
love notes
lifeboats

misquotes
outvotes
promotes
raincoats
rowboats
redcoats
sore throats
slowboats
sailboats
scapegoats
turncoats
wild oats

anecdotes
antidotes
billy goats
compare notes
overcoats
petticoats
root-beer floats
sugarcoats

sow one's wild oats
electoral votes

OTS

blots
cots
clots
dots
jots
knots
lots
pots
plots
plotz
rots
sots
shots
spots
slots
snots
Scots
swats
tots

trots
watts
yachts

allots
blind spots
big shots
boycotts
bloodclots
culottes
crackpots
cheap shots
dogtrots
ersatz
foxtrots
flower pots
gunshots
hot shots
have-nots
hot spots
inkblots
jackpots
mugshots
pot shots
robots
soft spots
snapshots
slingshots
upshots
whatnots

call the shots

haves and have-nots
hit the high spots

OT-sē

Nazi

hotsy-totsy
paparazzi

OT-sō

matzo
fought so

not so

palazzo
terrazzo

OT-su

lotsa
matzah

piazza

OT-sum

blots 'em
brought some
bought some
caught some
dot some
flotsam
got some
plots 'em
rots 'em
shot some
spot some
sought some
taught some
thought some

ŌT-u
(See ŌD-u)

OT-u
(See OD-u)

ŌT-u-bul
(See ŌD-u-bul)

OT-u-bul
(See OD-u-bul)

ŌT-ud
(See ŌD-ud)

OT-ud
(See OD-ud)

ŌT-ul
(See ŌD-ul)

OT-ul
(See OD-ul)

OT-u-lē
(See OD-u-lē)

OT-ul-us
(See OD-ul-us)

ŌT-um
(See ŌD-um)

OT-um
(See OD-um)

OT-um-ē
(See OD-um-ē)

OT-un

blottin'
clottin'
cotton
dottin'
gotten
jottin'
knottin'
oughten
plottin'
rotten
spottin'
squattin'
swattin'
tauten

trottin'

au gratin
allottin'
begotten
boycottin'
dogtrottin'
foxtrottin'
forgotten
ill-gotten
misgotten
spoiled rotten

counterplottin'
misbegotten
sauerbraten
turkey trottin'
unforgotten

OT-un-ē

botany
cottony

monotony

OT-un-us

gotten us
spottin' us
swattin' us

allottin' us
begotten us
boycottin' us
forgotten us
monotonous

**ŌT-ur
(See ŌD-ur)**

**OT-ur
(See OD-ur)**

**ŌT-ur-ē
(See ŌD-ur-ē)**

**OT-ur-ē
(See OD-ur-ē)**

**ŌT-ur-īz
(See ŌD-ur-īz)**

**OT-us
(See OD-us)**

Ō-u

boa
Noah
stoa

aloha
Alcoa
Balboa
Samoa

Figueroa
Krakatoa
Mauna Loa
protozoa
Shenandoah

spermatozoa

**Ō-ul
(See ŌL)**

Ō-up

blow up
flow up
go up
grow up
sew up
show up
slow up
throw up

Ō-ur

blower
crower

goer
grower
hoer
know 'er
mower
owe 'er
rower
sewer
sower
slower
show 'er
thrower

churchgoer
flamethrower
lawnmower
mindblower

partygoer

Ō-ut

blow it
go it
grow it
hoe it
know it
mow it
owe it
poet
row it
sew it
sow it
show it
slow it
throw it
tow it

below it
bestow it
forego it
outgrow it

Ō-u-wā

blow away
crow away

flow away
go away
row away
stowaway
towaway
throwaway

ŌV

cove
clove
dove
drove
grove
hove
loave(s)
mauve
rove
stove
strove
trove
wove

alcove
by jove
rewove

interwove
pirate cove
treasure trove

OV

mauve
Slav

improv

mazel tov
Molotov
Stroganov

OV-ē

mauvy

Mondavi
Mohave

OV-el
(See OV-ul)

ŌV-en
(See ŌV-un)

ŌV-ē-u

Monrovia
Segovia

OV-ē-ur

mauvier

Xavier

OV-ō

bravo

centavo

ŌV-u

nova
ova

Canova
Jehovah

bossa nova
Casanova
supernova
Villanova

OV-u

brava
guava
java
kava
lava

lavalava

OV-ul

grovel
hovel
novel

ŌV-un

cloven
rovin'
woven

Beethoven
rewoven

interwoven

ŌV-ur

clover
drove 'er
Dover
over
rover

all over
boil over
bowl over
blow over
changeover
do over
flip over
fork over
hangover
holdover
hand over
knock over
Land Rover
layover
leftover
make over
once-over
pick over
Passover
pullover
popover
pushover

roll over
run over
sleep over
strikeover
spillover
switchover
turnover
takeover
throw over
think over
talk over
work over
warmed-over

carryover
Cliffs of Dover
death warmed over
four-leaf clover
going-over

over and over

ŌV-ur-ē

clovery
ovary

Madame Bovary

ŌV-urt

covert
overt

OW

bough
bow
brow
cow
ciao
chow
how
now
ow
pow
prow

plough
plow
row
scow
sow
thou
tau
vow
wow

avow
allow
and how
bow wow
dinghao
endow
eyebrow
highbrow
hausfrau
hoosegow
hofbrau
kowtow
know-how
lowbrow
luau
landau
Macao
Mau Mau
meow
Moscow
nohow
powwow
somehow
snowplow

anyhow
cat's meow
curaçao
disallow
disavow
even now
here and now
holy cow
Mindanao
marriage vow
solemn vow

sacred cow
take a bow

holier than thou

OWCH

couch
crouch
grouch
ouch
pouch
slouch
vouch

mail pouch

casting couch

OWCH-ē

grouchy
ouchy
pouchy
slouchy

OWCH-ēng

couching
crouching
grouching
slouching
vouching

OWCH-ur

coucher
croucher
groucher
oucher
sloucher
voucher

OWD

boughed
bowed
cowed

crowd
cloud
loud
proud
plowed
shroud
vowed
wowed

aloud
allowed
avowed
bow-wowed
kowtowed
enshroud
eyebrowed
endowed
highbrowed
in-crowd
lowbrowed
meowed
outloud
pow-wowed
raincloud
unbowed
uncloud
unplowed
war cloud

bushy-browed
disavowed
disallowed
mushroom cloud
madding crowd
overcrowd
thundercloud
three's a crowd

atomic cloud

for crying out loud

OWD-ē

cloudy
dowdy
doughty

gouty
howdy
pouty
rowdy
snouty

cum laude
uncloudy

apple pandowdy
magna cum laude
summa cum laude

OWD-ēng

crowding
clouding
doubting
flouting
grouting
outing
pouting
routing
spouting
scouting
sprouting
shouting
touting

enshrouding
overcrowding
overclouding

OWD-ē-nus

cloudiness
dowdiness
goutiness
poutiness
rowdiness

OWD-est
(See OWD-ust)

OWD-u-bul

doubtable
floutable

routable
shoutable
toutable

redoubtable

OWD-ur

chowder
doubter
flouter
grouter
louder
outer
pouter
powder
prouder
router
shouter
scouter
sprouter
stouter
touter

bath powder
clam chowder
enshrouder
gun powder
mail router

overcrowder
take a powder

OWD-ust

flautist
loudest
proudest
stoutest

devoutest

OW-ē

Howie
Maui
powie

wowie
zowie

OW-ēng

bowing
cowing
chowing
plowing
vowing
wowing

allowing
avowing
bow-wowing
kowtowing
endowing
meowing
snowplowing

disallowing
disavowing

OW-es
(See OW-us)

OWL
(See also OW-ul)

bowel
cowl
dowel
fowl
foul
growl
howl
jowl
owl
prowl
scowl
towel
vowel
yowl

afoul
befoul

hoot owl
night owl

crying towel
disembowel
fish or fowl
on the prowl
waterfowl
wise old owl

throw in the towel
technical foul
wise as an owl

neither fish nor fowl

OWL-ē

Crowley
growly
howly
scowly

OWL-ēng

fouling
growling
howling
prowling
scowling

befouling

OWL-ur

fouler
growler
howler
prowler
scowler
yowler

befoul 'er

disemboweler

OWN

brown
clown

crown
down
drown
frown
gown
noun
town

aroun'
burn down
Bean Town
back down
boomtown
ballgown
breakdown
countdown
crosstown
comedown
chow down
close down
clampdown
cow town
crackdown
downtown
face-down
goose down
Georgetown
ghosttown
hometown
hands down
hoedown
hick town
Jamestown
knockdown
lowdown
lay down
letdown
markdown
Miltown
meltdown
nightgown
pronoun
putdown
renown
rubdown

sundown
shakedown
showdown
shutdown
slowdown
sit down
scale-down
splashdown
small-town
touchdown
thumbs-down
takedown
uptown
wash down
wind down

buttoned-down
broken-down
circus clown
chocolate brown
cap and gown
Cooperstown
Chinatown
dressing-down
dressing gown
evening gown
eiderdown
go to town
hand-me-down
knuckle down
out-of-town
on the town
paint the town
shantytown
tumbledown
triple crown
trickle-down
upside down
up and down
watered-down
wedding gown

Koreatown
man about town
out on the town

take lying down

only game in town

OWND

bound
browned
crowned
clowned
downed
drowned
frowned
found
gowned
ground
hound
mound
pound
round
sound
wound
zound(s)

around
aground
all-round
astound
abound
bloodhound
background
break ground
chowhound
confound
compound
campground
dogpound
dumbfound
earthbound
expound
fairground
foreground
greyhound
hardbound
hidebound
high ground

impound
inbound
icebound
newfound
outbound
profound
playground
propound
renowned
redound
rebound
snowbound
spellbound
surround
unfound
unwound
unbound
unsound
wolfhound
year-round

above ground
all around
breeding ground
battleground
duty-bound
fool around
fox and hound
hallowed ground
homeward bound
honorbound
kiss the ground
leather-bound
lost and found
musclebound
neutral ground
off the ground
outward-bound
pitcher's mound
proving ground
round and round
run aground
runaround
stand one's ground
stamping ground

solid ground
underground
ultrasound
westward bound
wraparound

burial ground
ear to the ground
get off the ground
in and around
merry-go-round
run rings around
up and around

happy hunting ground
pussyfoot around
run into the ground

theater in the round

OWND-ēng

bounding
founding
grounding
hounding
pounding
rounding
sounding

astounding
abounding
confounding
compounding
dumbfounding
expounding
high-sounding
impounding
inbounding
propounding
rebounding
surrounding
strange sounding

OWND-lē

roundly
soundly

profoundly
unsoundly

OWND-lus

boundless
groundless
soundless

OWND-rē

boundary
foundry

OWND-ud

bounded
founded
hounded
pounded
rounded
sounded

astounded
abounded
confounded
compounded
dumbfounded
expounded
impounded
inbounded
propounded
redounded
rebounded
surrounded
unfounded
well-founded
well-rounded

OWND-up

bound up
ground up
roundup
wound up

OWND-ur

bounder
browned 'er
crowned 'er
downed 'er
drowned 'er
founder
flounder
grounder
gowned 'er
hounder
pounder
rounder
sounder
wound 'er

astounder
around 'er
confounder
co-founder
compounder
dumbfound 'er
expounder
impounder
inbounder
profounder
rebounder
surrounder
unwound 'er

all around 'er
musclebounder
quarter pounder

OWNDZ
(See OWNZ)

OWN-ē

brownie
clowny
downy
frowny
townie

OWN-ēng

browning
clowning
crowning
downing
drowning
frowning

OWNJ

lounge
scrounge

OWNS

bounce
counts
flounce
founts
mounts
ounce
pounce
trounce

announce
accounts
amounts
denounce
discounts
dismounts
headcounts
miscounts
no-counts
pronounce
recounts
renounce
remounts
surmounts

bank accounts
body counts
mispronounce
no accounts
ounce for ounce

OWNS-ēng

bouncing
flouncing
pouncing
trouncing

announcing
denouncing
pronouncing
renouncing

mispronouncing

OWNS-ment

announcement
denouncement
pronouncement
renouncement

OWNST

bounced
flounced
pounced
trounced

announced
denounced
pronounced
renounced

mispronounced

OWNS-ur

bouncer
flouncer
pouncer
trouncer

announcer
denouncer
pronouncer
renouncer

mispronouncer

OWNT

count
fount
mount

account
amount
blood count
discount
dismount
head count
miscount
no-count
recount
remount
surmount

body count
bank account
catamount
do without
no-account
on account
paramount
tantamount

down for the count
expense account
on no account

take into account

OWNT-ē

bounty
county
mountie

OWNT-ēng

counting
mounting

accounting
amounting
discounting
dismounting

miscounting
recounting
remounting
surmounting

cost accounting

**OWNT-es
(See OWNT-us)**

**OWNTS
(See OWNS)**

OWNT-u-bul

countable
mountable

accountable
discountable
dismountable
recountable
remountable
surmountable

insurmountable
unaccountable

OWNT-un

countin'
fountain
mountain
mountin'

accountin'
amountin'
discountin'
dismountin'
miscountin'
recountin'
remountin'
surmountin'

drinking fountain
Magic Mountain
soda fountain

OWNT-ur

counter
mounter

accounter
discounter
dismounter
encounter
lunch counter
miscounter
recounter
remounter
surmounter

bargain counter
chance encounter
checkout counter
do without 'er
Geiger counter

over the counter
under the counter

OWNT-us

countess
count us
mount us

discount us
dismount us
miscount us

OWNZ

bounds
browns
clowns
crowns
downs
drowns
frowns
gowns
hounds
mounds
nouns
rounds

sounds
towns
zounds

astounds
abounds
bloodhounds
backgrounds
countdowns
cow towns
chowhounds
confounds
compounds
campgrounds
dumbfounds
expounds
grand rounds
greyhounds
hashbrowns
hoedowns
impounds
inbounds
knockdowns
letdowns
markdowns
nightgowns
playgrounds
pronouns
propounds
rebounds
rubdowns
surrounds
shakedowns
showdowns
slowdowns
touchdowns
fox and hounds
leaps and bounds
make the rounds
out of bounds
wraparounds

**OWR
(See also OW-ur)**

bower

Bauer
cower
dour
flour
flower
hour
our
power
shower
sour
scour
tower

cornflower
cold shower
deflower
devour
empower
gray power
gay power
horsepower
half hour
H-hour
lunch hour
lung power
Mayflower
manpower
manhour
noonhour
rainshower
rush hour
sea power
safflower
sweet-sour
wallflower
world power
wildflower
willpower
watchtower

after hour(s)
bridal shower
baby shower
candlepower
cauliflower
control tower

cocktail hour
dinner hour
Eiffel Tower
Eisenhower
happy hour
hearts and flower(s)
miles per hour
overpower
office hour(s)
passion flower
superpower
sweet and sour
veto power
whiskey sour
woman power
witching hour
zero hour

atomic power
balance of power
ivory tower
nuclear power
Water and Power

OWRD
(See also OW-urd)

coward
cowered
floured
flowered
Howard
powered
showered
soured
scoured
towered

deflowered
devoured
empowered

overpowered

OWR-ē
(See OW-ur-ē)

OWR-ēng

cowering
flouring
flowering
souring
showering
scouring
towering

deflowering
devouring
empowering

overpowering

OWR-lē

dourly
hourly
sourly

OWRZ

bowers
cowers
flowers
hours
ours
powers
showers
sours
scours
towers

cold showers
deflowers
devours
empowers
lunch hours
manhours
rainshowers
wallflowers
world powers
war powers
watchtowers

after hours

April showers
bankers' hours
hearts and flowers
overpowers
office hours
superpowers
whiskey sours

ivory towers

OWS

blouse
douse
grouse
house
louse
Laos
mouse
souse
spouse
Strauss

bughouse
boathouse
beachhouse
birdhouse
bathhouse
cathouse
courthouse
clubhouse
churchmouse
doghouse
delouse
dollhouse
espouse
ex-spouse
firehouse
flophouse
field house
field mouse
full house
greenhouse
guest house
guardhouse
hot house

jailhouse
lighthouse
madhouse
outhouse
penthouse
playhouse
poorhouse
powerhouse
roundhouse
row house
roughhouse
roadhouse
storehouse
steak house
smokehouse
townhouse
treehouse
titmouse
teahouse
White House
warehouse
whorehouse

boarding house
coffeehouse
cat and mouse
house-to-house
haunted house
halfway house
Mickey Mouse
open house
overblouse
on the house
porterhouse
slaughterhouse
set up house
the big house
Westinghouse

big as a house
bring down the house

quiet as a mouse
Speaker of the House

OWS-ē

blousy
mousy

OWS-ēng

blousing
dousing
grousing

delousing
espousing

OWST

bloused
doused
Faust
groused
joust
oust
roust
soused

espoused

OWST-ēng

jousting
ousting
rousting

OWT

bout
clout
doubt
drought
flout
gout
grout
kraut
lout
out
pout
rout
route

scout
sprout
spout
stout
snout
shout
tout
trout

all out
about
blowout
bugout
belt out
boy scout
blackout
bail out
breakout
bean sprout
burnout
cub scout
cutout
campout
close-out
cookout
cross out
downspout
devout
dugout
dropout
dine out
drag out
fade-out
far out
fallout
flame-out
girl scout
hangout
handout
holdout
knockout
lights out
lookout
lockout
layout

make out
no doubt
pass out
psych-out
rain spout
rained out
reroute
sauerkraut
shutout
stakeout
standout
self-doubt
sellout
shoot-out
smoke out
sold-out
strung out
throughout
take-out
turnout
tryout
without
walkout
washout
wipeout
way out
washed out
workout

all about
Brussels sprout
bring about
beyond doubt
coming-out
chicken out
do without
down and out
dish it out
falling-out
figure out
gadabout
go without
in and out
inside out
knockabout

live without
long-drawn-out
out-and-out
odd man out
overshout
rainbow trout
roundabout
roustabout
runabout
sauerkraut
scenic route
turnabout
talent scout
truth will out
without doubt
waterspout
walkabout

bandy about
day in, day out
eat one's heart out
easy way out
knock-down-drag-out
on or about
over and out
stick one's neck out
up and about
with or without
without a doubt
year in, year out

reasonable doubt
shadow of a doubt

benefit of the doubt

**OWT-ē
(See OWD-ē)**

**OWT-ēng
(See OWD-ēng)**

OWTH

mouth
south

bad-mouth
big mouth
deep South
loudmouth

blabbermouth
hand-to-mouth
hoof and mouth
mouth-to-mouth
shut one's mouth
Solid South
word of mouth

OWT-ist
(See OWD-ust)

OWT-lē

stoutly

devoutly

OWT-nus

stoutness

devoutness

OWT-owt

rout out
scout out
shout out
spout out

about out
without doubt

OWTS

bouts
doubts
droughts
flouts
louts
outs
pouts

routs
routes
scouts
sprouts
spouts
snouts
shouts
touts

blowouts
Boy Scouts
blackouts
breakouts
burnouts
cub scouts
cutouts
cookouts
downspouts
dugouts
dropouts
Girl Scouts
handouts
holdouts
knockouts
shutouts
stakeouts
sellouts
shoot-outs
tryouts
walkouts
wipeouts
workouts

Brussels sprouts
hereabouts
ins and outs
overshouts
roundabouts
runabouts
scenic routes
thereabouts
talent scouts
whereabouts
waterspouts
walkabouts

OWT-ur
(See OWD-ur)

O-wu

agua

Chihuahua
Misawa

OW-u-bul

plowable
wowable

allowable
endowable

disallowable
disavowable
unallowable

OW-ul
(See also OWL)

bowel
dowel
Powell
towel
trowel
vowel

avowal

disembowel

throw in the towel

OW-ur
(See also OWR)

bower
cower
flower
power
plower
shower
tower

vower
wower

avower
allower
bell tower
brain power
cornflower
cold shower
clock tower
kowtower
deflower
endower
empower
firepower
gray power
gay power
horsepower
lung power
meower
Mayflower
manpower
rain shower
snowplower
sea power
sunflower
safflower
wallflower
world power
wildflower
willpower
watchtower

bridal shower
baby shower
candlepower
cauliflower
control tower
disallower
disavower
Eiffel Tower
Eisenhower
overpower
passion flower
superpower
veto power

womanpower

atomic power
balance of power
electric power
ivory tower
nuclear power
Water and Power

separation of power(s)

OW-urd
(See also OWRD)

coward
cowered
floured
flowered
glowered
Howard
powered
soured
showered
scoured
towered

deflowered
devoured
empowered
high-powered

Noel Coward
overpowered

OW-ur-ē

bowery
dowry
flowery
floury
showery

OW-ur-ēng
(See OWR-ēng)

OW-urz
(See OWRZ)

OW-us

prowess
wow us

allow us
endow us

disallow us
disavow us

OW-wow

bow-wow
pow-wow

OWZ

browse
boughs
bows
brows
cows
chows
drowse
house
nows
ows
pows
prows
plows
rouse
rows
souse
sows
vows
wows

arouse
allows
avows
bow-wows
carouse
espouse
endows
eyebrows
highbrows

hausfraus
hoosegows
kowtows
know-hows
lowbrows
luaus
meows
milk cows
powwows

disallows
disavows
marriage vows
pepper boughs
rabble-rouse
sacred cows

OWZD

browsed
drowsed
housed
roused
soused

aroused
caroused
espoused

rabble-roused

OWZ-ē

drowsy
frowsy
lousy

OWZ-ēng

browsing
drowsing
housing
rousing

arousing
carousing
espousing
roughhousing

warehousing

rabble-rousing

OWZ-ul

spousal
tousle

arousal
carousal
espousal

OWZ-ur

bowser
browser
drowser
houser
pows 'er
rouser
souser
schnauzer
trouser(s)
wows 'er

allows 'er
arouser
carouser
endows 'er
espouser

rabble-rouser

ŌX

blokes
Cokes
chokes
cloaks
croaks
coax
folks
hoax
jokes
oaks
pokes
soaks

spokes
stokes
strokes
smokes
toques
yolks
yokes

convokes
chain-smokes
downstrokes
evokes
egg yolks
heatstrokes
invokes
in-jokes
provokes
revokes
unyokes

artichokes
Diet Cokes
dirty jokes
holy smokes
just plain folks
masterstrokes

OX

achs
box
blocks
Bach's
clocks
cox
crocks
chocks
chalks
cocks
docks
docs
flocks
frocks
fox
gawks
hocks

hawks
jocks
knocks
Knox
lox
locks
mocks
ox
pox
pocks
rocks
shocks
schlocks
socks
stocks
stalks
smocks
squawks
sox
talks
walks
woks

boardwalks
boondocks
bandbox
breadbox
black box
beanstalks
cellblocks
crosswalks
chalk talks
catwalks
cashbox
call box
cornstalks
defrocks
dumb ox
deadlocks
detox
flowerbox
fast-talks
Fort Knox
fuse box
gravlax

gridlocks
gift box
headlocks
hard knocks
ham hocks
hatbox
icebox
jaywalks
knee socks
landlocks
lunchbox
lockbox
mailbox
Mohawks
matchbox
outtalks
outwalks
outfox
poor box
pillbox
press box
postdocs
pep talks
padlocks
peacocks
roadblocks
restocks
Reboks
soap box
shoebox
sidewalks
sweet-talks
shellshocks
sleepwalks
smallpox
squeezebox
sweat socks
shylocks
sandbox
shamrocks
sunblocks
squawk box
snuff box
sweatbox
strongbox

tick-tocks
toy box
unlocks
voice box
woodblocks
warlocks
windsocks
woodcocks
Xerox

aftershocks
argyle socks
alarm clocks
ballot box
bobby sox
blue-chip stocks
butcher blocks
chickenpox
cardboard box
chatterbox
crackerbox
chickenhawks
cuckoo clocks
cigar box
cement blocks
double-talks
equinox
Goldilocks
hollyhocks
hammerlocks
interlocks
jury box
jewelry box
laughingstocks
letter box
music box
money talks
mental blocks
nature walks
on the rocks
orthodox
overstocks
paradox
shuttlecocks
stumbling blocks

shadowbox
silver fox
starting blocks
tomahawks
tic-a-locks
tinderbox
windowbox
walks and talks
weathercrocks
witness box

collection box
celery stalks
digital clocks
electric shocks
grandfather clocks
jack-in-the-box
post office box
penalty box
Pandora's box
sly as a fox
school of hard knocks
suggestion box
unorthodox

security locks
vernal equinox

biological clocks
first crack out of the
    box
opportunity knocks

ŌX-ē

coaxy
folksy

OX-ē

boxy
foxy
moxie
proxy
Roxie

Biloxi

epoxy
unfoxy

orthodoxy
vote by proxy

OX-en
(See OX-un)

OX-ēng

boxing
foxing

detoxing
outfoxing
Xeroxing

OX-ik

toxic

paradoxic

OX-ik-ul

toxical

paradoxical

OX-ix

coccyx
toxics

OX-u-bul

boxable

detoxable
outfoxable
Xeroxable

OX-un

boxin'
coxswain
oxen
toxin

outfoxin'

shadowboxin'

OX-ur

boxer
blocks 'er
clocks 'er
cocks 'er
docks 'er
knocks 'er
mocks 'er
rocks 'er
shocks 'er
socks 'er
walks 'er

detoxer
outtalks 'er
outwalks 'er
outfox 'er
sweet-talks 'er
Xeroxer

bobby soxer
orthodoxer

OX-yus

noxious

obnoxious

O-yur

lawyer
Sawyer

Arkansawyer

ŌZ

bows
blows
beaus
crows
chose

close
clothes
doze
does
foes
floes
flows
froze
goes
grows
glows
hose
hoes
knows
lows
mows
nose
noes
ohs
owes
O's
pose
prose
pros
rose
rows
sows
schmos
sews
stows
slows
snows
shows
toes
tows
those
throws
throes
woes
whoas

airhose
arose
brown-nose
bimbos

bluenose
bestows
bozos
bandeaux
bon mots
bulldoze
cache pots
compose
crossbows
chapeaus
case close(d)
châteaus
depose
disclose
dispose
dodos
dildoes
enclose
expose
foreclose
forgoes
fire hose
floorshows
golf pros
hardnose
heave-hos
hum-hos
impose
ice floes
KOs
low blows
no-shows
no-nos
oppose
outflows
plainclothes
propose
primrose
pug nose
quiz shows
rainbows
repose
red rose
scarecrows
suppose

ski nose
sideshows
transpose
tiptoes
talk shows
tea rose
unfroze
yo-yos

afterglows
audios
barrios
by a nose
buffaloes
bungalows
cameos
change of clothes
Cheerios
come to blows
curios
dominoes
decompose
damask rose
dynamos
embryos
Eskimos
folios
garden hose
gigolos
heaven knows
interpose
Irish rose
juxtapose
long agos
nose-to-nose
oleos
olios
Oreos
on the nose
overflows
overgrows
overthrows
on one's toes
presuppose
purple prose

predispose
panty hose
piccolos
porticos
quelque chose
radios
Romeos
rodeos
runny nose
ratios
recompose
Roman nose
Scorpios
status quos
so-and-sos
stereos
studios
tallyhos
tippytoes
tic tac toes
thumb one's nose
thar she blows
tournedos
twinkle toes
undertows
undergoes
videos
water hose

anything goes
buttons and bows
cut of one's clothes
designer clothes
lead by the nose
overexpose
open and close
pay through the nose
superimpose
turn up one's nose
underexpose

my wild Irish rose
no skin off one's nose
step on someone's toes
which way the wind
  blows

OZ

awes
blahs
bras
bahs
baas
cause
caws
chaws
craws
claws
clause
Claus
craws
daws
flaws
fas
gauze
gnaws
hahs
jaws
laws
las
mas
nahs
Oz
paws
pas
pause
Roz
rahs
saws
straws
spas
shahs
schnozz
thaws
vase

applause
ah-hahs
because
buzz saws
bear claws
bylaws

Crenshaws
cha-chas
draw straws
faux pas
guffaws
hacksaws
ha-has
hee-haws
health spas
hooplas
hurrahs
in-laws
jigsaws
jackdaws
lost cause
La Paz
macaws
niçoise
outlaws
outdraws
pshaws
papas
quickdraws
ripsaws
rickshaws
southpaws
state laws
seesaws
ta-tas
withdraws

brouhahas
common cause
Chickasaws
Chippewas
civil laws
clutch at straws
escape clause
grandmamas
grasp at straws
Häagen-Dazs
hems and haws
just because
menopause
nursing bras

oompah-pahs
ohs and ahs
overawes
overdraws
Santa Claus
tra-la-las
training bras
vichyssoise

father-in-laws
grandfather clause
mother-in-laws
male menopause
probable cause
Wizard of Oz

ŌZD

closed
dozed
hosed
nosed
posed

bulldozed
composed
case closed
deposed
disclosed
disposed
enclosed
exposed
foreclosed
hardnosed
imposed
opposed
proposed
reposed
supposed
transposed

decomposed
ill-disposed
indisposed
juxtaposed
presupposed
predisposed

recomposed
self-imposed

overexposed
superimposed

OZD

caused
paused

ŌZ-ē

cozy
mosey
nosy
posy
rosy
Rosie
toesy

tea cozy

OZ-ē

gauzy
Ozzie

kamikaze

ŌZ-en
(See ŌZ-un)

ŌZ-ēng

closing
dozing
hosing
nosing
posing

bulldozing
composing
deposing
disclosing
disposing
enclosing

exposing
foreclosing
imposing
opposing
proposing
reposing
supposing
transposing

decomposing
interposing
presupposing
predisposing
recomposing
unimposing

overexposing
superimposing

OZ-ēng

causing
pausing

ŌZ-es
(See ŌZ-us)

OZ-et
(See OZ-ut)

OZ-ē-u
(See OZH-u)

ŌZ-ē-ur

cozier
nosier
rosier

OZH

barrage
garage
mirage
ménage

camouflage
décolletage
entourage
fuselage
sabotage

double garage
espionage

ŌZH-u

knows ya
loggia
owes ya
shows ya
snows ya
throws ya

ambrosia

apologia

OZH-u

awes ya
cause ya
nausea
paws ya

ŌZH-un

corrosion
erosion
explosion
implosion

ŌZH-ur

closure

composure
disclosure
enclosure
exposure
foreclosure

keep one's composure

indecent exposure

OZ-ib-ul
(See OZ-ub-ul)

ŌZ-i-lē

cozily
nosily
rosily

OZ-in
(See OZ-un)

OZ-it
(See OZ-ut)

OZ-it-iv
(See OZ-ud-iv)

OZ-it-ōr-ē
(See OZ-ut-ōr-ē)

OZM
(See OZ-um)

ŌZ-ub-ul

closable
hosable
posable

bulldozable
composable
disclosable
disposable
enclosable
exposable
supposable
transposable

indisposable
interposable
juxtaposable

OZ-ub-ul

causable
pausable
plausible

implausible

OZ-ud-iv

causative
positive

ŌZ-ul

deposal
disposal
proposal

at your disposal
garbage disposal
marriage proposal

OZ-ul

causal
nozzle

ŌZ-ul-ē

cozily
nosily
Rosalee
rosily

OZ-um

awes 'em
cause 'em
chaws 'em
claws 'em
draws 'em
gnaws 'em
paws 'em
saws 'em

outlaws 'em
pshaws 'em

withdraws 'em

Ashkenazim
microcosm
macrocosm

ŌZ-un

chosen
closin'
dozin'
frozen
hosin'
nosin'
posin'
Rosen

bulldozin'
deposin'
disposin'
enclosin'
exposin'
fresh frozen
foreclosin'
imposin'
opposin'
proposin'
reposin'
supposin'
transposin'
unfrozen
unchosen

decomposin'
interposin'
lederhosen
presupposin'
recomposin'

OZ-un

causin'
pausin'
rosin

ŌZ-ur

chose 'er
dozer
froze 'er
knows 'er
owes 'er
poser
shows 'er
slows 'er
tows 'er
throws 'er

bulldozer
brown-noser
composer
deposer
exposer
forecloser
imposer
opposer
proposer
supposer
transposer
unfroze 'er

ŌZ-us

blows us
chose us
close us
froze us
hose us
knows us
Moses
owes us
pose us
snows us
slows us
shows us
tows us
throws us

bulldoze us
compose us
depose us
disclose us

enclose us
expose us
foreclose us
forgoes us
impose us
oppose us
propose us
transpose us
unfroze us

decompose us
juxtapose us
overthrows us
presuppose us
predispose us

overexpose us

OZ-ut

bahs it
cause it
closet
claws it
draws it
gnaws it
paws it
posit
saws it

buzz-saws it
composite
clothes closet
deposit
pshaws it
withdraws it

overawes it
overdraws it
redeposit
safe deposit

out of the closet

skeleton in the closet

OZ-ut-ōr-ē

causatory

depository
suppository

U Sounds

Ū

boo
blue
blew
brew
clue
crew
chew
cue
due
do
dew
drew
ewe
few
flew
flu
flue
glue
goo
grew
gnu
hue
Jew
knew
lieu
loo

moo
new
nu
ooh
pooh
pew
q
queue
rue
roux
spew
shoe
shrew
sue
stew
slew
screw
slue
true
threw
through
to
two
too
u
view
woo
who

you
zoo

askew
all through
add to
adieu
ado
anew
accrue
ah-choo
breakthrough
beaucoup
blue flu
bamboo
Bantu
boo-boo
brand new
boo-hoo
big do
bless you
church pew
curfew
cashew
Corfu
come to
can-do
come through

corkscrew	old shoe	whereto
construe	Peru	work crew
choo-choo	pass-through	withdrew
cuckoo	past due	world-view
canoe	pooh-pooh	yoo-hoo
come true	pull through	yahoo
doo-doo	pursue	
dim view	PU	avenue
debut	purlieu	bugaboo
dog-doo	perdu	bill and coo
drive-through	Purdue	black and blue
ensue	revue	*billet-doux*
eschew	review	book review
et tu	ragout	ballyhoo
fall through	renew	break in two
fondue	redo	buckaroo
froufrou	shampoo	BTU
goo-goo	snowshoe	baby shoe
ground crew	sky-blue	boogaloo
gumshoe	says who?	barbecue
hairdo	subdue	bird's-eye view
home-brew	snafu	curlicue
how-to	see-through	cleaning crew
horseshoe	skiddoo	caribou
hereto	soft-shoe	cockatoo
imbue	tutu	cockapoo
I do	thumbscrew	countercoup
IQ	thank you	countersue
in lieu	to-do	*cordon bleu*
into	thereto	*déjà vu*
kazoo	taboo	dipsy-doo
kerchoo	tattoo	dream come true
kung fu	true blue	derring-do
lean-to	too too	double U
love to	untrue	*entre nous*
lulu	updo	follow through
misdo	unto	field of view
muumuu	unglue	flopperoo
milieu	undo	honeydew
me too	unscrew	hitherto
miscue	undue	I love you
on view	voodoo	interview
outgrew	woo-woo	in full view
outdo	walk-through	*ingénue*
on cue	who's who	impromptu

in a stew
Irish stew
in situ
jujitsu
kangaroo
Katmandu
kickapoo
looky-loo
law review
misconstrue
midnight blue
Malibu
marabou
much ado
mountain dew
navy blue
no can do
overdo
overdue
oyster stew
overthrew
Oahu
overshoe
overview
ocean view
PDQ
parvenu
peek-a-boo
point of view
petting zoo
postage due
QE II
quite a few
revenue
royal blue
rendezvous
residue
retinue
switcheroo
Sigma Nu
shiatsu
Swiss fondue
sockeroo
smackeroo
Super Glue

stinkaroo
tried and true
toodle-oo
Timbuktu
through and through
two-by-two
tennis shoe
w
whoop-de-do
well-to-do
wooden shoe
Waterloo
worm's-eye view
witches' brew
World War II
wrecking crew

ACLU
Bartholomew
bully for you
brand spanking new
bolt from the blue
corrective shoe
catch-22
how do you do?
hullabaloo
Kalamazoo
mulligan stew
merci beaucoup
out of the blue
pass in review
poo poo pee doo
red, white, and blue
room with a view
skeleton crew
Tippecanoe
up the kazoo
Winnie the Pooh

cock-a-doodle-doo
drop the other shoe
musical review
judicial review
panoramic view
Saks Fifth Avenue
VFW

Internal Revenue
win a few, lose a few

ŪB

boob
cube
lube
rube
tube

boob tube
Danube
flashcube
ice cube
test tube

down the tube(s)
inner tube
picture tube
Rubik's cube

UB

bub
blub
cub
chub
club
dub
drub
flub
grub
hub
nub
pub
rub
sub
stub
snub
scrub
shrub
tub

bridge club
bear cub
bathtub

backrub
check stub
fan club
flubdub
golf club
glee club
hot tub
hubbub
health club
handrub
nightclub
well-scrub(bed)
washtub

auto club
billy club
Beelzebub
flub the dub
lion cub
mile-high club
ol' boys' club
ticket stub

alcohol rub
Rotary Club
rub a dub dub

ŪB-ē

boobie
booby
looby
ruby
you be

UB-ē

cubby
clubby
chubby
grubby
hubby
nubby
stubby
scrubby
tubby

**ŪB-en
(See ŪB-un)**

ŪB-ēng

cubing
lubing
tubing

UB-ēng

clubbing
dubbing
drubbing
flubbing
rubbing
subbing
stubbing
snubbing
scrubbing

backrubbing
nightclubbing

UB-ē-nus

chubbiness
grubbiness
stubbiness

ŪB-ik

cubic
pubic
Rubik

**UB-in
(See UB-un)**

UB-ish

clubbish
rubbish
snubbish

UB-lēng

bubbling
doubling
troubling

redoubling
untroubling

**UB-lin
(See UB-lun)**

UB-lun

bubblin'
Dublin
doublin'
troublin'

redoublin'

ŪB-rē-us

lugubrious
salubrious

ŪB-u

Cuba
tuba

Aruba

UB-u

Bubba

hubba-hubba

ŪB-ul

lubal
ruble
tubal

UB-ul

bubble
double

hubble
nubble
rubble
stubble
trouble

air bubble
car trouble
in trouble
mixed double(s)
redouble
see double
soap bubble

borrow trouble
daily double
double trouble
on the double
too much trouble
takeout double

UB-ul-sum

bubble some
double some
troublesome

redouble some

ŪB-un

lubin'
Reuben
Steuben
tubin'

UB-un

clubbin'
dubbin'
drubbin'
flubbin'
nubbin
rubbin'
subbin'
snubbin'

scrubbin'

down to the nubbin

ŪB-ur

goober
tuber

UB-ur

blubber
clubber
dubber
drubber
flubber
grubber
lubber
rubber
snubber
scrubber

burn rubber
foam rubber
landlubber
pot scrubber
sponge rubber
whale blubber

money grubber

UB-urd

blubbered
cupboard
rubbered

kitchen cupboard
Mother Hubbard

UB-ur-ē

blubbery
rubbery
shrubbery

ŪB-ur-unt

exuberant
protuberant

ŪCH

brooch
hooch
mooch
pooch
smooch

hootchy-kootch

UCH

clutch
crutch
dutch
hutch
much
smutch
such
touch

as such
go Dutch
light touch
not much
retouch
soft touch
some such
too much

common touch
final touch
inasmuch
insomuch
Midas touch
overmuch
pretty much
rabbit hutch
such-and-such
thank you much

ever so much

ŪCH-ē

Gucci
moochy
poochy
smoochy

Il Duce

Chattahoochee
hootchy-kootchy
Yamaguchi

Amerigo Vespucci

ŪCH-ēng

mooching
pooching
smooching

UCH-ēng

clutching
touching

retouching

UCH-es
(See UCH-us)

ŪCH-ur

future
moocher
smoocher
suture

wave of the future

UCH-us

clutch us
duchess
touch us

ŪD

booed
brewed

brood
crude
clued
crewed
chewed
cued
dude
food
feud
glued
hewed
hued
lewd
mood
mewed
mooed
nude
prude
poohed
queued
rood
rude
rued
spewed
shrewd
shoed
snood
sued
stewed
screwed
viewed
wooed
who'd
you'd

adieued
allude
accrued
ah-chooed
boo-hooed
canoed
construed
collude
conclude
cuckooed

denude
delude
dog food
elude
etude
exude
exclude
ensued
eschewed
fast food
health food
imbued
intrude
include
miscued
occlude
obtrude
pursued
plant food
protrude
preclude
pooh-poohed
Quaalude
renewed
reviewed
Saint Jude
seclude
subdued
seafood
shampooed
soul food
tabooed
tattooed
unglued
unscrewed
yahooed

attitude
altitude
aptitude
amplitude
baby food
billed and cooed
ballyhooed
barbecued

certitude
come unglued
consuetude
crassitude
desuetude
fortitude
family feud
finger food
gratitude
interlude
in the nude
in the mood
interviewed
lassitude
latitude
longitude
misconstrued
magnitude
multitude
platitude
pulchritude
plenitude
quietude
rendezvoused
rectitude
solitude
servitude
sanctitude
toodle-ooed
turpitude
unpursued
unrenewed

beatitude
disquietude
decrepitude
exactitude
high altitude
inaptitude
ineptitude
not in the mood
poo-poo-pee-dooed
solicitude
vicissitude

moral turpitude
out of gratitude

UD

bud
blood
cud
crud
dud
flood
HUD
mud
spud
stud
scud
thud

blue blood
bad blood
flash flood
hot blood
lifeblood
Milk Dud
new blood
rosebud
sweat blood
taste blood
tired blood
taste bud
young blood

chew one's cud
creeping crud
draw first blood
flesh and blood
in cold blood

curdle one's blood
nip in the bud
stick in the mud

ÛD

could
good

hood
stood
should
wood
would

boyhood
backwood(s)
childhood
driftwood
do-good
dry good(s)
dogwood
deadwood
falsehood
firewood
for good
girlhood
knighthood
manhood
make good
milkwood
no-good
plywood
priesthood
redwood
rainhood
sainthood
saw wood
Westwood
withstood
wildwood

adulthood
babyhood
bill of good(s)
bachelorhood
brotherhood
cottonwood
damaged good(s)
fatherhood
Hollywood
knock on wood
likelihood
livelihood

motherhood
maidenhood
not so good
neighborhood
nationhood
pretty good
parenthood
Robin Hood
sisterhood
spinsterhood
understood
womanhood
widowhood

babe in the wood(s)
come to no good
misunderstood
out of the wood(s)
Planned Parenthood
Red Riding Hood
second childhood
so far so good
unlikelihood

finger-licking good

ŪD-ē

beauty
broody
bootie
booty
cootie
cutie
duty
fruity
hooty
Judy
moody
nudie
snooty
Trudy
tootie

guard duty
night duty
off duty

on duty
spring beauty
ya-hootie

active duty
bathing beauty
call of duty
do one's duty
double-duty
heavy-duty
howdy doody
jury duty
line of duty
Punch and Judy
Sleeping Beauty
sweet patooty
tutti-frutti
tour of duty

military duty

UD-ē

buddy
bloody
cruddy
fuddy
gutty
jutty
muddy
mutty
nutty
putty
ruddy
rutty
study
smutty
slutty

golf buddy
good buddy
peanutty
unmuddy
walnutty

buddy-buddy
coconutty

drinking buddy
fuddy-duddy
nature study
Silly Putty
understudy

character study

ÛD-ē

goody
sooty
woody

goody-goody

ŪD-ed
(See ŪD-ud)

UD-ed
(See UD-ud)

ÛD-ed
(See ÛD-ud)

UD-en
(See UD-un)

ÛD-en
(See ÛD-un)

ŪD-ēng

booting
feuding
hooting
looting
muting
scooting
shooting
suiting
tooting
alluding

crapshooting
concluding
commuting
computing
denuding
disputing
deluding
diluting
eluding
exuding
excluding
imputing
intruding
including
occluding
polluting
protruding
permuting
precluding
refuting
recruiting
secluding
saluting
transmuting
uprooting

constituting
convoluting
executing
instituting
overshooting
parachuting
prostituting
prosecuting
persecuting
substituting
troubleshooting
undershooting

electrocuting
reconstituting

up to and including

UD-ēng

butting
budding
cutting
flooding
gutting
jutting
putting
shutting
strutting
thudding

abutting
precutting
rebutting
recutting

undercutting

ÛD-eng

footing
putting
pudding

uprooting

hasty pudding
pussyfooting
Yorkshire pudding

ŪD-ens
(See ŪD-uns)

ŪD-ent
(See ŪD-unt)

ŪD-ē-us

beauteous
snooty us
studious

ŪD-i-ful

beautiful
dutiful

ŪD-ik

pharmaceutic
therapeutic

ŪD-i-kul

cuticle

pharmaceutical
therapeutical

ŪD-in-us

denudin' us
deludin' us
excludin' us
includin' us
precludin' us
secludin' us

multitudinous
pulchritudinous
platitudinous

ŪD-ist

Buddhist
cutest
crudest
flutist
lewdest
nudist
nudest
rudest
shrewdest

parachutist

ŪD-it-ē
(See ŪD-ut-ē)

UDJ
(See UJ)

ŪD-lē

crudely
lewdly
rudely

ŪD-lēng

boodling
doodling
tootling

canoodling

UD-lēng

cuddling
huddling
muddling
scuttling
shuttling

befuddling
bemuddling
rebuttling

ŪD-nus

crudeness
lewdness
nudeness
prudeness
rudeness
shrewdness

ŪD-ō

judo
kudo
pseudo
Pluto

prosciutto

ŪD-ū

to do
voodoo
who do
you do

ŪD-u

Buddha
Gouda
Judah

Bermuda

barracuda

ŪD-ub-ul

bootable
broodable
feudable
hootable
lootable
mutable
scootable
shootable
suitable
tootable

alludable
concludable
commutable
computable
dilutable
denudable
disputable
deludable
exudable
excludable
immutable
intrudable
inscrutable
imputable
immutable
includable
permutable

protrudable
precludable
pollutable
pursuitable
refutable
recruitable
salutable
secludable
transmutable
uprootable
unsuitable

convolutable
executable
indisputable
prosecutable
persecutable
substitutable
undilutable

electrocutable
reconstitutable

ŪD-ud

booted
brooded
feuded
fruited
fluted
hooted
looted
mooted
rooted
routed
scooted
suited
tooted

alluded
colluded
concluded
commuted
computed
confuted
disputed
diluted

denuded
deluded
eluded
exuded
excluded
intruded
included
imputed
occluded
obtruded
polluted
protruded
precluded
refuted
reputed
recruited
saluted
secluded
transmuted
uprooted

constituted
convoluted
executed
instituted
parachuted
prostituted
prosecuted
persecuted
substituted

electrocuted
reconstituted

UD-ud

budded
butted
flooded
glutted
gutted
jutted
putted
strutted
studded
tutted

thudded

abutted
blue-blooded
cold-blooded
full-blooded
red-blooded
rebutted
star-studded

ÛD-ud

footed
hooded
rooted
sooted
wooded

big-footed
barefooted
clubfooted
deep-rooted
flat-footed
four-footed
light-footed
two-footed
web-footed
uprooted

pussyfooted

ŪD-ud-ē

crudity
lewdity
nudity
prudity
rudity

ŪD-ul

brutal
boodle
doodle
feudal
futile
noodle

oodle(s)
poodle
strudel
tootle
utile

caboodle
canoodle
French poodle
limp noodle
refutal
recruital
whangdoodle

apple strudel
dipsy-doodle
use one's noodle
Yankee Doodle

kit and caboodle
limp as a noodle

UD-ul

buttle
cuddle
fuddle
huddle
muddle
puddle
subtle
scuttle
shuttle
Tuttle

befuddle
bemuddle
mud puddle
rebuttle
space shuttle
unsubtle

water puddle

ŪD-ul-ē

brutally
feudally
futilely

ŪD-ul-ēng
(See ŪD-lēng)

UD-ul-ēng
(See UD-lēng)

UD-un

buddin'
floodin'
sudden
thuddin'

all of a sudden

ÛD-un

puddin'
wooden

ŪD-uns

prudence
students

protrudence

jurisprudence

ŪD-unt

prudent
student

ŪD-un-us
(See ŪD-in-us)

ŪD-ur

brooder
booed 'er
cruder
clued 'er
cued 'er
cuter
feuder

hooter
looter
lewder
muter
nuder
neuter
pewter
ruder
rooter
shoot 'er
shrewder
sued 'er
screwed 'er
shooter
suitor
scooter
tutor
tooter
Tudor
viewed 'er
wooed 'er

acuter
astuter
alluder
accouter
commuter
computer
concluder
crapshooter
denuder
deluder
diluter
disputer
exuder
eluder
excluder
intruder
includer
minuter
outshoot 'er
occluder
polluter
pursued 'er
protruder

peashooter
recruiter
refuter
reviewed 'er
subdued 'er
saluter
sharpshooter
tattooed 'er
uprooter
zoot-suiter

barbecued 'er
execute 'er
interviewed 'er
instituter
motor scooter
overshooter
parachuter
prosecutor
persecutor
substituter
troubleshooter

electrocuter

public prosecutor

UD-ur

budder
butter
cutter
clutter
flooder
flutter
gutter
glutter
jutter
mudder
mutter
putter
rudder
shutter
sputter
strutter
shudder
stutter

thudder
utter
udder

aflutter
abutter
clear cutter
golf putter
haircutter
rain gutter
unclutter
woodcutter

bread and butter
coast guard cutter
cookie cutter
peanut butter
paper cutter
undercutter
uppercutter

ÛD-ur

gooder
stood 'er

do-gooder
withstood 'er

understood 'er

ÛD-ur-ē

crudery
prudery

UD-ur-ē

buttery
cluttery
fluttery
sputtery
stuttery

ÛD-ur-ēng

neutering
tutoring

accoutering

UD-ur-ēng

buttering
cluttering
fluttering
muttering
puttering
sputtering
shuddering
stuttering
uttering

ÛD-ur-us

neuter us
tutor us
uterus

ÛD-us

booed us
boot us
Brutus
clued us
cued us
hoot us
Judas
loot us
sued us
scoot us
shoot us
screwed us
viewed us
wooed us

commute us
confute us
delude us
dispute us
exclude us
include us
impute us
miscued us
outshoot us
pollute us
pursued us

preclude us
refute us
renewed us
reviewed us
salute us
subdued us
shampooed us
tattooed us

execute us
overshoot us
parachute us
prostitute us
prosecute us
persecute us

electrocute us
reconstitute us

ÛD-ust
(See ÛD-ist)

ÛD-ut-ē
(See ÛD-ud-ē)

Û-ē

buoy
chewy
dewy
Dewey
gooey
hooey
Huey
Louis
phooey
sooey
screwy

chop suey
Drambuie
go blooey
kerflooey
mildewy
Mitsui

St. Louis
unchewy

ratatouille

Ū-ēng

booing
bluing
brewing
crewing
chewing
cuing
doing
gluing
mooing
poohing
queueing
ruing
spewing
shoeing
suing
stewing
screwing
viewing
wooing

accruing
boo-hooing
construing
cuckooing
canoeing
debuting
ensuing
eschewing
imbuing
miscuing
outdoing
pooh-poohing
pursuing
reviewing
renewing
redoing
shampooing
subduing
tattooing

undoing
unscrewing
wrongdoing
yoo-hooing

barbecuing
countersuing
interviewing
misconstruing
nothing doing
overdoing
peek-a-booing
rendezvousing
toodle-ooing
up-and-doing
whoopde-doing

Ū-ens
(See Ū-uns)

Ū-en-sē
(See Ū-un-sē)

Ū-ent
(See Ū-unt)

Ū-et
(See Ū-ut)

ŪF

goof
poof
proof
roof
spoof

aloof
childproof
disproof
fireproof
foolproof
flameproof
soundproof

bulletproof
galley proof
hot tin roof
Whiffenpoof
waterproof

burden of proof

UF

buff
bluff
cuff
duff
fluff
guff
gruff
huff
luff
muff
'nough
puff
rough
ruff
stuff
scruff
snuff
scuff
slough
tough

cream puff
enough
ear muff
French cuff
foodstuff
hard stuff
handcuff
hot stuff
hang tough
kid stuff
rebuff
rough stuff
restuff
right stuff

blindman's bluff

call one's bluff
Council Bluff(s)
fisticuff(s)
fair enough
huff and puff
in the buff
in the rough
overstuff
on the cuff
off the cuff
powder puff
rough and tough
sure enough
strut one's stuff
semitough
up to snuff

more than enough

diamond in the rough

ÛF

hoof
roof
wolf
woof

she-wolf
thatched roof
werewolf

Beowulf
big bad wolf
hit the roof
raise the roof
timber wolf

under one roof

ÛF-ē

goofy
poofy
spoofy

UF-ē

Duffy
fluffy
huffy
puffy
roughie
stuffy
snuffy
toughie

unstuffy

UF-el
(See UF-ul)

UF-en
(See UF-un)

ÛF-ēng

goofing
proofing
roofing
spoofing

childproofing
fireproofing
foolproofing
shockproofing

UF-ēng

buffing
bluffing
cuffing
fluffing
huffing
muffing
puffing
roughing
ruffing
stuffing
snuffing
scuffing

handcuffing
rebuffing

overstuffing

ÛF-ēng

hoofing
roofing
wolfing

UF-ē-nus

fluffiness
huffiness
puffiness
stuffiness
snuffiness

UF-et
(See UF-ut)

UF-in
(See UF-un)

UF-lur

muffler
ruffler
shuffler
scuffler
snuffler

ÛFT

goofed
proofed
roofed
spoofed

childproofed
fireproofed

UFT

buffed
bluffed

cuffed
fluffed
huffed
muffed
puffed
roughed
stuffed
snuffed
scuffed
tuft

French-cuffed
handcuffed
rebuffed
restuffed

huffed and puffed
overstuffed

UF-ul

duffel
muffle
ruffle
shuffle
scuffle
snuffle
truffle

dust ruffle
fast shuffle
reshuffle
unruffle

UF-un

buffin'
bluffin'
cuffin'
fluffin'
huffin'
muffin
muffin'
puffin'
roughen
roughin'
stuffin'

snuffin'
toughen

bread stuffin'
handcuffin'
rebuffin'
restuffin'

English muffin
overstuffin'
ragamuffin

ŪF-ur

goofer
proofer
roofer
spoofer
twofer

UF-ur

buffer
bluffer
cuffer
duffer
fluffer
gruffer
huffer
puffer
rougher
suffer
stuffer
snuffer
slougher
tougher

handcuffer
rebuffer
restuffer

candlesnuffer
stocking stuffer

huffer and puffer
rougher and tougher

ÛF-ur

hoofer
roofer
woofer

UF-ut

buffet
buff it
bluff it
cuff it
fluff it
muff it
puff it
rough it
stuff it
tuffet
tough it

Miss Muffet

UG

bug
chug
dug
drug
glug
hug
jug
lug
mug
pug
plug
rug
shrug
smug
snug
slug
thug
tug
ugh

bear hug
bear rug
bedbug

beer mug
earplug
fireplug
firebug
humbug
June bug
light plug
nose plug
spark plug
unplug

bunny hug
chug-a-lug
cut a rug
doodlebug
jitterbug
litterbug
ladybug
lightning bug
pull the plug
shutterbug
whiskey jug
wonder drug

designer drug
miracle drug
potato bug
prescription drug

fertility drug
Oriental rug

crazy as a bedbug

snug as a bug in a rug

UGD

bugged
chugged
drugged
hugged
lugged
mugged
plugged
shrugged
slugged

tugged

unplugged

jitterbugged

UG-ē

buggy
chuggy
huggy
muggy
snuggy

dune buggy

horse and buggy

ÛG-ē

boogie
noogie

boogie-woogie

UG-ēng

bugging
chugging
drugging
hugging
lugging
mugging
plugging
shrugging
slugging
tugging

humbugging
unplugging

jitterbugging
litterbugging

UG-et
(See UG-ut)

UG-ē-ust

buggiest
muggiest

UG-ij

luggage
pluggage

UG-ist
(See UG-ust)

UG-lē

juggly
snugly
smugly
ugly

UG-lur

juggler
snuggler
struggler
smuggler

UG-lus

bugless
Douglas
drugless
hugless
rugless

ŪG-ō

Hugo
you go
Yugo

Verdugo

ŪG-u

beluga

Chattanooga

UG-u-bul

buggable
druggable
huggable
luggable
pluggable
sluggable
tuggable

unpluggable

ŪG-ul

bugle
fugal
frugal

MacDougal

UG-ul

juggle
smuggle
snuggle
struggle
tuggle

ŪG-ur

cougar
luger

ÛG-ur

booger
sugar

UG-ur-ē

humbuggery
scullduggery

UG-ust

druggist
smuggest
snuggest

UG-ut

bug it
drug it
hug it
lug it
nugget
slug it

gold nugget
unplug it

Ū-id
(See Ū-ud)

Ū-in
(See Ū-un)

Ū-in-us
(See Ū-un-us)

Ū-ish

bluish
Jewish
newish
shrewish

—

Ū-i-sīd
(See Ū-u-sīd)

Ū-it
(See Ū-ut)

Ū-it-ē
(See Ū-ud-ē)

Ū-it-us
(See Ū-ud-us)

ŪJ

huge
rouge
stooge
Scrooge

deluge
refuge
vin rouge

centrifuge
subterfuge

UJ

budge
drudge
fudge
grudge
judge
nudge
smudge
sludge
trudge

adjudge
begrudge
forejudge
hot fudge
misjudge
prejudge

here come da judge
sober as a judge

UJ-ē

fudgy
pudgy
smudgy

UJ-ēng

budging
judging
nudging

smudging

trudging

adjudging

begruding

forejudging

misjudging

prejudging

UJ-et
(See UJ-ut)

ŪJH
(See also ŪJ)

rouge

deluge

vin rouge

Baton Rouge

UJ-un

bludgeon

budgin'

drudgin'

dudgeon

fudgin'

grudgin'

judgin'

nudgin'

smudgin'

trudgin'

adjudgin'

begrudgin'

curmudgeon

misjudgin'

prejudgin'

UJ-ut

budget

budge it

judge it

nudge it

smudge it

trudge it

begrudge it

forejudge it

low-budget

misjudge it

prejudge it

ŪK

cuke

duke

fluke

gook

kook

Luke

nuke

puke

spook

uke

archduke

Baruch

Dubuque

Farouk

peruke

rebuke

antinuke

gobble-de-gook

UK

buck

chuck

cluck

duck

fuck

guck

luck

muck

puck

Puck

pluck

ruck

suck

stuck

shuck

struck

schmuck

tuck

truck

yucch

yuk

amok

awestruck

bad luck

cold duck

dumbstruck

dumb cluck

dead duck

dump truck

fire truck

fast buck

good luck

lovestruck

lame duck

mukluk

moonstruck

potluck

sawbuck

sound truck

starstruck

stagestruck

tough luck

tow truck

upchuck

unstuck

worse luck

woodchuck

come unstuck

chuck-a-luck

Donald Duck

hockey puck

horror-struck

Lady Luck

megabuck(s)

nip and tuck

out of luck

pass the buck
panel truck
Peking duck
push one's luck
run amok
rotten luck
sitting duck
thunderstruck
tummy tuck
terror-struck

beginner's luck
down on one's luck
high muck-a-muck
poverty-struck

high muckety-muck

ÛK

book
brook
cook
crook
hook
look
nook
rook
schnook
shook
snook
took

betook
blue book
cookbook
casebook
Chinook
checkbook
closed book
datebook
forsook
fishhook
fry cook
guidebook
handbook
logbook

mistook
matchbook
make book
notebook
new look
outlook
partook
passbook
retook
scrapbook
songbook
skyhook
textbook
unhook

by the book
backward look
Captain Cook
comic book
cozy nook
crack a book
donnybrook
dirty look
gourmet cook
hit the book(s)
knowing look
overlook
off the hook
overcook
overtook
open book
pocketbook
small-time crook
The Good Book
undertook
undercook

coloring book
faraway look
gobble-de-gook
little black book
library book
one for the book(s)
short-order cook
telephone book

by hook or by crook

ŪK-ē

fluky
gooky
kooky
pukey
spooky

kabuki
Suzuki

UK-ē

Chuckie
clucky
ducky
gucky
lucky
mucky
plucky
yucky

Kentucky
unlucky

rubber ducky

happy-go-lucky

ÛK-e

bookie
cookie
hooky
looky
nooky
rookie

play hooky
tough cookie

fortune cookie

ŪK-ēng

puking
spooking

rebuking

UK-ēng

bucking
chucking
clucking
ducking
fucking
plucking
sucking
shucking
tucking
trucking

upchucking

tummy-tucking

ÛK-ēng

booking
cooking
hooking
looking
rooking

fry-cooking
good-looking
unhooking
what's cooking?

advance booking
backward looking
forward looking
gourmet cooking
overlooking
overcooking

UK-et
(See UK-ut)

UK-lēng

buckling
chuckling
duckling
knuckling
suckling

belt buckling
swashbuckling
unbuckling

ÛK-owt

cookout
lookout
took out

UKS
(See UX)

UK-shun

suction

abduction
conduction
construction
destruction
deduction
induction
instruction
obstruction
production
reduction
seduction

child abduction
dance instruction
introduction
liposuction
mass production
reproduction
reconstruction
self-destruction

army induction
movie production
overproduction

ŪKT

nuked
puked

spooked

rebuked

UKT

bucked
chucked
clucked
duct
ducked
fucked
mucked
plucked
shucked
sucked
tucked
trucked

abduct
air duct
conduct
construct
destruct
deduct
induct
instruct
obstruct
tear duct
upchucked
unplucked

aqueduct
reconstruct
reinstruct
self-destruct
viaduct

auto-destruct

ÛKT

booked
cooked
hooked
looked
rooked

unhooked

overlooked
overcooked

UKT-ēng

ducting

abducting
conducting
constructing
deducting
inducting
instructing
obstructing

reconstructing
reinstructing
self-destructing

UKT-i-bul
(See UKT-u-bul)

UKT-iv

conductive
constructive
destructive
deductive
inductive
instructive
obstructive
productive
seductive

introductive
reconstructive
reproductive
self-destructive
unproductive

counterproductive

UKT-u-bul

abductible
conductible

constructible
destructible
deductible
inductible
instructible
obstructible

indestructible

UKT-ur

bucked 'er
chucked 'er
ducked 'er
plucked 'er
sucked 'er

abductor
conductor
constructor
deductor
inductor
instructor
obstructor
upchucked 'er

reconstructor
self-destructor
train conductor

ŪK-u

bazooka
palooka

UK-ul

buckle
chuckle
knuckle
suckle
truckle

belt buckle
brass knuckle(s)
pinochle
swashbuckle
unbuckle

white-knuckle

honeysuckle

UK-uld

buckled
cuckold
chuckled
knuckled
suckled

swashbuckled
unbuckled

UK-ū-lunt

succulent
truculent

UK-ulz

buckles
cuckolds
chuckles
knuckles
suckles
truckles

brass knuckles
swashbuckles
unbuckles

ŪK-ur

lucre
puker
spooker

rebuker

UK-ur

bucker
chucker
clucker
ducker
mucker

pucker
plucker
sucker
Smucker('s)
succor
shucker
tucker
trucker
yukker

awestruck 'er
bloodsucker
corn shucker
seersucker
thumb-sucker
upchucker
unpucker

bib and tucker
chicken plucker
tummy-tucker

ÛK-ur

booker
cooker
hooker
looker
rooker
snooker
shook 'er
took 'er

good-looker
onlooker
unhooker

advance booker
backward looker
forward looker
overlooker
pressure cooker

ÛK-us

Lucas
mucous

mucus
nuke us
spook us

rebuke us

UK-us

buck us
chuck us
duck us
fuck us
ruckus
suck us
stuck us
struck us
tuck us

UK-ut

bucket
buck it
chuck it
duck it
fuck it
pluck it
suck it
struck it
tuck it
truck it

gutbucket
lardbucket
Nantucket
paint bucket
slopbucket
upchuck it

kick the bucket
sink a bucket

ŪL
(See also Ū-ul)

cool
drool
fool

fuel
ghoul
mule
pule
pool
rule
spool
stool
school
tool
yule

air-cool
barstool
cesspool
carpool
damfool
granule
gag rule
high school
house rule
home rule
Kabul
law school
mob rule
module
night school
nodule
O'Toole
preschool
prep school
packmule
retool
sliderule
toadstool
tidepool
whirlpool

April fool
as a rule
blow one's cool
boarding school
dirty pool
football pool
golden rule
Istanbul

Liverpool
lose one's cool
minuscule
molecule
overrule
play it cool
ridicule
swimming pool
Sunday school
supercool
traffic school
unit rule
vestibule

finishing school
nobody's fool
nursery school

majority rule

exception to the rule

UL

cull
dull
gull
hull
lull
mull
null
scull
skull

annul
numskull
sea gull

out of one's skull

ÛL

bull
full
pull
wool

bell pull

cram full
chock-full
half-full
lamb's wool
push-pull
pit bull
steel wool

cock and bull
Istanbul
shoot the bull
Sitting Bull
taffy pull
virgin wool

dyed-in-the-wool

ULCH

gulch
mulch

ULCH-ur

culture
vulture

subculture

agriculture
culture vulture
counterculture
floriculture
horticulture
multiculture

ÛLD

cooled
drooled
fooled
fueled
Gould
puled
pooled
ruled
stooled
schooled

tooled

air-cooled
carpooled
retooled
unschooled

overruled
ridiculed

ULD

culled
dulled
hulled
lulled
mulled
sculled

annulled

ŪL-ē

coolly
coolie
cruelly
drooly
duly
newly
stooly
tule
truly

gilhooley
unduly
unruly
uncruelly

yours truly

UL-ē

dully
gully
sully

ÛL-ē

bully
fully
pulley
woolly

wild-and-woolly

UL-en
(See UL-un)

ÛL-en
(See ÛL-un)

ŪL-ēng

cooling
drooling
fooling
fueling
puling
pooling
ruling
tooling

carpooling
retooling

overruling
ridiculing

UL-ēng

culling
dulling
lulling
mulling
sculling

annulling

ŪL-ep
(See ŪL-up)

UL-et
(See UL-ut)

ÛL-et
(See ÛL-ut)

ŪL-ē-un

Julian

cerulean
Herculean

UL-gur

bulgur
Bulgar
vulgar

ŪL-ip
(See ŪL-up)

ŪL-ish

coolish
foolish
ghoulish
mulish
schoolish

penny wise, pound
  foolish

ŪL-it-ē
(See ŪL-ud-ē)

ULJ

bulge

divulge
indulge

overindulge

Battle of the Bulge

ULJ-ēng

bulging

divulging
indulging

overindulging

ULK

bulk
hulk
sulk
skulk

ULK-ē

bulky
hulky
sulky

ULK-ēng

hulking
sulking
skulking

UL-min-āt

culminate
fulminate

ULP

gulp
pulp

ULP-it
(See ULP-ut)

ULPT

gulped
pulped
sculpt

ULP-ut

gulp it
pulpit

ULS

cults
pulse
Schultz

adults
convulse
consults
exults
insults
occults
results
repulse

catapults

consenting adults

ULS-ēng

pulsing

convulsing
repulsing

UL-shun

compulsion
convulsion
divulsion
expulsion
emulsion
impulsion
propulsion
repulsion
revulsion

UL-siv

convulsive
compulsive
impulsive

repulsive
revulsive

UL-sur

pulser
ulcer

convulser
consults 'er
exults 'er
insults 'er
repulser

ULT

cult

adult
consult
exult
insult
occult
penult
result
tumult

catapult
difficult
end result
young adult

antepenult

consenting adult

personality cult

ULT-chur
(See UL-chur)

ULT-ēng

consulting
exulting
insulting
resulting

catapulting

ULT-rē

sultry

adultery

ULTS
(See ULS)

ULT-ud

consulted
exulted
insulted
resulted

catapulted

ULT-ur-ē
(See ULT-rē)

ŪL-ū

lulu
Zulu

Honolulu

ŪL-u

Beulah
hula

Abdullah
Missoula

Boula Boula

ŪL-u-bul

coolable
foolable
fuelable
poolable
rulable
schoolable

retoolable

unschoolable

overrulable

ŪL-ud-ē

credulity
garrulity

incredulity

UL-un

lullin'
mullin'
scullin'
sullen

ÛL-un

bullin'
pullin'
woolen

ŪL-up

julep
tulip

mint julep

ŪL-ur

crueler
cooler
dueler
drooler
fooler
jeweler
Mueller
pooler
ruler
stooler
schooler
tooler

bejeweler
preschooler

retooler
wine cooler

overruler
water cooler

UL-ur

color
duller
huller
luller
muller

annuller
discolor
off color
true color(s)

flying color(s)
Technicolor

horse of a different
    color

UL-urd

colored
dullard

discolored
off-colored
rose-colored

ŪL-ur-ē

foolery
jewellery

tomfoolery

UL-ut

dull it
gullet

annul it

ÛL-ut

bullet
pullet
pull it

bite the bullet

ŪL-ut-ē
(See ŪL-ud-ē)

ŪLZ

cools
drools
fools
fuels
ghouls
mules
pules
pools
rules
spools
stools
schools
tools

air-cools
barstools
cesspools
damfools
gag rules
ground rules
packmules
retools
toadstools
tidepools
uncools
whirlpools

bend the rules
football pools
molecules
overrules
ridicules
Robert's Rules

swimming pools
vestibules

Queensbury Rules
majority rules

ŪM

boom
broom
bloom
doom
flume
fume
groom
gloom
loom
plume
rheum
room
spume
tomb
vroom
whom
womb
zoom

abloom
assume
bridegroom
boardroom
bathroom
bazoom
barroom
boom-boom
bedroom
ballroom
backroom
costume
checkroom
consume
classroom
cloakroom
card room
courtroom
dark room

exhume
entomb
guest room
heirloom
headroom
homeroom
ka-boom
Khartoum
legume
leg room
mushroom
men's room
make room
no room
presume
perfume
pump room
resume
restroom
rec room
showroom
spare room
storeroom
stateroom
subsume
taproom
tack room
tea room
well-groom(ed)
whiskbroom

anteroom
baby boom
breathing room
bride and groom
elbow room
fuss and fume
gloom and doom
love in bloom
ladies' room
locker room
nom de plume
powder room
reassume
sonic boom

standing room
smoke-filled room
women's room
waiting room

fruit of the loom
lower the boom
reception room

UM

bum
chum
come
crumb
drum
dumb
'em
from
glum
gum
hum
mum
numb
plum
plumb
rum
scum
slum
some
strum
swum
sum
thumb
yum

alum
all thumb(s)
beach bum
bay rum
become
bass drum
bread crumb
benumb
come from
dumdum

eardrum
first-come
green thumb
ho-hum
humdrum
how come?
hear from
hail from
lump sum
outcome
oil drum
rum-dum
succumb
Tom Thumb
yum-yum

bubblegum
beat one's gum(s)
cookie crumb
chewing gum
deaf and dumb
fife and drum
kingdom come
kettle drum
overcome
rule of thumb
to and from
Tweedledum

chrysanthemum
fe fi fo fum
hot buttered rum
twiddle one's thumb(s)
under one's thumb

UMB-lĕng

bumbling
fumbling
grumbling
humbling
jumbling
mumbling
rumbling
stumbling
tumbling

UM-blur

bumbler
fumbler
grumbler
humbler
jumbler
mumbler
rumbler
stumbler
tumbler

UM-bō

Dumbo
gumbo
jumbo

mumbo jumbo

UM-bul

bumble
crumble
fumble
grumble
humble
jumble
mumble
rumble
stumble
scumble
tumble

rough-and-tumble
take a tumble

UM-bunt

incumbent
procumbent
recumbent

UM-bur

lumber
number
slumber

umber

call number
cucumber
encumber
hot number
outnumber
renumber
wrong number

by the number(s)
disencumber
lucky number
paint by number
unencumber
without number

cardinal number

cool as a cucumber

UM-bur-ēng

lumbering
numbering
slumbering

encumbering
outnumbering
renumbering

disencumbering

UM-bur-sum

cumbersome
number some

encumber some
outnumber some

ŪMD

boomed
bloomed
doomed
fumed
groomed
loomed

plumed
roomed
zoomed

assumed
costumed
consumed
exhumed
entombed
presumed
perfumed
resumed
subsumed
well-groomed

reassumed

UMB

bummed
chummed
crumbed
drummed
gummed
hummed
numbed
plumbed
slummed
strummed
summed
thumbed

benumbed
succumbed

ŪM-ē

clue me
do me
drew me
flew me
gloomy
grew me
knew me
plumy
roomy
roomie

rheumy
sue me
to me
who me?
woo me

perfumy
so sue me
unroomy
ungloomy

UM-ē

chummy
crummy
dummy
gummy
glummy
mummy
rummy
slummy
scummy
tummy
yummy

gin rummy

**UM-el
(See UM-ul)**

ŪM-ēng

booming
blooming
grooming
looming
rooming
zooming

assuming
costuming
consuming
exhuming
entombing
good grooming
presuming

resuming

reassuming
time-consuming
unassuming

UM-ēng

bumming
chumming
coming
drumming
gumming
humming
numbing
plumbing
slumming
strumming
summing
thumbing

becoming
benumbing
forthcoming
homecoming
nose-thumbing
oncoming
succumbing
shortcoming

overcoming
second coming
unbecoming
up and coming

ŪM-ē-nus

gloominess
roominess

**UM-et
(See UM-ut)**

**ŪM-id
(See ŪM-ud)**

ŪM-ij

bloomage
plumage

ŪM-in
(See ŪM-un)

ŪM-in-āt

luminate
ruminate

illuminate

ŪM-in-us

doomin' us
groomin' us
luminous
roomin' us

bituminous
consumin' us
voluminous

UM-it
(See UM-ut)

UM-nī

come nigh
alumni

UMP

bump
clump
chump
dump
frump
grump
hump
jump
lump
mump(s)

pump
plump
rump
sump
stump
slump
schlump
thump
trump
ump

broad jump
breast pump
goose bump(s)
gas pump
high jump
long jump
mugwump
no trump
ski jump
speed bump
trash dump
tree stump

city dump
in a slump
overtrump
quantum jump
stomach pump
sugar lump
suction pump
triple jump
take one's lump(s)
up a stump
umpty-ump
water pump

dowager's hump
down in the dump(s)
hop, skip, and jump
over the hump
parachute jump

UMP-ē

bumpy
clumpy

dumpy
frumpy
grumpy
humpy
jumpy
lumpy
stumpy
slumpy
thumpy

UMP-ēng

bumping
clumping
dumping
grumping
humping
jumping
lumping
pumping
plumping
stumping
slumping
thumping
trumping
umping

broad jumping
high jumping
no dumping

overtrumping
triple jumping

UMP-et
(See UMP-ut)

UMP-kin

bumpkin
pumpkin

UMP-lēng

crumpling
dumpling

rumpling

uncrumpling

apple dumpling

chicken dumpling

UMP-shun

gumption

assumption

consumption

presumption

resumption

conspicuous
    consumption

UMP-shus

bumptious

scrumptious

presumptuous

UMPT

bumped

clumped

dumped

grumped

humped

jumped

lumped

pumped

plumped

stumped

slumped

thumped

trumped

umped

broad jumped

overtrumped

UMP-tiv

assumptive

consumptive

presumptive

resumptive

heir presumptive

UMP-un-ē

company

accompany

UMP-ur

bumper

dumper

jumper

pumper

plumper

stumper

thumper

trumper

broad jumper

claim-jumper

high jumper

long jumper

Bible-thumper

overtrumper

puddle jumper

triple jumper

bumper to bumper

parachute jumper

UMP-us

bump us

compass

dump us

jump us

pump us

rumpus

stump us

trump us

thump us

encompass

overtrump us

UMP-ut

bump it

crumpet

dump it

hump it

jump it

pump it

strumpet

thump it

trumpet

trump it

ear trumpet

tea and crumpet(s)

like it or lump it

ŪM-u

puma

summa

Yuma

Zuma

Montezuma

Petaluma

ŪM-u-bul

assumable

consumable

exhumable

entombable

presumable

perfumable

resumable

subsumable

reassumable

unassumable

unconsumable

UM-u-bul

crumbable

gummable

hummable

numbable
plumbable
strummable
thumbable

ŪM-ud

humid
tumid

UM-uks
(See UM-ux)

UM-ul

pommel

Beau Brummel

ŪM-un

boomin'
bloomin'
cumin
doomin'
fumin'
groomin'
human
loomin'
Newman
roomin'
Schumann
Truman
zoomin'

acumen
albumen
assumin'
consumin'
exhumin'
entombin'
inhuman
mushroomin'
presumin'
resumin'

subhuman

super human

UM-unz

comin's
drummin's
hummin's
summons

goin's and comin's

ŪM-ur

boomer
bloomer
doomer
fumer
groomer
humor
loomer
roomer
rumor
tumor
zoomer

assumer
black humor
brain tumor
costumer
consumer
exhumer
entomber
good humor
ill humor
late bloomer
presumer
perfumer
pet groomer
resumer

baby boomer
doom and gloomer
early bloomer
reassumer
sonic boomer

UM-ur

bummer
comer
crumber
dumber
drummer
glummer
gummer
hummer
mummer
number
plumber
summer
slummer
strummer
thumber

becomer
benumber
humdrummer
latecomer
midsummer
newcomer
nose-thumber

fife and drummer
overcomer
overcome 'er
table crumber
up-and-comer

Indian summer

ŪM-ur-ē

plumery

costumery
perfumery

UM-ur-ē

mummery
summary
summery

Montgomery

ŪM-ur-ēng

humoring
rumoring

ŪM-ur-us

humorous
humor us
numerous
tumorous

UM-ut

bum it
crumb it
from it
gum it
hum it
plummet
slum it
strum it
summit
thumb it

become it

UM-ux

lummox
stomachs

UM-zē

clumsy
mumsy

ŪN

boon
coon
croon
dune
goon
hewn
June
loon
moon

noon
prune
rune
soon
spoon
strewn
swoon
tune

attune
balloon
bestrewn
buffoon
baboon
bassoon
cocoon
cartoon
Calhoun
commune
doubloon
dragoon
festoon
fine-tune
full moon
hit tune
high noon
harpoon
half-moon
immune
impugn
jejune
lagoon
lampoon
maroon
monsoon
Neptune
new moon
oppugn
poltroon
pontoon
platoon
quadroon
racoon
Rangoon
repugn

saloon
spittoon
soup spoon
tycoon
teaspoon
typhoon
too soon

afternoon
Brigadoon
blue lagoon
Clair de Lune
call the tune
Cameroon
croon a tune
crescent moon
change one's tune
Daniel Boone
full of prune(s)
greasy spoon
honeymoon
harvest moon
importune
loony tune
lick one's wound(s)
lead balloon
macaroon
opportune
out of tune
overstrewn
picayune
pretty soon
silver spoon
trial balloon
tablespoon

carry a tune
hot-air balloon
inopportune
man in the moon
twelve o'clock noon

crazy as a loon
once in a blue moon
wrinkled as a prune

UN

bun
dun
done
fun
gun
hon
Hun
none
nun
one
pun
run
sun
son
spun
shun
stun
ton
tun
won

all done
begun
burp gun
blowgun
cap gun
dog run
dry run
day one
end run
earned run
finespun
grandson
great gun(s)
homespun
home run
hired gun
make fun
no one
outdone
outrun
poke fun
popgun
rerun

redone
square one
squirt gun
six gun
ski run
short run
shogun
shotgun
someone
trial run
top gun
undone
unrun
unwon
well done
year one

anyone
Air Force One
all or none
BB gun
cut and run
cattle run
everyone
favorite son
Gatling-gun
hit-and-run
hot dog bun
hole in one
honeybun
jump the gun
just begun
murder one
midnight sun
native son
number one
noonday sun
911
overdone
one by one
overrun
one-on-one
on the run
pack a gun
smoking gun

setting sun
underdone
unbegun
unearned run
World War I

back to square one
cost overrun
fun in the sun
favorite son
hamburger bun
in the long run
Mohammedan
over and done
prodigal son
place in the sun
son of a gun
stick to one's gun(s)
under the gun
under the sun

Attila the Hun
committee of one
every other one
each and every one

UNCH

brunch
bunch
crunch
grunch
hunch
lunch
munch
punch
scrunch

box lunch
do lunch
free lunch
fruit punch
keypunch
pull punch(es)
school lunch
whole bunch

business lunch
counterpunch
honeybunch
out to lunch
one-two punch
on a hunch
pleased as punch
rabbit punch
sucker-punch
Sunday brunch

energy crunch
Hawaiian Punch
roll with the
    punch(es)

three-martini lunch

UNCH-ē

crunchy
munchy
punchy

UNCH-ēng

brunching
bunching
crunching
hunching
lunching
munching
punching
scrunching

keypunching

counterpunching

UNCH-un

brunchin'
bunchin'
crunchin'
luncheon
lunchin'
munchin'
punchin'

scrunchin'
truncheon

UNCH-ur

cruncher
muncher
puncher

cowpuncher
keypuncher

ŪND

crooned
mooned
spooned
swooned
tuned
wound

attuned
ballooned
cartooned
communed
fine-tuned
harpooned
impugned
lampooned
marooned

honeymooned
importuned

UND

dunned
fund
funned
gunned
punned
sunned
shunned
stunned

refund
rotund
slush fund

trust fund

cummerbund
moribund
orotund
pension fund
rubicund

UND-ē

Monday
Sunday
sundae
undie(s)

Burundi
blue Monday

hot-fudge sundae
salmagundi

never on Sunday

forty ways to Sunday

UND-it

fund it
gunned it
pundit
shunned it
stunned it

UND-rus

thunderous
wondrous

UND-ul

bundle
rundle
trundle

unbundle

drop a bundle

UND-un

fundin'
London
undone

refundin'

UND-unt

abundant
redundant

overabundant

UND-ur

blunder
dunned 'er
funder
gunned 'er
plunder
sunder
shunned 'er
stunned 'er
thunder
under
wonder

asunder
boy wonder
down under
go under
no wonder
rotunder
refunder
work wonder(s)

blood and thunder
knuckle under
loot and plunder
out from under

ninety-day wonder
steal someone's
     thunder

UND-ur-ēng

blundering
plundering
thundering
wondering

UND-ur-us

blunderous
plunder us
thunderous
under us

ŪN-ē

croony
goony
loony
moony
puny
Rooney
SUNY
Zuni

UN-ē

bunny
funny
funnie(s)
honey
money
punny
runny
sonny
sunny

beach bunny
blood money
Bugs Bunny
dumb bunny
hush money
mad money

even money
Easter bunny
easy money

for love or money
one for the money
right on the money

a run for one's money
land of milk and
     honey

UN-el
(See UN-ul)

ŪN-ēng

crooning
mooning
pruning
spooning
swooning
tuning

attuning
ballooning
communing
fine-tuning
harpooning
impugning
lampooning
marooning
oppugning

honeymooning
importuning

UN-ēng

cunning
dunning
funning
gunning
punning
running
sunning
shunning
stunning

frontrunning

off and running

ŪN-ful

croonful
spoonful
tuneful

untuneful

UNG

brung
Chung
clung
dung
flung
hung
lung
rung
strung
swung
sung
sprung
stung
slung
tongue
wrung
young

among
cow dung
far-flung
forked tongue
high-strung
hamstrung
shantung
unsung
unhung
unstrung
well hung

bite one's tongue
egg foo yung
hold one's tongue
iron lung
mother tongue
speak in tongue(s)
underslung

forever young
slip of the tongue

on the tip of one's
   tongue

UNG-ul

bungle
fungal
jungle

antifungal
concrete jungle

law of the jungle

UNG-ur

hunger
younger

fishmonger
newsmonger
warmonger

die of hunger
gossipmonger
ironmonger
rumormonger
scandalmonger

UNG-ur-ēng

hungering

warmongering

scandalmongering

UNG-us

fungus

humongous

ŪN-ik
(See ŪN-uk)

UN-ish

nunnish
punish
punnish

ŪN-ist

soonest

balloonist
bassoonist
cartoonist
harpoonist
jejunest
lampoonist

opportunist

ŪN-it
(See ŪN-ut)

UN-it
(See UN-ut)

ŪN-it-ē
(See ŪN-ud-ē)

UNJ

grunge
lunge
plunge
sponge

expunge

take the plunge

throw in the sponge

UNJ-ē

bungee
grungy
spongy

UNJ-ēng

lunging
plunging
sponging

expunging

UNJ-un

dungeon
lungin'
plungin'

expungin'

UNK

bunk
chunk
clunk
dunk
drunk
funk
flunk
hunk
junk
lunk
monk
punk
plunk
skunk
sunk
stunk
slunk
spunk
shrunk
thunk
trunk
unk

blue funk
chipmunk
debunk
kerplunk
preshrunk
Podunk

punch-drunk
slam dunk
undrunk

Chinese junk
pile of junk
steamer trunk

drunk as a skunk

UNK-chur

juncture
puncture

grand juncture
tire puncture

acupuncture

UNK-ē

chunky
clunky
funky
flunky
hunky
junky
monkey
punky
spunky

grease monkey

junk-food junky

UNK-en
(See UNK-un)

UNK-ēng

bunking
clunking
dunking
flunking
junking
plunking

debunking
slam-dunking

UNK-et
(See UNK-ut)

UNK-shun

function
junction
unction

adjunction
compunction
conjunction
disjunction
dysfunction
expunction
injunction
malfunction
rambunction

railroad junction

UNK-shus

unctuous

rambunctious

UNKT

bunked
chunked
clunked
dunked
flunked
junked
plunked
skunked

adjunct
conjunct
debunked
defunct
disjunct
injunct

kerplunked
slam-dunked

UNKT-iv

adjunctive
conjunctive
disjunctive
injunctive
subjunctive

UNK-ul

uncle

carbuncle
Dutch uncle
say uncle

UNK-um

bunkum
dunk 'em
drunk 'em
flunk 'em
junk 'em
sunk 'em
shrunk 'em

UNK-un

clunkin'
drunken
Duncan
dunkin'
flunkin'
junkin'
plunkin'
sunken
shrunken

debunkin'
kerplunkin'
preshrunken
slam-dunkin'

UNK-ur

bunker
clunker
dunker
drunker
flunker
hunker
junker
punker
plunker
shrunk 'er
sunk 'er

debunk 'er
old clunker
slam-dunker
spelunker

Archie Bunker

UNK-ut

dunk it
drunk it
flunk it
junket
junk it
plunk it
sunk it
shrunk it
thunk it

debunk it

ŪN-ō

Bruno
do know
Juneau
Juno
uno
you know

numero uno

UNS

brunts
bunts
blunts
dunce
fronts
grunts
hunts
months
once
punts
runts
shunts
stunts

affronts
at once
storefronts
witch hunts

all at once
ambulance

UNT

bunt
brunt
blunt
front
grunt
hunt
punt
runt
shunt
stunt

affront
beachfront
confront
cold front
forefront
fox hunt
homefront
manhunt
out front
storefront

up front
witch hunt

elephant
oceanfront
treasure hunt

UNT-ēng

bunting
blunting
fronting
grunting
hunting
punting
shunting

affronting
confronting
foxhunting
manhunting
witch hunting

treasure hunting

UNTS
(See UNS)

UNT-ul

frontal

confrontal
disgruntle

UNT-ur

bunter
blunter
fronter
grunter
hunter
punter
shunter
stunter

affronter

confronter
headhunter
manhunter

ŪN-u

luna
tuna

Altoona
lacuna
laguna
vicuna

ŪN-u-dē

punity
unity

community
disunity
impunity
immunity

importunity
opportunity

equal opportunity
photo opportunity

diplomatic immunity

ŪN-uk

eunuch
Munich
tunic

ŪN-ul

communal
tribunal

UN-ul

funnel
tunnel

wind tunnel

ŪN-um

croon 'em
moon 'em
prune 'em
tune 'em

harpoon 'em
maroon 'em

importune 'em

e pluribus unum

ŪN-ur

crooner
lunar
mooner
pruner
sooner
schooner
spooner
swooner
tuner

ballooner
communer
fine-tuner
harpooner
impugner
lampooner
marooner

honeymooner
importuner
opportuner

piano tuner

UN-ur

gunner
oner
punner
runner
sunner
shunner
stunner

front-runner
roadrunner
tailgunner

UN-ur-ē

gunnery
nunnery

ŪN-us

newness
trueness

askewness

**ŪN-ust
(See ŪN-ist)**

ŪN-ut

croon it
moon it
prune it
spoon it
strewn it
tune it
unit

harpoon it
impugn it
lampoon it

importune it

UN-ut

done it
gun it
run it
spun it
shun it
stun it

begun it
outdone it
outrun it

rerun it
redone it
undone it
whodunit

ŪN-yu

moon ya

harpoon ya
impugn ya
maroon ya
petunia
vicuna

importune ya

ŪN-yun

union

communion
reunion

labor union

UN-yun

bunion
Bunyan
grunion
onion

ŪP

bloop
coop
croup
dupe
droop
goop
group
hoop
loop
oop(s)
poop
soup
stoop

stupe
snoop
sloop
swoop
scoop
stoup
troop
whoop

age group
duck soup
door stoop
in-group
pea soup
peer group
recoup
regroup
rap group
scout troop
youth group

alley oop
Betty Boop
chicken coop
chicken soup
ethnic group
fly the coop
Guadeloupe
hula hoop
in the soup
interest group
inside scoop
loop-the-loop
nincompoop
one fell swoop
party poop
pooper-scoop
pressure group
splinter group

encounter group
knock for a loop
not worth a whoop
newspaper scoop

UP

cup
pup
sup
up
whup
yup

act up
bring up
buildup
bust-up
backup
bucks up
blowup
buck up
B-cup
bone up
burn up
breakup
crackup
catch up
cut-up
closeup
checkup
cleanup
dress-up
egg cup
'fess up
fix up
flare-up
foul-up
grown-up
gear up
get up
give up
hiccup
hard up
holdup
heads up
hookup
hang-up
knock up
lay up
let up

lineup
lockup
makeup
matchup
mixup
mess up
mop up
own up
pent up
pickup
pinup
push-up
roundup
roll up
rough up
stuck up
setup
sunup
stickup
size up
show up
shut up
speak up
slip up
spruce up
stand up
shakeup
spit up
straight up
tuneup
tank up
teacup
turn up
trip up
throw up
tossup
touchup
wind up
wrap-up
wake up
World Cup
write-up
wrought-up
walkup
washed-up

what's up?

all shook up
ante up
all washed up
bottoms up
buckle up
belly up
bundle up
butter up
buttercup
bring it up
coffee cup
cover-up
cuddle up
double up
divvy up
fill 'er up
giddy-up
higher-up
listen up
loving cup
pick-me-up
paper cup
runner up
straighten up
7UP
shoot 'em-up
Stanley Cup
suction cup
training cup
up and up
whoop it up
wickiup

sunnyside up

America's Cup
curtain going up
on the up-and-up
put up or shut up

tempest in a teacup

ŪP-ē

croupy
droopy

goopy
groupie
kewpie
loopy
poopy
rupee
snoopy
soupy
swoopy
whoopee

UP-ē

guppy
puppy
Yuppie

hush puppy

ŪP-ēng

blooping
duping
drooping
grouping
looping
pooping
stooping
snooping
swooping
scooping
trooping
whooping

recouping
regrouping

UP-ēng

cupping
supping
upping

UP-et
(See UP-ut)

ŪP-id

cupid
stupid

Dan Cupid

ŪP-il
(See ŪP-ul)

ŪP-on

coupon
poop on
Poupon
snoop on

UPS

cups
pups
sups
ups
whups

bankrupts
corrupts
disrupts
erupts

buttercups
cover-ups
higher-ups
interrupts
in one's cups

UP-shun

corruption
disruption
eruption

interruption

UPT

cupped
supped

upped
whupped

abrupt
bankrupt
corrupt
disrupt
erupt
hiccupped
one-upped

interrupt
uncorrupt

UPTS
(See UPS)

UPT-ud

bankrupted
corrupted
disrupted
erupted

interrupted
uncorrupted

uninterrupted

ŪP-ud
(See ŪP-id)

ŪP-ul

pupil
scruple

octuple
quadruple
quintuple

UP-ul

couple
supple

unsupple

married couple
smooth and supple

UP-uns

tuppance
uppance

comeuppance

ŪP-ur

blooper
cooper
duper
drooper
grouper
hooper
looper
pooper
super
stupor
stooper
snooper
swooper
scooper
trooper
trouper
whooper

recouper
regrouper
state trooper

hula hooper
ice cream scooper
party pooper
pooper scooper
paratrooper
super-duper

UP-ur

supper
upper

grown-upper
hiccupper

Last Supper

fixer-upper
pepper-upper
picker-upper

ŪP-us

dupe us
group us
lupus
poop us
scoop us

UP-ut

Muppet
puppet
sup it
up it

ŪR
(See also Ū-ur)

boor
Coor(s)
cure
dour
ewer
fleur
lure
moor
poor
pure
skewer
spoor
sure
tour
your
you're

assure
azure
abjure
amour
allure
bon jour

brochure
cocksure
coiffure
cook's tour
contour
chauffeur
couture
demure
detour
dirt poor
endure
ensure
fer sure
grand tour
impure
insure
inure
liqueur
l'amour
mature
make sure
masseur
obscure
procure
piss-poor
rest cure
secure
unsure
up your(s)
velour

amateur
aperture
connoisseur
curvature
de rigueur
Cote d'Azur
epicure
haute couture
immature
insecure
manicure
overture
pedicure
premature

paramour
plat du jour
reassure
reinsure
raconteur
sinecure
soupe du jour
saboteur
simon-pure
take the cure

affaire d'amour
affaire de coeur
chanson d'amour

Kuala Lumpur

UR

burr
blur
br-r-r
cur
err
fir
fur
gr-r-r
her
Kerr
myrrh
per
purr
sir
stir
slur
spur
were
whir

aver
astir
bestir
Ben Hur
Big Sur
concur
confer
defer

demur
deter
incur
inter
infer
larkspur
occur
prefer
recur
refer
yessir

as it were
cockleburr
de rigueur
disinter
Edinburgh
emperor
him and her

URB

blurb
curb
herb
Serb
verb

adverb
acerb
disturb
news blurb
perturb
proverb
suburb
superb

do not disturb

URB-ē

blurby
derby
Herbie
Kirby

URB-ēng

curbing

disturbing
perturbing

URB-et
(See URB-ut)

URB-ē-ul

adverbial
proverbial

URB-ik

Serbic

acerbic

URB-ish

blurbish

refurbish

URB-ul

gerbil
Herb'll
herbal
verbal

URB-ul-ē

herbally
verbally

hyperbole

URB-un

bourbon
curbin'
turban
urban

disturbin'

perturbin'
suburban

URB-ur

curber
Gerber

disturber
perturb 'er
superber

URB-ut

curb it
sherbet
turbot

disturb it
perturb it

URCH

birch
church
lurch
perch
search
smirch

besmirch
research
soul-search
strip-search

body-search

leave in the lurch

URCH-ēng

lurching
perching
searching

besmirching
researching
soul-searching

strip-searching

body-searching

URCH-in
(See URCH-un)

URCH-un

lurchin'
perchin'
searchin'
urchin

besmirchin'
researchin'
soul-searchin'
sea urchin
strip-searchin'

URCH-ur

lurcher
nurture
percher
searcher

besmircher
researcher
soul-searcher
strip-searcher

body-searcher

URCH-us

purchase
search us

besmirch us
strip-search us

ŪRD

cured
lured
moored
skewered

toured

assured
contoured
detoured
endured
ensured
inured
insured
matured
obscured
procured
secured

manicured
reassured
unsecured

URD

bird
burred
br-r-r-ed
blurred
curd
erred
furred
gr-r-r-ed
gird
herd
heard
purred
stirred
spurred
slurred
turd
third
whirred
word

averred
absurd
byword
bean curd
blackbird
Big Bird
bird turd

buzzword
bluebird
code word
crossword
conferred
concurred
demurred
deterred
deferred
F word
God's Word
incurred
interred
inferred
jailbird
jaybird
lovebird
last word
occurred
one-third
preferred
password
recurred
referred
reword
railbird
send word
snowbird
songbird
swearword
transferred
unheard
watchword
yardbird

afterward
calendared
dirty word
disinterred
eat one's word(s)
early bird
for the bird(s)
hummingbird
household word
have a word

just a word
keep one's word
ladybird
massacred
mark my word
mockingbird
not mince word(s)
overheard
play on word(s)
reoccurred
reconferred
seen not heard
say the word
solemn word
self-assured
take my word
tax-deferred
word for word

eat like a bird
free as a bird
four-letter word
in other word(s)
Mortimer Snerd

as good as one's word

naked as a jaybird

theater of the absurd

URD-ē

blurty
Bertie
birdie
dirty
flirty
Gertie
nerdy
perty
spurty
sturdy
squirty
thirty
wordy

down and dirty

Dirty Gertie
hurdy-gurdy
overwordy
over thirty
watch the birdie

URD-en
(See URD-un)

URD-ēng

blurting
curding
flirting
girding
hurting
herding
squirting
spurting
skirting
wording

asserting
averting
converting
diverting
deserting
exerting
everting
inserting
inverting
perverting
reverting
rewording
subverting

disconcerting

overexerting

URD-ē-us

courteous
dirty us

discourteous

URD-lēng

curdling
girdling
hurdling

bloodcurdling

URD-u

Gerda

Alberta

URD-ub-ul

blurtable
flirtable
girdable
herdable
hurtable
skirtable
spurtable
wordable

alertable
avertable
assertable
convertible
desertable
divertible
exertable
evertable
insertable
invertible
revertible
rewordable
subvertible

disconcertable
unassertable

incontrovertible

URD-ud

blurted
curded
flirted

girded
herded
spurted
squirted
skirted
worded

asserted
averted
alerted
converted
diverted
deserted
exerted
inserted
inverted
perverted
reworded
reverted
subverted

disconcerted
extroverted
introverted

overexerted

URD-ul

curdle
fertile
girdle
hurdle
hurtle
myrtle
turtle

crape myrtle
engirdle
infertile
mock turtle

URD-un

burden
girdin'
herdin'

wordin'

rewordin'
unburden

beast of burden
overburden

URD-ur

blurter
curter
flirter
girder
hurter
herder
heard 'er
murder
perter
squirter
spurter
worder

absurder
asserter
averter
alerter
coverter
converter
diverter
deserter
exerter
frankfurter
inserter
inerter
inverter
overter
perverter
reverter
reworder
subverter

bloody murder
disconcerter

ŪR-ē

brewery
Curie
Drury
fury
jury

de jure
grand jury
Missouri
Tandoori

UR-ē

blurry
curry
furry
flurry
hurry
Murray
purry
surrey
slurry
scurry
whirry
worry

Missouri

Arthur Murray
hurry-scurry
not to worry

ŪR-ē-āt

infuriate
luxuriate

UR-ēd

curried
hurried
scurried
worried

unhurried

UR-ē-ēng

currying
flurrying
hurrying
scurrying
worrying

ŪR-ēng

during
luring
mooring
touring

assuring
alluring
contouring
chauffeuring
detouring
enduring
maturing
unerring

reassuring

UR-ēng

burring
blurring
erring
purring
stirring
slurring
spurring
whirring

concurring
conferring
deferring
demurring
deterring
incurring
interring
inferring
occurring
preferring

recurring
referring
unerring

disinterring

UR-ent
(See UR-unt)

ŪR-est
(See ŪR-ist)

UR-ē-sum

hurry some
worrisome

ŪR-ē-ul

Muriel

mercurial

UR-ē-un

hurryin'
worryin'

Arthurian
Ben-Gurion
centurion
Manchurian
Missourian

epicurean

ŪR-ē-unt

prurient

luxuriant

UR-ē-ur

blurrier
courier
furrier
hurrier

scurrier
worrier

mail courier

ŪR-ē-us

curious
furious

injurious
luxurious
penurious
uncurious

UR-ē-us

hurry us
spurious
worry us

UR-ēz

curries
flurries
hurries
Murray's
surreys
scurries
worries

snow flurries

URF

serf
surf
smurf
turf

windsurf

Astroturf
body surf

URG

berg
burg

iceberg
Pittsburgh
Salzburg

Gettysburg
Hindenburg
Luxembourg

Johannesburg

tip of the iceberg

URG-lēng

burgling
gurgling

URG-lur

burglar
gurgler

URG-ul

burgle
gurgle

UR-ij

courage
moorage

discourage
encourage

badge of courage

**ŪR-in
(See ŪR-un)**

ŪR-ish

boorish
flourish
nourish

amateurish
undernourish

UR-ish-ment

flourishment
nourishment

ŪR-ist

dourest
jurist
purist
poorest
purest
surest
tourist

coiffurist
demurest
maturest
securest
obscurest

immaturest
insecurest
manicurist

caricaturist

**ŪR-it-ē
(See ŪR-ud-ē)**

URJ

dirge
merge
purge
serge
surge
splurge
scourge
urge
verge

converge
diverge
deterge
emerge
resurge

submerge
upsurge

on the verge
resubmerge
reemerge

funeral dirge

URJ-ē

clergy
splurgy

metallurgy

benefit of clergy

URJ-ēng

merging
purging
surging
splurging
urging
verging

converging
diverging
emerging
resurging
submerging
upsurging

resubmerging
reemerging

URJ-ent
(See URJ-unt)

URJ-ik-ul

surgical
liturgical

URJ-in
(See URJ-un)

URJ-un

burgeon
mergin'
purgin'
surgin'
surgeon
splurgin'
scourgin'
sturgeon
urgin'
virgin
vergin'

convergin'
divergin'
emergin'
resurgin'
smoked sturgeon
submergin'

plastic surgeon
resubmergin'
reemergin'
vestal virgin

URJ-uns

mergence

convergence
divergence
detergents
emergence
insurgence
insurgents
resurgence
submergence

URJ-uns-ē

urgency

convergency
divergency
emergency
insurgency
resurgency

URJ-unt

urgent

abstergent
convergent
detergent
divergent
emergent
insurgent
resurgent

URJ-ur

merger
purger
perjure
surger
splurger
urger
verger
verdure

converger
emerger
resurger
submerger

URJ-ur-ē

perjury
surgery

URK

Berk
clerk
dirk
irk
jerk
kirk
lurk
murk
perk
quirk
smirk
shirk

Turk
work

artwork
brainwork
bulwark
bridgework
bookwork
berserk
clockwork
daywork
file clerk
footwork
fieldwork
flatwork
firework(s)
fast work
framework
groundwork
guesswork
homework
housework
knee jerk
legwork
network
patchwork
piecework
rework
schoolwork
teamwork
town clerk
woodwork

busy work
clear and jerk
dirty work
handiwork
line of work
latticework
men at work
needlework
overwork
out of work
right-to-work
underwork
women's work

URK-ē

jerky
murky
perky
quirky
smirky
turkey

beef jerky
cold turkey
talk turkey

Albuquerque
herky-jerky
turkey-lurkey

URK-ēng

clerking
irking
jerking
lurking
perking
smirking
shirking
working

networking
not working
reworking
tearjerking

URK-in
(See URK-un)

URK-it
(See URK-ut)

URKT

clerked
irked
jerked
lurked
perked

smirked
shirked
worked

overworked

URK-ū-lur

circular

tubercular

URK-un

clerkin'
gherkin
irkin'
jerkin
jerkin'
lurkin'
merkin
perkin'
smirkin'
shirkin'
workin'

URK-ur

irker
jerker
lurker
smirker
shirker
worker

berserker
caseworker
dayworker
tearjerker

migrant worker

URK-us

circus
irk us
jerk us
perk us

shirk us
work us

rework us

overwork us
three-ring circus
underwork us

URK-ut

circuit
jerk it
shirk it
work it

URL

burl
curl
churl
earl
furl
girl
hurl
pearl
purl
squirrel
swirl
twirl
whorl
whirl

awhirl
call girl
dream girl
pincurl
recurl
show girl
spitcurl
unfurl
uncurl

attagirl
cover girl
string of pearl(s)
working girl
mother-of-pearl

URLD

curled
furled
hurled
purled
pearled
swirled
twirled
world
whirled

dream world
pincurled
recurled
Third World
uncurled
unfurled

out of this world

on top of the world

ŪRL-ē

dourly
purely
poorly
surely

demurely
impurely
maturely
obscurely
securely
unsurely

amateurly
immaturely
insecurely
prematurely

URL-ē

burly
curly
churly
early

girly
pearly
Shirley
surly
squirrelly
swirly
twirly
whirly

hurly-burly

URL-ēng

curling
furling
hurling
purling
sterling
whirling

hair curling
uncurling
unfurling

URL-ē-ur

burlier
curlier
churlier
earlier
pearlier
surlier

URL-ish

churlish
girlish

URL-ōēn

purloin
sirloin

URL-ur

curler
furler

hurler
purler
swirler
twirler
whirler

hair curler
recurler
unfurler
uncurler

baton twirler
eyelash curler

URM

derm
firm
germ
perm
squirm
sperm
term
worm

affirm
bookworm
confirm
deworm
earthworm
full-term
glowworm
infirm
long-term
midterm
ringworm
silkworm
short-term
tapeworm

angleworm
can of worm(s)
come to term(s)
disaffirm
epiderm
pachyderm
reconfirm

reaffirm
wiggleworm

on speaking term(s)

URM-ē

germy
per me
stir me
spur me
squirmy
wormy

affirm me
confirm me
defer me
deter me
inter me
prefer me
refer me
unwormy

taxidermy

URM-ēng

firming
perming
squirming
terming
worming

affirming
confirming
deworming

disaffirming
reconfirming
reaffirming

UR-ment

deferment
determent
interment

URM-in
(See URM-un)

URM-in-āt

germinate
terminate

exterminate

URM-in-ul
(See URM-un-ul)

URM-ish

firmish
squirmish
skirmish
wormish

URM-u

Burma
Erma

terra firma

URM-ul

dermal
thermal

epidermal
hypothermal
pachydermal

URM-un

Berman
ermine
firmin'
German
Herman
merman
sermon
squirmin'
Sherman
vermin
wormin'

affirmin'

confirmin'
dewormin'
determine

disaffirmin'
predetermine
reconfirmin'
reaffirmin'

URM-un-ul

germinal
terminal

URM-ur

firmer
murmur
permer
squirmer
termer
wormer

affirmer
confirmer
dewormer
heart murmur
infirmer
mid-termer

disaffirmer
reconfirmer

URM-us

firm us
dermis
perm us
thermos
term us

affirm us
confirm us

epidermis
reconfirm us

URN

burn
churn
durn
ern
earn
fern
learn
stern
spurn
turn
tern
urn
yearn

adjourn
Ahern
astern
concern
discern
dad-burn
downturn
epergne
goldurn
heartburn
intern
Jules Verne
lectern
nocturne
return
sojourn
slow burn
sauterne
sunburn
upturn
unlearn
U-turn
windburn

live and learn
overturn
out of turn
taciturn
tax return
toss and turn

unconcern

at every turn
done to a turn
money to burn
third-degree burn

point of no return

URND

burned
churned
earned
learned
spurned
turned
yearned

adjourned
concerned
discerned
interned
returned
sojourned
sunburned
unearned
upturned
unlearned
windburned

overturned
unconcerned

leave no stone
    unturned

URN-ē

ferny
gurney
journey
tourney
yearny

attorney

Bert and Ernie

district attorney
power of attorney

URN-ēng

burning
churning
earning
learning
spurning
turning
yearning

adjourning
book-learning
cross-burning
concerning
discerning
interning
returning
sojourning
sunburning
unlearning

overturning
undiscerning

URN-est
(See URN-ust)

URN-ib-ul
(See URN-ub-ul)

URN-ish

burnish
furnish

refurnish
unfurnish(ed)

URN-it-ē
(See URN-ud-ē)

URN-ō

Sterno

inferno

URN-owt

burnout
churn out
turnout

URNT

burnt
learnt
weren't

URN-u-bul

burnable
churnable
earnable
learnable
spurnable
turnable
yearnable

adjournable
discernible
returnable
unlearnable

indiscernible
overturnable

URN-ud-ē

discernity
eternity
fraternity
maternity
modernity
paternity

taciturnity

URN-ul

colonel
journal
kernel
vernal

external
eternal
fraternal
infernal
internal
maternal
nocturnal
paternal

chicken colonel
daily journal

URN-ul-īz

journalize

externalize
internalize

URN-um

burn 'em
churn 'em
durn 'em
earn 'em
learn 'em
spurn 'em
sternum
turn 'em

URN-ur

burner
churner
durn 'er
earner
learner
Lerner
sterner
spurner
turner

yearner

adjourner
bra-burner
back burner
barn-burner
concern 'er
discerner
front burner
returner
slow learner
sojourner
wage earner

butter churner
Bunsen burner
money earner
overturner
pancake turner

URN-us

burn us
durn us
earn us
furnace
learn us
spurn us

adjourn us
blast furnace
concern us
discern us
return us

unconcern us

URN-ust

earnest
Ernest
sternest

ŪR-ō

bureau
Euro
neuro

Census Bureau
Politburo

UR-ō

burro
borough
burrow
furrow
thorough

Marlborough
unthorough

URP

burp
chirp
syrup
slurp
twerp

Antwerp
corn syrup
usurp

little twerp
maple syrup
Wyatt Earp

URP-ē

burpy
chirpy
herpe(s)
syrupy
slurpy

URP-ēng

burping
chirping
slurping
twerping

usurping

URP-en-tīn
(See URP-un-tīn)

URPT

burped
chirped
slurped

excerpt
usurped

URP-un-tīn

serpentine
turpentine

URP-us

burp us
purpose
syrup us

all-purpose
cross-purpose
on purpose
usurp us

multipurpose

URS

curse
hearse
nurse
purse
terse
verse
worse

averse
asperse
adverse
accurse
blank verse
coerce
commerce
converse
disburse
disperse
diverse

inverse
immerse
obverse
perverse
reverse
rehearse
submerse
traverse
transverse
wet nurse

intersperse
reimburse
universe

chapter and verse
doggerel verse

for better or worse

URS-ē

Circe
mercy
nursey
Percy

at one's mercy
controversy

angel of mercy

URS-en
(See URS-un)

URS-ēng

cursing
nursing
pursing
versing

coercing
conversing
disbursing
dispersing
immersing
reversing

rehearsing
submersing
traversing
transversing

interspersing
reimbursing

UR-shul

commercial
coertial
inertial

UR-shun

assertion
desertion
exertion
insertion

disconcertion

overexertion

URS-i-bul
(See URS-u-bul)

URS-it-ē
(See URS-ud-ē)

URS-iv

cursive

aversive
coercive
conversive
diversive
discursive
inversive
perversive
subversive

URS-ment

coercement
disbursement

dispersement
perversement

interspersement
reimbursement

URST

burst
cursed
erst
first
Hearst
nursed
pursed
thirst
versed
worst

accursed
Amherst
at worst
bratwurst
coerced
conversed
cloudburst
disbursed
dispersed
feetfirst
headfirst
immersed
knackwurst
lips pursed
outburst
reversed
rehearsed
sunburst
submersed
traversed
unversed
well-versed

die of thirst
interspersed
ladies first
liverwurst
reimbursed

safety first
unrehearsed
untraversed

if worst comes to
worst

URST-ē

first tee
thirsty
worse tea

bloodthirsty

URST-ēng

bursting
thirsting

URS-u-bul

cursable
nursable

coercible
conversible
disbursible
dispersible
immersible
reversible
rehearsable
submersible
traversable

interspersible
reimbursible

URS-ud-ē

adversity
diversity
perversity

multiversity
university

URS-ul

disbursal
dispersal
rehearsal
reversal

dress rehearsal
role reversal
universal

URS-un

cursin'
nursin'
pursin'
person
versin'
worsen

chairperson
coercin'
conversin'
disbursin'
dispersin'
immersin'
layperson
MacPherson
nonperson
reversin'
rehearsin'
spokesperson
traversin'

anchor person
displaced person
interspersin'
reimbursin'

person-to-person

URS-ur

cursor
curser
Mercer
nurser
purser

terser
verser
worser

coercer
converser
disburser
disperser
diverser
immerser
precursor
perverser
reverser
rehearser
submerser
traverser
transverser

intersperser
reimburser

URS-ur-ē

cursory
nursery
tersory

coercery

anniversary

URS-us

curse us
nurse us
versus

coerce us
disperse us
reverse us
rehearse us

reimburse us

URS-ut-ē
(See URS-ud-ē)

URT

blurt
Bert
curt
Cert(s)
dirt
flirt
hurt
pert
squirt
shirt
spurt
skirt

assert
avert
alert
covert
convert
divert
desert
dessert
exert
eat dirt
avert
Frankfurt
hair shirt
insert
inert
invert
nightshirt
overt
pay dirt
pervert
redshirt
revert
subvert
stuffed shirt
unhurt

controvert
dish the dirt
disconcert
extrovert
hula skirt

introvert
lose one's shirt
miniskirt
red alert
smog alert
underskirt
undershirt

animadvert
overexert
yellow alert

URT-ē
(See URD-ē)

URT-ēng
(See URD-ēng)

URT -ē-us
(See URD-ē-us)

URTH

birth
berth
dearth
earth
firth
girth
mirth
Perth
worth

childbirth
Fort Worth
net worth
rebirth
self-worth
stillbirth
unearth
Woolworth
Wordsworth

afterbirth
down-to-earth

Leavenworth
money's worth
what on earth?

for all it's worth
heaven on earth
salt of the earth

move heaven and
    earth

URTH-ē

earthy
girthy
mirthy

URTHE-ē

worthy
blameworthy
noteworthy
newsworthy
praiseworthy
unworthy

URTH-ēng

birthing

unearthing

URTH-lus

berthless
girthless
mirthless
worthless

URT-i-bul
(See URD-u-bul)

URT-il
(See URD-ul)

URT-iv

furtive

assertive
concertive
divertive
exertive
invertive
revertive
unfurtive

extrovertive
introvertive
self-assertive

URT-ub-ul
(See URD-ub-ul)

URT-ud
(See URD-ud)

URT-ul
(See URD-ul)

URT-un

Burton
blurtin'
curtain
certain
flirtin'
hurtin'
squirtin'
spurtin'
skirtin'

assertin'
avertin'
alertin'
convertin'
divertin'
exertin'
for certain
invertin'

make certain
pervertin'
redshirtin'
revertin'
subvertin'
uncertain

bamboo curtain
blackout curtain
disconcertin'
final curtain
iron curtain

ring down the curtain

URT-ur
(See URD-ur)

UR-ū

guru
Peru

ŪR-ub-ul

curable
durable

assurable
endurable
incurable
insurable
procurable
securable

unsecurable
uninsurable
unendurable

ŪR-ud-ē

Curity
purity
surety

impurity
maturity

obscurity
security
unsurety

immaturity
insecurity
prematurity

lack of security
social security

UR-uj
(See UR-ij)

ŪR-ul

mural
neural
plural
rural

intramural

UR-ul

conferral
deferral
referral

ŪR-un

curin'
lurin'
moorin'
tourin'
Turin
urine

assurin'
allurin'
contourin'
detourin'
endurin'
inurin'
maturin'

obscurin'

procurin'
securin'
Van Buren

ŪR-uns

assurance
endurance
insurance
procurance

life insurance
reassurance
self-assurance

UR-unt

current
currant

concurrent
crosscurrent
deterrent
referent
recurrent

undercurrent

UR-up

stirrup
stir up
syrup
were up

ŪR-ur

curer
furor
juror
lurer
poorer
purer
surer
tourer

assurer
allurer

contourer
demurer
ensurer
endurer
grand juror
insurer
maturer
obscurer
procurer
securer
unsurer

immaturer
insecurer
manicurer
reassurer

UR-ur

purrer
stirrer
slurrer
spurrer
whirrer

concurrer
conferrer
deferrer
deterrer
inferrer
preferrer
transferrer

ŪR-us

cure us
lure us

assure us
endure us
Honduras
insure us
obscure us

Epicurus

URV

curve
nerve
serve
swerve
verve

conserve
deserve
hors d'oeuvre
observe
preserve
reserve
subserve
self-serve
unnerve

brown-and-serve
gold reserve
in reserve
on the curve
throw a curve

bundle of nerve(s)
first-come first-
    serve(d)

URVD

curved
served
swerved

conserved
deserved
observed
preserved
reserved
unnerved

unreserved
well-preserved

first-come first-served

URV-ē

curvy
nervy

scurvy
swervy

topsy-turvy

URV-ēng

curving
Irving
serving
swerving

conserving
deserving
observing
preserving
reserving
self-serving
unnerving

**URV-ent
(See URV-unt)**

**URV-is
(See URV-us)**

URV-ish

curvish
dervish

observish

whirling dervish

**URV-u-div
(See URV-u-tiv)**

URV-un-sē

fervency

conservancy
observancy

URV-unt

fervent
servant

maidservant
manservant
observant

civil servant
unobservant

URV-ur

curver
fervor
server
swerver

conserver
deserver
observer
preserver
reserver
unnerver

life preserver
process server

URV-us

nervous
service
serve us

disservice
deserve us
lip service
maid service
observe us
preserve us
room service
reserve us
self-service
unnerve us
unnervous
wire service
civil service

out of service
saints preserve us
secret service

URV-u-tiv

conservative
preservative

archconservative

URV-u-tōr-ē

conservatory
observatory

URX

clerks
dirks
irks
jerks
kirks
lurks
perks
quirks
smirks
shirks
Turks
works

fireworks
reworks
skunk works
waxworks

in the works
overworks
shoot the works

URZH-un

Persian
version

aspersion
aversion
coercion

conversion
diversion
dispersion
emersion
excursion
immersion
incursion
inversion
perversion
recursion
reversion
short version
subversion
submersion

cast aspersion(s)
extroversion
introversion

holiday excursion

ŪS

Bruce
deuce
goose
juice
loose
moose
mousse
noose
puce
ruse
spruce
sluice
truce
use
Zeus

abuse
abstruse
au jus
adduce
burnoose
Bull Moose
caboose
cayuse

cooked goose
chartreuse
chanteuse
deduce
disuse
diffuse
educe
excuse
footloose
gone goose
hang loose
hangnoose
induce
misuse
masseuse
mongoose
no use
obtuse
profuse
papoose
produce
refuse
reduce
recluse
Spruce Goose
seduce
turn loose
traduce
Toulouse
unloose
vamoose
wild goose

Ballet Russe
Christmas goose
child abuse
call a truce
calaboose
charlotte russe
cook one's goose
disabuse
Dr. Seuss
fast and loose
hangman's noose
introduce

lemon juice
Mother Goose
mass-produce
no excuse
out of use
orange juice
on the loose
overuse
reproduce
silly goose
what's the use?

chocolate mousse
hypotenuse
have a screw loose
no earthly use
overproduce
put to good use

stew in one's own
   juice

US

bus
buss
cuss
fuss
muss
pus
plus
truss
thus
us

cost-plus
discuss
nonplus
school bus

blunderbus
between us
gloomy Gus
minibus
make a fuss

no muss, no fuss

ÛS

puss
schuss

sourpuss

drizzlepuss
glamourpuss
octopus
omnibus
Oedipus
picklepuss
platypus

ŪS-ē

goosy
juicy
Lucy
moosey
U.C.
who see
you see

DeBussy

acey-deucy

US-ē

fussy
gussy
hussy
mussy

ŪS-en
(See ŪS-un)

ŪS-ēng

goosing
juicing
sprucing
sluicing

adducing
deducing

educing
inducing
producing
reducing
seducing
traducing
unloosing

introducing
mass-producing
reproducing

overproducing

US-ēng

busing
bussing
cussing
fussing
mussing
trussing

discussing

US-et
(See US-ut)

ŪS-ful

useful

abuseful
induceful

ŪSH

douche
swoosh
whoosh

cartouche

USH

blush
brush
crush

flush
gush
hush
lush
mush
plush
rush
slush
shush
thrush

agush
airbrush
ablush
bulrush
bum's rush
cheek blush
clothes brush
gold rush
hush-hush
hairbrush
onrush
paintbrush
sagebrush
straight flush
toothbrush

at first blush
bottlebrush
royal flush
underbrush

ÛSH

bush
push
shoosh
tush
whoosh

ambush
rosebush

beat around the bush

ŪSH-ē

mooshy
swooshy
sushi

USH-ē

gushy
mushy
plushy
slushy

ÛSH-ē

bushy
cushy
gushy
pushy
tushie

ŪSH-ēng

douching
swooshing
whooshing

USH-ēng

blushing
brushing
crushing
flushing
gushing
hushing
mushing
rushing
slushing
shushing

airbrushing
bone-crushing
toothbrushing

ÛSH-ēng

Cushing
pushing

shooshing
whooshing

ambushing

USHT

blushed
brushed
crushed
flushed
gushed
hushed
mushed
rushed
slushed
shushed

airbrushed

ÛSHT

bushed
pushed
shooshed
whooshed

ŪSH-u

fuchsia

minutia

USH-u
(See USH-yu)

USH-u-bul

brushable
crushable
flushable
gushable
hushable
rushable
shushable

ŪSH-un

douchin'
swooshin'
whooshin'

ablution
Aleutian
Confucian
dilution
locution
pollution
solution

air pollution
absolution
attribution
contribution
convolution
constitution
distribution
diminution
dissolution
destitution
evolution
elocution
execution
institution
Lilliputian
persecution
prosecution
prostitution
retribution
resolution
revolution
restitution
smog pollution
substitution

circumlocution
electrocution
redistribution
water pollution

counterrevolution
marriage dissolution
New Year's resolution

stay of execution
U.S. Constitution

USH-un

blushin'
brushin'
crushin'
flushin'
gushin'
hushin'
mushin'
Prussian
rushin'
Russian
slushin'
shushin'

bone-crushin'
concussion
discussion
percussion

repercussion

ÛSH-un

cushion
pushin'
shooshin'
whooshin'

ambushin'
pincushion

whoopee cushion

ÛSH-un-ar-ē

evolutionary
revolutionary

ÛSH-un-ist

douchin'est

evolutionist
revolutionist

ÛSH-un-ul

constitutional
distributional
evolutional
institutional

USH-ur

blusher
brusher
crusher
flusher
gusher
husher
lusher
musher
plusher
rusher
slusher
shusher
usher

bone crusher
four-flusher
oil gusher

movie usher
toilet flusher

ÛSH-ur

pusher
shoosher

ambusher
dope pusher

pedal pusher(s)

ÛSH-us

douche us
Lucius
swoosh us

Confucius

USH-us

brush us
crush us
hush us
luscious
rush us
shush us

USH-yu

brush ya
crush ya
Prussia
Russia
rush ya
shush ya

ŪS-i-bul
(See ŪS-u-bul)

ŪS-i-fur

crucifer
Lucifer

ŪS-iv

abusive
allusive
conducive
collusive
conclusive
diffusive
delusive
elusive
exclusive
effusive
infusive
illusive
intrusive
inclusive
obtrusive
occlusive
profusive
protrusive

preclusive
reclusive
seclusive

inconclusive
unobtrusive

USK

brusque
dusk
husk
musk
tusk

cornhusk
dehusk

USK-ē

dusky
husky
musky

Siberian husky

US-lur

bustler
hustler
muscler
rustler
tussler

ŪS-ō

blew so
Crusoe
do so
knew so
trousseau
you sow
you sew

Caruso

ŪST

boost
deuced
goosed
juiced
loosed
roost
sluiced
spruced

adduced
deduced
educed
induced
produced
reduced
seduced
unloosed
vamoosed

chicken roost
introduced
mass-produced
reproduced
rule the roost
self-induced

come home to roost
overproduced
underproduced

UST

bust
bussed
bused
cussed
crust
dust
fussed
gust
just
lust
must
mussed
plussed

rust
trust
trussed
thrust

adjust
august
a must
beer bust
brain-trust
coal dust
combust
crop-dust
distrust
drug bust
discussed
disgust
encrust
entrust
gold dust
mistrust
nonplussed
pie crust
robust
stardust
sawdust
tongue-thrust
unjust
unmussed
untrussed

angel dust
antitrust
breach of trust
boom-or-bust
bite the dust
dry as dust
public trust
readjust
uppercrust
undiscussed
wanderlust

UST-ē

busty
crusty

dusty
gusty
lusty
musty
rusty
trusty
trustee

ŪST-ēng

boosting
roosting

UST-ēng

busting
crusting
dusting
gusting
lusting
rusting
trusting
thrusting

adjusting
combusting
crop-dusting
distrusting
disgusting
entrusting
encrusting
mistrusting

readjusting

UST-i-bul
(See UST-u-bul)

ŪST-ik

blue stick
do stick
new stick

acoustic

UST-is
(See UST-us)

UST-lur
(See US-lur)

UST-ment

adjustment

maladjustment
readjustment

UST-rē-us

industrious
illustrious

UST-ub-ul

bustable
dustable
lustable
rustable
trustable

combustible

noncombustible

ŪST-ud

boosted
roosted

UST-ud

busted
crusted
dusted
gusted
lusted
rusted
trusted

adjusted
combusted

distrusted
disgusted
entrusted
encrusted
mistrusted

flat-out busted
readjusted

UST-um

bust 'em
custom
dust 'em
thrust 'em
trust 'em

accustom
distrust 'em
discussed 'em
mistrust 'em

readjust 'em
unaccustom

ŪST-un

boostin'
Houston
roostin'

ŪST-ur

booster
Brewster
goosed 'er
rooster
Schuster
Worcester

induced 'er
produced 'er
reduced 'er
seduced 'er

UST-ur

buster
bluster

cluster
Custer
duster
fluster
juster
luster
muster
ruster
truster
thruster

auguster
adjuster
backbuster
ball-buster
blockbuster
crop duster
crimebuster
Dustbuster
discussed 'er
disgust 'er
distruster
entruster
fuzzbuster
gangbuster
lackluster
mistruster
pass muster
robuster
sodbuster
trustbuster
unjuster

bronco buster
filibuster
feather duster

UST-urd

blustered
clustered
custard
flustered
mustered
mustard

egg custard

unflustered

cut the mustard

UST-ur-ē

blustery
clustery
flustery

UST-ur-ēng

blustering
clustering
flustering
mustering

UST-us

bust us
bussed us
bused us
cussed us
dust us
justice
just us
mussed us
rust us
trust us
trussed us

Augustus
chief justice
distrust us
discussed us
disgust us
injustice
mistrust us
nonplussed us

Hall of Justice

poetic justice

miscarriage of justice

ŪS-u

Azusa
Medusa

Appaloosa
Bogalusa

ŪS-u-bul

crucible
goosable

deducible
inducible
producible
reducible
seducible

introducible
irreducible
mass-producible
reproducible

ŪS-u-fur
(See ŪS-i-fur)

US-ul

bustle
Brussel(s)
hustle
muscle
mussel
Russell
rustle
tussle

corpuscle

flex one's muscle(s)
hustle bustle

ŪS-um

blew some
brew some
chew some
do some
drew some
gruesome
grew some

goose 'em
knew some
rue some
sue some
stew some
slew some
screw some
threw some
through some
to some
twosome
woo some

accrue some
deduce 'em
induce 'em
outgrew some
produce 'em
pursue some
run through some
renew some
redo some
reduce 'em
subdue some
seduce 'em
tattoo some
undo some
unscrew some
withdrew some

mass-produce 'em
misconstrue some
overthrew some
reproduce 'em

ŪS-un

goosin'
loosen
sprucin'
sluicin'

adducin'
deducin'
inducin'
producin'
Rasmussen

reducin'
seducin'
traducin'
unloosen

introducin'
mass-producin'
reproducin'

overproducin'

US-unt

mustn't

discussant

ŪS-ur

gooser
juicer
looser
sprucer
you, sir

deducer
inducer
obtuser
profuser
producer
reducer
seducer
vamooser

introducer
mass-producer

US-ur

busser
cusser
fusser
muss 'er

discusser

US-ut

bus it
buss it

cuss it
gusset
muss it
russet
truss it

ŪT

beaut
boot
butte
brute
cute
chute
coot
flute
fruit
hoot
jute
loot
lute
moot
mute
newt
root
route
scoot
shoot
snoot
suit
toot
zoot

acute
astute
Beirut
breadfruit
cheroot
crapshoot
commute
compute
confute
deaf mute
dispute
dilute
en route

en croûte
file suit
galoot
grapefruit
hirsute
impute
jumpsuit
lawsuit
long suit
minute
mail route
offshoot
outshoot
patoot
pollute
pursuit
permute
refute
repute
recruit
salute
strong suit
square root
spacesuit
trade route
to boot
trump suit
tribute
trapshoot
transmute
uproot
wet suit
zoot suit

absolute
attribute
arrowroot
birthday suit
bet your boot(s)
bathing suit
constitute
convolute
cowboy boot
chute-the-chute
disrepute

dissolute
diving suit
destitute
Denver boot
execute
follow suit
hot pursuit
in cahoot(s)
ice-cream suit
involute
institute
ill repute
leisure suit
laundry chute
malemute
monkey suit
overshoot
passionfruit
parachute
Puss in Boot(s)
prostitute
prosecute
persecute
retribute
resolute
restitute
substitute
tutti-fruit
troubleshoot
turkey shoot
three-piece suit
undershoot

alternate route
class action suit
electrocute
forbidden fruit
irresolute
not give a hoot
not worth a hoot
reconstitute

house of ill repute
Trivial Pursuit

twenty-one gun salute

UT

but
butt
cut
glut
gut
hut
jut
mutt
nut
putt
rut
shut
strut
slut
smut
tut

all but
abut
clear-cut
catgut
clean-cut
crewcut
cold cut(s)
chestnut
haircut
King Tut
low-cut
precut
putt-putt
rebut
recut
rough cut
rotgut
shortcut
uncut
woodcut

butternut
bust a gut
coconut
hazelnut
halibut
in a rut

Lilliput
nothing but
paper cut
pitch-and-putt
scuttlebutt
stingy gut
split a gut
undercut
uppercut

anything but
cigarette butt
emerald cut
open-and-shut

ŪT

foot
put
root
soot
toot(s)

afoot
Blackfoot
Bigfoot
barefoot
caput
crow's foot
clubfoot
flatfoot
hotfoot
hard-put
input
kaput
light foot
lead foot
output
square foot
six foot
slewfoot
stay put
square root
shotput
uproot

webfoot
athlete's foot
gingerroot
hand and foot
pussyfoot
rabbit's foot
tenderfoot
underfoot

ŪTCH
(See ŪCH)

UTCH
(See UCH)

ŪT-ē
(See ŪD-ē)

UT-ē
(See UD-ē)

ÛT-ē
(See ÛD-ē)

ÛT-ed
(See ÛD-ud)

ŪT-ēng
(See ŪD-ēng)

UT-ēng
(See UD-ēng)

ÛT-ēng
(See ÛD-ēng)

ŪT-ē-us
(See ŪD-ē-us)

ŪTH

booth
couth
Ruth
sleuth
sooth
tooth
truth
youth

Babe Ruth
bucktooth
Duluth
eyetooth
forsooth
false tooth
half-truth
phone booth
sawtooth
sweet tooth
shark's tooth
toll booth
uncouth
untruth
vermouth
whole truth

baby tooth
gospel truth
kissing booth
naked truth
polling booth
snaggletooth
supersleuth
sabertooth
voting booth
wisdom tooth

fountain of youth
moment of truth
projection booth
telephone booth

nothing but the truth

ŪTH-ē

Ruthie
sleuthy
toothy

ŪTHE

soothe
smooth

UTHE-ur

brother
druther(s)
mother
'nother
other
smother

another
blood brother
big brother
each other
Earth Mother
godmother
housemother
none other
oh, brother
queen mother
stepmother
some other

any other
Holy Mother
one another
Ringling Brother(s)
Whistler's Mother

one or another
somehow or other

one thing or another
one way or the other
significant other

ŪTH-ful

sleuthful
toothful
truthful
youthful

uncouthful
untruthful

ŪTH-lus

boothless
couthless
ruthless
toothless
truthless
youthless

ŪTH-ur

couther
Luther
sleuther

uncouther

ŪT-i-ful
(See ŪD-i-ful)

ŪT-ik
(See ŪD-ik)

ŪT-i-kul
(See ŪD-i-kul)

ŪT-in
(See ŪT-un)

ŪT-in-ē

mutiny
scrutiny

UT-in-ē

buttony
gluttony
muttony

ŪT-ist
(See ŪD-ist)

UT-lur

butler
subtler
shuttler

silent butler

UT-lur-ē

butlery
cutlery

ŪT-lus

bootless
chuteless
fruitless
rootless

recruitless

ŪT-ō
(See ŪD-ō)

UT-owt

butt out
cut out
gut out
jut out
shutout

UTS

buts
butts
cuts

futz
guts
gluts
huts
juts
klutz
mutts
nuts
putts
ruts
shuts
Stutz
struts
sluts
schmutz
tuts

abuts
cold cuts
chestnuts
crewcuts
Grape Nuts
precuts
putt-putts
recuts
rebuts
shortcuts
woodcuts
walnuts

blood and guts
coconuts
nothing buts
paper cuts
spill one's guts
stingy guts
undercuts
uppercuts

cigarette butts
emerald cuts
from soup to nuts

no ifs, ands, or buts

ŪT-sē

footsie
tootsie

play footsie

ŪT-ub-ul
(See ŪD-ub-ul)

ŪT-ud
(See ŪD-ud)

UT-ud
(See UD-ud)

ÛT-ud
(See ÛD-ud)

ŪT-ul
(See ŪD-ul)

UT-ul
(See UD-ul)

ŪT-un

bootin'
hootin'
lootin'
mutin'
rootin'
scootin'
tootin'

commutin'
computin'
darn tootin'
dilutin'
disputin'
pollutin'
Rasputin
recruitin'

refutin'
reputin'
salutin'
transmutin'
trapshootin'
uprootin'

highfalutin

UT-un

button
buttin'
cuttin'
glutton
mutton
nuttin
puttin'
Sutton

push button
unbutton

bellybutton
E. F. Hutton
leg-of-mutton
on the button
panic button

ŪT-un-ē
(See ŪT-in-ē)

UT-un-ē
(See UT-in-ē)

UT-up

cutup
jut up
strut up
shut up

ŪT-ur
(See ŪD-ur)

ŪT-ur
(See UD-ur)

ŪT-ur-ē
(See UD-ur-ē)

ŪT-ur-ēng
(See UD-ur-ēng)

UT-ur-ēng
(See UD-ur-ēng)

ŪT-ur-us
(See ŪD-ur-us)

ŪT-us
(See ŪD-us)

Ū-u-bul

brewable
chewable
doable
suable
screwable
viewable

accruable
construable
ensuable
eschewable
pursuable
reviewable
renewable
redoable
shampooable
subduable
undoable
unscrewable

Ū-ud

druid
fluid

Ū-ud-ē

annuity
congruity
circuity
fortuity
gratuity
vacuity

ambiguity
contiguity
continuity
exiguity
ingenuity
incongruity
promiscuity
perpetuity
superfluity

Ū-ud-us

circuitous
fortuitous
gratuitous

Ū-ul

cruel
crewel
duel
dual
fuel
gruel
jewel
who'll
you'll

accrual
bejewel
crown jewel
pursual
renewal

subdual
uncruel

family jewel(s)
license renewal
urban renewal

Ū-ul-ē
(See ŪL-ē)

Ū-un

bruin
brewin'
crewin'
chewin'
doin'
ruin
ruin'
screwin'
shoein'
suin'
wooin'

accruin'
construin'
ensuin'
mildewin'
outdoin'
pursuin'
renewin'
redoin'
shampooin'
subduin'
tattooin'
undoin'
unscrewin'

misconstruin'
overdoin'
peek-a-booin'
rendezvousin'
rack and ruin

Ū-uns

affluence
congruence
confluence
influence
pursuance

incongruence

Ū-un-sē

fluency
truancy

affluency
congruency

incongruency

Ū-unt

fluent
truant

affluent
congruent
confluent
pursuant

incongruent

Ū-un-us

booin' us
cuin' us
doin' us
ruinous
ruin us
suin' us
screwin' us
viewin' us

Ū-ur
(See also ŪR)

bluer
brewer
boo 'er

cooer
chewer
doer
dour
drew 'er
ewer
fewer
gluer
knew 'er
newer
ruer
sewer
suer
screwer
shoer
stewer
skewer
truer
threw 'er
to 'er
viewer
who're
wooer
you're

construer
ensuer
horseshoer
into 'er
manure
outdoer
outgrew 'er
pursuer
renewer
redoer
reviewer
shampooer
subduer
tattooer
undoer
unscrewer
withdrew 'er
wrongdoer

barbecuer
countersuer

evildoer
horse manure
interviewer
misconstruer
overdoer
overdue 'er
overthrew 'er
revenuer

entrepreneur

Ū-urd

steward
skewered

Ū-us

cue us
due us
do us
drew us
flew us
knew us
Louis
pooh us
sue us
screw us
threw us
through us
view us
woo us

imbue us
miscue us
outgrew us
outdo us
pursue us
review us
shampoo us
St. Louis
subdue us
see through us
undo us

Ū-u-sīd

blew aside
drew aside
suicide
threw aside

Ū-ut

blew it
brew it
chew it
cruet
do it
drew it
flew it
glue it
grew it
knew it
rue it
suet
screw it
to it
threw it
through it
view it

accrue it
can do it
conduit
go to it
imbue it
into it
live through it
misdo it
outgrew it
pass through it
pull through it
pursue it
review it
run through it
renew it
shampoo it
subdue it
undo it

walk through it
withdrew it

Ū-ut-us
(See Ū-ud-us)

ŪV

groove
hoove(s)
move
prove
who've
you've

amove
approve
behoove
disprove
false move
improve
remove
reprove

disapprove
in the groove
on the move

UV

dove
glove
Gov
love
of
shove

above
hereof
kid glove
sort of
self-love
thereof
true love
white-glove
whereof

boxing glove
fall in love
get rid of
grow tired of
hand and glove
ladylove
puppy love
rise above
rubber glove
secret love
turtledove
unheard of
up above
well-thought-of

a cut above
brotherly love
fit like a glove
in favor of
illicit love
labor of love
motherly love
make a mess of
push comes to shove
platonic love
tunnel of love

none of the above
over and above

ŪVD

grooved
hooved
moved
proved

approved
behooved
disproved
improved
removed
reproved

disapproved
once removed

unapproved
unimproved

UVD

gloved
loved
shoved

beloved

ŪV-ē

groovy
movie

UV-ē

covey
dovey
lovey
shovey

lovey-dovey

UV-el
(See UV-ul)

UV-en
(See UV-un)

ŪV-ēng

grooving
moving
proving

approving
behooving
disproving
improving
removing
reproving

disapproving

UV-ēng

loving
shoving

everloving

UV-et
(See UV-ut)

ŪV-ē-ul

fluvial

alluvial
effluvial

ŪV-ment

movement

improvement

bowel movement
self-improvement

ŪV-u-bul

groovable
movable
provable

approvable
disprovable
immovable
improvable
removable
reprovable

ŪV-ul

approval
removal
reproval

disapproval
on approval

UV-ul

grovel
hovel
shovel

steam shovel

UV-ul-ēng

groveling
shoveling

UV-un

coven
lovin'
oven
shovin'
sloven

ŪV-ur

groover
Hoover
louver
mover
prover

approver
behoove 'er
disprover
earthmover
improver
maneuver
prime mover
reprove 'er
remover
Vancouver

disapprover
Herbert Hoover
outmaneuver
people mover
stain remover

Heimlich maneuver
polish remover

UV-ur

cover
hover
lover
love 'er
of her
shover

above 'er
book cover
book lover
cloud cover
dustcover
ground cover
hardcover
recover
slipcover
take cover
uncover

blow one's cover
rise above 'er
run for cover
red-hot lover
undercover
up above 'er

UV-urd

covered
hovered

recovered
uncovered

UV-ur-ē

discovery
recovery

UV-ur-ēng

covering
hovering

recovering
uncovering

UV-ut

covet
love it
of it
shove it

above it

rise above it
up above it

in favor of it

over and above it

UX

bucks
crux
chucks
clucks
ducks
flux
lucks
lux
plucks
pucks
shucks
sucks
schmucks
tux
tucks
trucks

aw-shucks
big bucks
deluxe
dumb clucks
dump trucks
fire trucks
influx
lame ducks
mukluks
potlucks
sawbucks
upchucks
woodchucks

hockey pucks
million bucks
megabucks
tummy-tucks

ÛX

books
brooks
cooks
crooks
hooks
looks
nooks
rooks
schnooks
snooks

Chinooks
outlooks
songbooks
unhooks

backward looks
comic books
cozy nooks
donnybrooks
dirty looks
hit the books
knowing looks
overlooks
overcooks
pocketbooks
tenterhooks

one for the books

UX-um

buxom
bucks 'em
chucks 'em
ducks 'em
plucks 'em
shucks 'em
sucks 'em
tucks 'em

Ū-yu

countersue ya
cotton to ya
due ya
do ya
give it to ya
give in to ya
hallelujah
interview ya
knew ya
miscue ya
outgrew ya
outdo ya
overdue ya
overthrew ya
pooh-pooh ya
pursue ya
review ya
redo ya
shampoo ya
subdue ya
see through ya
screw ya
sue ya
threw ya
through ya
to ya

ŪZ

boos
blues
brews
booze
bruise
cues
choose
Cruz
cruise
clues
crews
chews
do's
dues
fuse

glues
gnus
Hughes
hues
Jews
lose
moos
muse
mews
news
ooze
poohs
pews
queues
rues
ruse
spews
shoes
snooze
shrews
sues
stews
screws
twos
use
views
whose
woos
who's
yous
zoos

abuse
amuse
accuse
ados
adieus
accrues
ah-choos
bad news
boo-hoos
boo-boos
bemuse
bamboos
bayous

confuse
curfews
church pews
construes
chanteuse
choo-choos
chartreuse
charmeuse
canoes
cashews
corkscrews
cuckoos
defuse
diffuse
disuse
excuse
effuse
ensues
enthuse
eschews
froufrous
flight crews
gurus
gumshoes
good news
horseshoes
infuse
kazoos
lean-tos
muumuus
milieus
masseuse
make news
misuse
miscues
pooh-poohs
peruse
pursues
refuse
revues
reviews
renews
subdues
shampoos
snowshoes

suffuse
short fuse
transfuse
tutus
thumbscrews
to-dos
tattoos
taboos
unscrews
unglues
venues
voodoos
yahoos

avenues
ballyhoos
born to lose
buckaroos
baby shoes
baby blues
BTUs
blow a fuse
barbecues
caribous
cleaning crews
cockatoos
derring-dos
dancing shoes
double u's
disabuse
high-heeled shoes
honeydews
ingenues
in the news
interviews
kangaroos
misconstrues
nose for news
p's and q's
peek-a-boos
pick and choose
parvenus
pay one's dues
revenues
rendezvous

residues
retinues
Syracuse
sing the blues
Santa Cruz
sneak previews
win or lose
wrecking crews
Waterloos

corrective shoes
fill someone's shoes
hullabaloos
poo poo pee doos
membership dues
mulligan stews
skeleton crews
rhythm and blues

cock-a-doodle-doos
Caribbean cruise
elevator shoes
musical reviews
panoramic views

an offer one can't
   refuse

UZ

buzz
cuz
coz
does
fuzz
scuzz
'twas
was

abuzz
becuz

ŪZD

boozed
bruised
cruised

fused
mused
oozed
snoozed
used

abused
amused
accused
bemused
confused
defused
diffused
excused
enthused
infused
misused
perused
refused
suffused
transfused
unused

disabused
new or used

ŪZ-ē

boozy
choosy
doozie
floozy
newsy
oozy
Suzie
woozy

Jacuzzi

UZ-ē

buzzy
does he?
fuzzy
hussy
scuzzy
was he?

UZ-en
(SeeUZ-un)

ŪZ-ēng

boozing
bruising
choosing
cruising
fusing
losing
oozing
snoozing
using

abusing
amusing
accusing
bemusing
confusing
defusing
diffusing
excusing
infusing
misusing
perusing
refusing
suffusing
transfusing

disabusing
self-abusing

can't win for losing

cruising for a bruising

UZ-ēng

buzzing
fuzzing

defuzzing

ŪZH-un

fusion

allusion

confusion
conclusion
contusion
collusion
delusion
diffusion
effusion
exclusion
infusion
inclusion
illusion
intrusion
occlusion
obtrusion
perfusion
protrusion
preclusion
profusion
seclusion
transfusion

blood transfusion
disillusion
in conclusion
malocclusion

foregone conclusion

optical illusion

UZ-in
(See UZ-un)

UZ-lun

guzzlin'
muslin
muzzlin'
nuzzlin'
puzzlin'

UZ-lur

guzzler
muzzler
nuzzler

puzzler

gas guzzler

ŪZ-u

Sousa

Medusa

lalapalooza

ŪZ-ub-ul

bruisable
choosable
cruisable
fusable
losable
usable

abusable
amusable
accusable
confusable
defusable
diffusable
excusable
effusable
infusible
perusable
refusable
reusable
transfusible
unusable

inexcusable

ŪZ-ul

accusal
bamboozle
perusal
refusal

UZ-ul

guzzle
muzzle

nuzzle
puzzle

UZ-un

buzzin'
cousin
cozen
dozen
fuzzin'

abuzzin'

baker's dozen
country cousin
dime a dozen
kissing cousin

ŪZ-ur

bruiser
boozer
chooser
cruiser
cues 'er
fuser
glues 'er
loser
muser
oozer
snoozer
user
views 'er

abuser
amuser
accuser
bemuser
born loser
bad loser
confuser
defuser
drug user
diffuser
excuser
good loser
infuser

misuser
miscues 'er
nonuser
refuser
reviews 'er

child abuser
cabin cruiser
disabuser
interviews 'er
two-time loser

UZ-ur

buzzer
does 'er
fuzzer

ŪZ-ur-ē

usury

illusory

INDEX OF SOUNDS

ĀD-ist
(See ĀD-ust)
AD-ist
(See AD-ust)
AD-it
(See AD-ut)
AD-i-tūd
ĀD-iv
AD-ix
(See AD-ux)
ADJ
(See AJ)
AD-lē
ĀD-lēng
AD-lēng
AD-lur
ĀD-nus
AD-nus
ĀD-ō
AD-ō
ĀD-u
AD-u
ĀD-u-bul
AD-u-bul
ĀD-ud
AD-ud
AD-u-fī
AD-uk
AD-uk-lē
ĀD-ul
AD-ul
AD-uld
ĀD-ul-ēng
(See ĀD-lēng)
AD-ul-ēng
(See AD-lēng)
ĀD-um
AD-um
AD-um-ē
ĀD-un
AD-un
AD-un-ēng
ĀD-ur
AD-ur
AD-urd
AD-ur-ē
ĀD-ur-ēng

AD-ur-ēng
AD-ur-īz
AD-urn
AD-ur-ul
AD-ur-ur
ĀD-us
AD-us
ĀD-ust
AD-ust
AD-ut
AD-ux
Ā-est
(See Ā-ust)
ĀF
AF
AF-ē
ĀF-ēng
AF-ēng
AF-ik
(See AF-uk)
AF-i-kul
(See AF-u-kul)
AF-lēng
AFS
AFT
AFT-ē
AFT-ed
(See AFT-ud)
AFT-ēng
AFT-u-bul
AFT-ud
AFT-un
AFT-ur
AF-ub-lē
AF-u-bul
AF-uk
AF-u-kul
ĀF-ul
AF-ul
AF-uld
ĀF-ur
AF-ur
ĀG
AG
AG-ē
ĀG-en
(See ĀG-un)

AG-en
(See AG-un)
ĀG-ēng
AG-ēng
AG-ē-nus
AG-lēng
AG-nun
ĀG-ō
ĀG-runt
ĀG-u
AG-u-bul
AG-ud
ĀG-ul
AG-ul
AG-ul-ēng
(See AG-lēng)
ĀG-un
AG-un
AG-un-ē
AG-un-ist
AG-un-ul
ĀG-ur
AG-ur
AG-urd
ĀG-ur-ē
AG-ur-ēng
AG-urt
AG-ur-us
ĀG-us
AG-ut
Ā-ik
(See Ā-uk)
Ā-is
(See Ā-us)
Ā-i-tē
(See Ā-ud-ē)
ĀJ
AJ
ĀJ-ēng
ĀJ-es
(See ĀJ-us)
AJ-et
(See AJ-ut)
AJ-ik
AJ-ik-lē
AJ-il
(See AJ-ul)

AJ-in-ul
(See AJ-un-ul)
ĀJ-lus
ĀJ-ment
AJ-ud-ē
AJ-ul
ĀJ-un
AJ-un
AJ-un-ul
ĀJ-ur
AJ-ur
ĀJ-ur-ēng
ĀJ-us
ĀJ-us-lē
AJ-ut
AJ-u-tē
(See AJ-u-dē)
ĀJ-uz
ĀK
AK
ĀK-āt
AK-chur
AK-chū-ul
ĀK-ē
AK-ē
ĀK-en
(See ĀK-un)
AK-en
(See AK-un)
ĀK-ēng
AK-ēng
ĀK-ē-nus
AK-ē-nus
AK-et
(See AK-ut)
AK-et-ē
(See AK-ud-ē)
ĀK-ful
AK-ij
ĀK-il-ē
(See ĀK-ul-ē)
ĀK-in
(See ĀK-un)
AK-in
(See AK-un)
AK-ish

AK-it
(See AK-ut)
AK-lē
AK-lēng
AK-mē
AK-nē
AK-nus
ĀK-ō
ĀK-ō
ĀK-owt
AK-owt
AK-pot
AK-run
AKS
(See AX)
AK-shun
AK-shun-ul
AK-shus
AK-sun
(See AX-un)
ĀKT
AKT
AKT-ēng
AKT-ful
AKT-ī
AKT-i-bul
(See AKT-u-bul)
AKT-ik
AKT-i-kul
AKT-is
(See AKT-us)
AKT-iv
AKT-iv-nus
AKT-lē
(See AK-lē)
AKTS
(See AX)
AKT-u-bul
AKT-u-kul
(See AKT-i-kul)
AKT-ul
AKT-ur
AKT-ur-ē
AKT-us
AK-u-dē
AK-uj
(See AK-ij)

AK-ul
ĀK-u-lē
AK-ū-lur
ĀK-un
AK-un
AK-un-ēng
ĀK-up
AK-up
ĀK-ur
AK-ur
AK-urd
ĀK-ur-ē
AK-ur-ē
AK-ur-un
ĀK-us
AK-us
AK-ust
AK-ut
AK-ut-ē
(See AK-ud-ē)
AK-yū-lur
(See AK-ū-lur)
ĀL
(See also Ā-ul)
AL
ĀL-ā
AL-ā
ĀL-burd
ĀLD
Ā-lē
AL-ē
ĀL-ē-en
(See ĀL-ē-un)
AL-ē-ēng
AL-ek
(See AL-uk)
ĀL-em
(See ĀL-um)
Ā-lēn
ĀL-ēng
AL-ēng
AL-en-jur
AL-ens
(See AL-uns)
AL-ent
(See AL-unt)

ANS-el
(See ANS-ul)
ANS-el-ur
(See ANS-ul-ur)
ANS-ēng
AN-shē
AN-shul
(See AN-chul)
AN-shun
(See AN-chun)
ANS-ment
ANST
AN-sul
ANS-u-lot
AN-sul-ur
AN-sum
AN-sum-ur
AN-sur
AN-sur-us
ĀNT
ANT
ĀNT-ē
ANT-ē
ĀNT-ēng
ANT-ēng
ANTH-u
ANT-ik
ANT-ik-lē
ANT-is
(See ANT-us)
ANT-lur
ĀNTS
(See ĀNS)
ANTS
(See ANS)
ANTS-ē
(See ANS-ē)
ANT-u
ĀNT-ud
ANT-ud
ANT-uk
(See ANT-ik)
ANT-ul
ANT-u-lōp
ANT-um
ĀNT-ur
ANT-ur

ANT-ur-ēng
ANT-us
ĀNT-ust
AN-u
AN-u-bul
AN-u-dē
AN-u-gun
(See AN-i-gun)
AN-uk
(See AN-ik)
AN-u-kul
ĀN-ul
AN-ul
AN-ul-ēng
AN-ul-ist
AN-um
AN-u-mus
(See AN-i-mus)
AN-un
ĀN-ur
AN-ur
AN-urd
ĀN-ur-ē
AN-ur-ē
ĀN-us
AN-us
AN-us
AN-ut
AN-u-tē
(See AN-u-dē)
AN-ū-ul
ANX
AN-yul
AN-yun
AN-yū-ul
(See AN-ū-ul)
ANZ
ANZ-ē
ANZ-u
ANZ-us
Ā-of
Ā-on
ĀP
AP
AP-chur
AP-ē
ĀP-en
(See ĀP-un)

AP-en
(See AP-un)
ĀP-ēng
AP-ēng
AP-ē-nus
ĀP-ē-ur
AP-ē-ur
AP-id
(See AP-ud)
AP-i-lē
(See AP-u-lē)
ĀP-in
(See ĀP-un)
AP-in
(See AP-un)
ĀP-ist
AP-lē
AP-lēng
AP-lin
(See AP-lun)
AP-lun
ĀP-lus
AP-lus
ĀPS
APS
APS-ēng
AP-shun
ĀPT
APT
APT-lē
(See AP-lē)
APT-un
APT-ur
ĀP-u-bul
AP-ud
ĀP-ul
AP-ul
AP-uld
AP-u-lē
AP-ul-us
ĀP-un
AP-un
ĀP-ur
AP-ur
ĀP-ur-ē
ĀP-ur-ēng
ĀP-ur-us

ĀP-ust
(See ĀP-ist)
AR
(See also Ā-ur)
ÄR
AR-āt
ÄRB
ÄRB-ul
ÄRB-ur
ÄRB-urd
ÄRB-ur-ēng
ÄRCH
ÄRCH-ē
ÄRCH-ēng
ÄRCH-ur
ARD
ÄRD
ÄRD-ē
ÄRD-ed
(See ÄRD-ud)
ÄRD-en
(See ÄRD-un)
ÄRD-ēng
ÄRD-ent
(See ÄRD-unt)
ÄRD-ē-nus
ÄRD-ē-un
ÄRD-ik
ÄRD-i-kul
ÄRD-i-zun
ÄRD-lē
ÄRD-lus
ÄRD-ō
ARD-ū
ÄRD-u
ÄRD-ud
ÄRD-uk
(See ÄRD-ik)
ÄRD-u-kul
(See ÄRD-i-kul)
ÄRD-um
ÄRD-un
ÄRD-un-ēng
ÄRD-unt
ÄRD-ur
ÄRD-ur-dum
ÄRD-ur-ē

ÄRD-ur-ēng
ÄRD-ust
AR-ē
ÄR-e
AR-ēd
AR-ē-ēng
AR-ē-et
(See AR-ē-ut)
AR-e-fī
(See AR-u-fī)
AR-el
(See AR-ul)
ÄR-el
(See ÄR-ul)
AR-em
(See AR-um)
AR-en
(See AR-un)
AR-ēng
ÄR-ēng
AR-ēng-lē
AR-ent
(See AR-unt)
AR-en-ur
(See AR-un-ur)
ÄR-ē-ō
AR-e-sē
(See AR-u-sē)
AR-est
(See AR-ust)
AR-et
(See AR-ut)
AR-ē-u
AR-ē-ul
AR-ē-um
AR-ē-un
AR-ē-ur
ÄR-e-ur
AR-ē-us
AR-ē-ut
AR-ēz
ÄRF
AR-fõr
AR-ful
ÄR-gō
ÄR-gun

AR-i-bul
(See AR-u-bul)
AR-if
(See AR-uf).
AR-if-ī
(See AR-uf-ī)
AR-ij
AR-ik
(See AR-uk)
AR-i-ku
AR-ik-ul
AR-il
(See AR-ul)
AR-il-ē
(See AR-ul-ē)
AR-il-us
(See AR-ul-us)
AR-in
(See AR-un)
AR-i-nur
(See AR-u-nur)
AR-is
(See AR-us)
AR-ish
AR-ish-ēng
AR-ist
AR-is-un
Ā-rīt
AR-it
(See AR-ut)
AR-it-ē
(See AR-ud-ē)
AR-i-tõr-ē
(See AR-u-tõr-ē)
AR-it-u-bul
(See AR-ut-u-bul)
AR-i-tun
(See AR-u-tun)
AR-it-us
(See AR-ud-us)
ÄRJ
ÄRJ-ēng
ÄRJ-u-bul
ÄRJ-un
ÄRJ-ur
ÄRK
AR-kās

ÄRK-ē
ÄRK-en
(See ÄRK-un)
ÄRK-ēng
ÄRK-et
(See ÄRK-ut)
ÄRK-ik
ÄRK-le
ÄRK-nus
ÄRKT
ÄRK-ul
ÄRK-un
ÄRK-un-ēng
ÄRK-ur
ÄRK-us
ÄRK-ust
ÄRK-ut
ÄRL
ARL-ē
ÄRL-ē
ÄRL-ēng
AR-les
(See AR-lus)
ÄRL-et
(See ÄRL-ut)
AR-līn
ÄRL-ō
ÄRL-um
ÄRL-ur
AR-lus
ÄRL-ut
ÄRLZ
ÄRM
ÄRMD
ÄRM-ē
ÄRM-ēng
ÄRM-ent
(See ÄRM-unt)
ÄRM-ful
ÄRM-int
(See ÄRM-unt)
ÄRM-lus
AR-mun
ÄRM-un
ÄRM-unt
ÄRM-ur
ÄRN

ÄRN-ē
ÄRN-ish
ÄRN-ur
AR-nus
ÄR-nus
AR-ō
ÄR-ō
AR-ō-ēng
AR-ō-in
(See AR-ō-un)
Ä-rōl
AR-ō-un
ÄRP
ÄRP-ē
ÄRP-ist
ÄRP-ur
ÄRS
ÄRS-el
(See ÄRS-ul)
ÄRSH
ÄRSH-ul
ÄRS-i-tē
(See ÄRS-u-dē)
ÄRS-lē
ÄRS-u-dē
ÄRS-ul
ÄRS-un
ÄRT
ÄRT-ē
(See ÄRD-ē)
ÄRT-ed
(See ÄRD-ud)
ÄRT-en
(See ÄRT-un)
ÄRT-ēng
(See ÄRD-ēng)
ÄRT-ē-nus
(See ÄRD-ē-nus)
ÄRT-ik
(See ÄRD-ik)
ÄRT-ik-ul
(See ÄRD-ik-ul)
ÄRT-ist
(See ÄRD-ust)
ÄRT-iz-un
(See ÄRD-iz-un)
ÄRT-lē

ÄRT-lus
ÄRT-ment
ÄRT-nur
ÄRT-nus
ART-ō
ÄRT-rij
ÄRTS
ÄRT-u
(See ÄRD-u)
ÄRT-ud
(See ÄRD-ud)
ÄRT-um
(See ÄRD-um)
ÄRT-un
ÄRT-ur
(See ÄRD-ur)
ÄRT-ur-dum
(See ÄRD-ur-dum)
ÄRT-ur-ē
(See ÄRD-ur-ē)
ÄRT-ur-ēng
(See ÄRD-ur-ēng)
AR-u
ÄR-u
AR-ub
AR-u-bul
AR-ud
AR-u-dē
AR-ud-ēng
AR-u-div
AR-u-du-bul
AR-u-dus
AR-uf
AR-u-fī
AR-u-gon
AR-uk
AR-ul
ÄR-ul
AR-uld
AR-u-lē
AR-ul-ēng
AR-u-lus
AR-um
AR-um-ē
AR-un
AR-und
AR-un-et

AR-uns
AR-unt
AR-unts
(See AR-uns)
AR-un-ur
AR-unz
AR-ur
AR-us
ÄR-us
AR-u-sē
AR-u-sēng
AR-us-ment
ÄR-ust
(See ÄR-ist)
AR-us-un
(See AR-is-un)
AR-u-tē
(See AR-u-dē)
AR-ut
AR-ut-ēng
AR-u-tiv
(See AR-u-div)
AR-u-tõr-ē
AR-u-tu-bul
AR-u-tun
ÄRV
ÄRV-ēng
ÄRV-on
ÄRV-un
AR-wā
ÄRX
ÄS
AS
AS-ā
AS-chun
ÄS-ē
AS-ē
ÄS-ē-āt
(See ÄSH-ē-āt)
AS-el
(See AS-ul)
ÄS-en
(See ÄS-un)
AS-en
(See AS-un)
ÄS-ēng
AS-ēng

ÄS-ens
(See ÄS-uns)
ÄS-ent
(See ÄS-unt)
AS-ē-nus
AS-et
(See AS-ut)
AS-ez
(See AS-uz)
ÄS-ful
ASH
ASH-ē
ÄSH-ē-āt
ÄSH-en
(See ÄSH-un)
ASH-en
(See ASH-un)
ASH-ēng
ÄSH-ē-ō
ASH-ful
ASH-ist
ASH-lē
ASH-nus
ÄSH-u
ÄSH-ul
ÄSH-un
ASH-un
ASH-und
ÄSH-un-ēng
ÄSH-un-ēng
ÄSH-unt
ÄSH-un-ul
ASH-un-ul
ASH-un-ul-īz
ASH-un-ut
ÄSH-ur
ASH-ur
ÄSH-us
ÄSH-us-nus
ASH-ust
(See ASH-ist)
ASH-uz
AS-i-bul
(See AS-u-bul)
AS-id
(See AS-ud)

AS-if-ī
(See AS-uf-ī)
ÄS-ik
AS-ik
AS-il
(See AS-ul)
ÄS-in
(See ÄS-un)
AS-in
(See AS-un)
AS-in-āt
ÄS-is
(See ÄS-us)
AS-ist
AS-it
(See AS-ut)
AS-it-ē
(See AS-ud-ē)
ÄS-iv
AS-iv
ASK
ASK-ēng
ASK-et
(See ASK-ut)
ASK-ō
ASK-ot
ASK-u
ASK-u-bul
ASK-ur
ASK-us
ASK-ut
AS-lē
ÄS-lus
ÄS-ment
ÄS-ō
AS-ō
ASP
ASP-ē
ASP-ēng
ASP-u-bul
ASP-un
ASP-ur
ÄST
AST
ÄST-ē
AST-ē

AT-lur
(See AD-lur)
ĀT-lus
AT-lus
ĀT-ment
ĀT-nus
AT-nus
ĀT-ō
(See ĀD-ō)
AT-rik
ĀT-rix
AT-rix
ĀT-run
AT-sō
ĀT-u
(See ĀD-u)
AT-u
(See AD-u)
ĀT-ub-ul
(See ĀD-ub-ul)
AT-ub-ul
(See AD-ub-ul)
ĀT-ud
(See ĀD-ud)
AT-ud
(See AD-ud)
AT-u-fī
(See AD-u-fī)
ĀT-ul
(See ĀD-ul)
AT-ul
(See AD-ul)
ĀT-um
(See ĀD-um)
AT-um
(See AD-um)
AT-um-ē
(See AD-um-ē)
ĀT-un
AT-un
ĀT-unt
AT-unt
ĀT-ur
(See ĀD-ur)
AT-ur
(See AD-ur)

AT-urd
(See AD-urd)
AT-ur-ē
(See AD-ur-ē)
ĀT-ur-ēng
(See ĀD-ur-ēng)
AT-ur-ēng
(See AD-ur-ēng)
AT-ur-īz
(See AD-ur-īz)
AT-urn
(See AD-urn)
AT-ur-ul
(See AD-ur-ul)
AT-ur-ur
(See AD-ur-ur)
ĀT-us
(See ĀD-us)
AT-us
(See AD-us)
Ā-u
Ā-ub-ul
Ā-u-dē
Ā-uk
Ā-ul
(See ĀL)
Ā-um
Ā-uns
Ā-ur
(See also AR)
Ā-urz
Ā-us
Ā-ust
Ā-u-tē
(See Ā-u-dē)
ĀV
AV
ĀVD
ĀV-ē
AV-ē
ĀV-el
(See ĀV-ul)
AV-el
(See AV-ul)
ĀV-en
(See ĀV-un)
ĀV-ēng

AV-ē-u
ĀV-ē-un
AV-ij
AV-il
(See AV-ul)
ĀV-in
(See ĀV-un)
ĀV-is
(See ĀV-us)
AV-is
(See AV-us)
AV-ish
AV-ish-ēng
ĀV-it
AV-it-ē
(See AV-ud-ē)
ĀV-ment
AV-u
AV-ud-ē
ĀV-ul
AV-ul
AV-ul-ēng
ĀV-un
ĀV-ur
AV-ur
ĀV-urd
ĀV-ur-ē
ĀV-ur-ēng
AV-ur-is
(See AV-ur-us)
ĀV-ur-it
AV-urn
ĀV-ur-u-bul
AV-ur-us
ĀV-us
AV-us
ĀV-ust
ĀV-yur
AX
AXD
AX-ē
AX-en
(See AX-un)
AX-ēng
AX-ē-um
AX-im
(See AX-um)

AX-is
(See AX-us)
AX-u-bul
AX-um
AX-un
AX-ur
AX-us
ĀZ
AZ
ĀZD
AZD
ĀZ-ē
AZ-ē
ĀZ-el
(See ĀZ-ul)
ĀZ-en
(See ĀZ-un)
ĀZ-ēng
ĀZH-u
ĀZH-un
ĀZH-ur
ĀZH-ur-ēng
ĀZH-ur-u-bul
ĀZH-ur-ur
ĀZ-il
(See ĀZ-ul)
AZ-lēng
ĀZ-ment
AZ-mu
ĀZ-ul
AZ-ul
AZ-um
ĀZ-un
ĀZ-ur
AZ-ur
AZ-urd

Ē
EB
ĒB-ē
EB-ēng
ĒB-ō
ĒB-ru
ĒB-u
EB-ul
ĒCH
ECH

ĒCH-ē
ECH-ē
ĒCH-ēng
ECH-ēng
ĒCHT
ECHT
ĒCH-ub-ul
ECH-ub-ul
ECH-un
ĒCH-ur
ECH-ur
ECH-ur-ē
ECH-ur-us
ĒD
ED
ĒD-ē
ED-ē
ED-ē-ēng
ĒD-ē-ent
(See ĒD-ē-unt)
ĒD-en
(See ĒD-un)
ED-en
(See ED-un)
ĒD-ēng
ED-ēng
ĒD-ē-nus
ED-ē-nus
ĒD-ē-u
ĒD-ē-um
ĒD-ē-un
ĒD-ē-uns
ĒD-ē-unt
ĒD-ē-ur
ED-ē-ur
ĒD-ē-us
ĒD-ē-ut
ĒD-ēz
ED-ēz
ĒD-ful
ED-ib-ul
(See ED-ub-ul)
ÈD-ik
ED-ik
ED-i-kāt
ED-i-ket
(See ED-i-kut)

ED-ik-lē
ED-i-kul
ED-i-kut
ĒD-i-lē
(See ĒD-u-lē)
ED-i-lē
(See ED-u-lē)
ED-i-ment
ĒD-ish
ED-ish
ED-is-un
ED-it
(See ED-ut)
ED-it-ur
(See ED-ut-ur)
ĒD-ix
ED-ix
EDJ
(See EJ)
EDJ-ē
(See EJ-ē)
EDJ-ur
(See EJ-ur)
ED-lē
ĒD-lēng
ED-lēng
ED-līn
ED-lok
ĒD-lur
ED-lur
ĒD-lus
ED-nus
ĒD-ō
ED-ō
ĒD-ō-ēng
ĒD-u
ED-u
ĒD-ub-ul
ED-ub-ul
ĒD-ud
ED-ud
ĒD-ul
ED-ul
ĒD-ul-ē
ED-ul-ē
ĒD-ul-dum
ED-ul-sum

ED-ūl-us
ĒD-um
ĒD-un
ED-un
ĒD-uns
ĒD-unt
ĒD-ur
ED-ur
ED-urd
ĒD-ur-ē
ĒD-ur-ēng
ED-ur-ēng
ĒD-ur-ship
ED-ur-un
ED-ur-ut
ĒD-us
ED-us
ĒD-ust
ED-ust
ED-ut
ĒD-us-uz
ED-ut
ED-ut-ēng
ED-ut-iv
ED-ut-ud
ED-ut-ur
ĒD-uz
ED-wûd
ED-yū-lus
(See ED-ū-lus)
È-ēng
ĒF
EF
ĒF-ē
EF-en
(See EF-un)
ÈF-ēng
EF-ēng
EFT
EFT-ē
EF-un
ĒF-ur
EF-ur
EF-ur-uns
ĒG
EG
EG-ē

ĒG-ēng
EG-ēng
ĒG-ō
ĒG-ul
ĒG-ul-ē
ĒG-ur
EG-ur
ĒG-ur-lē
Ē-ist
Ē-i-tē
(See Ē-u-dē)
ÈJ
EJ
EJD
ĒJ-ē
EJ-ē
EJ-ēng
EJ-i-bul
(See EJ-u-bul)
ÈJ-ik
ÈJ-is
(See ĒJ-us)
EJ-u-bul
ÈJ-un
EJ-ur
ÈJ-us
ĒK
EK
EK-chur
EK-chur-ur
ĒK-chū-ul
(See EX-ū-ul)
ĒK-ē
ĒK-en
(See ĒK-un)
ÈK-ēng
EK-ēng
ĒK-ē-nus
ĒK-lē
EK-lē
EK-lus
ĒK-nus
EK-nus
ĒK-ō
EK-ō
EK-owt

ĒKS
(See ĒX)
EKS
(See EX)
EK-shun
EK-shun-ist
EK-shun-ul
EK-shun-ut
EK-shur
(See EK-chur)
EK-shū-ul
(See EX-ū-ul)
ĒKT
EKT
EKT-ēng
EKT-ful
EKT-ī
EKT-i-fī
(See EKT-u-fī)
EKT-ik
EKT-iv
EKT-lē
(See EK-lē)
EKT-nus
(See EK-nus)
EKT-rik
EKT-u-bul
EKT-ud
EKT-u-fī
EKT-u-kul
EKT-um
EKT-um-ē
EKT-ur
EKT-ur-ē
EKT-ur-ul
EKT-ur-ut
EKT-us
ĒK-u
EK-u
ĒK-u-bul
EK-u-bul
EK-ū-div
EK-ul
EK-ūl-ur
ĒK-un
EK-un
EK-und

ĒK-un-ēng
EK-un-ēng
EK-up
ĒK-ur
EK-ur
EK-urd
EK-urz
ĒK-ust
EK-ū-tiv
(See EK-ū-div)
ĒK-wul
ĒK-wens
(See ĒK-wuns)
ÈL
EL
ELCH
ĒLD
ELD
ĒLD-ēng
ELD-ēng
ĒLD-u-bul
ĒLD-ud
ELD-um
ĒLD-ur
ELD-ur
ĒLDZ
(See ĒLZ)
ELDZ
(See ELZ)
ÈL-ē
EL-ē
EL-e-gāt
(See EL-u-gāt)
ÈL-ēng
EL-ēng
ĒL-ē-nus
EL-et
(See EL-ut)
EL-e-tun
(See EL-u-tun)
ĒL-ē-u
(See ĒL-yu)
ELF
ELF-ish
EL-i-bul
(See EL-u-bul)
EL-ik

Ē-līn
EL-ish
EL-ish-ment
EL-ist
EL-it
(See EL-ut)
EL-it-ē
(See EL-ud-ē)
ÈL-ix
EL-jun
ELM
ELM-ur
ĒL-ō
EL-ō
EL-ō-ēng
ELP
ELP-ur
ELS
ELS-ē
ELS-ur
ELT
ELT-ēng
ELTH
ELTH-ē
ELTS
(See ELS)
ELTS-ur
(See ELS-ur)
ELT-ur
ELT-ur-ēng
ĒL-u
EL-u
ĒL-u-bul
EL-u-bul
EL-ud-ē
EL-u-gāt
EL-uk
(See EL-ik)
EL-um
EL-un
EL-un-ē
EL-unt
EL-up
ĒL-ur
EL-ur
EL-ur-ē
EL-us

EL-ust
(See EL-ist)
EL-ut
EL-u-tun
ELV
ELV-ēng
ELV-et
(See ELV-ut)
ELV-is
(See ELV-us)
ELV-us
ELV-ut
ELVZ
ĒL-yu
EL-yun
ĒLZ
ELZ
ĒM
EM
Ē-man
EM-blē
EM-bul
EM-bur
EM-bur-ēng
ĒM-ē
EM-ē
EM-e-dē
(See EM-u-dē)
ĒM-en
(See ĒM-un)
ĒM-ēng
EM-ēng
ĒM-ēng-lē
ĒM-ē-u
ĒM-ē-ur
ĒM-ik
EM-ik
EM-ik-ul
(See EM-uk-ul)
EM-i-nāt
(See EM-u-nāt)
EM-i-nē
(See EM-un-ē)
ĒM-ish
EM-ish
ĒM-ist
ĒM-lē

EM-lun
ĒM-lus
EM-ni-tē
(See EM-nu-dē)
EM-nu-dē
ĒM-ō
EM-ō
EMP
EMP-ō
EMPT
EMPT-ē
EMPT-ēng
EMPT-i-bul
EMP-ur-ur
ĒM-u
EM-u
ĒM-u-bul
EM-u-dē
EM-uk-ul
ĒM-un
EM-un
EM-u-nāt
EM-un-ē
ĒM-ur
EM-ur
ĒM-ur-ē
EM-ur-ē
ĒMZ
EMZ
ĒN
EN
ENCH
ENCH-ēng
ENCH-mun
ENCH-u
ENCH-ul
(See EN-shul)
ENCH-un
(See EN-shun)
ENCH-un-ul
(See EN-shun-ul)
ENCH-ur
(See EN-shur)
ENCH-ur-ē
(See EN-shur-ē)
ENCH-ur-sum
(See EN-shur-sum)

ENCH-us
ENCH-us-nus
ENCH-ū-ul
(See EN-shū-ul)
ĒND
END
END-ē
END-ēng
END-en-sē
(See END-un-sē)
END-ent
(See END-unt)
END-id
(See END-ud)
END-ij
END-ix
END-lus
END-ō
END-u
END-u-bul
END-ud
END-um
END-un
END-uns
END-un-sē
END-unt
END-ur
END-ur-ēng
END-ur-īz
END-ur-lē
END-ur-nus
END-us
ĒNDZ
(See ĒNZ)
ENDZ
(See ENZ)
ĒN-ē
EN-ē
ĒN-ē-ens
(See ĒN-ē-uns)
ĒN-ē-ent
(See ĒN-ē-unt)
EN-e-mē
(See EN-u-mē)
ĒN-ēng
EN-ēng

ĒN-est
(See ĒN-ust)
ĒN-ē-u
ĒN-ē-ul
EN-ē-ul
ĒN-ē-uns
ĒN-ē-unt
ĒN-ē-us
ĒN-ēz
EN-ēz
ĒNG
ĒNG-dum
ĒNG-ē
ĒNG-ēng
ĒNG-ē-nus
ĒNG-lē
ĒNG-lēng
ĒNG-lish
ĒNG-ō
ENGTH
ENGTH-un
ĒNG-ul
ĒNG-ur
ĒNG-ur-ēng
ĒNGZ
ĒN-ik
EN-ik
EN-im
(See EN-um)
ĒN-is
(See ĒN-us)
EN-is
(See EN-us)
EN-ish
ĒN-ist
(See ĒN-ust)
EN-i-sun
(See EN-u-sun)
EN-it-ē
(See EN-ud-ē)
ĒN-ix
EN-ix
ENJ
ĒNK
ĒNK-ē
ĒNK-ēng

ĒNK-et
(See ĒNK-ut)
ĒNK-lē
ĒNK-lēng
ĒNK-lur
ĒNK-ō
ĒNKS
(See ĒNX)
ĒNK-shun
ĒNKT
ĒNKT-iv
ĒNKT-lē
(See ĒNK-lē)
ĒNKT-ur
ĒNK-u-bul
ĒNK-ul
ĒNK-un
ĒNK-ur
ĒNK-ut
ĒN-nus
ĒN-ō
ENS
ĒNS-ē
ENS-ēng
EN-shul
EN-shun
EN-shun-ēng
EN-shun-u-bul
EN-shun-ul
EN-shur
EN-shurd
EN-shur-ē
EN-shur-ēng
EN-shur-sum
EN-shus
(See ENCH-us)
EN-shus-nus
(See ENCH-us-nus)
EN-shū-ul
ENS-i-bul
(See ENS-u-bul)
ENS-ik-ul
(See ENS-uk-ul)
ENS-il
(See ENS-ul)
ENS-it-ē
(See ENS-ud-ē)

ENS-iv
ENS-iv-lē
ENS-lus
ENST
ENS-u-blē
ENS-u-bul
ENS-ud-ē
ENS-uk-ul
ENS-ul
ENS-ur
ENS-ur-ē
ENS-ur-ut
ENS-us
ENS-uz
ENT
ENT-ē
ENT-ēng
ENT-ens
(See ENT-uns)
ENT-ful
ENT-ik-ul
(See ENT-uk-ul)
ENT-il
(See ENT-ul)
ENT-is
(See ENT-us)
ENT-ist
ENT-it-ē
(See ENT-ud-ē)
ENT-iv
ENT-lē
ENT-lus
ENT-ment
ENT-ō
ENT-rē
ENT-rik
ENT-rik-ul
ENTS
(See ENS)
ENT-u
ENT-ub-ul
ENT-ud
ENT-ud-ē
ENT-uk-ul
ENT-ul
ENT-ul-ē
ENT-ul-ust

ENT-um
ENT-uns
ENT-ur
ENT-urd
ENT-ur-ē
ENT-ur-ēng
ENT-us
ENT-ust
(See ENT-ist)
EN-tu-tiv
ĒN-u
EN-u
EN-ū
ĒN-u-bul
EN-u-bul
EN-ud-ē
EN-ud-ur
ĒN-ul
EN-um
EN-um-ē
EN-uns
EN-unt
ĒN-ur
EN-ur
EN-ur-āt
ĒN-ur-ē
EN-ur-ē
EN-ur-jē
(See IN-ur-jē)
ĒN-us
EN-us
ĒN-ust
EN-u-sun
EN-ut
EN-ut-ur
(See EN-ud-ur)
EN-ū-us
ĒNX
ĒN-yō
EN-yū
(See EN-ū)
ĒN-yu
ĒN-yus
(See ĒN-ē-us)
EN-yū-us
(See EN-ū-us)
ĒNZ

IM-ē
ĪM-en
(See ĪM-un)
IM-en
(See IM-un)
ĪM-ēng
IM-ēng
ĪM-ē-nus
IM-est
(See IM-ust)
IM-e-trē
(See IM-u-trē)
IM-e-tur
(See IM-u-dur)
IM-ē-un
IMF
IM-ij
IM-ik
IM-ik-rē
IM-il-ē
(See IM-ul-ē)
IM-in-āt
(See IM-un-āt)
IM-in-ul
(See IM-un-ul)
IM-it
(See IM-ut)
IM-i-tā-shun
IM-it-ē
(See IM-ud-ē)
ĪM-lē
IM-nus
IMP
IMP-ē
IMP-ēng
IMP-lē
IMP-lēng
IMPS
IMP-tum
IMP-ul
IMP-ur
IMP-ur-ēng
IM-ud-ē
IM-ud-ur
IM-uk
(See IM-ik)

IM-uk-rē
(See IM-ik-rē)
IM-ūl-āt
IM-ul-ē
IM-ū-lunt
ĪM-un
IM-un
IM-un-āt
IM-un-ul
ĪM-ur
IM-ur
IM-ur-ēng
IM-us
ĪM-ust
IM-ust
ĪM-ut
IM-ut
IM-ut-ē
(See IM-ud-ē)
IM-u-trē
IM-u-tur
(See IM-u-dur)
IM-utz
IM-yū-lāt
(See IM-ū-lāt)
ĪMZ
IMZ
IM-zē
ĪN
IN
INCH
INCH-ē
INCH-ēng
INCH-ur
ĪND
IND
IND-ē
ĪND-ed
(See ĪND-ud)
IND-ed
(See ĪND-ud)
ĪND-ēng
IND-ēng
IND-i-kāt
ĪND-lē
IND-lē
IND-lēng

ĪND-nus
ĪND-ud
IND-ud
IND-ul
ĪND-ur
IND-ur
ĪN-ē
IN-ē
IN-en
(See IN-un)
ĪN-ēng
IN-ēng
IN-es
(See IN-us)
IN-et
(See IN-ut)
IN-ē-u
(See IN-yu)
IN-ē-ul
IN-ē-um
IN-ē-un
ĪN-ē-ur
IN-ē-ur
IN-ful
ING
(See ĒNG)
ING-dum
(See ĒNG-dum)
ING-ē
(See ĒNG-ē)
ING-ēng
(See ĒNG-ēng)
ING-lēng
(See ĒNG-lēng)
ING-lish
(See ĒNG-lish)
ING-ō
(See ĒNG-ō)
ING-ul
(See ĒNG-ul)
ING-ur
(See ĒNG-ur)
INGZ
(See ĒNGZ)
ĪN-ī
IN-ik

OB-lō
OB-lun
OB-lur
ŌB-ō
OB-ōn
OB-ru
OB-stur
OB-ub-ul
ŌB-ul
OB-ul
OB-un
ŌB-ur
OB-ur
OB-ur-ē
OB-ur-ēng
ŌB-ust
ŌCH
OCH
OCH-ē
ŌCH-ēng
OCH-ēng
OCH-ō
ŌCH-u-bul
ŌCH-ur
OCH-ur
ŌD
OD
ŌD-ē
OD-ē
ŌD-ed
(See ŌD-ud)
OD-ēd
OD-ed
(See OD-ud)
ŌD-el
(See ŌD-ul)
OD-el
(See OD-ul)
OD-en
(See OD-un)
ŌD-ēng
OD-ēng
OD-ē-nus
OD-ē-ō
OD-es
(See OD-us)

OD-es-ē
(See OD-us-ē)
OD-est
(See OD-ust)
ŌD-ē-um
ŌD-ē-un
ŌD-ē-us
OD-i-bul
(See OD-u-bul)
OD-i-fī
(See OD-u-fī)
OD-ij
OD-ik
OD-i-kul
OD-i-lē
(See OD-u-lē)
OD-is
(See OD-us)
OD-is-ē
(See OD-us-ē)
OD-ish
OD-it
(See OD-ut)
OD-it-ē
(See OD-ut-ē)
OD-i-tŏr-ē
(See OD-u-tŏr-ē)
OD-i-tur
(See OD-u-tor)
ŌD-iv
ODJ
(See OJ)
ODJ-ē
(See OJ-ē)
ODJ-ur
(See OJ-ur)
OD-lē
ŌD-lēng
(See ŌD-ul-ēng)
OD-lēng
(See OD-ul-ēng)
OD-lin
(See OD-lun)
OD-lun
OD-lur
ŌD-ō
OD-ō

Ō-down
OD-rē
ŌD-u
OD-u
ŌD-u-bul
OD-u-bul
ŌD-ud
OD-ud
OD-ud-ē
(See OD-ut-ē)
OD-u-fī
OD-u-kul
(See OD-i-kul)
ŌD-ul
ŌD-ūl
OD-ul
ŌD-ul-ē
ŌD-ul-ēng
OD-ul-ēng
OD-ul-us
ŌD-um
OD-um
OD-um-ē
OD-un
ŌD-ur
OD-ur
ŌD-ur-ē
OD-ur-ē
OD-ur-ēng
ŌD-ur-īz
OD-ur-īz
OD-ur-ut
ŌD-us
OD-us
OD-us-ē
OD-ust
OD-ut
OD-ut-ē
OD-u-tŏr-ē
OD-wā
Ō-ē
(See also ŌĒ)
ŌĒ
ŌĒD
ŌĒD-ēng
ŌĒD-ud
ŌĒD-ur

ŌĒD-ur-ēng
ŌĒD-us
ŌĒ-ēng
ŌĒK
ŌĒL
ŌĒLD
ŌĒL-ē
ŌĒL-ēng
ŌĒL-et
(See ŌĒL-ut)
ŌĒL-ist
(See ŌĒL-ust)
ŌĒL-tē
ŌĒL-ur
ŌĒL-ust
ŌĒL-ut
ŌĒ-ment
ŌĒN
ŌĒND
Ō-ēng
O-ēng
ŌĒNT
ŌĒNT-ed
(See ŌĒNT-ud)
ŌĒNT-ēng
ŌĒNT-ment
ŌĒNT-ud
ŌĒS
ŌĒS-ēng
ŌĒST
ŌĒST-ēng
ŌĒST-ur
ŌĒST-ur-us
ŌĒ-sum
ŌĒT
Ō-et
(See Ō-ut)
ŌĒT-ēng
(See ŌĒD-ēng)
ŌĒT-ur
(See ŌĒD-ur)
ŌĒT-ur-ēng
(See ŌĒD-ur-ēng)
ŌĒT-us
(See ŌĒD-us)
ŌĒ-u
(See ŌĒ-yu)

ŌĒ-ul
(See ŌĒL)
ŌĒ-uns
ŌĒ-unt
ŌĒ-ur
ŌĒ-us
ŌĒ-yu
ŌĒ-yur
(See ŌĒ-ur)
ŌĒZ
ŌĒZ-ē
ŌĒZ-un
ŌF
OF
ŌF-ē
OF-ē
OF-el
(See OF-ul)
OF-en
(See OF-un)
OF-ēng
OF-en-ur
(See OF-un-ur)
OF-et
(See OF-ut)
OF-ik
OF-in
(See OF-en)
OF-is
(See OF-us)
OF-ish
OF-it
(See OF-ut)
OFT
OFT-ē
OFT-en
(See OFT-un)
OFT-un
OF-ul
OF-un
OF-un-ē
OF-un-ur
OF-un-us
ŌF-ur
OF-ur
ŌF-ur-ēng
OF-ur-ēng

OF-us
OF-ut
ŌG
OG
ŌG-ē
OG-ē
OG-ēng
OG-in
(See OG-un)
ŌG-ish
OG-lēng
ŌG-ō
OG-ō
OG-ruf-ē
OG-ruf-ur
ŌG-u
OG-u-div
(See OG-u-tiv)
ŌG-ul
OG-ul
OG-um-ē
ŌG-un
OG-un
OG-ur
OG-ur-ē
OG-ur-ul
OG-ust
OG-u-tiv
OG-u-tōr-ē
OJ
(See also OJH)
OJ-ē
OJ-en-ē
(See OJ-un-ē)
OJ-ēng
ŌJH
OJH
OJ-ik
OJ-ik-ul
OJ-un-ē
OJ-ur
ŌK
OK
(See also OLK)
ŌK-ē
OK-ē

ŌK-el
(See ŌK-ul)
ŌK-en
(See ŌK-un)
OK-ēng
OK-ēng
OK-ē-nus
ŌK-ē-ō
OK-et
(See OK-ut)
ŌK-ē-ul
OK-ē-ur
OK-ēz
OK-ī
OK-i-lē
(See OK-u-lē)
OK-nē
ŌK-ō
OK-ō
OK-ri-sē
(See OK-ru-sē)
OK-ru-sē
OK-ru-tēz
ŌKS
(See ŌX)
OKS
(See OX)
OK-shun
OK-shus
(See OX-yus)
OKS-ik
(See OX-ik)
ŌKT
OKT
OKT-ur
ŌK-u
ŌK-ul
OK-ul
OK-u-lē
OK-ū-lur
ŌK-um
ŌK-un
OK-up
ŌK-ur
OK-ur
OK-ur-ē
ŌK-us

OK-us
ŌK-ust
OK-ut
OK-ut-iv
OK-ū-us
OK-wu
OK-wurd
OK-yū-lur
(See OK-ū-lur)
ŌL
OL
ŌLD
OLD
ŌLD-ē
OLD-ē
ŌLD-en
(See ŌLD-un)
ŌLD-ēng
OLD-ēng
ŌLD-un
OLD-un
ŌLD-ur
OLD-ur
ŌLD-ur-ēng
ŌL-ē
OL-ē
OL-ej
(See OL-ij)
OL-em
(See OL-um)
OL-en
(See ŌL-un)
OL-en
(See OL-un)
OL-eng
OL-ēng
ŌL-ē-ō
OL-es
(See OL-us)
OL-et
(See OL-ut)
ŌL-ē-u
OL-ē-u
ŌL-ē-um
ŌL-ē-un
OLF
ŌL-ful

ŌL-gu
OL-id
(See OL-ud)
OL-i-fī
(See OL-u-fī)
OL-ij
OL-ik
OL-ik-ul
OL-ip
(See OL-up)
ŌL-ish
OL-ish
OL-ish-ēng
OL-it
(See OL-ut)
OL-it-ē
(See OL-ut-ē)
ŌL-jur
ŌLK
(See ŌK)
OLK
(See also OK)
OLK-ēng
(See also OK-ēng)
OLK-un
OLK-ur
(See also OK-ur)
OLM
(See also OM)
OLM-ē
(See OM-ē)
OLM-ēng
(See also OM-ēng)
OLM-ist
(See OM-ist)
OLM-ur
(See OM-ur)
ŌL-ō
OL-ō
Ol-ō-ēng
OL-o-jē
(See OL-u-jē)
OL-o-jist
(See OL-u-jist)
OL-ō-ur
OL-owt
ŌLS

OP-les
(See OP-lus)
OP-lur
ŌP-lus
OP-lus
OP-o-lis
(See OP-u-lus)
OPS
OP-sē
OP-shun
ŌPT
OPT
OPT-ēng
OPT-ik
OPT-ur
OP-u-bul
OP-uk
(See OP-ik)
OP-uk-ul
ŌP-ul
OP-ul
OP-u-lāt
OP-ul-ē
OP-ū-lur
OP-u-lus
ŌP-un
ŌP-un-ur
ŌP-ur
OP-ur
ŌP-ur-ē
OP-ur-ē
OP-ur-u-tiv
ŌP-us
OP-ut
OP-yū-lur
(See OP-ū-lur)
ŌR
ŌRB
ORB-ut
ŌRCH
ŌRCH-ēng
ŌRCH-un
ŌRCH-un-ut
ŌRCH-ur
ŌRCH-urd
ŌRD
ŌRD-ē

ŌRD-ed
(See ŌRD-ud)
ŌRD-en
(See ŌRD-un)
ŌRD-ēng
ŌRD-ē-un
ŌRD-id
(See ŌRD-ud)
ŌRD-i-fī
(See ORD-u-fī)
ŌRD-in-ut
(See ORD-un-ut)
ŌRD-iv
ŌRD-u
ŌRD-u-bul
ŌRD-ud
ŌRD-u-fī
ŌRD-ul
ŌRD-um
ŌRD-un
ŌRD-uns
ŌRD-un-ut
ŌRD-ur
ŌRD-ur-ēng
ŌRD-ur-lē
ŌR-ē
ŌR-ēd
ŌR-el
(See ŌR-ul)
ŌR-en
(See ŌR-un)
ŌR-ēng
ŌR-ēng-lē
ŌR-en-ur
(See ŌR-un-ur)
ŌR-ent
(See ŌR-unt)
ŌR-ē-ō
ŌR-est
(See ŌR-ust)
ŌR-ē-u
ŌR-ē-ul
ŌR-ē-um
ŌR-ē-un
ŌR-ē-us
ŌRF
ŌRF-un

ŌRF-us
ORG-un
ŌR-ib-ul
(See ŌR-ub-ul)
ŌR-id
(See ŌR-ud)
ŌR-idj
(See ŌR-ij)
ŌR-if-ī
ŌR-ij
ŌR-ik
ŌR-ik-ul
(See ŌR-uk-ul)
ŌR-ist
(See ŌR-ust)
ŌR-it-ē
(See ŌR-ud-ē)
ŌRJ
ŌRJ-ē
ŌRJ-ur
ŌRJ-us
ŌRK
ŌRK-ē
ŌRK-u
ŌRK-ur
ŌRL
(See ŌR-ul)
ŌR-lē
ŌRM
ŌRM-at
ŌRMD
ŌRM-ē
ŌRM-ēng
ŌRM-ist
ŌRM-it-ē
(See ŌRM-ud-ē)
ŌRM-lē
ŌRM-lus
ŌRM-ōst
ŌRM-ud-ē
ŌRM-ul
ŌRM-ul-īz
ŌRM-un
ŌRM-uns
ŌRM-unt
ŌRM-ur
ŌRM-us

OX-ix
OX-u-bul
OX-un
OX-ur
OX-yus
O-yur
ŌZ
OZ
ŌZD
OZD
ŌZ-ē
OZ-ē
ŌZ-en
(See ŌZ-un)
ŌZ-ēng
OZ-ēng
ŌZ-es
(See ŌZ-us)
OZ-et
(See OZ-ut)
OZ-ē-u
(See OZH-u)
ŌZ-ē-ur
OZH
ŌZH-u
OZH-u
ŌZH-un
ŌZH-ur
OZ-ib-ul
(See OZ-ub-ul)
ŌZ-il-ē
OZ-in
(See OZ-un)
OZ-it
(See OZ-ut)
OZ-it-iv
(See OZ-ud-iv)
OZ-it-ōr-ē
(See OZ-ut-ōr-ē)
OZM
(See OZ-um)
ŌZ-ub-ul
OZ-ub-ul
OZ-ud-iv
ŌZ-ul
OZ-ul
ŌZ-ul-ē

OZ-um
ŌZ-un
OZ-un
ŌZ-ur
ŌZ-us
OZ-ut
OZ-ut-ōr-ē

Ū
ŪB
UB
ŪB-ē
UB-ē
ŪB-en
(See ŪB-un)
ŪB-ēng
UB-ēng
UB-ē-nus
ŪB-ik
UB-in
(See UB-un)
UB-ish
UB-lēng
UB-lin
(See UB-lun)
UB-lun
ŪB-rē-us
ŪB-u
UB-u
ŪB-ul
UB-ul
UB-ul-sum
ŪB-un
UB-un
ŪB-ur
UB-ur
UB-urd
UB-ur-ē
ŪB-ur-unt
ŪCH
UCH
ŪCH-ē
ŪCH-ēng
UCH-ēng
UCH-es
(See UCH-us)
ŪCH-ur

UCH-us
ŪD
UD
ÛD
ŪD-ē
UD-ē
ÛD-ē
ÛD-ed
(See ÛD-ud)
UD-ed
(See UD-ud)
ŪD-ed
(See ÛD-ud)
UD-en
(See UD-un)
ÛD-en
(See ÛD-un)
UD-ēng
UD-ēng
ÛD-ēng
ŪD-ens
(See ŪD-uns)
ŪD-ent
(See ŪD-unt)
ŪD-ē-us
ŪD-i-ful
ŪD-ik
ŪD-i-kul
ŪD-in-us
ŪD-ist
ŪD-it-ē
(See ŪD-ut-ē)
UDJ
(See UJ)
UDJ-ē
(See UJ-ē)
UDJ-et
(See UJ-ut)
UDJ-un
(See UJ-un)
UDJ-ur-ē
(See UJ-ur-ē)
ŪD-lē
ŪD-lēng
UD-lēng
ŪD-nus
ŪD-ō

UKT-ur
ŪK-u
UK-ul
UK-uld
UK-ū-lunt
UK-ulz
ŪK-ur
UK-ur
ÛK-ur
ŪK-us
UK-us
UK-ut
ŪL
(See also Ū-ul)
UL
ÛL
ULCH
ULCH-ur
ŪLD
ULD
ŪL-ē
UL-ē
ÛL-ē
UL-en
(See UL-un)
ÛL-en
(See ÛL-un)
ŪL-ēng
UL-ēng
ŪL-ep
(See ŪL-ip)
UL-et
(See UL-ut)
ÛL-et
(See ÛL-ut)
ŪL-ē-un
UL-gur
ŪL-ip
(See ŪL-up)
ŪL-ish
ŪL-it-ē
(See ŪL-ud-ē)
ULJ
ULJ-ēng
ULK
ULK-ē
ULK-ēng

UL-min-āt
ULP
ULP-it
(See ULP-ut)
ULPT
ULP-ut
ULS
ULS-ēng
UL-shun
UL-siv
UL-sur
ULT
ULT-chur
(See UL-chur)
ULT-ēng
ULT-rē
ULTS
(See ULS)
ULT-ud
ULT-ur-ē
(See ULT-rē)
ŪL-ū
ŪL-u
ŪL-u-bul
ŪL-ud-ē
UL-un
ÛL-un
ŪL-up
ŪL-ur
UL-ur
UL-urd
ŪL-ur-ē
UL-ut
ÛL-ut
ŪL-ut-ē
(See ŪL-ud-ē)
ŪLZ
ŪM
UM
UMB-lēng
UM-blur
UM-bō
UM-bul
UM-bunt
UM-bur
UM-bur-ēng
UM-bur-sum

ŪMD
UMD
ŪM-ē
UM-ē
UM-el
(See UM-ul)
ŪM-ēng
UM-ēng
ŪM-ē-nus
UM-et
(See UM-ut)
ŪM-id
(See ŪM-ud)
ŪM-ij
ŪM-in
(See ŪM-un)
ŪM-in-āt
ŪM-in-us
UM-it
(See UM-ut)
UM-nī
UMP
UMP-ē
UMP-ēng
UMP-et
(See UMP-ut)
UMP-kin
UMP-lēng
UMP-shun
UMP-shus
UMPT
UMP-tiv
UMP-ul
UMP-un-ē
UMP-ur
UMP-us
UMP-ut
ŪM-u
ŪM-u-bul
UM-u-bul
ŪM-ud
UM-uks
(See UM-ux)
UM-ul
ŪM-un
UM-unz
ŪM-ur

UM-ur
ŪM-ur-ē
UM-ur-ē
ŪM-ur-ēng
ŪM-ur-us
UM-ut
UM-ux
UM-zē
ŪN
UN
UNCH
UNCH-ē
UNCH-ēng
UNCH-un
UNCH-ur
ŪND
UND
UND-ē
UND-it
UND-rus
UND-ul
UND-un
UND-unt
UND-ur
UND-ur-ēng
UND-ur-us
ŪN-ē
UN-ē
UN-el
(See UN-ul)
ŪN-ēng
UN-ēng
ŪN-ful
UNG
UNG-ul
UNG-ur
UNG-ur-ēng
UNG-us
ŪN-ik
(See ŪN-uk)
UN-ish
ŪN-ist
ŪN-it
(See ŪN-ut)
UN-it
(See UN-ut)

ŪN-it-ē
(See ŪN-ud-ē)
UNJ
UNJ-ē
UNJ-ēng
UNJ-un
UNK
UNK-chur
UNK-ē
UNK-en
(See UNK-un)
UNK-ēng
UNK-et
(See UNK-ut)
UNK-shun
UNK-shus
UNKT
UNKT-iv
UNK-ul
UNK-um
UNK-un
UNK-ur
UNK-ut
ŪN-ō
UNS
UNT
UNT-ēng
UNTS
(See UNS)
UNT-ul
UNT-ur
ŪN-u
ŪN-u-dē
ŪN-uk
ŪN-ul
UN-ul
ŪN-um
ŪN-ur
UN-ur
UN-ur-ē
ŪN-us
ŪN-ust
(See ŪN-ist)
ŪN-ut
UN-ut
ŪN-yu
ŪN-yun

UN-yun
ŪP
UP
ŪP-ē
UP-ē
UP-ēng
UP-ēng
UP-et
(See UP-ut)
ŪP-id
ŪP-il
(See ŪP-ul)
ŪP-on
UPS
UP-shun
UPT
UPTS
(See UPS)
UPT-ud
ŪP-ud
(See ŪP-id)
ŪP-ul
UP-ul
UP-uns
ŪP-ur
UP-ur
ŪP-us
UP-ut
ŪR
(See also Ū-ur)
UR
URB
URB-ē
URB-ēng
URB-et
(See URB-ut)
URB-ē-ul
URB-ik
URB-ish
URB-ul
URB-ul-ē
URB-un
URB-ur
URB-ut
URCH
URCH-ēng

URCH-in
(See URCH-un)
URCH-un
URCH-ur
URCH-us
ŪRD
URD
URD-ē
URD-en
(See URD-un)
URD-ēng
URD-ē-us
URD-lēng
URD-u
URD-ub-ul
URD-ud
URD-ul
URD-un
URD-ur
ŪR-ē
UR-ē
ŪR-ē-āt
UR-ēd
UR-ē-ēng
ŪR-eng
UR-ēng
UR-ent
(See UR-unt)
UR-est
(See UR-ust)
UR-ē-sum
ŪR-ē-ul
UR-ē-un
ŪR-ē-unt
UR-ē-ur
ŪR-ē-us
UR-ē-us
UR-ēz
URF
URG
URG-lēng
URG-lur
URG-ul
UR-ij
ŪR-in
(See ŪR-un)
UR-ish

UR-ish-ment
ŪR-ist
ŪR-it-ē
(See ŪR-ud-ē)
URJ
URJ-ē
URJ-ēng
URJ-ent
(See URJ-unt)
URJ-ik-ul
URJ-in
(See URJ-un)
URJ-un
URJ-uns
URJ-uns-ē
URJ-unt
URJ-ur
URJ-ur-ē
URK
URK-ē
URK-ēng
URK-in
(See URK-un)
URK-it
(See URK-ut)
URKT
URK-ū-lur
URK-un
URK-ur
URK-us
URK-ut
URL
URLD
ŪRL-ē
URL-ē
URL-ēng
URL-ē-ur
URL-ish
URL-ōēn
URL-ur
URM
URM-ē
URM-ēng
UR-ment
URM-in
(See URM-un)
URM-in-āt

URM-in-ul
(See URM-un-ul)
URM-ish
URM-u
URM-ul
URM-un
URM-un-ul
URM-ur
URM-us
URN
URN-ē
URN-ēng
URN-est
(See URN-ust)
URN-ib-ul
(See URN-ub-ul)
URN-ish
URN-it-ē
(See URN-ud-ē)
URN-ō
URN-owt
URNT
URN-u-bul
URN-ud-ē
URN-ul
URN-ul-īz
URN-um
URN-ur
URN-us
URN-ust
ŪR-ō
UR-ō
URP
URP-ē
URP-ēng
URP-en-tīn
(See URP-un-tīn)
URPT
URP-un-tīn
URP-us
URS
URS-ē
URS-en
(See URS-un)
URS-ēng
UR-shul
UR-shun

UV-ul-ēng
UV-un
ŪV-ur
UV-ur
UV-urd
UV-ur-ē
UV-ur-ēng
UV-ut
UX
ÛX
UX-um
Ū-yu
ŪZ
UZ
ŪZD
ŪZ-ē
UZ-ē
UZ-en
(See UZ-un)
ŪZ-ēng
UZ-ēng
ŪZH-un
UZ-in
(See UZ-un)
UZ-lun
UZ-lur
ŪZ-u
ŪZ-u-bul
ŪZ-ul
UZ-ul
UZ-un
ŪZ-ur
UZ-ur
ŪZ-ur-ē